Rick Steves

SNAPSHOT

Sevilla, Granada & Andalucía

CONTENTS

Post-Pandemic Travels: Expect a Warm Welcome...and a Few Changes
Research for this guidebook was limited by the COVID-19 outbreak, and the long-term impact of the crisis on our recommended destinations is unclear. Some details in this book will change for post-pandemic travelers. Now more than ever, it's smart to reconfirm specifics as you plan and travel. As always, you can find major updates at RickSteves.com/update.

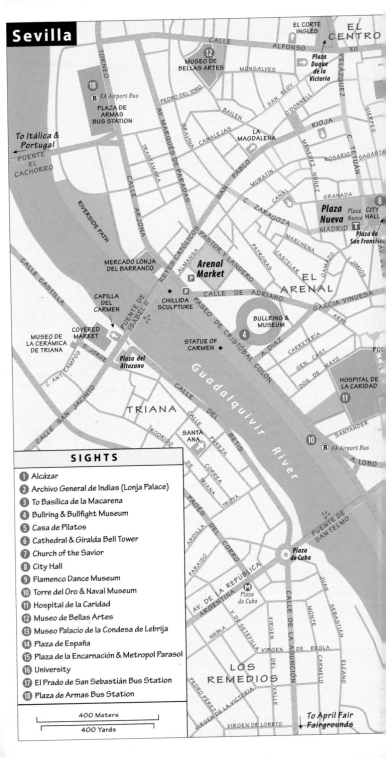

Sevilla

EL CENTRO

EL CORTE INGLÉS

CALLE ALFONSO XII

Plaza Duque de la Victoria

MONSALVES

MUSEO DE BELLAS ARTES **12**

18 EA Airport Bus **B**

PLAZA DE ARMAS BUS STATION

TORNEO

PEDRO DEL TORO

GRAJINA

CANALEJAS

BAILEN

SAN ELOY

O'DONNELL

LA MAGDALENA

RIOJA

MENÉNDEZ NÚÑEZ

ROSARIO

SAGASTA

C. TETUÁN

SIERPES

To Itálica & Portugal

PUENTE EL CACHORRO

TRASTÁMARA

CALLE ARJONA

AV. MARQUES DE PARADAS

SAN PABLO

MORATIN

GRANADA

8

Plaza Nueva

Plaza Nueva

CITY HALL

MADRID

Plaza de San Francisco **T**

RIVERSIDE PATH

C. ZARAGOZA

CANAL

MARCHENA

CASTELAR

GAMAZO

JIMIOS

CALLE CASTILLA

MERCADO LONJA DEL BARRANCO

REYES CATÓLICOS

PASTOR Y LANDERO

ALMANSA

Arenal Market P

CALLE DE ADRIANO

EL ARENAL

GARCÍA VINUESA

ARFE

CAPILLA DEL CARMEN

PUENTE DE ISABEL II

CHILLIDA SCULPTURE

PASEO DE CRISTÓBAL COLÓN

BULLRING & MUSEUM **4**

A. DIAZ

CARRETERÍA

GEN. CAST.

DOS DE MAYO

POS

MUSEO DE LA CERÁMICA DE TRIANA

COVERED MARKET

S. JORGE

STATUE OF CARMEN

HOSPITAL DE LA CARIDAD **11**

C. ANT CAMPOS

Plaza del Altozano

CALLE SAN JACINTO

TRIANA

CALLE DE BETIS

Guadalquivir River

SANTANDER

10

EA Airport Bus **B**

A. LOBO

RODRIGO

SANTA ANA

CALLE PUREZA

DE TRIANA

CORREA

PAGÉS DEL CORRO

PUENTE DE SAN TELMO

ARDILLA DEL CORRO

PARAÍSO

Plaza de Cuba

SIGHTS

1 Alcázar
2 Archivo General de Indias (Lonja Palace)
3 To Basílica de la Macarena
4 Bullring & Bullfight Museum
5 Casa de Pilatos
6 Cathedral & Giralda Bell Tower
7 Church of the Savior
8 City Hall
9 Flamenco Dance Museum
10 Torre del Oro & Naval Museum
11 Hospital de la Caridad
12 Museo de Bellas Artes
13 Museo Palacio de la Condesa de Lebrija
14 Plaza de España
15 Plaza de la Encarnación & Metropol Parasol
16 University
17 El Prado de San Sebastián Bus Station
18 Plaza de Armas Bus Station

AV. DE LA REPÚBLICA ARGENTINA

M Plaza de Cuba

NIEBLA

V. DE SETEFILA

VIRGEN DE LA ASUNCIÓN

VIRGEN DEL

CARMELO

ELCANO

CALLE DE LA ASUNCIÓN

JUAN

MONTE

SEBASTIÁN

REGLA

LOS REMEDIOS

PEDRO PÉREZ

VIRGEN DE LA VICTORIA

VIRGEN DE LORETO

To April Fair Fairgrounds

400 Meters

400 Yards

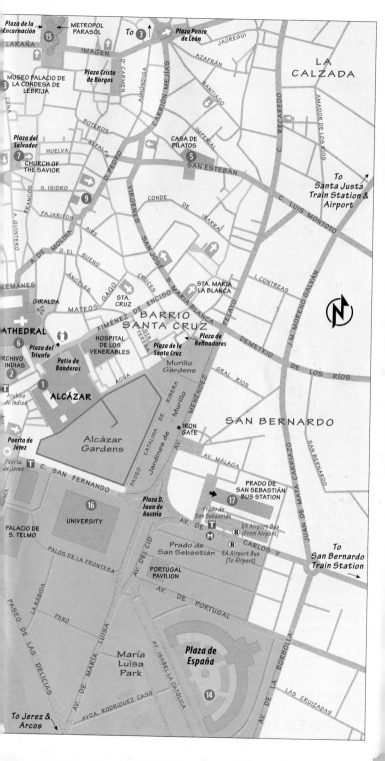

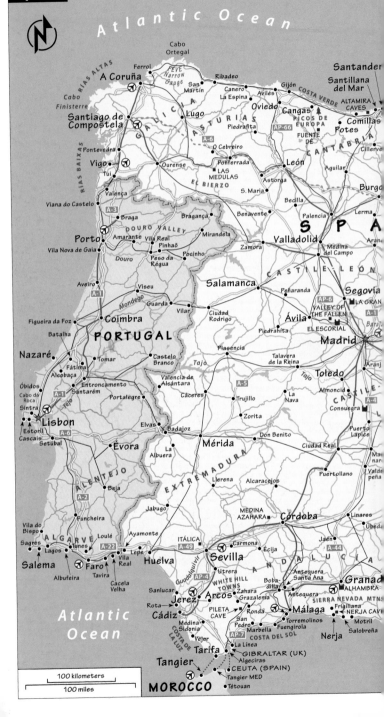

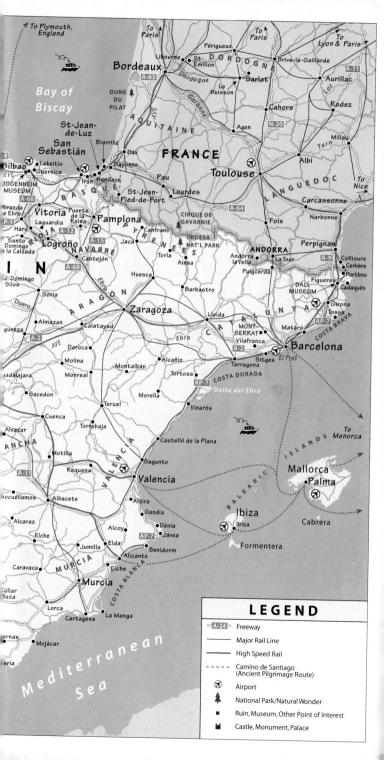

INTRODUCTION

This Snapshot guide, excerpted from my guidebook *Rick Steves Spain*, introduces you to southern Spain's two top cities—Sevilla and Granada—and the surrounding Spanish heartland. When Americans think of Spain, they often picture this region, with its massive cathedrals, Moorish palaces, vibrant folk life, whitewashed villages, bright sunshine, and captivating rat-a-tat-tat of flamenco.

Sevilla is the soulful cultural heart of southern Spain, with an atmospheric old quarter and riveting flamenco shows. Granada, formerly the Moorish capital, is home to the magnificent Alhambra palace. Córdoba features Spain's top surviving Moorish mosque, the Mezquita. Make time to delve into Andalucía's sleepy, whitewashed hill towns: Arcos de la Frontera, Ronda, and Grazalema. Spain's south coast, the Costa del Sol, is a palm-tree jungle of beach resorts and concrete, but has some appealing destinations—Nerja, Tarifa, and Gibraltar—beyond the traffic jams. And since it's so easy, consider an eye-opening side-trip to another continent by hopping the ferry to Tangier, the revitalized gateway to Morocco (and to Africa).

To help you have the best trip possible, I've included the following topics in this book:

- **Planning Your Time,** with advice on how to make the most of your limited time
- **Orientation,** including tourist information offices (abbreviated as TI), tips on public transportation, local tour options, and helpful hints
- **Sights** with ratings and strategies for meaningful and efficient visits
- **Sleeping** and **Eating,** with good-value recommendations in every price range

• **Connections,** with tips on trains, buses, and driving

Practicalities, near the end of this book, has information on money, staying connected, hotel reservations, transportation, and other helpful hints, plus Spanish survival phrases.

To travel smartly, read this little book in its entirety before you go. It's my hope that this guide will make your trip more meaningful and rewarding. Traveling like a temporary local, you'll get the absolute most out of every mile, minute, and dollar.

Buen viaje! Happy travels!

Rick Steves

SEVILLA

Flamboyant Sevilla (seh-VEE-yah) thrums with flamenco music, sizzles in the summer heat, and pulses with passion. It's a place where bullfighting is still politically correct and little girls still dream of being flamenco dancers. While Granada has the great Alhambra and Córdoba has the remarkable Mezquita, Sevilla has soul. As the capital of Andalucía, Sevilla offers a sampler of every Spanish icon, from sherry to matadors to Moorish heritage to flower-draped whitewashed lanes. It's a wonderful-to-be-alive-in kind of place.

As the gateway to the New World in the 1500s, Sevilla boomed when Spain did. The explorers Amerigo Vespucci and Ferdinand Magellan sailed from its great river harbor, discovering new trade routes and abundant sources of gold, silver, cocoa, and tobacco. For more than a century, it all flowed in through the port of Sevilla, bringing the city into a Golden Age. By the 1600s, Sevilla had become Spain's largest and wealthiest city, home to artists like Diego Velázquez and Bartolomé Murillo, who made it a cultural center. But by the 1700s, Sevilla's Golden Age was ending, as trade routes shifted, the harbor silted up, and the Spanish empire crumbled.

Nevertheless, Sevilla remained a major stop on the Grand Tour of Europe. European nobles flocked here in the 19th century, wanting to see for themselves the legendary city from story and song: the daring of *Don Giovanni* (Don Juan), the romance of *Carmen*, the spine-tingling cruelty of the Spanish Inquisition, and the comic gaiety of *The Barber of Seville.* To build on this early tourism, Sevilla planned a grand world's fair in 1929. Bad year. But despite the worldwide depression brought on by the US stock market crash, two million visitors flocked to see Sevilla's new parks and new

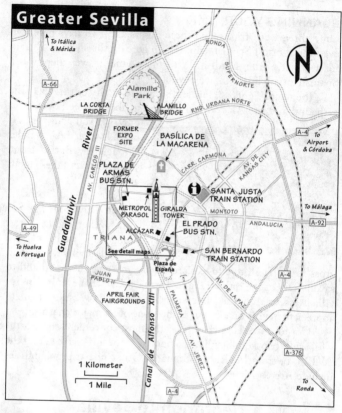

Greater Sevilla

neighborhoods, which are still beautiful parts of the city. In 1992, Sevilla got a second chance, and this world's fair was an even bigger success, leaving the city with impressive infrastructure: a new airport, six sleek bridges, a modern train station, and the super AVE bullet train (making Sevilla a 2.5-hour side-trip from Madrid). In 2007, the main boulevards—once thundering with noisy traffic and mercilessly cutting the city in two—were pedestrianized, enhancing Sevilla's already substantial charm.

Today, Spain's fourth-largest city (pop. 700,000) is Andalucía's leading destination, buzzing with festivals, color, guitars, castanets, and street life, and enveloped in the fragrances of orange trees and myrtle. Sevilla also has its share of impressive sights. It's home to the world's largest Gothic cathedral. The Alcázar is a fantastic royal palace and garden ornamented with Islamic flair. But the real magic is the city itself, with its tangled former Jewish Quarter, riveting flamenco shows, thriving bars, and teeming evening paseo. As James Michener wrote, "Sevilla doesn't *have* ambience, it *is* ambience."

PLANNING YOUR TIME

On a three-week trip, spend three nights and two days here. On even the shortest Spanish trip, I'd zip here on the slick AVE train for a day trip from Madrid. With more time, if ever there was a Spanish city to linger in, it's Sevilla.

The major sights are few and simple for a city of this size. The cathedral and the Alcázar can be seen in about three hours—but only if you buy tickets in advance. A wander through the Barrio Santa Cruz district takes about an hour.

You could spend a second day touring Sevilla's other sights. Stroll along the bank of the Guadalquivir River and cross Isabel II Bridge to explore the Triana neighborhood and to savor views of the cathedral and Torre del Oro. An evening in Sevilla is essential for the paseo and a flamenco show. Stay out late to appreciate Sevilla on a warm night—one of its major charms.

Córdoba (see later chapter) is the most convenient and worthwhile side-trip from Sevilla, or a handy stopover if you're taking the AVE to or from Madrid or Granada. Other side-trip possibilities include Arcos or Jerez.

Orientation to Sevilla

For the tourist, this big city is small. The bull's-eye on your map should be the cathedral and its Giralda bell tower, which can be

seen from all over town. Nearby are Sevilla's other major sights, the Alcázar (palace and gardens) and the lively Barrio Santa Cruz district. The central north-south pedestrian boulevard, Avenida de la Constitución, stretches north a few blocks to Plaza Nueva, gateway to the shopping district. A few blocks west of the cathedral are the bullring and the Guadalquivir River, while Plaza de España is a few blocks south. The colorful Triana neighborhood, on the west bank of the Guadalquivir River, has a thriving market and plenty of tapas bars, but no major tourist sights. While most sights are within walking distance, don't hesitate to hop in a taxi to avoid a long, hot walk (they are plentiful and cheap).

TOURIST INFORMATION

Sevilla has tourist offices at the **airport** (Mon-Fri 9:00-19:30, Sat-Sun 9:30-15:00, +34 954 782 035), at **Santa Justa train station** (just inside the main entrance, same hours as airport TI, +34 954 782 002), and near the cathedral on **Plaza del Triunfo** (Mon-Fri 9:00-19:30, Sat-Sun from 9:30, +34 954 210 005).

At any TI, ask for the English-language magazine *The Tourist* (also available at www.thetouristsevilla.com) and a current listing of sights with opening times. The free monthly events guide—*El Giraldillo*, written in Spanish basic enough to be understood by travelers—covers cultural events throughout Andalucía, with a focus on Sevilla. You can also ask for information you might need for elsewhere in the region (for example, if heading south, pick up the free *Route of the White Towns* brochure and a Jerez map). Helpful websites are www.turismosevilla.org and www.andalucia.org.

Steer clear of the "visitors centers" on Avenida de la Constitución (near the Archivo General de Indias) and at Santa Justa train station (overlooking tracks 6-7), which are private enterprises.

ARRIVAL IN SEVILLA

By Train: All long-distance trains arrive at modern **Santa Justa** station, with banks, ATMs, and a TI. Baggage storage is below track 1 (follow signs to *consigna*, security checkpoint open 6:00-24:00). The easy-to-miss TI sits by the sliding doors at the main entrance, to the left before you exit. The plush little AVE Sala Club, designed for business travelers, welcomes those with a first-class AVE ticket and reservation (across the main hall from track 1). The town center is marked by the ornate Giralda bell tower, peeking above the apartment flats (visible from the front of the station—with your back to the tracks, it's at 1 o'clock). To get into the center, it's a flat and boring 25-minute walk or about an €8 taxi ride. By city bus, it's a short ride on #C1 or #21 to the El Prado de San Sebastián bus station (find bus stop 100 yards in front of the train station, €1.40, pay driver), then a 10-minute walk or short tram ride (see "Getting Around Sevilla," later).

Regional trains use **San Bernardo** station, linked to the center by a tram (see "Getting Around Sevilla," later).

By Bus: Sevilla's two major bus stations—El Prado de San Sebastián and Plaza de Armas—both have information offices, basic eateries, and baggage storage.

The **El Prado de San Sebastián bus station,** or simply "El Prado," covers most of Andalucía (information desk, daily 8:00-20:00, +34 955 479 290, generally no English spoken; baggage lockers/*consigna* at the far end of station, same hours). From the bus station to downtown (and Barrio Santa Cruz hotels), it's about a 15-minute walk: Exit the station straight ahead. When you reach

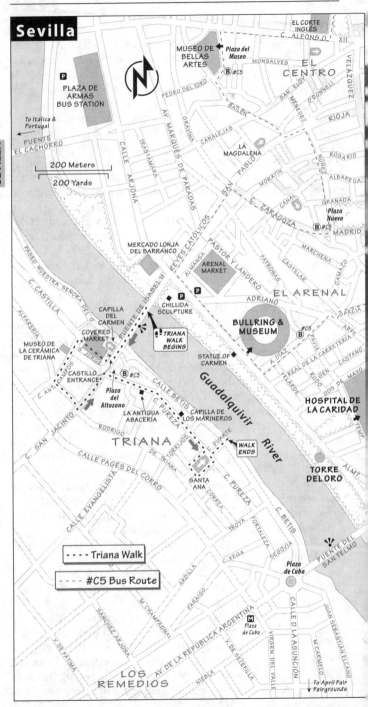

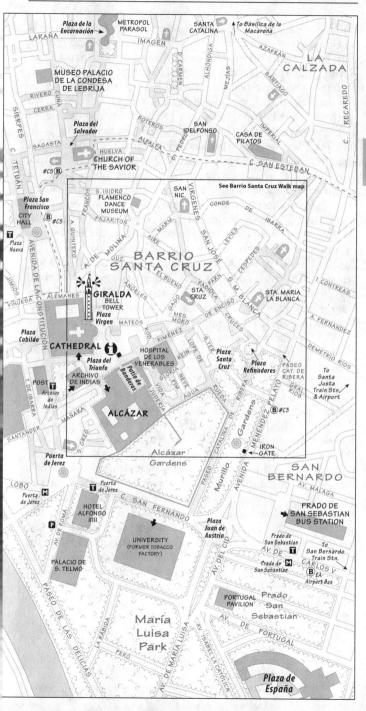

the busy avenue (Menéndez Pelayo) turn right to find a crosswalk and cross the avenue. Enter the Murillo Gardens through the iron gate, emerging on the other side in the heart of Barrio Santa Cruz. Sevilla's tram connects the El Prado station with the city center (and many of my recommended hotels): Turn left as you exit the bus station and walk to Avenida de Carlos V (€1.40, buy ticket at machine before boarding; ride it two stops to Archivo General de Indias to reach the cathedral area, or three stops to Plaza Nueva).

The **Plaza de Armas bus station** (near the river, opposite the Expo '92 site) serves long-distance destinations such as Madrid, Barcelona, Lagos, and Lisbon. Ticket counters line one wall, an information kiosk is in the center, and at the end of the hall are pay luggage lockers (buy tokens at info kiosk). Taxis to downtown cost around €7. Or, to take the bus, exit onto the main road (Calle Arjona) to find bus #C4 into the center (stop is to the left, in front of the taxi stand; €1.40, pay driver, get off at Puerta de Jerez).

By Car: To drive into Sevilla, follow *Centro Ciudad* (city center) signs. The city is no fun to drive in and parking can be frustrating. If your hotel lacks parking or a recommended plan, I'd pay for a garage (€24/day) and grab a taxi to your hotel from there. For hotels in the Barrio Santa Cruz area, the handiest parking is the Cano y Cueto garage near the corner of Calle Santa María la Blanca and Avenida de Menéndez Pelayo (open daily 24 hours, at edge of big park, underground).

By Plane: Sevilla's San Pablo Airport sits about six miles east of downtown and has several car rental agencies in the arrivals hall (airport code: SVQ, +34 954 449 000, www.aena.es). The Especial Aeropuerto (EA) bus connects the airport with Santa Justa and San Bernardo train stations, both bus stations, and several stops in the town center (4/hour, less in off-peak hours, runs 4:30-24:00, 40 minutes, €4, pay driver). The two most convenient stops downtown are south of the Murillo gardens on Avenida de Carlos V, near El Prado de San Sebastián bus station (close to my recommended Barrio Santa Cruz hotels); and on the Paseo de Cristóbal Colón, near the Torre del Oro. Look for the small *EA* sign at bus stops. If you're going from downtown Sevilla *to* the airport, the bus stop is on the side of the street closest to Plaza de España. To taxi into town, go to an airport taxi stands to ensure a fixed rate (€23 by day, €27 at night and on weekends, luggage extra, confirm price with driver before your journey).

HELPFUL HINTS

Festivals: Sevilla's peak season is April and May, and it has two one-week spring festival periods when the city is packed: Holy Week and April Fair.

While **Holy Week** (Semana Santa) is big all over Spain,

it's biggest in Sevilla. Held the week between Palm Sunday and Easter Sunday, locals prepare for the big event starting up to a year in advance. What would normally be a five-minute walk can take an hour if a religious procession crosses your path, and many restaurants stop serving meat during this time. But any hassles become totally worthwhile as you listen to the *saetas* (spontaneous devotional songs) and give in to the spirit of the festival.

Then, after taking two weeks off to catch its communal breath, Sevilla holds its **April Fair** (April 18-24 in 2021). This is a celebration of all things Andalusian, with plenty of eating, drinking, singing, and merrymaking (though most of the revelry takes place in private parties at a large fairground).

Book rooms well in advance for these festival times. Prices can be sky-high and many hotels have four-night minimums.

Rosemary Scam: In the city center, and especially near the cathedral, you may encounter women thrusting sprigs of rosemary into the hands of passersby, grunting, *"Toma! Es un regalo!"* ("Take it! It's a gift!"). The twig is free...but then they grab your hand and read your fortune for a tip. Coins are "bad luck," so the minimum payment they'll accept is €5. They can be very aggressive, but you don't need to take their demands seriously—don't make eye contact, don't accept a sprig, and say firmly but politely, *"No, gracias."*

Laundry: Lavandería Tintorería Roma offers quick and economical drop-off service (Mon-Fri 10:00-14:00 & 17:30-20:30, Sat 10:00-14:00, closed Sun, a few blocks west of the cathedral at Calle Arfe 22, +34 954 210 535). Near the recommended Barrio Santa Cruz hotels, **La Segunda Vera Tintorería** has two self-service machines (Mon-Fri 9:30-14:00 & 17:30-20:30, Sat 10:00-13:30, closed Sun, about a block from the eastern edge of Barrio Santa Cruz at Avenida de Menéndez Pelayo 11, +34 954 536 376). For locations, see the "Sevilla Hotels" map, later.

Bike Rental: This biker-friendly city has designated bike lanes and a public bike-sharing program (€14 one-week subscription, first 30 minutes of each ride free, €2 for each subsequent hour, www.sevici.es). Ask the TI about this and other bicycle-rental options.

GETTING AROUND SEVILLA

Most visitors have a full and fun experience in Sevilla without ever riding public transportation. The city center is compact, and most of the major sights are within easy walking distance.

By Taxi: Sevilla is a great taxi town; they're plentiful and cheap. Two or more people should go by taxi rather than public

Sevilla at a Glance

▲▲▲**Flamenco** Flamboyant, riveting music-and-dance performances, offered at clubs throughout town. See page 73.

▲▲**Sevilla Cathedral** The world's largest Gothic church, with Columbus' tomb and climbable bell tower. **Hours:** Tue-Sat 11:00-17:00 (July-Aug until 18:00), Sun 14:30-18:00 (July-Aug 14:00-19:00), Mon 11:00-15:30. See page 26.

▲▲**Royal Alcázar** Palace built by the Moors in the 10th century, revamped in the 14th century, and still serving as royal digs. **Hours:** Daily 9:30-19:00, Oct-March until 17:00. See page 37.

▲▲**Hospital de la Caridad** Former charity hospital (funded by likely inspiration for Don Juan) with gorgeously decorated chapel. **Hours:** Daily 10:30-19:30. See page 48.

▲▲**Church of the Savior** Sevilla's second-biggest church and home to some of its most beloved statues used for religious festivals. **Hours:** Mon-Sat 11:00-18:00 (July-Aug from 10:00), Sun 15:00-19:30. See page 52.

▲▲**Basílica de la Macarena** Church and museum with much-venerated Weeping Virgin statue and Holy Week floats. **Hours:** Daily 9:00-14:00 & 18:00-21:30, mid-Sept-May daily 9:00-14:00 & 17:00-21:00 except Sun from 9:30. See page 59.

▲▲**Triana** Energetic, colorful neighborhood on the west bank of the river. See page 62.

▲▲**Bullfight Museum** Guided tour of the bullring and its museum. **Hours:** Daily 9:30-21:00, Nov-March until 19:00, until 15:00 on fight days. See page 66.

▲▲**Evening Paseo** Locals strolling around the city. **Hours:** Best paseo scene 19:00-21:00, until very late in summer. See page 68.

▲**Museo Palacio de la Condesa de Lebrija** 18th-century aristocratic mansion. **Hours:** Daily 10:30-19:30. See page 54.

▲**Flamenco Dance Museum** High-tech museum on the history and art of flamenco. **Hours:** Daily 10:00-19:00. See page 55.

▲**Museo de Bellas Artes** Andalucía's top paintings, including works by Murillo and Zurbarán. **Hours:** Tue-Sat 9:00-21:00, until 15:00 on Sun and in summer, closed Mon year-round. See page 56.

transit. You can hail one showing a green light anywhere, or find a cluster of them parked by major intersections and sights (€1.35 drop rate, €1/kilometer, €3.60 minimum; about 20 percent more on evenings and weekends; calling for a cab adds about €3). A quick daytime ride in town will generally fall within the €3.60 minimum. Although I'm quick to take advantage of taxis, note that because of one-way streets and traffic congestion it's often just as fast to hoof it between central points.

By Bus, Tram, and Metro: A single trip on any form of city transit costs €1.40. Skip the various transit cards—they are a hassle to get and not a good value for most tourists. Various #C **buses,** which are handiest for tourists, make circular routes through town (note that all of them except the #C6 eventually wind up at Basílica de La Macarena). For all buses, buy your ticket from the driver or from machines at bus stops. The #C3 stops at Murillo Gardens, Triana, then La Macarena. The #C4 goes the opposite direction, but without entering Triana. And the spunky **#C5** minibus winds through the old center of town, including Plaza del Salvador, Plaza de San Francisco, the bullring, Plaza Nueva, the Museo de Bellas Artes, La Campana, and La Macarena, providing a relaxing joyride that also connects some farther-flung sights (see route on "Sevilla" map).

A **tram** *(tranvía)* makes just a few stops in the heart of the city but can save you a bit of walking. Buy your ticket at the machine on the platform before you board (runs about every 7 minutes Sun-Thu until 23:00, Fri-Sat until 1:45 in the morning). It makes five city-center stops (from south to north): San Bernardo (at the San Bernardo train station), Prado San Sebastián (next to El Prado de San Sebastián bus station), Puerta Jerez (south end of Avenida de la Constitución), Archivo General de Indias (next to the cathedral), and Plaza Nueva (beginning of shopping streets).

Sevilla also has a one-line underground **Metro,** but it's of little use to travelers since its primary purpose is to connect the suburbs with the center. Its downtown stops are at the San Bernardo train station, El Prado de San Sebastián bus station, and Puerta Jerez.

Tours in Sevilla

🎧 To sightsee on your own, download my free Sevilla City Walk audio tour.

ON FOOT

Sevilla Walking Tours

A joy to listen to, **Concepción Delgado** is an enthusiastic teacher who takes small groups on English-only walks. Although you

can just show up, it's smart to confirm departure times and reserve a spot (4-person minimum, none on Sun or holidays, mobile +34 616 501 100, www. sevillawalkingtours.com, info@ sevillawalkingtours.com). Because she's a busy mom, Concepción sometimes sends her equally excellent colleagues to lead these tours.

City Walk: This fine two-hour introduction to Concepción's hometown is a fascinating cultural show-and-tell in which she skips the famous monuments and shares intimate insights the average visitor misses. Other than seeing the cathedral and Alcázar, this to me is the most interesting two hours you could spend in Sevilla (€15/person, Mon-Sat at 10:30, check website for Dec-Feb and Aug schedule, meet at statue in Plaza Nueva).

Cathedral and Alcázar Tours: For those wanting to really understand the city's two most important sights, Concepción offers 75-minute visits to the **cathedral** (€12 plus admission) and the **Alcázar** (€28 including admission, must book in advance). These tours are scheduled to fit efficiently after Concepción's city walk (€2 discount if combined). Meet at 13:00 at the statue in Plaza del Triunfo (cathedral tours—Mon, Wed, and Fri; Alcázar tours—Tue, Thu, and Sat).

Other Tours: Concepción offers a Tasty Culture tour covering social life and popular traditions (€26, includes a drink and tapa), and a *Game of Thrones* add-on to the Alcázar tour.

All Sevilla Guided Tours

This group of three licensed guides (Susana, Jorge, and Elena) offers quality private tours (€160/3 hours). They also run a Monuments Tour covering the Sevilla basics: cathedral, Alcázar, and Barrio Santa Cruz (€25/person plus admissions, Mon-Sat at 14:00, 2.5 hours, leaves from Plaza del Triunfo, mobile +34 606 217 194, www.allsevillaguides.com).

Sevilla a la Carta

Julia Rozet adopted Sevilla as her home 12 years ago and specializes in themed tours that explore different facets of the city such as its industrial and seafaring past, Magellan and the history of spices, and locations used for famous operas set in Sevilla. If you visit during one of Sevilla's many festivals, Julia can explain the traditions behind all the commotion (€20, families with children welcome, mobile +34 633 083 961, www.sevillalacarta.com).

"Free" Walks

Free tour companies dominate the walking tour scene in Sevilla. They are not "free," as you're aggressively hit up for a tip at the end, and you'll spend a good part of the tour hearing a sales pitch for the companies' paid offerings. The walk spiel is entertaining but with little respect for history or culture, and your "guide" is often a student who has memorized a script. Still—it's "free" and you get what you pay for. You'll see these guides with color-coded umbrellas at various starting points around the city.

Food Tours

For information on tapas tours and cooking lessons, see the sidebar on page 85.

BY BUS AND BUGGY
Hop-On, Hop-Off Bus Tours

Two competing city bus tours leave from the curb near the riverside Torre del Oro. You'll see parked buses and salespeople handing out fliers. Each tour does about an hour-long swing through the city with recorded narration. The tours, which allow you to hop on and off at 14 stops, are heavy on Expo '29 and Expo '92 neighborhoods—of limited interest nowadays. While the narration does its best, Sevilla is most interesting in places buses can't go (daily 10:00-22:00, off-season until 18:00, €22 for red bus: www.city-sightseeing.com; €18 online in advance for green bus: http://sevilla.busturistico.com).

Horse-and-Buggy Tours

A carriage ride is a classic, popular way to survey the city and to enjoy María Luisa Park (€45 for a 45-minute clip-clop, much more during Holy Week and the April Fair, find a likable English-speaking driver for better narration). There are several departure points around town: Look for rigs at Plaza de América, Plaza del Triunfo, the Archivo General de Indias, the Alfonso XIII Hotel, and Plaza de España.

SEVILLA

Holy Week (Semana Santa)

Holy Week—the week between Palm Sunday and Easter—is a major holiday throughout the Christian world, but nowhere is it celebrated with as much fervor as in Andalucía, especially Sevilla. Holy Week is all about the events of the Passion of Jesus Christ: his entry into Jerusalem, his betrayal by Judas and arrest, his crucifixion, and his resurrection. In Sevilla, on each day throughout the week, 60 neighborhood groups (brotherhoods, called *hermandades* or *cofradías*) parade from their neighborhood churches to the cathedral with floats depicting some aspect of the Passion story. (With the help of my Sevilla guides and friends, this amazing event was featured in my *Rick Steves' European Easter* public television special, viewable at RickSteves.com/watch-read-listen.)

As the week approaches, anticipation grows: Visitors pour into town, grandstands are erected along parade routes, and TV stations anxiously monitor the weather report. (The floats are so delicate that rain can force the processions to be called off—a crushing disappointment.)

By midafternoon of any day during Holy Week, thousands line the streets. The parade begins. First comes a line of "penitents" carrying a big cross, candles, and incense. The *penitentes* perform their penance publicly but anonymously, their identities obscured by pointy, hooded robes. (The penitents' traditional hooded garb has been worn for centuries—long before such hoods became associated with racism in the American South.) Some processions are silent, but others are accompanied by beating drums, brass bands, or wailing singers.

A hush falls over the crowd as the floats (*los pasos*) approach.

Barrio Santa Cruz Walk

The soul of Sevilla is best found in the narrow lanes of its oldest quarter—the Barrio Santa Cruz. Of Sevilla's once-thriving Jewish neighborhood, only the tangled street plan and a wistful Old World ambience survive. This classy maze of lanes (too tight for most cars), small plazas, tile-covered patios, and whitewashed houses with wrought-

First comes a Passion float, showing Christ in some stage of the drama—being whipped, appearing before Pilate, or carrying the cross to his execution. More penitents follow—with hundreds or even thousands of participants, a procession can stretch out over a half-mile. All this sets the stage for the finale—typically a float of the Virgin Mary, who represents the hope of resurrection.

The elaborate floats feature carved wooden religious sculptures, most embellished with gold leaf and silverwork. They can be adorned with fresh flowers, rows of candles, and even jewelry on loan from the congregation. Each float is carried by 30 to 50 men *(los costaleros),* who labor unseen—although you might catch a glimpse of their shuffling feet. The bearers wear turban-like headbands to protect their heads and necks from the crushing weight (the floats can weigh as much as three tons). Two "shifts" of float carriers rotate every 20 minutes. As a sign of their faith, some men carry the float until they collapse.

As the procession nears the cathedral, many pass through the square called La Campana, south along Calle Sierpes, and through Plaza de San Francisco. (Some parades follow a parallel route a block or two east.) Grandstands and folding chairs are filled by VIPs and Sevilla's prominent families. Thousands of candles drip wax along the well-trod parade routes, forming a waxy buildup that causes shoes and car tires to squeal for days to come.

Being in Sevilla for Holy Week is both a blessing and a curse. It's a remarkable spectacle, but it's extremely crowded. Parade routes can block your sightseeing for hours. Check printed schedules if you want to avoid them. But, if a procession blocks your way, look for a crossing point marked by a red-painted fence, or ask a guard. Even if all you care about on Easter is a chocolate bunny, the intense devotion of the Andalusian people during their Holy Week traditions is an inspiration to behold.

iron latticework draped in flowers is a great refuge from the summer heat and bustle of Sevilla. The streets are narrow—some with buildings so close they're called "kissing lanes." A happy result of the narrowness is shade: Locals claim the Barrio Santa Cruz is three degrees cooler than the rest of the city.

The *barrio* is made for wandering. Getting lost is easy, and I recommend doing just that. But to get started, here's a self-guided plaza-to-plaza walk that loops you through the *corazón* (heart) of the neighborhood and back out again. Along the way, we'll get an introduction to some of the things that give Sevilla its unique charm.

🎧 Download my free Sevilla City Walk audio tour, which

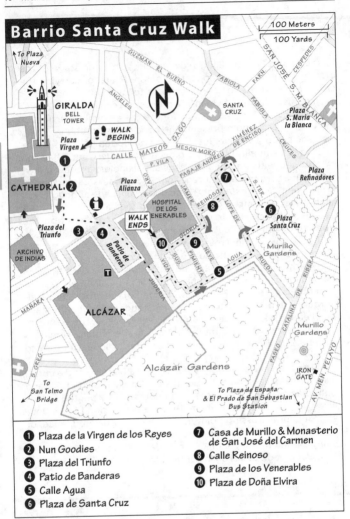

Barrio Santa Cruz Walk

❶ Plaza de la Virgen de los Reyes
❷ Nun Goodies
❸ Plaza del Triunfo
❹ Patio de Banderas
❺ Calle Agua
❻ Plaza de Santa Cruz
❼ Casa de Murillo & Monasterio de San José del Carmen
❽ Calle Reinoso
❾ Plaza de los Venerables
❿ Plaza de Doña Elvira

complements this walk (following stops at the Sevilla Cathedral and Royal Alcazar).

When to Go: Tour groups often trample the *barrio*'s charm in the morning. I find that early evening—around 19:00—is the ideal time to explore the quarter.

• *Start in the square in front of the cathedral, at the lantern-decked fountain in the middle that dates from Expo '29.*

❶ Plaza de la Virgen de los Reyes

Do a 360-degree spin and take in some of Sevilla's signature sights. There's the gangly cathedral with its soaring Giralda

bell tower—ground zero of the
city. To the right is the ornate red
Archbishop's Palace, a center of
power since Christians first conquered the city from the Moors in
1248. Continuing your spin, the
next building is almost a cliché
of early 20th-century (and now
government-protected) Sevillian
architecture—whitewashed with
goldenrod trim and ironwork balconies. The street stretching away
from the cathedral is lined with another Sevillian trademark—tapas

bars, housed in typical Andalusian buildings with their ironwork.
Continuing your spin, there's a row of Sevilla's signature orange
trees. Hiding in the orange trees is a statue of Pope John Paul II,
who performed Mass here before a half-million faithful Sevillians during a 1982 visit. Finally, you return to the Giralda bell
tower.

The Giralda encapsulates Sevilla's 2,000-year history. The
large blocks that form the very bottom of the tower date from when
Sevilla was a Roman city. (Up close, you can actually read some
Latin inscriptions.) The tower's main trunk, with its Islamic patterns and keyhole arches, was built by the Moors (with bricks made
of mud from the river) as a call-to-prayer tower for a mosque. The
top (16th-century Renaissance), with its bells and weathervane
figure representing Faith, was added after Christians reconquered
Sevilla, tore down the mosque, built the sprawling cathedral—and
kept the minaret as their bell tower.

This square is dedicated to that Christian reconquest, and to
the Virgin Mary. Turn 90 degrees to the left as you face the cathedral and find (hiding behind the orange trees) the Virgin of the
Kings (see her blue-and-gold tiled plaque on the white wall). This
is one of the many different versions of Mary you'll see around
town—some smiling, some weeping, some triumphant—each appealing to a different type of worshipper.

Notice the columns and chains that ring the cathedral, as if
put there to establish a border between the secular and Catholic
worlds. Indeed, that's exactly the purpose they served for centuries,
when Sevillians running from the law merely had to cross these
chains to find sanctuary—like crossing the county line. Many of
these columns are far older than the cathedral, having originally
been made for Roman and Visigothic buildings and later recycled
by medieval Catholics.

• *Facing the cathedral, turn left and walk toward the next square to find some...*

❷ Nun Goodies

The white building on your left was an Augustinian convent. Step inside the door at #3 to meet (but not see) a cloistered nun behind a fancy *torno* (a lazy Susan the nuns spin to sell their goods while staying hidden). The sisters raise money by selling rosaries, prayer books, and communion wafers (*tabletas*—bland, but like sin-free cookies). Consider buying something here just as a donation. The sisters, who speak only Spanish, have a sense of humor—have fun practicing your Spanish with them (Mon-Sat 9:15-13:00 & 16:45-18:15, Sun 10:00-13:00).

• *Step into the square marked with a statue of the Virgin atop a pillar. This is...*

❸ Plaza del Triunfo

Bordered by three of Sevilla's most important buildings—the cathedral, the walled Alcázar, and the Archivo General de Indias (filled with historic papers)—this place was the center of the action during the Golden Age of the 16th and 17th centuries. Businessmen from all over Europe gathered here to trade in the exotic goods pouring in from the New World. That wealth produced a flowering of culture, including Sevilla's most beloved painter, Bartolomé Murillo, who is honored at the base of the pillar (the sculptor used a famous painting by Murillo for his model of the Immaculate Conception on top).

The "Plaza of Triumph" is named for yet another Virgin statue atop a smaller pillar at the far end of the square. This Virgin helped the city miraculously "triumph" over the 1755 earthquake that destroyed Lisbon but only rattled Sevilla.

• *Before leaving the square, consider stopping at the TI. Then pass through the arched opening in the Alcázar's spiky, crenellated wall. You'll emerge into a white-and-goldenrod courtyard called the...*

❹ Patio de Banderas

The Banderas Courtyard (as in "flags," not Antonio) was part of the Alcázar, the Spanish king's residence when he was in town. This square was a military parade ground, and the barracks surrounding it housed the king's bodyguards.

Before the Alcázar was the palace of the Christian king, it was the palace of the Muslim Moors who ruled Sevilla. Archaeologists

found remains of this palace (as well as 2,000-year-old Roman ruins) beneath the courtyard. They excavated it, then covered the site to protect it.

Orange trees abound. Because they never lose their leaves, they provide constant shade. But forget about eating the oranges. They're bitter and used only to make vitamins, perfume, cat food, and that marmalade you can't avoid in British B&Bs. But when they blossom (for three weeks in spring, usually in April), the aroma is heavenly. (You can identify a bitter orange tree by its leaves—they have a tiny extra leaf between the main leaf and the stem.)

Head for the arch at the far-left corner of this square, do a 180, and enjoy the view of the Giralda bell tower.

• *Exit the courtyard through the Judería arch. Go down the long, narrow passage still paved with its original herringbone brickwork. Emerging into the light, you'll be walking alongside the red Alcázar wall. Take the first left at the corner lamppost and you'll pass another gate. A gate here was locked each evening—at first to protect the Jewish community (when they were the privileged elite—bankers, merchants, tax collectors) and later during times of persecution to isolate them (until they were finally expelled in 1492). Passing the gate, go right, through a small square, and follow the long narrow alleyway called...*

❺ Calle Agua

This narrow lane is typical of the *barrio*'s tight quarters, born when the entire Jewish community was forced into a small seg-
regated ghetto. As you walk, on your right is one of the older walls of Sevilla, dating back to Moorish times. Glancing to the left, peek through iron gates for occasional glimpses of the flower-smothered patios of restaurants and exclusive private residences (sometimes open for viewing). The patio at #2 is a delight—ringed with columns, filled with flowers, and colored with glazed tiles. The tiles are not merely decorative—they keep buildings cooler in the summer heat. If the gate is closed, try the next door down, or just look up for

a hint of the garden's flowery bounty. Admire the expensive ornamental mahogany eaves.

The plaque above and to the left of #1 remembers Washington

Sevilla's Jews

In the summer of 1391, smoldering anti-Jewish sentiment flared up in Sevilla. On June 6, Christian mobs ransacked the city's Jewish Quarter (Judería). Approximately 4,000 Jews were killed, and 5,000 Jewish families were driven from their homes. Synagogues were stripped and transformed into churches. The former Judería eventually became the neighborhood of the Holy Cross—Barrio Santa Cruz. Sevilla's uprising spread through Spain (and Europe), the first of many nasty pogroms during the next century.

Before the pogrom, Jews had lived in Sevilla for centuries as the city's respected merchants, doctors, and bankers. They flourished under the Muslim Moors. After Sevilla was "liberated" by King Ferdinand III (1248), Jews were given protection by Castile's kings and allowed a measure of self-government, though they were confined to the Jewish neighborhood. But by the 14th century, Jews were increasingly accused of everything from poisoning wells to ritually sacrificing Christian babies. Mobs killed suspected Jews, and some of Sevilla's most respected Jewish citizens had their fortunes confiscated.

After 1391, Jews were forced to make a choice: Be persecuted (even killed), relocate, or convert to Christianity. The newly Christianized—called conversos (converted) or marranos (swine)—were constantly under suspicion of practicing their old faith in private, and thereby undermining true Christianity. Fanning the mistrust were the perceptions of longtime Christians, who felt threatened by this new social class of converted Jews, who now had equal status.

To root out the perceived problem of underground Judaism, the "Catholic Monarchs," Ferdinand and Isabel, established the Inquisition in Spain (1478). Under the direction of Grand Inquisitor Tomás de Torquemada, these religious courts arrested and interrogated conversos suspected of practicing Judaism. Using long solitary confinement and torture, they extracted confessions.

On February 6, 1481, Sevilla hosted Spain's first auto-da-fé ("act of faith"), a public confession and punishment for heresy. Six accused conversos were paraded barefoot into the cathedral, forced to publicly confess their sins, then burned at the stake. Over the next three decades, thousands of conversos were tried and killed in Spain.

In 1492, the same year the last Moors were driven from Spain, Ferdinand and Isabel decreed that all remaining Jews convert or be expelled. In what became known as the Sephardic Diaspora, Spain's Jews left mostly for Portugal and North Africa (many ultimately ended up in Holland). Spain emerged as a nation unified under the banner of Christianity.

Irving. He and Romantic novelists, poets, and painters of his era inspired early travelers and popularized the Grand Tour. Aristocrats back in the 19th century had their favorite stops as they gallivanted around Europe, and Sevilla—with its operettas (like *Carmen*), bullfighting, and flamenco—was hard to resist.

Emerging at the end of the street, turn around and look back at the openings of two old pipes built into the wall. These 12th-century Moorish pipes once carried fresh spring water to the Alcázar (and today give the street its name—Agua). They were part of a 10-mile-long aqueduct system that was originally built by the ancient Romans and expanded by the Moors, serving some parts of Sevilla until the 1600s. You're standing at an entrance into the pleasant Murillo Gardens (through the iron gate), formerly the fruit-and-vegetable gardens for the Alcázar.

• *Don't enter the gardens now, but instead cross the square diagonally, and continue 20 yards down a lane to the...*

❻ Plaza de Santa Cruz

Arguably the heart of today's *barrio*, this pleasant square is graced with orange trees and draping vines, with a hedged garden in the center.

This square encapsulates the history of the neighborhood. In early medieval times, it was the *Judería*, with a synagogue standing where the garden is today. When the Jews were rousted in the 1391 pogrom, the synagogue was demolished, and a Christian church was built on the spot (the Church of Santa Cruz). It was the neighborhood church of the Sevillian painter Bartolomé Murillo (and later his burial site). But when the French (under Napoleon) invaded, the church was demolished. A fine 17th-century iron cross in the center of the square now marks the former site of the church. This "holy cross" *(santa cruz)*, from a renowned Sevillian forge, has inspired similar-looking crosses still carried in Holy Week processions, and gave this former Jewish Quarter its Christian name.

At #9, you can peek into a lovely courtyard that's proudly been left open so visitors can enjoy it. It's a reminder of the traditional Andalusian home, built around an open-air courtyard. The square is also home to the recommended Los Gallos flamenco bar, which puts on nightly performances (see "Nightlife in Sevilla," later).

• *Exit the square right of Los Gallos, going uphill (north) on Calle Santa Teresa. Notice millstones in the walls. Tour guides like to say this was a way for a wealthy miller to show off (like someone today parking a fancy car in their driveway). Notice also the well-worn ancient column functioning as a cornerstone. With the ruins of Roman Itálica nearby, Sevilla had a ready quarry for such ornamental corner pieces.*

After the kink in the road, find #8 (on the left).

SEVILLA

❼ Casa de Murillo and Monasterio de San José del Carmen

Sevilla's famous painter, Bartolomé Esteban Murillo, lived here in the 17th century. Born and raised in Sevilla, Murillo spent his final years here in this plush two-story mansion with a central patio. He soaked in the ambience of street life in this characteristic *barrio* and reproduced it in his paintings of cute beggar children. He also painted iconic versions of local saints and took Sevilla's devotion to the Virgin to another level with his larger-than-life Immaculate Conceptions. Wedding extreme religiosity with down-to-earth street life, he captured the Sevillian spirit.

Directly across from Casa de Murillo is the enormous wooden doorway of the Monasterio de San José del Carmen. This convent was founded by the renowned mystic, St. Teresa of Ávila. When she arrived in Sevilla in 1575, it was Spain's greatest city, and she stayed here for 10 years. Today, the Baroque convent keeps some of Teresa's artifacts and spiritual manuscripts, but it's closed to the public except for early morning Mass (Mon-Fri at 8:45 and Sun at 9:00).

• *Continue north on Calle Santa Teresa, then take the first left on Calle Lope de Rueda (just before the popular Las Teresas café). Here you enter a series of very narrow lanes. Take a left again, then right on...*

❽ Calle Reinoso

This street—so narrow that the buildings almost touch—is one of the *barrio's* "kissing lanes." A popular explanation suggests the buildings were so close together to provide maximum shade. But the history is more complex than that: This labyrinthine street plan goes back to Moorish times when this area was a tangled market. Later, this was the densely populated Jewish ghetto.

• *Leaving the "kissing zone," just to the left, the street spills onto...*

❾ Plaza de los Venerables

This tiny square is another candidate for "heart of the *barrio*," as it captures the romantic ambience that inspired so many operettas in Sevilla (from *Don Giovanni* and *Carmen* to *The Barber of Seville* and *The Marriage of Figaro*). The square also serves as the lively hub for several narrow streets that branch off it, oozing local color. With its vibrant buildings and visitor-oriented businesses, it typifies the *barrio* today: traditional and touristy at the same time.

The harmonious red-and-white Sevillian-Baroque Hospital

de los Venerables (1675) was once a retirement home for old priests (the "venerable" ones). It's now a cultural foundation worth visiting for its ornate church and small but fine collection of Sevillian paintings (see listing later, under "Sights in Sevilla"). The ceramic shop at the far end of the square welcomes tourists to use its bustour-friendly WCs.

• *Pass through the square. On Calle de Gloria is an interesting tile map of the Jewish Quarter. (Find yourself in the lower left, second row up, third tile from the left.) Now continue west on Calle de Gloria, where you'll soon emerge into...*

⑩ Plaza de Doña Elvira

This square—with orange trees, tile benches, and a stone fountain—sums up our *barrio* walk. Shops sell work by local artisans,

such as ceramics, embroidery, and fans. The plaza has a long history. In the 19th century, aristocrats flocked here to see the supposed home of the legendary lady love of the legendary Don Juan. At night, with candlelight and Spanish guitars playing, this is indeed a romantic place to dine.

But the plaza we see today reflects the fate of much of the *barrio*. After the neighborhood's Jews were expelled in 1492, the area went into slow decline. Napoleon's invasion furthered the destruction. By the early 1900s it was deserted and run down. Sevilla began an extensive urban renewal project, which culminated in the 1929 world's fair. They turned much of the *barrio*, including this plaza, into a showcase of Andalusian style. Architects renovated with traditional-style railings, tile work, orange trees, and other too-cute, Epcot-like adornments. The Barrio Santa Cruz may not be quite as old as it appears, but the new and improved version respects tradition while carrying the neighborhood's 800-year legacy into the future.

• *Our walk is over. To return to the area near the start of this walk, cross the plaza and head north along Calle Rodrigo Caro; keep going until you enter the large Plaza de la Alianza. From here, a narrow lane (Calle Joaquín Romero Murube) leads left back to the Alcázar.*

Sights in Sevilla

▲▲SEVILLA CATHEDRAL

Sevilla's cathedral (Catedral de Sevilla) is the third-largest church in Europe (after St. Peter's at the Vatican in Rome and St. Paul's in London) and the largest Gothic church anywhere. When they ripped down a mosque of brick on this site in 1401, the Reconquista Christians vowed they'd build a cathedral so huge that "anyone who sees it will take us for madmen." When it was finished in 1528, it was indeed the  world's biggest, and remained so for a century until St. Peter's came along. Even today, the descendants of those madmen proudly point to a *Guinness Book of Records* letter certifying, "Santa María de la Sede in Sevilla is the cathedral with the largest area."

On this self-guided tour, we'll marvel at the vast interior, over-the-top altars, world-class art, a stuffed crocodile, and the final resting place of Christopher Columbus.

Cost: €10 combo-ticket also includes Giralda bell tower and entry to the Church of the Savior—buy online in advance.

Hours: Tue-Sat 11:00-17:00 (July-Aug until 18:00), Sun 14:30-18:00 (July-Aug 14:00-19:00), Mon 11:00-15:30.

Information: www.catedraldesevilla.es.

Advance Tickets Recommended: It's smart to buy your ticket online (dates are available starting five weeks in advance) to avoid the long, time-consuming line. Without advance tickets, consider buying your combo-ticket at the Church of the Savior first (though lines there can also be long). Ticket in hand, walk boldly to the front and find the special entry line for advance ticketholders.

If you booked a tour of the rooftop (see later), you can enter the cathedral any time before your scheduled tour. Otherwise, after your tour, the guide can add your name to a list for approved entry the following day.

Tours: The €4 **audioguide** is excellent. The cathedral offers a **guided tour** that provides only a little extra information and is overpriced at €17; consider joining Concepción Delgado's guided tour instead (see "Tours in Sevilla," earlier).

The cathedral offers a 90-minute

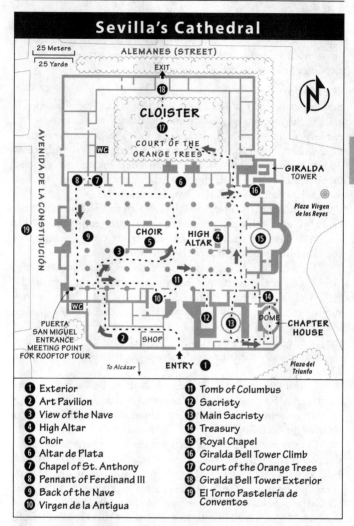

Sevilla's Cathedral

25 Meters
25 Yards

ALEMANES (STREET)

EXIT
18

CLOISTER
17

COURT OF THE
ORANGE TREES

WC

GIRALDA
TOWER

8 7 6
16

Plaza Virgen
de los Reyes

9

CHOIR
5

HIGH
ALTAR
4

15

3

19

11

10

14

WC

PUERTA
SAN MIGUEL
ENTRANCE
MEETING POINT
FOR ROOFTOP TOUR

12

13

DOME

CHAPTER
HOUSE

2

SHOP

To Alcázar

ENTRY 1

Plaza del
Triunfo

AVENIDA DE LA CONSTITUCIÓN

SEVILLA

1 Exterior
2 Art Pavilion
3 View of the Nave
4 High Altar
5 Choir
6 Altar de Plata
7 Chapel of St. Anthony
8 Pennant of Ferdinand III
9 Back of the Nave
10 Virgen de la Antigua

11 Tomb of Columbus
12 Sacristy
13 Main Sacristy
14 Treasury
15 Royal Chapel
16 Giralda Bell Tower Climb
17 Court of the Orange Trees
18 Giralda Bell Tower Exterior
19 El Torno Pastelería de
   Conventos

guided rooftop visit (€16, includes cathedral entrance, book on-line, English tours daily June-Sept at 10:30 and 18:00, Oct-May at 12:00 and 16:30, meet at west facade 15 minutes before tour). I prefer the last entry of the day for a more intimate experience. If you do this tour, skip the Giralda tower climb.

 My free Sevilla City Walk **audio tour** includes background detail and descriptions of the cathedral exterior, but doesn't cover the interior.

Visitor Services: A WC and drinking fountain are just inside the entrance and in the courtyard near the exit.

➋ Self-Guided Tour

• *You'll enter the church at the south facade (closest to the Alcázar). But before you head inside, take time to circle clockwise around the exterior (you can also do this at the end of the tour).*

❶ Exterior

Sevilla's cathedral has an odd exterior that is hard to fully appreciate. As the mosque was square and the cathedral was designed to entirely fill its footprint, the transepts don't show from the outside. And with no great square leading to the church, you hardly know where the front door is (it's on the west side). The church is circled by pillars and chains, which provided sanctuary to those escaping secular law (but not Christian law) 500 years ago.

Today's tourists enter through the south facade, which is 19th-century Neo-Gothic and unfinished—notice the empty niches that never got their statues. In the courtyard stands a full-size replica of the Giraldillo statue that caps the bell tower.

The west facade faces the trams, horses, and commotion of Avenida de la Constitución. Though this is the main entry to the cathedral, it seems totally ignored. The central door shows the Assumption of Mary, with the beloved Virgin rocketing up to heaven to be crowned by God with his triangular halo (reminding all of the Trinity). While this part wasn't finished until the 19th century, the side doors—with their red terra-cotta saints—date from the 15th century.

Continuing around the huge cathedral, at the next corner (across from Starbucks) you'll see animal-blood graffiti from 18th-century students celebrating their graduation—revealed in a recent cleaning project.

On the north side, the Puerta del Perdón (where you'll exit at the end of this tour) was once the entry to the mosque's courtyard. But, as with much of the Moorish-looking art in town, it's now actually Christian—the two coats of arms are a giveaway. The relief above the door shows the Bible story of Jesus ridding the temple of the merchants...a reminder to contemporaries that there will be no retail activity in the church. (German merchants gathered on this street—notice the name: Calle Alemanes.) The plaque on the right honors Miguel de Cervantes, the great 16th-century writer; this is one of many plaques scattered throughout town showing places mentioned in his books. (In this case, the topic was pickpockets.)

• *Circle back to the south facade and enter the cathedral. You'll pass through the...*

❷ Art Pavilion

This room features paintings that once hung in the church. You'll see a few by Sevilla's 17th-century master, Bartolomé Murillo, including paintings of beloved local characters who'll crop up again on our tour. King (and saint) Ferdinand III—usually shown with sword, crown, globe, and ermine robe—is the man who took Sevilla from the Moors and made this church possible. Santa Justa and Santa Rufina—Sevilla's patron saints—represent the city's Christian past. They were killed in ancient Roman times for their Christian faith. Potters by trade, they're easy to identify by their palm branches (symbolic of their martyrdom), their pots (at their feet or in their hands), and the Giralda bell tower symbolizing the town they protect. As you tour, play slug bug whenever you spot this dynamic hometown duo.

• *Now enter the actual church (passing a WC on the way) and take in the...*

❸ View of the Nave

The church is 137 yards long and 90 yards wide. That's more than two acres, the size of an entire city block in downtown Manhattan. Measured by area, this is still the world's largest church. (The church's footprint needed to be big enough to stamp out every trace of the mosque it replaced.) While most Gothic churches are long and tall, this nave is square and compressed. The pillars are massive. Like other Spanish churches, this nave is clogged in the middle by the huge rectangular enclosure called the choir.

• *Walk up the nave, past the choir, to the center of the church, where you can enjoy a view of the main altar. Look through the wrought-iron Renaissance grille at the...*

❹ High Altar

This dazzling 80-foot wall of gold covered with statues is considered the largest altarpiece *(retablo mayor)* ever made. Carved from

walnut and chestnut, and blanketed by a staggering amount of gold leaf, it took three generations to complete (1481-1564). Its 44 scenes tell the story of Jesus and Mary—left to right, bottom to top. Focus on the main spine of scenes running up the cen-

ter. At the bottom sits a 750-year-old silver statue of Baby Jesus and Mary—the cathedral's patroness since Christians first worshipped here in the old converted mosque. Above Mary, find the scene of Baby Jesus (with cow and donkey) being born in a manger. Above that, Mary (flanked by winged angels) is assumed into heaven. Above that, a shirtless, flag-waving Jesus stands atop his coffin, having been resurrected. And above that, he ascends past his disciples into heaven. Bible scholars can trace the entire story through

Bartolomé Murillo (1617-1682)

The son of a barber of Seville, Bartolomé Murillo (mur-EE-yoh) got his start selling paintings meant for export to the frontier churches of the Americas. In his 20s, he became famous after he painted a series of saints for Sevilla's Franciscan monastery. By about 1650, Murillo's sugary, simple, and accessible religious style was spreading through Spain and beyond.

Murillo painted street kids with cute smiles and grimy faces, and radiant young Marías with Ivory-soap complexions and rapturous poses (Immaculate Conceptions). His paintings view the world through a soft-focus lens, wrapping everything in warm colors and soft light, with a touch (too much, for some) of sentimentality.

Murillo became a rich, popular family man, and the toast of Sevilla's high society. In 1664, his wife died, leaving him heartbroken, but his last 20 years were his most prolific. At age 65, Murillo died after falling off a scaffold while painting. His tomb is lost somewhere under the bricks of Plaza de Santa Cruz.

the miracles, the Passion, and the Pentecost. Look way up to the tippy-top, where a Crucifixion adorns the dizzying summit: That teeny figure is six feet tall.

Now crane your neck skyward to admire the elaborate **ceiling** with its intricate interlacing arches. Though done in the 16th-century Spanish Renaissance style, this stonework is only about 100 years old. You're standing under the cathedral's central dome, which has collapsed three times in the past 500 years.

• *Don't even think about that. Turn around and check out the...*

❺ Choir

A choir area like this one—enclosed within the cathedral for more intimate services—is where church VIPs can gather close to the high altar. Choirs are common in Spain and England, but rare in churches elsewhere. They're called choirs because singers were also allowed here to accompany services. This one features an organ of more than 7,000 pipes (played Mon-Fri at the 10:00 Mass, Sun at the 10:00 and 13:00 Mass, not in July-Aug, free entry for worshippers). The big, spinnable book holder in the middle of the room held giant hymnals—large enough for all to chant from in an age when there weren't enough books to go around.

• *Now turn 90 degrees to the right to take in the enormous silver sunburst of the...*

❻ Altar de Plata

This gleaming silver altarpiece is meant to resemble a monstrance—that's the ceremonial vessel that displays a communion wafer in the center. This one is gargantuan, big enough for a card-table sized wafer (and made from more than 5,000 pounds of silver looted from Mexico by Spanish conquistadores in the 16th century). Amid the gleaming silver is a colorful statue of the Virgin. In 2014, Sevilla's celebration of La Macarena's 50th anniversary "jubilee" culminated here, remembering when this beloved icon was granted a canonical coronation by the pope.

• *From here, we'll tour some sights going counterclockwise around the church. Head left from the Altar de Plata, pass a few chapels where people come to pray to their chosen saint, and keep going to the last chapel on the right (with the big, marble baptismal font).*

❼ Chapel of St. Anthony

This chapel (Capilla de San Antonio) holds a special place in the hearts of Sevillians. Many were baptized in the big Renaissance-era font with the delightful carved angels dancing along its base. The chapel is also special for Murillo's tender painting of the *Vision of St. Anthony* (1656). The saint kneels in wonder as Baby Jesus comes down surrounded by a choir of angels. Anthony, one of Iberia's most popular saints, is the patron  saint of lost things—so people come here to pray for his help in finding jobs, car keys, and life partners. (In 1874, the cathedral had to find Anthony himself, when thieves stole this painting; it turned up in New York.) Above the *Vision* is *The Baptism of Christ*, also by Murillo. As for the stained glass, you don't need to be an art historian to know that it dates from 1685. And by now you must know who the women are—Santa Justa and Santa Rufina, the third-century Roman sisters eaten by lions at Itálica because of their faith.

• *Exiting the rear of the chapel, look for the enormous glass display case with the...*

❽ Pennant of Ferdinand III

This 800-year-old battle flag shows the castle of Castile and the lion of León—the two kingdoms Ferdinand inherited, forming the nucleus of a unified, Christian Spain two centuries later. This pennant was raised here over the minaret of the mosque on November 23, 1248, as Christian forces finally expelled the Moors from

Sevilla. For centuries afterward, it was paraded through the city on special days.

• *Continuing on, stand at the...*

❾ Back of the Nave

Face the choir and appreciate the ornate immensity of the church. Can you see the angels trumpeting on their Cuban mahogany? Any birds? On the floor before you (breaking the smooth surface) is the gravestone of Ferdinand Columbus (Hernando Colón), Christopher's second son. Having given the cathedral his collection of 6,000 precious books, he was rewarded with this prime burial spot. Behind you (behind an iron grille) is Murillo's *Guardian Angel* pointing to the light and showing an astonished child the way.

• *Continue counterclockwise, passing a massive wooden candlestick from 1560. That's old, but there's even older stuff here. Find a chapel (opposite the towering organ) with a big wall of statues whose centerpiece is a golden fresco of Mary and Baby Jesus.*

❿ Virgen de la Antigua

In this gilded fresco, the Virgin delicately holds a rose while the Christ Child holds a bird. It's some of the oldest art here (from the 1300s), even older than the cathedral itself. This chapel was once the site of the mosque's mihrab—the horseshoe-shaped prayer niche that points toward Mecca. When Christians moved in (1248), they initially used the mosque for their church services, covering the mihrab with this Virgin. The mosque served as a church for about 120 years—until it was completely torn down and replaced by today's cathedral. But the Virgin stayed, thanks to her beauty and her role as protector of sailors—crucial in this port city. Gaze up (above the metal gate) to find flags of all the New World countries where the Virgen de la Antigua is revered.

• *Just past the Virgen de la Antigua chapel is the...*

⓫ Tomb of Columbus

Four royal pallbearers carry the coffin of Christopher Columbus. It's appropriate that Columbus is buried here. His 1492 voyage departed just 50 miles away, and the port of Sevilla became the exclusive entry point for all the New World plunder that made Spain rich. Columbus' pallbearers represent the traditional kingdoms that formed the core of Spain: Castile, Aragon, León, and Navarre (identify them by their team shirts). The last kingdom, Granada, is also represented: Notice how Señor León's pike is stabbing a pomegranate, the symbol of

Immaculate Conception

Throughout Sevilla—and all of Spain—you'll see paintings titled *The Immaculate Conception,* all looking quite similar (see the example in the Bartolomé Murillo sidebar, earlier). Young, lovely, and beaming radiantly, these virgins look pure and untainted...you might even say "immaculate." According to Catholic doctrine, Mary, the future mother of Jesus, entered the world free from the original sin that other mortals share. When she died, her purity allowed her to be taken up directly to heaven (in the Assumption).

The doctrine of Immaculate Conception can be confusing, even to Catholics. It does not mean that the Virgin Mary herself was born of a virgin. Rather, Mary's mother and father conceived her in the natural way. But at the moment Mary's soul animated her flesh, God granted her a special exemption from original sin. The doctrine of Immaculate Conception had been popular since medieval times, though it was not codified until 1854. It was Murillo who painted the model of this goddess-like Mary, copied by so many lesser artists. In Counter-Reformation times (when Murillo lived), paintings of a fresh-faced, ecstatic Mary made abstract doctrines like the Immaculate Conception and the Assumption tangible and accessible to Catholics across Europe.

Most images of the Immaculate Conception show Mary wearing a radiant crown and with a crescent moon at her feet; she often steps on the heads of cherubs. Paintings by Murillo frequently portray Mary in a blue robe with long, wavy hair—young and innocent.

Granada—the last Moorish-ruled city to succumb to the Reconquista in that momentous year of 1492.

Columbus didn't just travel a lot while alive—he even kept it up posthumously. He died in 1506 in northwestern Spain (in Valladolid) where he was also buried. His remains were then moved to a monastery here in Sevilla, then to what's now the Dominican Republic (as he'd requested), then to Cuba. Finally—when Cuba gained independence from Spain in 1902—his remains sailed home again to Sevilla. After all that, are these really his remains? In 2006, a DNA test matched the bones of his son (buried just a few steps from here), giving Sevillians some evidence to substantiate their proud claim.

Columbus' tomb stands, appropriately, at the church entrance reserved for pilgrims, near a 1584 mural of St. Christopher, patron saint of travelers. The clock above has been ticking since 1788.

• *From here, our tour focuses on some of the artistic treasures of this rich church. For centuries, the faithful have donated their time and money to beautify their cathedral. The next chapel is the...*

❷ Sacristy

This space is where the priests get ready each morning before Mass. The painting above the altar is remarkable for several reasons: It's by the well-known artist Goya, it was specifically painted for this room, and it features our old friends Justa and Rufina with their trademark bell tower, pots, and palm leaves. Here they're bathed in a heavenly light, triumphing over a broken pagan statue, while the lion who was supposed to attack meekly licks their toes. Goya daringly portrayed the two third-century Romans dressed like fashionable women of his time.

• *Two chapels farther along is the entrance to the...*

❸ Main Sacristy

Marvel at the ornate, 16th-century dome of the main room, a grand souvenir from Sevilla's Golden Age. The intricate masonry, called Plateresque, resembles lacy silverwork (*plata* means "silver"). God is way up in the cupola. The three layers of figures below him show the heavenly host; relatives in purgatory—hands folded in prayer—looking to heaven in hope of help; and the wretched in hell, including naked sinners engulfed in flames and teased cruelly by pitchfork-wielding monsters.

Dominating the room is a nearly 1,000-pound, silver-plated monstrance (vessel for displaying the communion wafer). This is the monstrance used to parade the holy host through town during Corpus Christi festivities.

• *The next door down leads you through a few rooms, including one with a unique oval dome.*

This is the 16th-century chapter house *(sala capitular)*, where monthly meetings take place with the bishop (he gets the throne, while the others share the bench). The paintings here are by Murillo: *The Immaculate Conception* (1668, high above the bishop's throne) is one of his finest (and largest) depictions of Mary (in blue and white, standing amid a cloud of cherubs). To the right of her is Ferdinand (with sword and globe), along with more of Sevilla's favorite saints.

• *Now enter the...*

❹ Treasury

This wood-paneled Room of Ornaments shows off gold and silver reliquaries, which hold hundreds of holy body parts and splinters of the true cross. The star of the collection is Spain's most valuable crown—the Corona de la Virgen de los Reyes. Made in 1904, it sparkles with nearly 12,000 precious stones, including the world's largest pearl—used as the torso of an angel. This amazing treasure was completely paid for by devoted locals. Not fit for a human head, once a year the crown is taken out and placed on the head of a statue of the Virgin who represents Mary as patron of this cathedral.

• *Leave the treasury and continue around, passing (directly behind the high altar) the closed-to-tourists* ⓫ *Royal Chapel. Though it's only open for worship (access from outside), it's the holy-of-holies of Sevillian history, with the tombs of Sevilla's founder Ferdinand III, his enlightened successor Alfonso the Wise, and Pedro I, who built the Alcázar.*

In the far corner is the entry to the Giralda bell tower. It's time for some exercise (unless you're touring the rooftop later—then you can skip it).

⓰ Giralda Bell Tower Climb

Your church admission includes entry to the bell tower, a former minaret. Notice the beautiful Moorish simplicity as you climb to its top, 330 feet up (35 ramps plus 17 steps), for a grand city view. The graded ramp was designed to accommodate a donkey-riding muezzin, who clip-clopped up five times a day to give the Muslim call to prayer back when a mosque stood here. It's less steep the farther up you go, but if you get tired along the way, stop at balconies for expansive views over the entire city.

• *Back on the ground, head outside. As you cross the threshold, look up. Why is a **crocodile** hanging here? It's a reminder of the live crocodile given by the Islamic sultan of Egypt (in 1260) to the Christian king Alfonso the Wise as a show of goodwill. Alfonso proudly showed his croc off, and when it died he had the body stuffed for display. When that rotted, it was replaced with this wooden replica.*

You're now in an open-air courtyard (with WCs at the far end). This is the...

⓱ Court of the Orange Trees

This courtyard—one of the few things remaining from the original mosque—was the place for ritual ablutions. Muslims would enter through the keyhole-shaped archway, stop at the fountain to wash their hands, face, and feet, then proceed inside to pray. Another remnant is the Puerta del Perdón ("Door of Forgiveness"), the keyhole-arch entrance (and now tourist exit), with its original green doors of finely wrought bronze-covered wood. The lanes

SEVILLA

between the courtyard bricks were once irrigation streams—a reminder that the Moors introduced irrigation to Iberia. Otherwise, the Christians completely leveled the site and turned a mosque of brick into a cathedral of stone.

• *The biggest remnant of the original mosque ended up becoming the symbol of Sevilla itself—the Giralda bell tower. Find a spot near the Puerta del Perdón where you can look back and take in the tower.*

⑱ Giralda Bell Tower Exterior

This was the mosque's minaret from which Muslims were called to prayer. After the Reconquista, it still called the faithful to prayer...

but as a Christian bell tower. The tower offers a brief recap of the city's history: a strong foundation of precut blocks from ancient Rome; a middle section of brick made by the Moors; and the rebuilt tower from the Christian era (the original fell in 1356 and was rebuilt even higher in the 1550s).

Capping the tower is a 4,000-pound bronze female angel symbolizing the Triumph of Faith—specifically, the Christian faith over the Muslim one. The statue serves as a weather vane. (In Spanish, *girar* means "to rotate"; *la giralda* refers to this figure that turns with the wind.) A ribbon of letters (you can make out *Nomen Die* from this vantage point) proclaims, "The strongest tower is the name of God."

Now take in the whole scene—Giralda tower, courtyard, and the church with its flying buttresses and magnificent Gothic doorways. Enjoy the impressive remnants of the former mosque and the additions of today's church. And appreciate the significance of this site that was sacred to two great world religions.

• *Your cathedral tour is finished. If you haven't already done so, loop around the exterior of the cathedral (described at the start of the tour).*

Or for a truly religious experience, consider one more stop. After exiting the cathedral, make a U-turn left onto Avenida de la Constitución. At #24 (directly across from the church door), enter the passageway marked Plaza del Cabildo, which leads into a quiet courtyard with a humble little hole-in-the-wall shop.

⑲ El Torno Pastelería de Conventos

Here, nuns sell handicrafts (such as baptismal dresses for babies) and baked goods (Mon-Fri 10:00-13:30 & 17:00-19:30, Sat-Sun 10:30-14:00, closed Aug). You won't actually see the cloistered sisters, since this shop is staffed by laypeople, but the pastries they make are heavenly—Sevilla's best cookies, bar nun.

▲▲ROYAL ALCÁZAR

This palace has been a lavish residence for Spain's rulers for a thousand years. Originally a 10th-century palace built for the governors of the local Moorish state, it still functions as one of the royal family's homes—the oldest in Europe that's still in use. The core of the palace features an extensive 14th-century rebuild, done by Muslim workmen for the Christian king, Pedro I (1334-1369). Pedro was nicknamed either "the Cruel" or "the Just," depending on which end of his sword you were on. Pedro's palace embraces both cultural traditions.

Today, visitors can enjoy several sections of the Royal Alcázar. Spectacularly decorated halls and courtyards have distinctive Islamic-style flourishes. Exhibits call up the era of Columbus and Spain's New World dominance. The lush, sprawling gardens invite exploration.

Cost and Hours: €12.50, €18.50 includes worthwhile audioguide, buy tickets in advance online; open daily 9:30-19:00, Oct-March until 17:00; +34 954 502 324, www.alcazarsevilla.org. Your ticket gets you free admission to Museo de la Cerámica de Triana (see page 63).

Advance Tickets Recommended: You could line up for hours to buy a ticket, but why? The smart move is to buy a timed-entry ticket in advance. Book online as soon as you can, then use the short line for savvy travelers who did just that (show your printed or digital ticket).

Tours: The fast-moving **audioguide** gives you an hour of information as you wander. Or consider Concepción Delgado's **guided tour** (see "Tours in Sevilla," earlier).

𝛀 My free Sevilla City Walk **audio tour** includes background information and descriptions of the Royal Alcázar exterior, but not the interior.

Upper Royal Apartments Option (Cuarto Real Alto): With a little planning, you could fit in a visit to the 15 lavish, chandeliered, Versailles-like rooms used by today's monarchs, including the official dining room, living rooms, and stunning Mudejar-style Audience Room. Your group (15 people max) will be escorted on a 30-minute tour while using the included audioguide. It's a delightful and less-crowded part of the palace, but you'll need to book well in advance (€4.50, must check bags in lockers, check in 15 minutes early, last tour departs at 13:30). With this ticket, you become an Alcázar VIP and can enter the complex

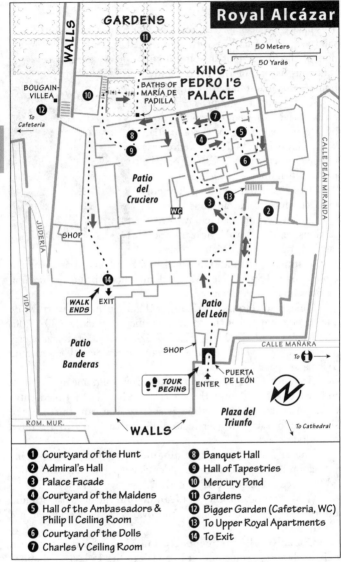

Royal Alcázar

1. Courtyard of the Hunt
2. Admiral's Hall
3. Palace Facade
4. Courtyard of the Maidens
5. Hall of the Ambassadors & Philip II Ceiling Room
6. Courtyard of the Dolls
7. Charles V Ceiling Room
8. Banquet Hall
9. Hall of Tapestries
10. Mercury Pond
11. Gardens
12. Bigger Garden (Cafeteria, WC)
13. To Upper Royal Apartments
14. To Exit

any time you like that day (go to the front of the line and present ticket).

○ Self-Guided Tour

This royal palace is decorated with a mix of Islamic and Christian elements—a style called Mudejar. It offers a thought-provoking glimpse of a graceful al-Andalus world that might have survived its Castilian conquerors...but didn't. The floor plan is intentionally confusing, to make experiencing the place more exciting and surprising. While Granada's Alhambra was built by Moors for Moorish rulers, what you see here is essentially a Christian ruler's palace, built in the Moorish style by Moorish artisans (after the Reconquista).

• *Just past the entrance, you'll go through the garden-like Lion Patio (Patio del León), with the rough original structure of the older Moorish fortress on your left (c. 913), and through the 12th-century arch into a courtyard called the...*

❶ Courtyard of the Hunt (Patio de la Montería)

For centuries, this has been the main gathering place in the Alcázar (and it's now where tourists converge). Get oriented. The palace's main entrance is directly ahead, through the elaborately decorated facade.

History is all around you. The Alcázar was built over many centuries, with rooms and decorations from the various rulers who've lived here. Behind you, the courtyard you passed through has remnants of the original 10th-century Moorish palace. The towering entrance facade before you dates from after Sevilla was Christianized, when King Pedro I built the most famous part of the complex. To the right are rooms dedicated to Spain's Golden Age, when the Alcázar was home to Ferdinand and Isabel and, later, their grandson Charles V (the most powerful man in Europe...the Holy Roman Emperor). Each successive monarch left their mark, adding still more luxury. And today's king and queen still use the palace's upper floor as one of their royal residences.

• *Before entering the heart of the palace, let's get a sense of its history. Start in the wing to the right of the courtyard.*

❷ Admiral's Hall (Salón del Almirante)

In the first room, filled with big canvases, find the **biggest painting** (and most melodramatic). This shows the crucial turning point in the Alcázar's history: The king who defeated the Moors in 1248, and turned the palace from Moorish to Christian, is kneeling humbly before the bishop, symbolically giving his life to God. Other paintings depict later royalty who made their mark on the Alcázar's history. (This particular room is still used today for fancy government receptions.)

Queen Isabel put her stamp on the Alcázar by building this series of rooms (1503). Having debriefed Columbus after his New World discoveries, she realized the potential business opportunity. She created this wing to administer Spain's New World ventures. In these halls, Columbus recounted his travels, Ferdinand Magellan planned his around-the-world cruise, and Amerigo Vespucci tried to come up with a catchy moniker for that newly discovered continent.

Continue into the pink-and-red Audience Chamber, once the Admiralty's chapel. The **altarpiece painting** is *St. Mary of the Navigators* (*Santa María de los Naveg-*

antes, Alejo Fernández, 1530s). The Virgin—the patron saint of sailors and a favorite of Columbus—keeps watch over the puny ships beneath her. Her cape seems to protect everyone under it—even the Native Americans in the dark background (the first time "Indians" were painted in Europe). Kneeling beside the Virgin (on the right, dressed in gold, almost joining his hands together in prayer) is none other than Christopher Columbus. He's on a cloud and this is heaven (this was painted a few decades after his death). Notice that Columbus is blond. Columbus' son said of his dad: "In his youth his hair was blond, but when he reached 30, it all turned white." Many historians believe this to be the earliest known portrait of Columbus. If so, it's also likely to be the most accurate. The man kneeling on the left side of the painting, with the big gold cape, is King Ferdinand.

Left of the painting is a **model** of Columbus' *Santa María*, his flagship and the only of his three ships not to survive the 1492 voyage. Columbus complained that

the *Santa María*—a big cargo ship, different from the sleek *Niña* and *Pinta* caravels—was too slow. On Christmas Day it ran aground off present-day Haiti and tore a hole in its hull. The ship was dismantled to build the first permanent structure in America, a fort for 39 colonists. (After Columbus left, the na-

tives burned the fort and killed the colonists.) Opposite the altarpiece (in the center of the back wall) is the family **coat of arms** of
Columbus' descendants, who now live in Spain and Puerto Rico.
Using Columbus' Spanish name, it reads: "To Castile and to León,
a new world was given by Colón."

As you return to the courtyard, don't miss the room (beyond
the grand piano) with display cases of ornate **fans** (mostly foreign
and well-described in English). A long painting (designed to be
gradually rolled across a screen and viewed like a primitive movie)
shows 17th-century Sevilla during Holy Week. Follow the procession, which is much like today's, with traditional floats carried by
teams of men along with a retinue of penitents.

• *Back in the Courtyard of the Hunt, face the impressive entrance to the...*

❸ Palace Facade

This is the entrance to **King Pedro I's Palace** (Palacio del Rey
Pedro I), the Alcázar's 14th-century
nucleus. Though it looks Islamic—
with lobed arches, slender columns,
and intricate stucco work—it's a classic example of the palace's Mudejar style. Looking closer you'll see
Christian motifs mixed in—coats of
arms of Spain's kings and heraldic
animals. About two-thirds of the
way up, find the inscription dedicated
to the man who built the gate (center
of the top row)—"Conquerador Don
Pedro." The facade's elaborate blend
of Islamic tracery and Gothic Chris-

tian elements introduces us to the unique style seen throughout
Pedro's part of the palace.

• *Enter the palace. Go left through the vestibule (impressive, yes, but
we'll see better), and emerge into the big courtyard with a long pool in
the center. This is the...*

❹ Courtyard of the Maidens (Patio de las Doncellas)

You've reached the center of King Pedro's palace. It's an open-air
courtyard, surrounded by
rooms. In the middle is a
long, rectangular reflecting pool. Like the Moors
who preceded him, Pedro
built his palace around
water.

King Pedro cruelly
abandoned his wife and

moved into the Alcázar with his mistress, then hired Muslim workers from Granada to re-create the romance of that city's Alhambra in Sevilla's stark Alcázar. The designers created a microclimate engineered for coolness: water, sunken gardens, pottery, thick walls, and darkness. This palace is considered Spain's best example of the Mudejar style. Stucco panels with elaborate designs, coffered wooden ceilings, and intricate lobed arches atop slender columns create a refined, pleasing environment. Ceramic tiles on the walls add color. The elegant proportions and symmetry of this courtyard are a photographer's delight.

Pedro's original courtyard was a single story; the upper floors were added by Isabel's grandson, Charles V, in the 16th century. Today, those upper-story rooms are part of the Spanish monarch's living quarters. See the different styles: Mudejar below (lobed arches and elaborate tracery) and Renaissance above (round arches and less decoration).

• *Let's explore some rooms surrounding the courtyard. Start with the room at the far end of the long reflecting pool—beneath the big octagonal tower. This is the palace's most important room.*

❺ Hall of the Ambassadors (Salón de Embajadores)

Here, in his throne room, Pedro received guests and caroused in luxury. The room is a cube topped with a half-dome, like many important Islamic buildings. In Islam, the cube represents the earth, and the dome is the starry heavens. In Pedro's world, the symbolism proclaimed that he controlled heaven and earth. Islamic horseshoe arches stand atop recycled columns with leafy golden capitals. As you marvel, remember that this is original, from the 1300s.

The stucco on the walls is molded with interlacing plants, geometrical shapes, and Arabic writing. Despite this being a Christian palace, the walls are inscribed with unapologetically Muslim sayings: "None but Allah conquers" and "Happiness and prosperity are benefits of Allah, who nourishes all creatures." The artisans added propaganda phrases, such as "Dedicated to the magnificent Sultan Pedro—thanks to God!" (Perhaps the Allah quotes survived because Muslims and Christians praise the same God, and in Arabic—Muhammad's native language—God is called Allah.)

The Mudejar style also includes Christian motifs. Find the row of kings, high up at the base of the dome, chronicling all of Castile's rulers from the 600s to the 1600s (portrayed as if on playing cards). Within the intricate patterns inside the dome, you can

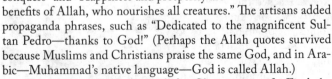

see a few coats of arms—including the castle of Castile and the lion of León. These symbols (along with another royal symbol with twin columns) are seen throughout the palace. The Mudejar style also incorporates birds, seashells, and other natural objects you wouldn't normally find in Islamic decor, as it traditionally avoids realistic images of nature.

Notice how it gets cooler as you go deeper into the palace. Straight ahead from the Hall of the Ambassadors, in the **Philip II Ceiling Room** (Salón del Techo de Felipe II), look above the arches to find peacocks, falcons, and other birds amid interlacing vines. Imagine day-to-day life in the palace—with VIP guests tripping on the tiny steps.

• *Make your way to the second courtyard (with your back to the Hall of the Ambassadors, circle right). This smaller courtyard (with the skylight) is the...*

❻ Courtyard of the Dolls (Patio de las Muñecas)

This delicate courtyard was reserved for the king's private family life. Originally, the center of the courtyard had a pool, cool-

ing the residents and reflecting decorative patterns that were once brightly painted on the walls. The columns—recycled from ancient Roman and Visigothic buildings— are of alternating white, black, and pink marble. The courtyard's name comes from the tiny doll faces found at the base of one of the arches. Circle the room and try to find them. (Hint: While just a couple of inches tall, they're eight feet up—kitty- corner from where you entered.)

• *Wander around before returning to the big Courtyard of the Maidens. In the middle of the right side an arch leads to the...*

❼ Charles V Ceiling Room (Salón del Techo del Carlos V)

Emperor Charles V ruled Spain at its peak and, flush with New World wealth, expanded the palace. His marriage to his beloved cousin Isabella—which took place in this room—joined vast realms of Spain and Portugal. Devoutly Christian, Charles celebrated his wedding night with a midnight Mass, and later ordered the Mudejar ceiling in this room to be replaced with the less Islamic (but no less impressive) Renaissance one you see today. At the base of the ceiling, find Charles' coat of arms—the black double eagle.

• *When you're ready to move on, return to the Courtyard of the Maidens, then turn right. In the corner, find the small staircase. Go up to rooms decorated with bright ceramic tiles and Gothic vaulting. Pass directly through the chapel (with its majestic mahogany altar on your right) and into a big, long room.*

❽ Banquet Hall (Salón Gótico)

This airy banquet hall is where Charles and Isabella held their wedding reception. Note the huge coats of arms: Charles' double eagle on one end and Isabella's shield of Portugal on the other. Both are painted cloth from the 1500s. Tiles of yellow, blue, green, and orange (from the 16th century) line the room, some decorated with whimsical human figures with vase-like bodies. Imagine a formal occasion here, as elegant guests took in the views of the gardens. To this day, city officials and VIPs still host receptions here.

• *Midhall, on the left, enter the...*

❾ Hall of Tapestries (Salón Tapices)

Next door, the walls are hung with 18th-century Spanish copies of 16th-century Belgian tapestries showing the power, conquests, and industriousness of Charles' prosperous reign. This series of scenes depicts the pivotal Conquest of Tunisia (1535), which stopped the Muslim Ottomans in North Africa at a time when they were threatening Europe on different fronts. (The highlights are described in Spanish along the top, and in Latin  along the bottom.) The map tapestry of the Mediterranean world has south pointing up. Find Genova, Italy, on the bottom; Africa on top; Lisbon (Lisboa) on the far right; the large city of Barcelona in between; and Tunisia (Tunis). The ships of the Holy Roman Empire gather in anticipation of a major battle. The artist included himself (far right) holding the legend—with a scale in both leagues and miles.

At the far end of the room is a big, dramatic portrayal of the Spanish Navy. With cannon-laden warships and a merchant fleet to haul goods and people, Spain ruled the waves—and thereby an empire upon which the sun never set. Its reign lasted from 1492 until the defeat of the Spanish Armada in 1588; after that, Britannia's navy took the helm, and it was her crown that controlled the next global empire.

• *Return to the Banquet Hall, then head outside at the far end to the extensive landscaped gardens. First up is the...*

⑩ Mercury Pond

The Mercury Pond is marked by a tiny bronze statue of the messenger of the gods, with his cute little winged feet. This was a reservoir fed by a 16th-century aqueduct that irrigated the palace's entire garden. As only elites had running water, the fountain was an extravagant show of power. The long stucco-studded wall along one side of the garden was part of the original Moorish castle wall. In the early 1600s, when fortifications were no longer needed here, that end was redesigned to be a grotto-style gallery.

• *From the Mercury Pond, steps lead into the formal gardens. Just past the bottom of the steps, a tunnel on the right leads under the palace to the coolest spot in the city—the* **Baths of María de Padilla.** *This long underground pool was a rainwater cistern, named for Pedro of Castile's mistress who frequented the place. Its mysterious medieval atmosphere is like something out of* Game of Thrones—*which actually did use this and other Alcázar settings in several episodes of the television series. Finally, explore the rest of the...*

⑪ Gardens

The intimate geometric zone nearest the palace is the Moorish garden. The far-flung garden beyond that was the backyard of the Christian ruler.

Here in the gardens, as in the rest of the palace, Christian and Islamic traditions merge and mingle. Both cultures used water and nature as essential parts of their architecture. The garden's pavilions and fountains only enhance this. Wander among palm trees, myrtle hedges, and fragrant roses. While tourists pay to be here, this is actually a public garden, and free to locals. It's been that way since 1931, when the king was exiled and Spanish citizens took ownership of royal holdings. In 1975, the Spanish people allowed the king back on the throne—but on their terms...which included keeping this garden.

From the Moors to Pedro I to Ferdinand and Isabel, and from Charles V to King Felipe VI, we've seen the home of a millennium of Spanish kings and queens. Feel free to explore the exotic landscape they created and create your own *Arabian Nights* fantasies.

• *Your Alcázar tour is over. When you're ready to leave these gardens, return to the Mercury Pond and step back into the palace into a small courtyard with palm trees. From here, consider your options:*

Just a few steps away, on the other side of the stucco wall, is a mas-

Christopher Columbus (1451-1506)

This Italian wool weaver ran off to sea, was shipwrecked in Portugal, married a captain's daughter, learned Portuguese and Spanish, and persuaded Spain's monarchs to finance his bold scheme to trade with the East by sailing west. On August 3, 1492, Columbus set sail from Palos (near Huelva, 60 miles west of Sevilla) with three ships and 90 men, hoping to land in Asia, which Columbus estimated was 3,000 miles away. Ten weeks—and yes, 3,000 miles—later, with a superstitious crew ready to mutiny after they'd seen evil omens (including a falling meteor and a jittery compass), Columbus landed on an island in the Bahamas, convinced he'd reached Asia. He and his crew traded with the "Indians" and returned home to Palos harbor, where they were received as heroes.

Columbus made three more voyages to the New World and became rich with gold. But he gained a bad reputation among the colonists for ruling with an iron fist. Further tarnishing his legacy was Columbus' mistreatment, forced labor, and enslavement of the indigenous people he encountered—establishing a cruel precedent that would linger for centuries. Eventually, Columbus was arrested and brought back to Spain in chains. Though pardoned, Columbus fell out of favor with the court. On May 20, 1506, he died in Valladolid. His son said he was felled by "gout and by grief at seeing himself fallen from his high estate," but historians speculate that diabetes or syphilis may have contributed. Columbus died thinking he'd visited Asia, unaware he'd opened up Europe to a New World.

sive bougainvillea and a **⑫ bigger garden with cafeteria and WCs.** Once a farm that provided for the royal community, the garden is now home to a cool and convenient cafeteria with a delightful terrace.

If you've booked a spot to visit the **⑬ Upper Royal Apartments,** return to the Courtyard of the Hunt, and head upstairs.

Otherwise, follow **⑭ exit** signs and head out through the **Patio de Banderas,** once the entrance for guests arriving by horse carriage. Enjoy a classic Giralda bell tower view as you leave.

BETWEEN THE CATHEDRAL AND THE RIVER
▲Archivo General de Indias
(General Archives of the Indies)

To the right of the Alcázar's main entrance, the Archivo General de Indias houses historic papers related to Spain's overseas territories. Its four miles of shelving contain 80 million pages documenting a once-mighty empire. While little of interest is actually on show, a visit is free, easy, and gives you a look at the Lonja Palace, one of the finest Renaissance edifices in Spain. Designed by royal architect Juan de Herrera, the principal designer of El Escorial, the building evokes the greatness of the Spanish empire at its peak (c. 1600).

🎧 Download my free Sevilla City Walk audio tour for background on the Archivo General de Indias.

Cost and Hours: Free, Tue-Sat 9:30-17:00, Sun 10:00-14:00, closed Mon, Avenida de la Constitución 3, +34 954 500 528.

Background: In the early 1500s, as exotic goods began pouring into Sevilla from newly discovered lands, this spot between the cathedral and the Alcázar was an open-air market, where businessmen met to trade. Sevilla was the only port licensed to trade with the New World, and merchants came here from across Europe, establishing the city as a commercial powerhouse. The area evolved as a hub of Spanish power, where the royal palace, business community, and cathedral all came together.

In 1583, this grand building was built as a place for those merchants, moneychangers, and accountants to do their business—an early stock market, or *lonja*. (On the cathedral-facing side of the building stands a stone cross where businessmen would "swear to God" to be honest in their trade.) Mapmakers, sea captains, and navigators also gathered here, as well as lawyers, accountants, and politicians who could administer Spain's far-flung colonies. Herrera designed a no-nonsense Renaissance building of symmetrical doors and windows, balustrades, and distinctive rooftop pinnacles.

By 1785, with Sevilla in decline (a victim of plagues, a silted-up harbor, and the rise of Cádiz as Spain's main port), the building was put to new use as an archive: the storehouse for documents the country was quickly amassing from its discovery, conquest, and administration of the New World.

Visiting the Archives: The **ground floor** houses a small rotating exhibit that tells the story of the building. You may see copies of famous documents here, like the Treaty of Tordesillas (1494, when Spain and Portugal divvied up the New World) or the Capitulations of Santa Fe (the contract Columbus signed with Ferdinand and Isabel for his 1492 voyage). There's often a cannon discovered by American treasure hunter Mel Fisher. He used information in the archives to find a Spanish galleon that sank off the Florida coast in 1616—with a huge treasure onboard. Fisher returned the cannon as a gesture of goodwill.

Upstairs (up an extravagant marble staircase) there are several exhibits clustered near the landing: Don't miss the huge 16th-century security chest—meant to store gold and important documents. Its elaborate locking mechanism (it fills the inner lid) could be opened only by following a set series of pushes, pulls, and twists—an effective way to keep prying eyes and greedy fingers from its valuable contents. Portraits depict some of the explorers whose discoveries made this building possible (Columbus, Cortés, et al.), scholars who archived the documents, and the powdered-wig administrators *(teniente general)* of the colonial empire. Nearby, find a curtained room with an interesting 15-minute video on Sevilla's New World connections and the archive's work. Then browse the wooden racks with (copies of) documents from the collection. The collection covers both "Indies"—East and West—so you'll see maps of Guatemala and the Philippines, maps by Amerigo Vespucci (who sailed from Sevilla in the 1490s and was one of the first to realize America wasn't India), manuscripts about Magellan's around-the-world voyage, Pizarro's conquest of Peru, and old sketches of Indian natives.

Finally, make a big circle around the rest of the (mostly empty) upstairs to check out the rows and rows of cedar and mahogany bookshelves, beautifully decorated domes, and occasional rotating exhibits.

Avenida de la Constitución

Old Sevilla is bisected by this grand boulevard. Its name celebrates the country's 1978 adoption of a democratic constitution, as the Spanish people moved quickly to reestablish their free government after the 1975 death of longtime dictator Francisco Franco (an understandable change, since it was previously named for the founder of Spain's Fascist Party, José Antonio Primo de Rivera).

The busy avenue was converted into a pedestrian boulevard in 2007. Overnight, the city's paseo route took on a new dimension. Suddenly cafés and shops here had fresh appeal. The tram line (infamously short, only about a mile long) is controversial, as it violates what might have been a more purely pedestrian zone.

▲▲Hospital de la Caridad

This charity hospital, which functioned as a place of final refuge for Sevilla's poor and homeless, was founded in the 17th century by the nobleman Don Miguel Mañara. Your visit includes an evocative courtyard, a church filled with powerful art, and a good audioguide that explains it all. This is still a working charity, so when you pay your entrance fee, you're advancing the work Mañara started back in the 17th century.

Cost and Hours: €8, includes audioguide, daily 10:30-19:30, Calle Temprado 3, +34 954 223 232, www.santa-caridad.es.

Background: Hospital founder Don Miguel Mañara (1626-1679) was the happy-go-lucky mayor of Sevilla at its peak of prosperity and sophistication. A big-time playboy and enthusiastic sinner, he had a massive change of heart late in life and dedicated his last years to strict worship and taking care of the poor. In 1674, Mañara acquired some empty warehouses in Sevilla's old shipyard and built this 150-ward "place of heroic virtues."

Mañara could well have been the inspiration for Don Juan, the quasi-legendary character from a play set in 17th-century Sevilla, popularized later by Lord Byron's poetry and Mozart's opera *Don Giovanni*. While no one knows for sure, it adds some fun to the visit. Regardless, the hospital's iconography is all built around a Don Juan theme: the sudden realization that, in the face of death, all of life's pleasures are fleeting, and only by doing acts of charity can we gain eternal life.

Visiting the Hospital: Entering the **courtyard** you're greeted by a statue of a woman and two ecstatic cherubs, filled with the love of mankind. It's Charity, the mission of this hospital. The statues come from Genoa, Italy, as Mañara's family were rich Genovese merchants who moved to Sevilla to get in on the wealth from New World discoveries. The Dutch tiles (from Delft), depicting scenes from the Old and New Testament, are a reminder that the Netherlands was under Spanish rule in centuries past. This charming red-and-white courtyard, surrounded by offices, was the administrative hub of the hospital's charitable work and its ongoing assistance to the poor. You're likely to see seniors shuffling in and out, as this is still a home for the poor—Mañara's legacy in action.

The **Sala de Cabildos,** a small room at the end of the courtyard, is Mañara's former office. It has rotating exhibits from Mañara's art collection.

Stepping out of the Sala de Cabildos, the chapel is on your right. But first, head left into a small, evocative courtyard. These arches are part of the 13th-century **shipyards.** Wander around and imagine the huge halls where the ships were produced that enabled Columbus, Vasco da Gama, and Magellan to broaden Europe's horizons and make Portugal a world power.

Next, cross the inner courtyard and head up a few steps into the highlight—the **chapel.** It's an over-the-top masterpiece of Sevillian Baroque—a fusion of architecture, painting, and sculpture. Don Miguel hired Sevilla's three greatest artists (who were also his friends): the painters Bartolomé Murillo and Juan de Valdés Leal and the sculptor Pedro Roldán. Mañara himself worked with them to design the church and its themes.

Start with the painting at the back of the **nave**, on the left wall. Worshippers would be greeted by Leal's *In the Blink of an Eye (In Ictu Oculi)*. In it, the Grim Reaper extinguishes the candle of life. Filling the canvas are the ruins of worldly goods, knowledge, power, and position. It's all gone in the blink of an eye—true in the 1670s...and true today. Don Miguel experienced that personally when his wife suddenly died—along with half of Sevilla—in a devastating plague.

Directly opposite is Leal's *The End of the Glories of the World*. The painting shows Mañara and a bishop decaying together in a crypt, with worms and assorted bugs munching away. Above, the hand of Christ—pierced by the nail—holds the scales of justice: sins ("Nimas," on the left) and good deeds ("Nimanos," on the right). The placement of both paintings gave worshippers plenty to think about during and after their visit.

Strolling up the nave, you'll see paintings and statues that show various good deeds and acts of self-sacrifice and charity performed by Jesus and the saints—the kinds of things that we should emulate to save us from eternal death. Most of the paintings leading up to the altar are replicas of Murillo's pieces, lost during Napoleonic times. On the left wall, Moses strikes a rock to bring water to the needy Israelites. A trademark Murillo beggar-boy atop a horse points at Moses as if saying, "Do what he did." On the right wall, Jesus gives loaves and fishes to thousands of hungry people. Murillo, a devoted member of this charity, was hammering home one of the institution's functions—give food and drink to the poor.

The giant **altar** is carved wood with gold leaf, with a dozen hardworking cupids providing support. Christ's lifeless body has been taken from the cross and some workers are bringing in the dark-gray tombstone. This illustrated the mission of the monks here—to provide a proper Christian burial to society's outcasts, like executed criminals. The carved-and-painted statues by Roldán are realistic and emotional, in the style of his famed *La Macarena* statue. Atop the altar are three female figures representing faith (left), hope (right), and—the star of this place—charity. Notice how the altar's painting blends seamlessly with the statues of his burial below. The rocks and shrubs of the painting morph into sculpted 3-D rocks and shrubs, as the events of the Crucifixion become the more tangible reality of Jesus' very dead body.

As you leave the church, do Don Miguel Mañara a favor. Step on his **tombstone.** It's located in the back, tucked within the big wooden entranceway. Set in the pavement, this tombstone has served as a humble doormat since 1679. He requested to be buried here so everyone would step on him as they entered. The tombstone reads, "Beneath this stone lies the worst man in the world." By focusing on the vanity of his own life and dedicating himself to charity, Don Miguel hoped to be saved from his sins.

Outside, more big shots—many of Sevilla's top families to this day—are featured on tombstones paving the exit.

Across the street from the entry is a park. Pop in and see Don Miguel—wracked with guilt—carrying a poor, sick person into his hospital. One thing's for certain: Don Miguel is on the road to sainthood. But since you need to perform miracles to become a saint, his supporters request that you report any miraculous answers to prayers to the Vatican.

Torre del Oro (Gold Tower) and Naval Museum

Sevilla's historic riverside Gold Tower was the starting and ending point for all shipping to the New World. It's named for the golden reflection of the sun off the Guadalquivir River—not for all the New World booty that landed here. Ever since the Moors built it in the 13th century, it's been part of the city's fortifications, and long anchored a heavy chain that draped from here across the river to protect the harbor. In 1248, King Ferdinand III's ships rammed the chain and broke through, taking the city from the Moors. Today, it houses a skippable, dreary naval museum with a mediocre river view.

SEVILLA

BARRIO SANTA CRUZ

For a self-guided walk through this neighborhood, see my "Barrio Santa Cruz Walk," earlier, or 🎧 download my free Sevilla City Walk audio tour.

Hospital de los Venerables

This former charity-run old-folks home and hospital comes with a Baroque church and an exquisite painting gallery that includes the Centro Velázquez, which displays works by one of Spain's premier artists. It merges local history, art, and architecture in one building. Everything is well explained by the audioguide.

Cost and Hours: €10, includes audioguide, open daily 10:00-18:00, closes at 14:00 July-Nov, Plaza de los Venerables 8, +34 954 562 696, www.focus.abengoa.es.

Visiting the Hospital: In the courtyard, you get a sense of how retired priests and Sevilla's needy mingled around its sunken fountain.

The church, which takes you back to the year 1700, is bursting with Baroque decor, one of Spain's best pipe organs, and frescoes by Juan de Valdés Leal. Of note is the *trompe l'oeil* he painted on the sacristy ceiling, turning a small room into a piece of heaven. The decor exalts the priesthood and Spain's role as standard-bearer of the pope.

The top-notch **painting gallery** is dedicated to one of the world's greatest painters, Diego Velázquez (1599-1660), who was born here in Sevilla, where he also worked as a young man. Velázquez's *Vista de Sevilla* helps you imagine the excitement of this thriving city in 1649 when, with 120,000 people, it was the fourth largest in Europe. You'll recognize landmarks like the Giralda bell tower, the cathedral, and the Torre del Oro. The pontoon bridge leads to Triana—where citizens of all ranks strolled the promenade together, as they still do today.

The Sevilla that shaped Velázquez was the gateway to the New World. There was plenty of stimulation: adventurers, fortune hunters, and artists passed through here, and many stayed for years. Of the few Velázquez paintings remaining in his hometown, three are in this gallery. Upstairs has little of interest, but the staircase dome is worth a look, as is the private box view into the church.

NORTH OF THE CATHEDRAL

Plaza Nueva

The pleasant "New Square" is a five-minute walk north of the cathedral and the end of the line for Sevilla's short tram system (which zips down Avenida de la Constitución to the San Bernardo train station).

At the center of the square is a **statue of King Ferdinand III,** who liberated Sevilla from the Moors in the 13th century and was later sainted. This is another example of Sevilla's devotion to the Virgin. If you look closely at the statue, you can see the horn of the king's saddle is actually his treasured Virgin of the Battles statuette. Made of hollowed ivory, it was carved to fit over the saddle horn, and he rode with it into battle many times. When his 13th-century tomb was opened in the 17th century, they found the same ivory Mary with his incorrupt body. (And that very statue is now in the cathedral's big sacristy).

For centuries after the Christian reconquest, a huge Franciscan **monastery** stood on this site; it was a spiritual home to many of the missionaries who colonized the California coast. But, in the 1800s, when the Jesuits threatened the secular government and stood in the way of modern, post-revolutionary thinking, the power of the monasteries was overturned and grand monasteries like this were destroyed.

Running along the square is the relatively modern **City Hall.** Couples use the grand salon upstairs for weekend weddings, then join their photographers on the front steps. For a more interesting look at this building, circle around to the other end (to the smaller square, called Plaza de San Francisco). This square—the site of the Spanish Inquisition's infamous *auto-da-fé*—has been used for executions, bullfights, and (today) big city events.

▲▲Church of the Savior (Iglesia del Salvador)

Sevilla's second-biggest church, built on the site of a ninth-century mosque, gleams with freshly scrubbed Baroque pride. While the larger cathedral is a jumble of styles, this church is uniformly

Andalusian Baroque—the architecture, decor, and statues are all from the same period. The church is home to some of Sevilla's most beloved statues that are paraded through town during religious festivals.

Cost and Hours: €6, includes audioguide, covered by cathedral combo-ticket, best to buy ticket in advance online; Mon-Sat 11:00-18:00 (July-Aug from 10:00), Sun 15:00-19:30; Plaza del Salvador, +34 954 211 679, www.catedraldesevilla.es.

Advance Tickets Recommended: While lines are generally shorter here than at the cathedral, they can still be long and slow. It's smart to purchase your combo-ticket online in advance. Ticket in hand, head straight to the exit, where a guard will let you in.

Visiting the Church and Semana Santa Statues: The spacious **nave** covers the same footprint as the ancient mosque it replaced from the year 830, and because of that it's oddly shaped (square, like the cathedral). This Baroque structure dates from around 1700, built to replace an earlier (run-down) church. The enormous **high altar** features a golden Jesus (being Transfigured) atop an eruption of black clouds. But the artistic stars here are the whirling pair of angels holding lamps with red ropes. Look high above to see frescoes that, once long forgotten, were revealed by a recent cleaning. (It's easy to forget how sooty Europe's art treasures were until the last generation or so.)

The church's many richly decorated **chapels** are the highlight. Each has a distinct statue, generally made of wood, painted, and expressive in the Sevillian style. The realistic statues depict events from the Passion (the week leading up to Easter), showing Jesus being tortured and crucified, and Mary mourning her son. Many are set atop floats during Holy Week—and many are on pedestals, making them portable. The rest of the year, they reside here and are cared for by brotherhoods dedicated to charitable works. (If you visit here just before Holy Week, you might see floats being assembled and bedecked in flowers in the nave.) Some of the better-known statues headquartered here include:

The **Little Donkey,** or *Borriquita* (right of altar), carries a statue of Jesus into Jerusalem to kick off Holy Week on Palm Sunday. All five statues in this corner of the church parade together during Holy Week. The grippingly beautiful **Christ of Love** (left of the donkey) dates from about 1600 and is one of the oldest in the parade.

Our Lady of the Waters (right of the Little Donkey) is a maternal pyramid filling an extravagantly Baroque chapel with a white marble baptismal font in front. She predates this church by about 400 years. Though permanently parked now, for centuries she was paraded through Sevilla in times of drought.

Christ Suffering for the Afflicted (left of the altar) shows

Christ laboring under his turquoise and silver cross for souls stranded in purgatory—see groups in flames at the bottom.

Christ of the Passion (left of the altar, in the left transept) shows Jesus carrying the cross to his death. Made in 1619 by Juan Martínez Montañés, this is one of the city's most beloved statues. It's so revered by pilgrims and worshippers that the chapel has a separate entrance (though it's sometimes visible through the bars, if the curtain is open).

To reach the Christ of the Passion **chapel,** exit the church, go right, and then right again. Under the stubby tower, go through a small door into a courtyard and then through a small pilgrims' shop (free, daily 10:00-14:00 & 17:00-21:00). For centuries, the faithful have come here to pray, marvel at the sadness that fills the chapel, then kiss Jesus' heel. (To join them, head up the stairs behind the altar.) Jesus is flanked by John the Evangelist and a grieving, red-eyed María Dolorosa, with convincing tears and a jeweled dagger in her heart. Flanking Jesus are two Jesuit missionaries who were martyred in Japan. Their skulls are under their feet. In the adjacent shop (above the cashier), a wall tile shows the Christ of the Passion statue in a circa-1620 procession.

Back outside, in the **courtyard,** you can feel the presence of the mosque that once stood on this spot. Its minaret is now the Christian bell tower and the mosque's arches are now halfway underground.

Nearby: Finish your visit by enjoying **Plaza del Salvador,** a favorite local meeting point. Strolling this square, you become part of the theater of life in Sevilla.

Casa de Pilatos

This 16th-century palace offers a scaled-down version of the royal Alcázar (with a similar mix of Gothic, Moorish, and Renaissance styles) and a delightful garden. The nobleman who built it was inspired by a visit to the Holy Land, where he saw the supposed mansion of Pontius Pilate. If you've seen the Alcázar, this probably isn't worth the time or money. Your visit comes in two parts: the stark ground floor and garden (a tile lover's fantasy, with good audioguide); and a plodding, 25-minute guided English/Spanish tour of the lived-in noble residence upstairs.

Cost and Hours: €12, includes entire house and guided tour; €10 covers just the ground floor and garden; audioguide included in both tickets; daily 9:00-19:00, off-season until 18:00, tours run 2/hour (check schedule at entry); Plaza de Pilatos 1, www.fundacionmedinaceli.org.

▲Museo Palacio de la Condesa de Lebrija

This aristocratic mansion takes you back to the 18th century like no other place in town. The Countess of Lebrija was a passionate collector of antiquities. Her home's ground floor is paved with Roman mosaics (that you can actually walk on) from nearby Itálica and lined with musty old cases of Phoenician, Greek, Roman, and Moorish artifacts—mostly pottery. The grand staircase and dining-room tiles came from a former Augustinian convent, and several rooms were even modified to fit the collectibles the countess bought (a good example is the octagonal room built to house an eight-sided Roman floor mosaic). To see a plush world from a time when the nobility had a private priest and their own chapel, take a quickie tour of the upstairs, which shows the palace as the countess left it when she died in 1938.

Cost and Hours: €5 for unescorted visit of ground floor (good English descriptions), €8 includes English/Spanish tour of "lived-in" upstairs—offered every 45 minutes; open daily 10:30-19:30, free and obligatory bag check, Calle Cuna 8, +34 954 227 802, www.palaciodelebrija.com.

Plaza de la Encarnación

Several years ago, in an attempt to revitalize this formerly nondescript square, the city unveiled what locals call "the mushrooms":

a gigantic, undulating canopy of five waffle-patterned, toadstool-esque, hundred-foot-tall wooden structures. Together, this structure (officially named *Metropol Parasol*) provides shade, a gazebo for performances, and a traditional market hall. While the market is busy each morning, locals don't know what to make of the avant-garde structure. A ramp under the canopy leads down to ancient-Roman-era street level, where a museum displays Roman ruins found during the building process. From the museum level, a pay elevator takes you up top, where you can do a loop walk along the terrace to enjoy its commanding city views—but I found it not worth the time or trouble. Other views in town are free and just as good (such as from the rooftop bar of the EME Catedral Hotel, across the street from the cathedral).

Cost and Hours: Plaza level always open and free; €3 viewpoint elevator ride includes drink at the top and runs daily 10:00-23:30, shorter hours off-season; free with Alcázar ticket; www.setasdesevilla.com.

▲Flamenco Dance Museum (Museo del Baile Flamenco)

Though small and pricey, this museum is worthwhile for anyone looking to understand more about the dance that embodies the spirit of southern Spain. The main exhibit, on floor 1, takes about 45 minutes to see. It features well-produced videos, flamenco costumes, and other artifacts collected by the grande dame of flamenco, Cristina Hoyos. The top floor and basement house temporary exhibits, mostly of photography and other artwork. On the ground floor and in the basement, you can watch flamenco lessons in progress—or even take one yourself (one hour, first person-€60, €20/person after that, shoes not provided but yours are OK).

Cost and Hours: €10, €26 combo-ticket includes evening flamenco performance (see "Nightlife in Sevilla," later), daily 10:00-19:00, pick up English info sheet at front desk; about 3 blocks east of Plaza Nueva at Calle Manuel Rojas Marcos 3—follow signs for *Museo del Baile Flamenco*; +34 954 340 311, www.museoflamenco.com.

▲Museo de Bellas Artes

Sevilla's passion for religious art is preserved and displayed in its Museum of Fine Arts. While most Americans go for El Greco, Goya, and Velázquez (not a forte of this collection), this museum opens horizons and gives a fine look at other, less well-known Spanish masters: Zurbarán and Murillo. Rather than exhausting, the museum is pleasantly enjoyable.

Cost and Hours: €1.50; Tue-Sat 9:00-21:00, until 15:00 on Sun and in summer, closed Mon year-round; mandatory bag check (€1 deposit), +34 954-786-498, www.museosdeandalucia.es.

Getting There: The museum is at Plaza Museo 9, a 15-minute walk or cheap taxi ride from the cathedral. It's also on the #C5 bus route.

Background: As Spain's economic Golden Age (the 1500s) blossomed into its arts and literature Golden Age (the 1600s), wealthy Sevilla reigned as the sophisticated capital of culture while Madrid was still a newly built center of government. Several of Spain's top painters—Zurbarán, Murillo, and Velázquez—lived in Sevilla in the 1600s. They labored to make the spiritual world tangible, and forged the gritty realism that marks Spanish painting. You'll see balding saints and monks with wrinkled faces and sunburned hands, radiating an inner spirituality. This highly accessible style inspired the Catholic faithful in an age when Protestants were demanding a closer personal relationship with God.

Appropriately, this collection of (mostly) religious art is now displayed in the halls of what once was a convent for friars of the Order of Mercy. The building itself is an attraction: It was a particularly wealthy convent boasting some of the finest courtyards and decorative tiles in the city. In the early 1800s, Spain's ultra-secular government began disbanding convents and monasteries, and secular fanatics had a heyday looting churches. Fortunately, much of Andalucía's religious art was rescued and hung safely here.

● **Self-Guided Tour:** The permanent collection features 20 rooms in neat chronological order. It's easy to breeze through once with my tour, then backtrack to what appeals to you. Pick up the English-language floor plan, which explains the theme of each room.

• *Enter and follow signs to the permanent collection, which begins in Sala I (Room 1).*

Rooms 1-4: Medieval altarpieces of gold-backed saints, Virgin-and-babes, and Crucifixion scenes attest to the religiosity that nurtured Spain's early art. Spain's penchant for unflinching realism culminates in Room 2 with Michelangelo friend/rival Pietro Torrigiano's 1525 statue of an emaciated San Jerónimo, whose gaze never falters from the cross, and in Room 3 with the painted clay head of St. John the Baptist—complete with severed neck muscles, throat, and windpipe. This warts-and-all naturalism would influence the well-known Sevillian art teacher Francisco Pacheco (also Room 3) as well as his student and son-in-law, Velázquez (Room 4). Velázquez's *Head of an Apostle*—a sober portrait of a bearded, balding, wrinkled man—exemplifies how Sevillian painters could make once-inaccessible saints seem flesh and blood like you and me.

• *Continue through the pleasant outdoor courtyard (the convent's former cloister) to the grand, former church that is now Room 5.*

Room 5: Large-scale religious art now hangs in what was once a church nave. On the left wall is the *Apotheosis of St. Thomas Aquinas* (*Apoteosis de Santo Tomás de Aquino,* 1631) by **Francisco de Zurbarán** (thoor-ba-RAHN, 1598-1664). This is the artist's most important work, done at the height of his career. Zurbarán presents the pivotal moment when the great saint-theologian experiences his spiritual awakening. He's surrounded by ultra-realistic portraits of other saints, whose stately poses and simple gestures speak volumes. What's unique about Zurbarán is the setting. He strips away any semblance of 3-D background to portray how these real people are having a surreal experience. Thomas has suddenly found himself in a heavenly cloud surrounded by long-dead saints, while his contemporaries below gaze upward, sharing the vision. We'll see more of Zurbarán later in our tour.

As you approach the former church's main altar, you find works of another hometown boy, **Bartolomé Murillo,** including

several paintings of the Virgin Mary, his signature subject (for more on Murillo, see the sidebar on page 30). He portrayed the Immaculate Conception of Mary, the doctrine that she was born without the taint of original sin. Typically, Mary is depicted as young, dressed in white and blue, standing atop the moon (crescent or full). She clutches her breast and gazes up rapturously, surrounded by tumbling winged babies. Murillo's tiny *Madonna and Child* (*Virgen de la Servilleta*, 1665), at the end of the room in the center, shows the warmth and appeal of his work.

Murillo's sweet naturalism is quite different from the harsh realism of his fellow artists, so his work was understandably popular. For many Spaniards, Mary is their main connection to heaven. They pray directly to her, asking her to intercede on their behalf with God. Murillo's Marys are always receptive and ready to help.

Besides his *Inmaculadas*, Murillo painted popular saints. They often carry sprigs of plants, and cock their heads upward, caught up in a heavenly vision of sweet Baby Jesus. Murillo is also known for his "genre" paintings—scenes of common folk and rascally street urchins—but the museum has few of these.

• *Now head back outside to enjoy the coolness of the cloister and the beauty of its tiles, then go up the Imperial Staircase to the first floor.*

Rooms 6-9: In Rooms 6 and 7, you'll see more Murillos and Murillo imitators. Room 8 is dedicated to yet another native Sevillian (and friend of Murillo), Juan de Valdés Leal (1622-1690), whose work is also featured in the Hospital de la Caridad (see listing earlier). He adds Baroque motion and drama to religious subjects. His surreal colors and feverish, unfinished style create a mood of urgency. In Room 9, art students will recognize the work of José de Ribera—a Spaniard living in Italy—who merged Spanish realism with Caravaggio's strong dark-light contrast.

Room 10: Here you'll find more Zurbarán saints and monks, and the miraculous things they experienced, with an unblinking, crystal-clear, brightly lit, highly detailed realism. Browse the paintings, enjoying the weathered faces, voluminous robes, and precisely etched details. These photorealistic people are shown against a neutral background, as though existing in the landscape of an otherworldly vision. Monks and nuns could meditate upon Zurbarán's meticulous paintings for hours, finding God in the details.

In Zurbarán's *St. Hugo Visiting the Refectory* (*San Hugo en el Refectorio*), white-robed Carthusian monks gather for their simple meal in a communal dining hall. Above them hangs a painting of Mary, Baby Jesus, and John the Baptist. Zurbarán created paintings like this for monks' dining halls. His audience: celibate men and women who lived in isolation, as in this former convent, devoting their time to quiet meditation, prayer, and Bible study. Zurbarán shines a harsh spotlight on many of his subjects,

creating strong shadows. Zurbarán's people often stand starkly isolated against a single-color background—a dark room or the gray-white of a cloudy sky. He was the ideal painter for the austere religion of 17th-century Spain as it led the Counter-Reformation, standing strong against the rising tide of Protestantism in Europe.

Adjacent to *St. Hugo*, find *The Virgin of the Caves (La Virgen de las Cuevas)* and study the piety and faith in the monks' weathered faces. Zurbarán's Mary is protective, with her hands placed on the heads of two monks. Note the loving detail on the cape embroidery, the brooch, and the flowers at her feet.

Rest of the Museum: Spain's subsequent art, from the 18th century on, generally followed the trends of the rest of Europe. Room 11 is a hallway with a dozen joyous scenes from the 1700s of carriages and parade floats filing by Sevillian landmarks. Room 12 has creamy Romanticism and hazy Impressionism. You'll see typical Sevillian motifs such as matadors, cigar-factory girls, and river landscapes. Of particular interest is the large *Death of the Master* by José Villegas Cordero, in which bullfighters touchingly express their grief after their teacher, gored in the ring, dies in bed. Enjoy these painted slices of Sevilla, then exit to experience similar scenes today.

FAR NORTH OF THE CATHEDRAL
▲▲Basílica de la Macarena

Sevilla's Holy Week celebrations are Spain's grandest. During the week leading up to Easter, the city is packed with pilgrims witnessing 60 processions carrying about 100 religious floats. If you miss the actual event, you can get a sense of it by visiting the Basílica de la Macarena and its accompanying museum to see the two most impressive floats and the darling of Semana

Santa, the statue of the Virgen de la Macarena. Although far from the city center, it's located on Sevilla's ring road and easy to reach. (While La Macarena is the big kahuna, for a more central look at beloved procession statues, consider stopping by the Church of the Savior or Triana's Church of Santa Ana, both described in this chapter.)

Cost and Hours: Church-free, treasury museum—€5; daily 9:00-14:00 & 18:00-21:30, mid-Sept-May daily 9:00-14:00 & 17:00-21:00 except Sun from 9:30, closed a few weeks before Holy Week for float preparation; audioguide-€1, +34 954 901 800, www.hermandaddelamacarena.es.

Getting There: A taxi is about €6 from the city center. The quickest bus routes are #C3 and #C4 from Puerta de Jerez (near the Torre del Oro) or Avenida de Menéndez Pelayo (the ring road east of the cathedral). Buses #C1 through #C5 also go there.

Visiting the Church: Despite the long history of the Macarena statue, the Neo-Baroque church was only built in 1949 to give the oft-moved sculpture a permanent home. Grab a pew and study the statue.

Weeping Virgin: La Macarena is known as the "Weeping Virgin" for the five crystal teardrops trickling down her cheeks.

She's like a Baroque doll with human hair and articulated arms, and even has underclothes. Sculpted in the late 17th century (probably by Pedro Roldán), she's become Sevilla's most popular image of Mary.

Her beautiful expression—halfway between smiling and crying—is ambiguous, letting worshippers project their own emotions onto her. Her weeping can be contagious—look around you. She's also known as La Esperanza, the Virgin of Hope, and she promises better times after the sorrow.

Installed in the left side chapel is the **Christ of the Judgment** (from 1654), showing Jesus on the day he was condemned. This statue and La Macarena stand atop the two most important floats of the Holy Week parades. The side chapel on the right has an equally remarkable image of the **Virgen del Rosario**, which is paraded around the city on the last Sunday of October.

Tesoro (Treasury Museum): To see the floats and learn more, head to the museum (to reach the entrance—on the church's left side—either exit the church or go through a connecting door at the rear). This small, three-floor museum tells the history of the Virgin statue and the Holy Week parades. Though rooted in medieval times, the current traditions developed around 1600, with the formation of various fraternities *(hermandades)*. During Holy Week, they demonstrate their dedication to God by parading themed floats throughout Sevilla to retell the story of the Crucifixion and Resurrection of Christ (for more, see sidebar on page 16). The museum displays ceremonial banners, scepters, and costumed mannequins; videos show the parades in action (some displays in English).

The three-ton **float** that carries the Christ of the Judgment is slathered in gold leaf and shows a commotion of figures acting out the sentencing of Jesus. (The statue of Christ—the one you saw in the church—is placed before this crowd for the Holy Week procession.) Pontius Pilate is about to wash his hands. Pilate's wife cries as a man reads the death sentence. During the Holy Week procession, pious Sevillian women wail in the streets while relays of 48 men carry this float on the backs of their necks—only their feet showing under the drapes—as they shuffle through the streets from midnight until 14:00 in the afternoon every Good Friday. The men rehearse for months to get their choreographed footwork in sync.

La Macarena follows the Christ of the Judgment in the procession. Mary's smaller 1.5-ton float seems all silver and candles—"strong enough to support the roof, but tender enough to quiver in the soft night breeze." Mary has a wardrobe of three huge mantles, worn in successive years; these are about 100 years old, as is her six-pound gold crown/halo. This float has a mesmerizing effect on the crowds. They line up for hours, then clap, weep, and throw roses as it slowly sways along the streets, working its way through town. A Sevillian friend once explained, "She knows all the problems of Sevilla and its people; we've been confiding in her for centuries. To us, she is hope."

The museum collection also contains some **matador paraphernalia**. La Macarena is the patron saint of bullfighters, and they give thanks for her protection. Copies of her image are popular in bullring chapels. In 1912, bullfighter José Ortega, hoping for protection, gave La Macarena the five emerald brooches she wears. It worked for eight years...until he was gored to death in the ring. For a month, La Macarena was dressed in widow's black—the only time that has happened.

Macarena Neighborhood: Outside the church, notice the best surviving bit of Sevilla's old walls. Originally Roman, what remains today was built by the Moors in the 12th century to (unsuccessfully) keep the Christians out. And yes, it's from this city that a local dance band (Los del Río) changed the world by giving us the popular 1990s song, "The Macarena." He-e-y-y, Macarena!

SOUTH OF THE CATHEDRAL
University
Today's university was yesterday's *fábrica de tabacos* (tobacco factory), which employed 10,000 young female *cigareras*—including the saucy femme fatale of Bizet's opera *Carmen*. In the 18th century, it was the second-largest building in Spain, after El Escorial. Today it boasts a gallery of reproduced sculpture, a beautiful chapel, and a studious library. It's free to visit outside of school hours (Fri 9:30-12:30 & 16:00-18:00, Sat 9:30-14:00, closed to public Sun-Thu and Aug).

Plaza de España
This square, the surrounding buildings, and the adjacent María Luisa Park are the remains of the 1929 world's fair, where for a year the Spanish-speaking countries of the world enjoyed a mutual-admiration fiesta. With the restoration work here finished, this delightful area—the epitome of world's fair-style architecture—is once again great for people-watching (especially during the 19:00-20:00 peak paseo hour).

The park's highlight is this former Spanish Pavilion. Its tiles—a trademark of Sevilla—show historic scenes and maps from every province of Spain (arranged in alphabetical order, from Álava to Zaragoza). Climb to one of the balconies for a classic postcard view of Sevilla. Wandering around this zone, you may feel like you've been here before: Lots of filming has been done here, including bits of *Star Wars: Episode II* and *Lawrence of Arabia*.

▲▲TRIANA WALK
In Sevilla—as is true in so many other European cities that grew up in the age of river traffic—what was long considered the "wrong side of the river" is now the most colorful part of town. Sevilla's Triana, west of the river, is a proud neighborhood that identifies with its working-class origins and is famed for its flamenco soul (characterized by the statue that greets arrivals from across the river). Known for their independent spirit, locals describe crossing the bridge toward the city center as "going to Sevilla." To trace the route described next, see the "Sevilla" map on page 8.

• *To reach Triana from downtown Sevilla, head to the river and cross over…*

Puente de Isabel II: Note the bridge's distinctive design as you approach. It was inspired by an 1834 crossing over the Seine

River in Paris—look for the circles under each span that lead the way into Triana.

While crossing the Guadalquivir River, to the right you can see Sevilla's single skyscraper—designed by Argentine architect César Pelli of Malaysia's Twin Towers fame. Locals lament the Torre Sevilla because according to city law, no structure should be taller than the Giralda bell tower. But since this building doesn't sit within the city center, developers found a way to avoid that regulation. Today it houses a bank, offices, a swanky shopping center, and a fancy five-star hotel. Surrounding the skyscraper are leftover buildings from the 1992 Expo.

The **Capilla del Carmen** sits at the end of the bridge. Designed by 1929 world's fair architect Aníbal González, the bell tower and chapel add glamour to the entrance to Triana.

• *At the end of the bridge, walk down the staircase on the right.*

Triana's Castle and Market: The **Castillo de San Jorge** is a 12th-century castle that in the 15th century was the headquarters for Sevilla's Inquisition (free small museum and TI kiosk; Mon-Fri 11:00-18:30, Sat-Sun 10:00-15:00). Explore the castle briefly, then retrace your steps to visit the neighborhood's covered market. Built in 2005 in the Moorish Revival style, it sits within the ruins of the castle (you can see its remains as you exit at the other side). The market bustles in the mornings and afternoons with traditional fruit and vegetable stalls as well as colorful tapas bars and cafés. This is a great spot to stop for coffee, watch produce being sold, and see locals catching up on the latest gossip.

• *Exit the market downstairs, out the back door, and turn left.*

Ceramic Museum and Shops: Here you can discover the district's ceramic history, starting with the **Museo de la Cerámica de Triana,** which focuses on tile and pottery production. Located in the remains of a former riverside factory, the museum explains the entire process—from selecting the right type of earth to kiln firing—with a small collection of ceramics and well-produced videos of interviews with former workers (good English translations). Another short video highlights Triana's neighborhood pride (€2, free with Alcázar ticket, Tue-Sat 11:00-18:00, Sun 10:00-15:00, closed Mon, Calle Antillano Campos 14, +34 954 342 737).

After your museum visit, ponder what you can carry home from nearby shops. Walk along Calle Antillano Campos, then turn left on Calle Alfarería. This area is lined with the old facades of ceramic workshops that once populated this quarter. Most have closed up or moved to the outskirts of town, where rent is cheaper. But a few stalwarts remain, including the lavishly decorated Santa Ana and the large showroom Santa Isabel (at Calle Alfarería 12). Several recommended bars are in this area (see "Eating in Sevilla," later).

• *Continue down Calle Alfarería to...*

Calle San Jacinto: This is the main (pedestrian-only) street of the quarter. It's the hip center of the people scene—a festival of life each evening. Venturing down side lanes, you find classic 19th-century facades with fine ironwork and colorful tiles.

• *Walk down Calle San Jacinto in the direction of the bridge. The final cross-street (to the right) is...*

Calle Pureza: This street cuts through the historic center of Triana. As you wander, pop into bars and notice how the decor mixes bullfighting lore with Virgin worship. It's easy enough to follow your nose into Dulcería Manu Jara, at Calle Pureza 5, where tempting artisan pastries are made on the spot.

At #12 is La Antigua Abacería. An *abacería* is a traditional neighborhood grocer that also functions as a neighborhood bar. Step inside and feel the presence of the Virgin Mary, flamenco culture, wine, and ham hocks...beautiful ham hocks.

At #28, sculptor José Gómez is busy with his restoration work and sculpting. If it's early in the year, he's likely particularly busy, preparing for Holy Week.

Take a moment to gaze down the street—looking above the shops—and appreciate the real community feel of this colorful line of homes.

Chapel of the Mariners: Across from #54 is the Capilla de los Marineros, home of the beloved Virgin statue called *Nuestra Señora de la Esperanza de Triana* (Our Lady of Hope of Triana). She's a big deal here. In Sevilla, upon meeting someone, it's customary to ask not only which football team they support, but which Virgin Mary they favor. The top two in town are the Virgen de la Macarena and La Esperanza de Triana. On the Thursday of Holy Week, it's a battle royale of the Madonnas, as Sevilla's two favorite Virgins are both in processions on the streets at the same time. Step inside to see her presiding like a queen from the high altar. The adoration is palpable. In the pilgrims' shop adjacent, see the photo of this Mary in the streets being mobbed by what seems like the entire population of Triana. Jesus with his cross is almost second fiddle. The brotherhood of this Virgin runs a delightful (if you're into Mary) museum where you can see her actual float, lots of regalia, and video clips (€4 entry).

• *Continue down Calle Pureza to explore the...*

Rest of Triana: The next church is the **Church of Santa Ana,** nicknamed the "Cathedral of Triana." The recommended **Bar Santa Ana** (on the corner before the church) is a classic Virgin Mary bar (with a little bullfighting tossed in). Step inside. A sign behind the bar is counting down the days to the next Holy Week.

Walking around the little church, on the far side is a delightful square with two recommended eateries, **Bar Bistec** and **Taberna**

La Plazuela. Circling farther around, return to Calle Pureza and the tiny Calle Duarte, which leads to the river. Gazing across the water, imagine the ships that kicked off the Age of Discovery sailing from here—then consider making the neighborhood you just explored your destination for a tapas crawl.

NEAR SEVILLA
Itálica

One of Spain's most impressive Roman ruins is found outside the sleepy town of Santiponce, about six miles northwest of Sevilla. Founded in 206 BC for wounded soldiers recuperating from the Second Punic War, Itálica became a thriving town of great agricultural and military importance. It was the birthplace of the famous Roman emperors Trajan and Hadrian. Today its best-preserved ruin is its amphitheater—one of the largest in the Roman Empire—with a capacity for 25,000 spectators (and used as a backdrop for dragons in *Game of Thrones*). Other highlights include beautiful floor mosaics, such as the one in Casa de los Pájaros (House of the Birds), with representations of more than 30 species of birds. In summer, plan your visit to avoid the midday heat—arrive either early or late in the day, and definitely bring water. After being picked clean as a quarry for centuries by Sevillian builders, there's not much left here.

Cost and Hours: €1.50; Tue-Sun 9:00-15:00 (April-mid-June until 20:00 Tue-Sat), shorter hours off-season, closed Mon; +34 955 123 847, www.museosdeandalucia.es.

Getting There: You can get to Itálica on bus #M-172A or #M-172B from Sevilla's Plaza de Armas station (30-minute trip, 2/hour Mon-Sat, hourly on Sun). If you're driving, head west out of Sevilla in the direction of Huelva; after you cross the second branch of the river, turn north on SE-30, exit on to N-630, and after a few miles, get off at Santiponce. Drive past pottery warehouses and through the town to the ruins at the far (west) end.

Experiences in Sevilla

▲Bullfights

Some of Spain's most intense bullfighting happens in Sevilla's 14,000-seat bullring, Plaza de Toros. The arena hosts about 45 fights each year, which are held (generally at 18:30) on most Sundays in May and June; on Easter and

Corpus Christi; daily during the April Fair; and for two weeks in late September (during the Feria de San Miguel). These serious fights, with adult matadors, are called *corrida de toros* and often sell out in advance. On many Thursday evenings in July, the *novillada* fights take place, with teenage novices doing the killing and smaller bulls doing the dying. *Corrida de toros* seats range from €25 for high seats looking into the sun to €175 for the first three rows in the shade under the royal box; *novillada* seats are half that—and easy to buy at the arena a few minutes before showtime (ignore scalpers outside; get information at a TI, your hotel, by phone, or online; +34 954 560 759, www.plazadetorosdelamaestranza.com).

▲▲Bullring (Plaza de Toros) and Bullfight Museum (Museo Taurino)

This 50-minute tour (escorted with audioguide) takes you through the bullring's strangely quiet and empty arena, its museum, and the chapel where the matador prays before the fight. (Thanks to readily available blood transfusions, there have been no deaths here in three decades.) The two most revered figures of Sevilla, the Virgen de la Macarena and the Jesús del Gran Poder (Christ of All Power), are represented in the chapel. In the museum, you'll see great classic scenes and the heads of a few bulls—awarded the bovine equivalent of an Oscar for a particularly good fight. The city was so appalled when the famous matador Manolete was killed in 1947 that even the mother of the bull that gored him was destroyed. Matadors—dressed to kill—are heartthrobs in their "suits of light." Many girls have their bedrooms wallpapered with posters of cute bullfighters.

Cost and Hours: €8, includes audioguide, entrance with escorted tour only—no free time inside; 3/hour, daily 9:30-21:00—last tour at 20:30, Nov-March until 19:00; until 15:00 on fight days, when chapel and horse room are closed. While they take groups of up to 50, it's still wise to reserve a spot in the busy season (+34 954 210 315, www.sevilletourexperience.com).

April Fair

Two weeks after Easter, much of Sevilla packs into its vast fairgrounds for a grand party (April 18-24 in 2021). The fair, seeming to bring all that's Andalusian together, feels friendly, spontaneous, and very real. The passion for horses, flamenco, and sherry is clear—riders are ramrod straight, colorfully clad girls ride sidesaddle, and everyone's drinking sherry spritzers. Women sport out-

landish dresses that would look clownish elsewhere, but are somehow brilliant here en masse. Every day for one crazy week, horses clog the streets in an endless parade until about 20:00, when they clear out and the lanes fill with exuberant locals. The party goes on literally 24 hours a day.

Countless private party tents, called *casetas,* line the lanes. Each tent is the private party zone of a family, club, or association. You need to know someone in the group—or make friends quickly—to get in. Because of the exclusivity, it has a real family-affair feeling. In each *caseta,* everyone knows everyone. It seems like a thousand wedding parties being celebrated at the same time.

Any tourist can have a fun and memorable evening by simply crashing the party. The city's entire fleet of taxis (who can legally charge double) and buses seems dedicated to shuttling people from downtown to the fairgrounds. Given the traffic jams and inflated prices, you may be better off hiking: From the Torre del Oro, cross the San Telmo Bridge to Plaza de Cuba and hike down Calle Asunción. You'll see the towering gate to the fairgrounds in the distance. Just follow the crowds (there's no admission charge). Arrive before 20:00 to see the horses, but stay later, as the ambience improves after the *caballos* giddy-up on out. Some of the larger tents are sponsored by the city and open to the public, but the best action is in the streets, where party-goers from the livelier *casetas* spill out. Although private tents have bouncers, everyone is so happy that it's not tough to strike up an impromptu friendship, become a "special guest," and be invited in. The drink flows freely, and the food is fun, bountiful, and cheap.

Flamenco Classes

Energetic performances often leave people wanting more, so Eva Izquierdo shares her passion for flamenco culture with an inspiring **master class** at a studio in the city center (1.5 hours, daily at 12:00, also Mon-Fri at 15:30, Sat-Sun at 17:30). Eva introduces you to the essentials of flamenco: its origins, rhythms, and different styles *(palos).* Learn to clap properly—technique is everything—in order to accompany flamenco music and song. Once you've got the beat down, you'll get more out of any show. If flamenco captivates you with its passion and tension, learn some of the basic movements to express those feelings. After basic foot and leg work, Eva will guide you through a unique routine—*olé!* Reservations are required (€28, Calle Gravina 50, mobile +34 626 007 868, www.ishowusevilla. com).

Shopping in Sevilla

For the best local shopping experience in Sevilla, visit the popular pedestrian streets Sierpes, Tetuán, Velázquez, and Cuna near Plaza Nueva. They, and the surrounding lanes, are packed with people and shops. For details, see my "Shopping Paseo," below.

Clothing and shoe stores stay open all day. Other shops generally take a siesta, closing between 13:30 and 16:00 or 17:00 on weekdays, as well as on Saturday afternoons and all day Sunday. Big department stores such as **El Corte Inglés** stay open (and air-conditioned) right through the siesta. El Corte Inglés also has a supermarket downstairs, a pricey cafeteria, and the Gourmet Experience food court on the fifth floor, with several international options and a view terrace (Mon-Sat 10:00-22:00, closed Sun).

Souvenir Markets

Popular Sevillian souvenir items include ladies' fans, shawls, *mantillas* (ornate head scarves), other items related to flamenco (castanets, guitars, costumes), ceramics, and bullfighting posters. The following markets are worth a browse.

Collectors' markets hop on Sunday. You'll see stamps and coins, and kids trading soccer cards like American kids trade baseball cards, at Plaza del Cabildo (near the cathedral). You can browse art on Plaza del Museo (by the Museo de Bellas Artes).

The arts-and-crafts **Mercado El Postigo,** in an architecturally interesting old building behind the Hospital de la Caridad, features artisan wares of all types (Mon-Fri 10:00-19:00, Sat-Sun until 20:00, at the corner of Calles de Arfe and Dos de Mayo, +34 954 560 013).

Mercado del Arenal, the covered fish-and-produce market, is perfect for hungry photographers (see "Eating in Sevilla," later).

▲▲Shopping Paseo

Although many tourists never get beyond the cathedral and Barrio Santa Cruz, the lively pedestrianized shopping area north of the cathedral is well worth a wander. The best shopping streets—Calle Sierpes, and Calle Cuna—also happen to be part of the oldest section of Sevilla. A walk here is a chance to join one of Spain's liveliest paseos—that bustling celebration of life that takes place before dinner each evening, when everyone is out strolling, showing off their fancy shoes and checking out everyone else's. This walk, if done between 18:00 and 20:00, gives you a chance to experience the paseo scene while getting a look at the town's most popular shops. First, to get warmed up, we'll walk from Plaza Nueva down Calle Tetuán (a pedestrian mall with more trendy fashion). Then we'll double back on the much more interesting (and traditional) Calle Sierpes.

Start on the pedestrianized **Plaza Nueva**—the 19th-century square facing the ornate City Hall. From here wander the length of **Calle Tetuán,** where old-time standbys bump up against fashion-right boutiques. **Juan Foronda** (#28) has been selling flamenco attire and *mantillas* since 1926. A few doors down, you'll find the flagship store of **Camper** (#24), the proudly Spanish shoe brand that's become a worldwide favorite. The rest of the street showcases mainly Spanish brands, such as Massimo Dutti, Zara, and Mango.

Calle Tetuán (which changes names to Calle Velázquez) ends five blocks later at La Campana, a big intersection and popular meeting point, with the super department store, El Corte Inglés, just beyond, on Plaza del Duque de la Victoria.

Turn right at the end of the street. At the corner of Calle Sierpes awaits a venerable pastry shop, **Confitería La Campana,** with a fine 1885 interior...and Sevilla's most tempting sweets (take a break at the outdoor tables, or head to the back of the shop, where you can grab a coffee and pastry at the stand-up bar).

The green newsstand in front of the pastry shop is **Prensa Sierpes.** This traditional newsstand has been in Miquel's family for 100 years, and while times are tough as newspaper sales decrease, he still has his loyal customers.

You may see someone nearby selling lottery tickets, which benefits a charity named ONCE (the national organization for the blind of Spain). They not only raise money for the charity this way, but they also provide job opportunities for those in need.

A few steps down Calle Sierpes at #5 is **Papelería Ferrer,** where the Ferrer family has been selling traditional stationery and pens since 1856. Such elegance survives and is appreciated by the people of Sevilla.

Next, at #19, is the clock-covered, wood-paneled **El Cronómetro** shop, where master watchmakers have been doing business since 1901. If you've got a problem with your Rolex, drop in—they're an official retailer of all the luxury brands.

In front of the clock shop, the tall, green robot in the street is for depositing *basura* (waste), not postcards. Garbage in the summer heat really stinks. So put your apple core or orange peel in here, close the door, crank open the hatch, and it's sucked away to the city dump. Try it.

At #33 is another Juan Foronda shop, filled with traditional ladies' accessories for Sevilla's many festivals. For a fancy festival hat, stop at #40. **Sombrerería Maquedano** is a styling place—

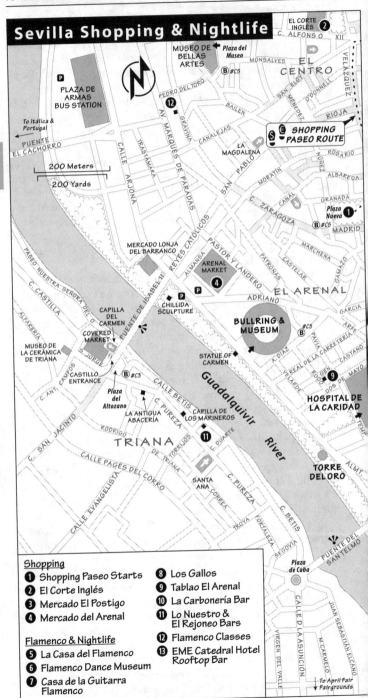

Sevilla Shopping & Nightlife

Shopping
1. Shopping Paseo Starts
2. El Corte Inglés
3. Mercado El Postigo
4. Mercado del Arenal

Flamenco & Nightlife
5. La Casa del Flamenco
6. Flamenco Dance Museum
7. Casa de la Guitarra Flamenco
8. Los Gallos
9. Tablao El Arenal
10. La Carbonería Bar
11. Lo Nuestro & El Rejoneo Bars
12. Flamenco Classes
13. EME Catedral Hotel Rooftop Bar

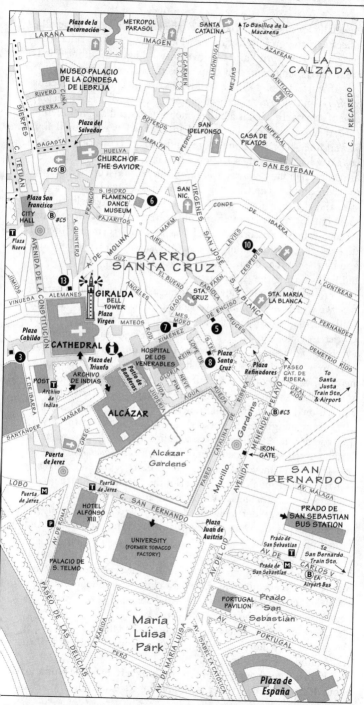

especially for men. They claim to be the oldest hat seller in Sevilla. Check out the great selection of wide-brimmed horse-rider hats, perfect for the April Fair. The inventory is huge but hiding—hats are stacked Pringles-style within boxes throughout the store.

If it's teatime, #45 is a handy next stop. Since 1910 **Ochoa** *confitería* and *salón de té* has been tempting locals with a long display case of sweets. In back is a buffet line for tapas and a light lunch.

At the corner of Sierpes and Jovellanos/Sagasta, you'll find several fine shops featuring more Andalusian accessories. **Abanicos Díaz** has a dazzling selection. Drop in to see how serious locals are about their fans, shawls, *mantillas,* and *peinetas* (combs designed to secure and prop up the *mantilla*). The most valuable *mantillas* are silk, and the top-quality combs are made of tortoiseshell (though most opt for much more affordable polyester and plastic). Andalusian women accessorize with fans, matching them to different dresses. The *mantilla* comes in black (worn only on Holy Thursday and by the mother of the groom at weddings) and white (worn at bullfights during the April Fair).

From here turn left down **Calle Sagasta.** Notice that the street has two names—the modern version and a medieval one: Antigua Calle de Gallegos ("Former Street of the Galicians"). With the Christian victory in 1248, the Muslims were given one month to evacuate. To consolidate Christian control during that time, settlers from Galicia, the northwest corner of Iberia, were planted here; this street was the center of their neighborhood.

The first shop on the right is **Lotería Sagasta,** the government-run national lottery. It's well known that the government makes a 30 percent margin on bettors; it's essentially a tax on those who aren't so bright. At Christmas time, a line of those hoping to strike it rich stretches down the street. Wish someone *"buena suerte."*

If you did win, you'd want to dress up. At #5, **Galán Camisería** is a traditional men's store that sells the "uniform" for the older gentlemen of Andalucía. While young men dress casually in T-shirts and jeans, older men still dress up to go out (especially for the Sunday paseo). Do a quick visual survey and see how the old formality persists.

Just before you hit the charming Plaza del Salvador, stop at #6 for a peek into the windows at **BuBi.** This *boutique infantil* displays pricey but exquisitely made baby clothes—knit, embroidered, starched, and beribboned—along with baptismal gowns with bonnets, tiny crocheted booties—you name it.

Now jump into **Plaza del Salvador**—it's teeming with life at the foot of the Church of the Savior (well worth a visit; described earlier, under "Sights in Sevilla").

Finish your shopping stroll by heading left up **Calle Cuna** for about 100 yards. This street is famous for its exuberant flamenco dresses and classic wedding dresses. Local women save up to have flamenco dresses custom-made for the April Fair: They're considered an important status symbol. At #46 a shop displays this year's dress fashions (or last year's at clearance prices). And at #42, **Galerias Madrid** has all the fabric that more talented shoppers need to save money, sew their own dress, and get it just right.

Nightlife in Sevilla

▲▲▲FLAMENCO

This music-and-dance art form has its roots in the Roma (Gypsy) and Moorish cultures. Even at a packaged "flamenco evening," sparks fly. The men do most of the flamboyant machine-gun footwork. The women often concentrate on the graceful turns and smooth, shuffling step of the *soleá* version of the dance. Watch the musicians. Flamenco guitarists, with their lightning-fast finger-roll strums, are among the best in the world. The intricate rhythms are set by castanets or the hand-clapping (called *palmas*) of those who aren't dancing at the moment. In the raspy-voiced wails of the singers, you'll hear echoes of the Muslim call to prayer.

Like jazz, flamenco thrives on improvisation. Also like jazz, good flamenco is more than just technical proficiency. A singer or dancer with "soul" is said to have *duende*. Flamenco is a happening, with bystanders clapping along and egging on the dancers with whoops and shouts. Get into it.

Hotels push tourist-oriented, nightclub-style flamenco shows, but they charge a commission. Fortunately, it's easy to book a place on your own.

Sevilla's flamenco offerings tend to fall into three categories: serious concerts (about €20 and about an hour long), where the singing and dancing take center stage; touristy dinner-and-drinks shows with table service (generally around €40—not including food—and 90 minutes long); and—the least touristy option—casual bars with late-night performances, where for the cost of a drink you can catch impromptu (or semi-impromptu) musicians at play. Here's the rundown for each type of performance. For venue locations, see the "Sevilla Shopping & Nightlife" map, earlier.

Serious Flamenco Concerts

While it's hard to choose among these three nightly, one-hour flamenco concerts, I'd say enjoying one is a must during your Sevilla visit. To the novice viewer, each company offers equal quality. They cost about the same, and each venue is small, intimate (congested seating in not-very-comfy chairs), and air-conditioned. For many, the concerts are preferable to the shows (listed next) because they're half the cost, length, and size (smaller audience), and generally start earlier in the evening. Also, shows are not appropriate for kids under six (or perhaps vice versa).

My recommended concerts are careful to give you a good overview of the art form, covering all the flamenco bases. At each venue you can reserve by phone and pay upon arrival, or drop by early to pick up a ticket. While La Casa del Flamenco is the nicest and most central venue, Flamenco Dance Museum has an exhibit that can add to the experience.

La Casa del Flamenco is in a delightful arcaded courtyard right in the Barrio Santa Cruz (€20, RS%—€2 discount with this book if you book directly and pay cash; shows nightly at 19:00 and 20:30, earlier or later performances added with demand—confirm on their website or stop by the venue; no drinks, 60 spacious seats, next to recommended Hotel Alcántara, Calle Ximénez de Enciso 28, +34 955 029 999, www.lacasadelflamencosevilla.com).

Flamenco Dance Museum, while the most congested venue (with 150 tightly packed seats), has a bar and allows drinks inside, and has a bigger production (six performers). It has festival seating—the doors open early so, for earlier performances, you can grab the seat of your choice, then tour the museum before the show (€22, nightly at 17:00, 19:00, 20:45, and 22:15; €26 combo-ticket includes the museum—described earlier under "Sights in Sevilla"; reservations smart, +34 954 340 311, www.museoflamenco.com). The museum also offers a more intimate "VIP show" in its basement. It's essentially the same performance but is under vaulted brick arches and includes a drink (€30, daily at 19:00 and 20:45).

Casa de la Guitarra Flamenco is another venue in the tourist zone with cramped seating (75 seats) and a strong performance (€18, daily at 19:30 and 21:00, no drinks, next to recommended Restaurante San Marco, Calle Mesón del Moro 12, +34 954 224 093, www.flamencoensevilla.com).

Razzle-Dazzle Flamenco Shows

These packaged shows can be a bit sterile—and an audience of mostly tourists doesn't help—but I find both Los Gallos and Tablao El Arenal entertaining and riveting. While El Arenal may have a slight edge on talent, and certainly feels slicker, Los Gallos has a cozier setting, with cushy rather than hard chairs, and is cheaper and less pretentious.

Los Gallos presents nightly 90-minute shows at 20:30 and 22:00 (€35 ticket includes drink, RS%—€3/person discount for 3 people with this book, arrive 30 minutes early for best seats, bar, no food served, Plaza de Santa Cruz 11, +34 954 216 981, www.tablaolosgallos.com, owners José and Blanca promise goose bumps). Their box office is open at 11:00 (you'll pass it on my Barrio Santa Cruz Walk).

Tablao El Arenal is more of an old-fashioned dinner show with arguably more professional performers and a classier setting. Dinner customers get preferred seating and servers work throughout the performance (€39 ticket includes drink, €62 includes tapas, €75 includes dinner, 1.25-hour shows at 19:15 and 22:00, likely later in summer, near bullring at Calle Rodo 7, +34 954 216 492, http://www.tablaoelarenal.com).

Impromptu Flamenco in Bars

Spirited flamenco singing still erupts spontaneously in bars throughout the old town after midnight—but you need to know where to look. Ask a local for the latest.

La Carbonería Bar, the sangria equivalent of a beer garden, is a few blocks north of the Barrio Santa Cruz. It's a big, open-tented area filled with young locals, casual guitar strummers, and nearly nightly flamenco music from about 22:30 to 24:00. Located just a few blocks from most of my recommended hotels, this is worth finding if you're not quite ready to end the day (no cover, daily 20:00-very late; near Plaza Santa María—find Hotel Fernando III, along the side alley Céspedes at #21; +34 954 214 460).

While the days of Gypsies and flamenco throbbing throughout Triana are mostly long gone, a few bars still host live dancing; **Lo Nuestro** and **El Rejoneo** are favorites (at Calle Betis 31A and 31B).

OTHER NIGHTLIFE
▲▲Evening Paseo

Sevilla is meant for strolling. The paseo thrives every evening (except in winter) in these areas: along either side of the river between the San Telmo and Isabel II bridges (Paseo de Cristóbal Colón and Triana district; see "Eating in Sevilla," later), up Avenida de la Constitución, around Plaza Nueva, at Plaza de España, and throughout the Barrio Santa Cruz. The best paseo scene is about 19:00 to 21:00, but on hot summer nights, even families with toddlers are out and about past midnight. Spend some time rafting through this river of humanity.

Nighttime Views

Savor the view of floodlit Sevilla by night from the Triana side of the river—perhaps over dinner. For the best late-night drink with a cathedral view, visit the trendy top floor of **EME Catedral Hotel** (at Calle Alemanes 27). Ride the elevator to the top, climb the staircases to the cocktail bar, and sit down at a tiny table with a big view (daily 12:00-24:00).

Sleeping in Sevilla

All of my listings are centrally located, mostly within a five-minute walk of the cathedral. The first are near the charming but touristy Barrio Santa Cruz. The last group is just as central but closer to the river, across the boulevard in a less touristy zone.

Room rates as much as double during the two Sevilla fiestas (Holy Week and the April Fair). In general, the busiest and most expensive months are April, May, September, and October. Hotels put rooms on the discounted push list in July and August—when people with good sense avoid this furnace—and from November through February.

If you do visit in July or August, you'll find the best deals in central, business-class places. They offer summer discounts and provide a (necessary) cool, air-conditioned refuge. But be warned that Spain's air-conditioning often isn't the icebox you're used to, especially in Sevilla.

BARRIO SANTA CRUZ

These places are off Calle Santa María la Blanca and Plaza Santa María. The most convenient parking lot is the underground Cano y Cueto garage (see page 10). A self-service launderette is a couple of blocks away up Avenida de Menéndez Pelayo (see "Helpful Hints" on page 10).

$$$$ Casa del Poeta offers peace, quiet, and a timeless elegance that seem contrary to its location in the heart of Santa Cruz. At the end of a side street, Trinidad and Ángelo have lovingly converted an old family mansion with 17 spacious rooms surrounding a large central patio into a home away from home. Evening guitar concerts plus a fantastic view terrace make it a worthwhile splurge (free breakfast if you reserve on their website, family room, air-con, elevator, Calle Don Carlos Alonso Chaparro 3, +34 954 213 868, www.casadelpoeta.es, info@casadelpoeta.es).

$$$$ Hotel Las Casas de la Judería has 178 quiet, classy rooms and junior suites, most of them tastefully decorated with hardwood floors and a Spanish Old-World ambience. The service can be too formal, but the rooms, which spread out through three connected buildings surrounding a series of peaceful courtyards, are

SEVILLA

a romantic splurge (air-con, elevator, pool in summer, valet parking, Plaza Santa María 5, +34 954 415 150, www.casasypalacios. com, juderia@casasypalacios.com).

$$$$ Hotel Casa 1800, well-priced for its elegance, is worth the extra euros. Located dead-center in the Barrio Santa Cruz (facing a boisterous tapas bar that quiets down after midnight), its 33 rooms are accessed via a lovely chandeliered patio lounge, where guests enjoy a daily free afternoon tea. With a rooftop terrace and swimming pool offering an impressive cathedral view, and tastefully appointed rooms with high, beamed ceilings, it's a winner (family rooms, air-con, elevator, Calle Rodrigo Caro 6, +34 954 561 800, www.hotelcasa1800.com, info@hotelcasa1800.com).

$$$ Hotel Palacio Alcázar is the former home and studio of John Fulton, an American who moved here to become a bullfighter and painter. This charming boutique hotel has 12 crisp, modern rooms, and each soundproofed door is painted with a different dreamy scene of Sevilla. Triple-paned windows keep out the noise from the plaza (air-con, elevator, rooftop terrace with bar and cathedral views, Plaza de la Alianza 11, +34 954 502 190, www. hotelpalacioalcazar.com, hotel@palacioalcazar.com).

$$$ Hotel Amadeus is a classy and comfortable gem, with welcoming public spaces and a very charming staff. The 30 rooms, lovingly decorated with a musical motif, are situated around small courtyards. Elevators take you to a two-tiered roof terrace with an under-the-stars hot tub. Breakfast is plentiful—enjoy it in your room, in the lounge, or on a terrace (air-con, elevator, iPads in some rooms, laundry service, pay parking nearby, Calle Farnesio 6, +34 954 501 443, www.hotelamadeussevilla.com, reservas@ hotelamadeussevilla.com, wonderfully run by María Luisa and her daughters Zaida and Cristina).

$$$ Hotel Murillo enjoys one of the most appealing locations in Santa Cruz, along one of the very narrow "kissing lanes." Above its elegant, antiques-filled lobby are 64 nondescript rooms with marble bathrooms. Skip the English-style breakfast in the basement and opt for the simple breakfast on the rooftop (air-con, elevator, Calle Lope de Rueda 7, +34 954 216 095, www.hotelmurillo. com, reservas@hotelmurillo.com). They also rent apartments with kitchens (see website for details).

$$ El Rey Moro encircles its spacious, colorful patio with 18 rooms. Colorful, dripping with quirky Andalusian character, and thoughtful about including extras (such as free loaner bikes, a welcome drink, afternoon snacks, and private rooftop whirlpool-bath time), it's a class act (free breakfast with this book, air-con, elevator, Reinoso 8, +34 954 563 468, www.elreymoro.com, hotel@ elreymoro.com).

$$ Hotel Alcántara offers clean and casual comfort in the

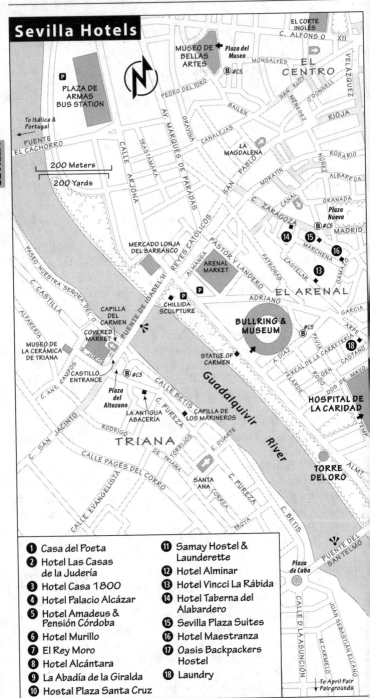

Sevilla Hotels

SEVILLA

1 Casa del Poeta
2 Hotel Las Casas de la Judería
3 Hotel Casa 1800
4 Hotel Palacio Alcázar
5 Hotel Amadeus & Pensión Córdoba
6 Hotel Murillo
7 El Rey Moro
8 Hotel Alcántara
9 La Abadía de la Giralda
10 Hostal Plaza Santa Cruz
11 Samay Hostel & Launderette
12 Hotel Alminar
13 Hotel Vincci La Rábida
14 Hotel Taberna del Alabardero
15 Sevilla Plaza Suites
16 Hotel Maestranza
17 Oasis Backpackers Hostel
18 Laundry

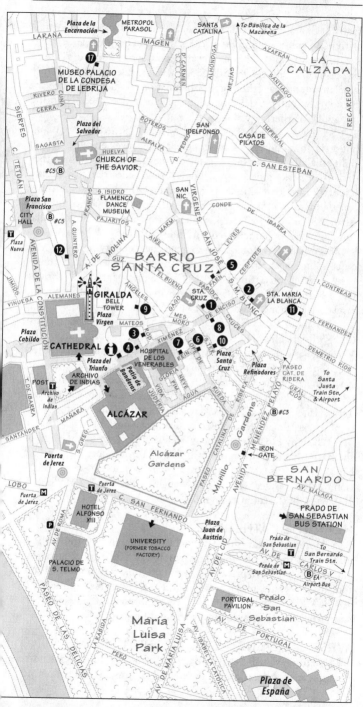

SEVILLA

heart of Santa Cruz. Well situated, it rents 23 slick rooms—most with patio views—at a good price (RS% if you pay cash, nice buffet breakfast available, air-con, elevator, outdoor patio, Calle Ximénez de Enciso 28, +34 954 500 595, www.hotelalcantara.net, info@hotelalcantara.net). The hotel also functions as the box office for the nightly La Casa del Flamenco show, next door (see "Nightlife in Sevilla," earlier).

$$ La Abadía de la Giralda, once an 18th-century abbots' house, is now a homey 14-room hotel tucked away on a little street right off Calle Mateos Gago, just a couple of blocks from the cathedral. The exterior rooms have windows onto a pedestrian street, and a few of the interior rooms have small windows that look into the inner courtyard; all rooms are basic but neatly appointed (air-con, Calle Abades 30, +34 954 228 324, www.alojamientosconencantosevilla.com, giralda@alojamientosconencantosevilla.com).

$ Pensión Córdoba, a homier and cheaper option, has 11 tidy, quiet rooms with cool-tone decor, and a showpiece tiled courtyard (air-con, on a tiny lane off Calle Santa María la Blanca at Calle Farnesio 12, +34 954 227 498, www.pensioncordoba.com, reservas@pensioncordoba.com, twins Ana and María).

$ Hostal Plaza Santa Cruz is a charming little place, with thoughtful touches that you wouldn't expect in this price range. The 17 clean, basic rooms surround a bright little courtyard that's buried deep in the Barrio Santa Cruz, just off Plaza Santa Cruz. They also have nine even-nicer rooms with a common terrace in a renovated residential palace on Calle Ximénez de Enciso (air-con, Calle Santa Teresa 15, +34 954 228 808, www.alojamientosconencantosevilla.com, plaza@alojamientosconencantosevilla.com).

¢ Samay Hostel, on a busy avenue a block from the edge of the Barrio Santa Cruz, is a youthful, well-run slumbermill with 80 beds in 17 rooms (shared kitchen, air-con, elevator, 24-hour reception, rooftop terrace, Avenida de Menéndez Pelayo 13, +34 955 100 160, www.hostelsamay.com, info@hostelsamay.com).

NEAR THE CATHEDRAL

$$$ Hotel Alminar, tidy and sophisticated, rents 11 fresh, slick, minimalist rooms. Double-pane windows keep it quiet at night, and two rooms have private terraces (air-con, elevator, loaner laptop, just 100 yards from the cathedral at Calle Álvarez Quintero 52, +34 954 293 913, www.hotelalminar.com, reservas@hotelalminar.com, run by well-dressed, never-stressed Francisco).

WEST OF AVENIDA DE LA CONSTITUCIÓN

$$$$ Hotel Vincci La Rábida, part of a big, impersonal hotel chain, offers four-star comfort with its 84 rooms and huge, inviting courtyard lounge (elevator, Calle Castelar 24, +34 954 501 280, www.vinccihoteles.com, larabida@vinccihoteles.com).

$$$$ Hotel Taberna del Alabardero has a special charm with seven spacious rooms occupying the top floor of a poet's mansion (above the classy recommended restaurant, Taberna del Alabardero). It's nicely located, a great value, and the ambience is perfectly circa-1900—notice the original Triana-made tiles in the lobby (air-con, elevator, pay parking, may close in Aug, Zaragoza 20, +34 954 502 721, www.tabernadelalabardero.es, info@ tabernadelalabardero.es).

$$$ Sevilla Plaza Suites rents 10 self-catering apartments with wood floors and kitchenettes. It's squeaky clean, family friendly, and well-located—and comes with an Astroturf sun terrace with a cathedral view. While service is scaled down, reception is open long hours (9:00-21:00) and rooms are cleaned daily (air-con, inside rooms are quieter, a block off Plaza Nueva at Calle Zaragoza 52, +34 955 038 533, www.suitessevillaplaza.com, info@ suitessevillaplaza.com, Javier).

$ Hotel Maestranza, sparkling with loving care and understated charm, has 17 simple, bright, clean rooms well-located on a street just off Plaza Nueva. It feels elegant for its price. Double-pane windows help to cut down on noise from the tapas bars below (family rooms available, 5 percent discount if you pay cash, air-con, elevator, Gamazo 12, +34 954 561 070, www.hotelmaestranza.es, sevilla@hotelmaestranza.es, Antonio).

NEAR PLAZA DE LA ENCARNACIÓN

¢ Oasis Backpackers Hostel is a good place for cheap beds, and perhaps Sevilla's best place to connect with young backpackers. Each of the eight rooms, with up to eight double bunks, comes with a modern bathroom and individual lockers. The rooftop terrace—with lounge chairs, a small pool, and adjacent kitchen—is well-used (includes breakfast, just off Plaza de la Encarnación on the tiny and quiet lane behind the church at Compañía 1, reception hours vary—confirm check-in time when you book, +34 955 228 287, www.oasissevilla.com, sevilla@hostelsoasis.com).

Eating in Sevilla

Eating in Sevilla is fun and affordable (visitors from more-expensive Madrid and Barcelona find it a wonderful value). Make a point to get out and eat well when you're here.

A dining trend in Sevilla is the rise of gourmet tapas bars, with spiffed-up decor and creative menus, at the expense of traditional restaurants. Old-school places survive, but they often lack energy, and their clientele is aging with them. My quandary: I like the

SEVILLA

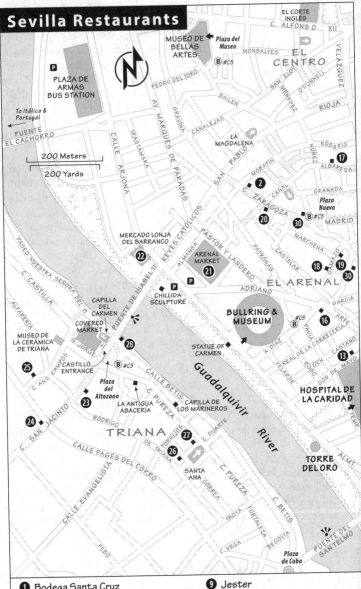

Sevilla Restaurants

EL CORTE
INGLÉS
C. ALFONS O   XII

MUSEO DE
BELLAS
ARTES   Plaza del
Museo   MONSALVES   EL
CENTRO
(B) #C5

P
PLAZA DE
ARMAS
BUS STATION   PEDRO DEL TORO   SAN ELOY   O'DONNELL   VELÁZQUEZ

To Itálica &
Portugal   BAILEN   RIOJA

PUENTE
EL CACHORRO   CALLE ARJONA   CANALEJAS   LA
MAGDALENA   MORATIN   ROSARIO   17
ALBAREDA

200 Meters   SAN PABLO   C.
ZARAGOZA   2   CANAL   GRANADA
Plaza
Nueva   MADRID
200 Yards   20   30   (B) #C5

MERCADO LONJA
DEL BARRANCO   22   PASTOR Y LANDERO   ARENAL
MARKET
21   MARCHENA   18   19   30
EL ARENAL

C. CASTILLA   CAPILLA
DEL
CARMEN   CHILLIDA
SCULPTURE   ADRIANO   GARCÍA

PASEO NUESTRA SEÑORA DEL O   P   BULLRING &
MUSEUM   (B) #C5   16

MUSEO DE
LA CERÁMICA
DE TRIANA   COVERED
MARKET   28   STATUE OF
CARMEN   13

25   CASTILLO
ENTRANCE   (B) #C5   HOSPITAL DE
LA CARIDAD

Plaza
del
Altozano   CALLE BETIS   Guadalquivir

23   LA ANTIGUA
ABACERÍA   C. PUREZA   CAPILLA DE
LOS MARINEROS   River   TORRE
DEL ORO

24   RODRIGO   27   E. DUARTE
DE TRIANA   26   TRIANA   SANTA
ANA   C. PUREZA

CALLE PAGES DEL CORRO   CORREA   PUENTE DEL
SAN TELMO

CALLE EVANGELISTA DEL CORRO   C. BETIS

FEBO   C. VEGA   SEGOVIA   Plaza
de Cuba

❶ Bodega Santa Cruz	❾ Jester
❷ La Azotea (2)	❿ La Canasta
❸ Las Teresas	⓫ Bodeguita Casablanca
❹ Donaire Azabache	⓬ La Casa del Tesorero
❺ Restaurante San Marco	⓭ El Postiguillo
❻ Freiduría Puerta de la Carne	⓮ La Isla
❼ Bar Restaurante El 3 de Oro	⓯ Bodega Morales
❽ Bolas Ice Cream	⓰ Bar Arenal

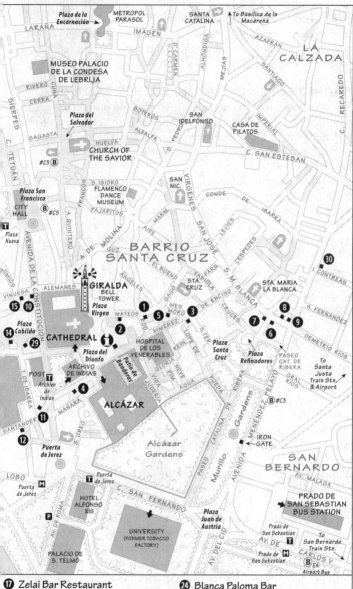

SEVILLA

17 Zelai Bar Restaurant
18 Bodeguita Antonio Romero
19 Abacería Casa Moreno
20 Taberna & El Bistro del Alabardero
21 Marisquería Arenal El Pesquero
22 Mercado Lonja del Barranco
23 Taberna Miami

24 Blanca Paloma Bar
25 Las Golondrinas Bar
26 Bar Bistec & Taberna La Plazuela
27 Bar Santa Ana
28 Fish Joints
29 El Torno Pastelería de Conventos
30 Grocery (3)

classic *típico* places. But the lively atmosphere and the best food are in the new places. One thing's for certain: if you want a good "restaurant" experience, your best value is a trendy tapas bar that offers good table seating—sit and enjoy some *raciones*.

BARRIO SANTA CRUZ AND CATHEDRAL AREA

For tapas, the Barrio Santa Cruz is *romántico* and *turístico*. Plenty of atmospheric joints fill the neighborhood near the cathedral. Walk up Calle Mateos Gago, where classic old bars—with the day's tapas scrawled on chalkboards—keep the tourists (and a few locals) well fed and watered.

$ Bodega Santa Cruz (a.k.a. **Las Columnas**) is a popular local standby with few tourists, affordable tapas, and an unforgettable scene. You can keep an eye on the busy kitchen from the bar or hang out like a cowboy at the tiny stand-up tables out front. To order, you'll need to muscle your way to the bar—a fun experience in itself (no table service). Separate chalkboards list tapas and *montaditos* (daily 11:30-24:00, Calle de Rodrigo Caro 1A, +34 954 218 618).

$$$ La Azotea is a modern place that makes up for its lack of traditional character with gourmet tapas—made with local, seasonal ingredients, explained with a fun and accessible menu. It's run by Juan Antonio and his partner from San Diego, Jeanine. You can dine elegantly on tapas for reasonable prices (served only at the bar) or enjoy a sit-down meal—but you need to arrive early. Half-sized *raciones* are big and the gazpacho is famous. They also serve breakfast (daily 9:00-24:00, Calle Mateos Gago 8, +34 954 215 878). Another branch is not far from Plaza Nueva (daily 13:30-24:00, Calle Zaragoza 5, +34 954 564 316).

$$ Las Teresas is a characteristic little bar draped in festival posters and memorabilia—with ham hocks dripping from the ceiling. It serves good tapas from a tight menu. Prices at the bar and outside tables (for fun tourist-watching) are the same, but tapas are only available inside at either the bar or tables (daily 10:00-24:00, Calle Santa Teresa 2, +34 954 213 069).

$$ Donaire Azabache offers tasty standards from Spain's south like *croquetas* and *salmorejo*, but they shine by inventing new dishes like *canelón ibérico* (cannelloni stuffed with grilled pork, covered with melted cheese) or serving a fancier version of *ensaladilla* with octopus *(pulpo)*. Bar service is quick and attentive, and a few tables are in back for casual dining. Outdoor tables are self-service—order and pick-up at the bar window (Mon-Fri 8:00-24:00, Sat from 9:00, Sun 9:00-17:00, Calle Santo Tomás 11, +34 954 224 702).

$$ Restaurante San Marco serves basic Italian dishes under the arches of what was a Moorish bath (1,000 years ago) and then a

Food Tours and Classes

Sevilla is one of Spain's great eating towns. The city's tourist information website is a great resource for local specialties and where to find them (www.visitasevilla.es). Below are some ways to immerse yourself deeper into the scene.

Tapas Tours: If ever a town was right for a tapas tour, it's Sevilla. Several hardworking little companies offer memorable experiences. For €80-90 you'll typically get four stops in three hours. At each stop your guide corrals a drink and a selection of local specialties, and adds cultural insights. Some tours go through the old center and others around Triana. I find them fun and educational...and time and money well spent. Companies come and go but **Azahar Sevilla Tapas**, run by Canadian Shawn Hennessey, has been into the tapas scene for 25 years offering unique food-and-wine experiences in her adopted city. Tours are kept small (2-6 people) to experience a typical *tapeo* the way locals would (€100/person, minimum 2 people, discount for 4 or more). Shawn also provides regional wine and sherry tastings (€50/person, minimum 4 people, mobile +34 608 636 290, www.azahar-sevilla.com).

Cooking Lessons: Taller Andaluz de Cocina offers a fun hands-on shopping/cooking/eating experience each morning in the colorful Triana neighborhood. You'll start your four-hour tour at 10:30 getting supplies in the market, then head to their shiny kitchen (fit for an episode of *Top Chef*), where you'll munch on olives, sip sangria, and whip up a traditional meal (typically a couple of starters, paella, and dessert). You then get to eat what you created (€60/person, Mon-Sat, none on Sun, reserve online, meets on the river side of the market, Mercado de Triana stall 75, mobile +34 672 162 621, www.tallerandaluzdecocina.com). They also offer an evening version without the shopping (€55, starts at 18:00).

disco (in the 1990s). The air-conditioned atmosphere feels upscale, but it's easygoing and family-friendly, with live Spanish guitar nightly after 20:30 (daily 13:00-16:15 & 19:30-24:00, Calle Mesón del Moro 6, +34 954 214 390, welcoming Ángelo).

$ Freiduría Puerta de la Carne is a fried-fish-to-go place, with great outdoor seating. Step into the fry shop and order a cheap cone of tasty fried fish, jumbo shrimp, or delicious chicken wings. Study the photos of your options; *un quarto* (250 grams, for €5-7) serves one person. Then head out front and grab a table. If you need a drink or even a small salad, flag down a server—technically from the El 3 de Oro restaurant across the lane, which shares the same owner (daily 13:00-17:00 & 20:00-24:30, usually no lunch service in summer; Calle Santa María la Blanca 34, +34 954 426 820).

$$ Bar Restaurante El 3 de Oro is a venerable place with old-school waiters and a fun energy. The menu offers the full range of Andalusian classics (long hours daily, Calle Santa María la Blanca 34, +34 954 422 759).

Ice Cream: The neighborhood favorite is **Bolas,** where *maestro heladero* Antonino has been making ice cream in Sevilla for the past 40 years, with a focus on fresh, natural, and inventive products. They are generous with samples and creative with their offerings, so try a few wild flavors before choosing. His wife, Cecilia, speaks English and doles out samples (daily 12:00-24:00, Calle Puerta de la Carne 3).

Healthy Option: Tiny **Jester** provides much-needed healthy choices (as well as tasty indulgences). Ramón and Zaneta crank out bagel sandwiches, homemade pastries, vegan options, smoothies, and acai bowls. With only five petite terrace tables, takeout is a smart option (daily 9:00-14:00 & 16:30-20:30 except closed Wed evening, Calle Puerta de la Carne 7a).

Groceries: Más is close to many of my recommended hotels (Mon-Sat 9:00-21:30, Sun until 15:00, Avenida Menéndez de Pelayo 50).

BETWEEN THE CATHEDRAL AND THE RIVER

The area between the cathedral and the river, just across Avenida de la Constitución, is a wonderland of tapas, cheap eats, and fine dining. Calle García de Vinuesa leads past several colorful and cheap tapas places to a busy corner surrounded by an impressive selection of happy eateries (where Calle Adriano meets Calle Antonia Díaz).

$$ La Canasta ("The Basket") is a modern diner facing the cathedral. While not particularly characteristic, it's bright, efficient, and air-conditioned, and the fun and accessible menu offers a nice break from tapas fare. It's also popular for breakfast, a bakery nibble, simple lunches, and smoothies (daily 7:30-23:00, across from the cathedral at corner of Calle García de Vinuesa and Avenida de la Constitución).

$$$ Bodeguita Casablanca is famously the choice of bullfighters—and even the king. Just steps from the touristy cathedral area, this feels like a neighborhood spot, with stylish locals and a great menu. I'm partial to the *solomillo* (tenderloin) and the artichokes. Tapas are available outside Monday through Thursday and inside anytime, while *raciones* are available inside or out. This is a good place to be bold and experiment with your order (Mon-Fri 12:30-17:00 & 20:00-24:00, Sat 12:30-17:30, closed Sun and Aug, reservations smart, across the way from Archivo General de Indias at Calle Adolfo Rodríguez Jurado 12, +34 954 224 114, www.bodeguitacasablanca.com).

$$$ La Casa del Tesorero is a good, dressy alternative to the tapas commotion, with mellow lighting and music (and with a full range of Italian options: salads, pastas, and pizzas). It creates its own world, with a calm, spacious, elegant interior built upon 12th-century Moorish ruins (look through the glass floor) and under historic arches of what used to be the city's treasury (daily 12:30-16:00 & 19:30-23:30, Calle Santander 1, +34 954 503 921).

$$ El Postiguillo has a fun ambience—sort of bullfighting-meets-*Bonanza*—where stuffed heads decorate the walls of a fanciful wooden stable. Locals come for the top-quality, traditional dishes, while tourists like the easy menu and snappy service. Try the *carrillada* (stewed pork cheeks), *rabo de toro* (bulltail stew), or the chilled *salmorejo* (a thicker, Córdoba-style gazpacho). Tapas are an option anywhere you sit (daily 12:00-24:00, Calle Dos de Mayo 2, +34 954 565 162).

$$$ La Isla, tucked away in a narrow alley behind the Postigo craft market, is dressy, expensive, and sought out for its food—locals say it serves some of the best seafood and paella in town. A nautical theme reminds diners of seafood specialties—the *albóndigas de pescado* (fish meatballs) are delectable. Classy service is the norm whether dining outside, at the bar, or in the restaurant (daily 12:30-24:00, Calle Arfe 25, +34 954 215 376).

$ Bodega Morales oozes old-Sevilla atmosphere. The front area is more of a drinking bar; for food, go to the back section (use the separate entrance around the corner). Here, sitting among huge adobe jugs, you can munch on affordable tiny sandwiches *(montaditos)* and tapas; both are just €2. Try the *salchicha al vino blanco*—tasty sausage braised in white wine—or the spinach with chickpeas (order at the bar, good wine selection, daily 13:00-16:00 & 20:00-24:00, Calle García de Vinuesa 11, +34 954 221 242).

$ Bar Arenal is a classic bull bar with tables spilling out onto a great street-corner setting. It's good for just a drink and to hang out with a crusty crowd. They sell cheap, old-school tapas (Tue-Sun 14:00-24:00, closed Mon, Calle Arfe 2).

Near Plaza Nueva

$$$ Zelai Bar Restaurant is utterly contemporary, without a hint of a historic-Sevilla feel or touristy vibe. Their pricey gourmet tapas and *raciones* are a hit with a smart local crowd, who enjoy the fusion of Basque, Andalusian, and international dishes. Study the English menu, which works in both the bar area and the dressy little restaurant out back, where reservations are generally required (daily 13:00-16:30 & 21:00-23:30, off Plaza Nueva at Calle Albareda 22, +34 954 229 992, www.restaurantezelai.com).

$$ Bodeguita Antonio Romero has served millions of *montaditos* (little sandwiches) over the years. It's a tight, stools-or-stand kind of place. They're known for their tasty *pringá* (a meaty mix of beef, pork, sausage, and fat simmered for hours), but my favorite is the *piripi* (mini mouthful of pork tenderloin, bacon, cheese, tomato, and mayo). They also offer many good wines by the glass (Tue-Sun 12:00-24:00, closed Mon, Gamazo 16, +34 954 210 585).

$$ Abacería Casa Moreno is a classic *abacería*, a neighborhood grocery store that doubles as a standing-room-only tapas bar. Squeeze into the back room and you're slipping back in time—and behind a tall language barrier. They're proud of their top-quality *jamón serrano, queso manchego,* and super-tender *mojama* (cured, dried tuna). Rubbing elbows here with local eaters, under a bull's head, surrounded by jars of peaches and cans of sardines, you feel like you're in on a secret (Mon-Fri 9:45-15:30 & 18:30-22:30, Sat 10:30-16:00, closed Sun, 3 blocks off Plaza Nueva at Calle Gamazo 7, +34 954 228 315).

$$$ Taberna del Alabardero, one of Sevilla's top restaurants, serves refined Spanish cuisine in chandeliered elegance. If you order à la carte, it adds up to about €50 a meal. Consider their €20/person (no sharing) starter sampler, followed by an entrée. For €64 you can have an elaborate, seven-course fixed-price meal with lots of little surprises from the chef (be sure to understand your bill, daily 13:00-16:30 & 20:00-23:30, air-con, reservations smart, Calle Zaragoza 20, +34 954 502 721, www.tabernadelalabardero.es).

$$ El Bistro del Alabardero, on the ground floor of the fancy Taberna del Alabardero, is part of a cooking school. They offer meals from the famed kitchen in an elegant setting at great prices. You're the dining guinea pig for their fixed menu (three delightful courses-€15 for weekday lunches, €20 for dinner and weekend lunches; daily 13:00-16:30 & 20:00-23:00, Calle Zaragoza 20, +34 954 502 721). To avoid a wait, arrive before 14:00 or opt for dinner (no reservations).

Groceries: Two handy markets are near Plaza Nueva. **Spar Express** has all the basics, plus a takeaway counter for sandwiches, salads, and smoothies (Mon-Sat 9:00-23:00, Sun from 10:30, Calle Zaragoza 31). **Carrefour Express** is stocked with prepared foods and picnic supplies (daily 9:30-22:30, Calle Harinas 7).

At or near the Arenal Market Hall

Mercado del Arenal, Sevilla's covered fish-and-produce market, is ideal for snapping photos and grabbing a cheap lunch. As with most markets, you'll find characteristic little diners with prices designed to lure in savvy shoppers, not to mention a crispy fresh world of picnic goodies—and a riverside promenade with benches just a block away (Mon-Sat 9:00-14:30, closed Sun, sleepy on Mon, on Calle Pastor y Landero at Calle Arenal, just beyond bullring).

$$$ Marisquería Arenal El Pesquero is a popular fish restaurant that thrives in the middle of the Arenal Market, and stays open after the market closes. In the afternoon and evening, you're surrounded by the empty Industrial Age market, with workers dragging their crates to and fro. It's a great family-friendly, finger-licking-good scene that's much appreciated by its enthusiastic local following. Fish is priced by weight, so be careful when ordering, and double-check the bill (Tue-Sat 13:00-17:00 & 21:00-24:00, Sun open for dinner only, closed Mon, reservations smart for dinner, enter on Calle Pastor y Landero 9, +34 954 220 881).

$$ Mercado Lonja del Barranco, an old fish market, is now a food hall with a wide variety of trendy, chain-like eateries filling a 19th-century building designed by Gustave Eiffel (of Parisian tower fame). It's just opposite Triana, facing the Isabel II Bridge (daily 10:00-24:00).

TRIANA

Colorful Triana, across the river from the city center, offers a nice range of eating options, especially around trendy Calle San Jacinto and the neighborhood scene behind the Church of Santa Ana (see my recommendations below).

Here are some other places to consider. The covered market is home to a world of tempting lunchtime eateries—take a stroll, take in the scene, and take your pick (busiest Tue-Sat morning through afternoon). The riverside fish joints at the Isabel II Bridge—El Mero and María Trifulca—change names and quality like hats and charge a little extra for their scenic setting, but they're worth considering if you want to eat on the river.

On or near Calle San Jacinto

The area's pedestrianized main drag is lined with the tables of several easy-to-enjoy restaurants.

$$ Taberna Miami is a reliable bet for seafood. Grab a table with a good paseo-watching perch right on the street (daily 11:30-24:00, Calle San Jacinto 21, +34 954 340 843).

$$ Blanca Paloma Bar is a classic wine bar offering a delightful bar (for tapas), plenty of small tables for a sit-down meal (no tapas), and a fine selection of good Spanish wines by the glass (listed on the blackboard). They serve tasty tapa standards such as *pisto con huevo frito* (ratatouille with fried egg) that look and taste homemade (Mon-Sat long hours, closed Sun, at the corner of Calle Pagés del Corro, +34 954 333 640).

$$ Las Golondrinas Bar ("The Swallows") is famed in Triana for its wonderful list of tasty tapas (from a fun and accessible menu). The dining area is limited to big and pricier *raciones* (ideal for groups). For one or two people, the tapas scene in the bar is best. Favorites here are the pork *punta de solomillo* (tenderloin) and *champiñones* (mushrooms). Complement your meat with a veggie plate from the *aliños* section of the menu. Cling to a corner of the bar and watch the amazingly productive little kitchen jam; be aggressive to get your order in. The clatter in the kitchen is the steady pounding of pork being tenderized (daily 13:00-16:00 & 20:00-24:00, Calle Antillano Campos 26, +34 954 338 235).

Behind the Church of Santa Ana

This is a more rustic and casual neighborhood scene, offering a charming setting where you can sit down under a big tree in the shade of the old church and dine with locals.

$$ Bar Bistec, with half of the square's tables, is enthusiastic about their cod fritters, fried zucchini *(calabacín)*, and calamari, and brags about their quail and snails in sauce. Before taking a seat out on the square, consider the indoor seating and the fun action at the bar (tapas only, daily 11:30-16:00 & 20:00-24:00, Plazuela de Santa Ana, +34 954 274 759).

$ Taberna La Plazuela, which shares the same square as Bar Bistec, is simpler, doing fried fish, grilled sardines, and *caracoles* (snails) in spring. They serve from the tapas menu in the bar and at tables on the square (long hours daily, Plazuela de Santa Ana 1, mobile +34 686 976 293).

$ Bar Santa Ana, just a block away alongside the church, is a rustic neighborhood bar—run by the same family for a century—with great seating on the street and a classic neighborhood-bar ambience inside. Peruse the interior, draped in Weeping Virgin and bullfighting memorabilia. It's always busy with the neighborhood gang, who enjoy fun tapas like *delicia de solomillo* (pork tenderloin) and appreciate the bar's willingness to serve even cheap tapas at the outdoor tables. I like to be engulfed in the scene—sitting at the bar, where they keep track of your bill by chalking it directly on the counter (long hours daily, facing the side of the church at Calle Pureza 82, +34 954 272 102).

Sevilla Connections

Note that many destinations are well served by both trains and buses.

BY TRAIN

All trains arriving and departing Sevilla, including high-speed AVE trains, leave from the larger, more distant **Santa Justa** station. But many *cercanías* and regional trains heading south to Granada, Jerez, Cádiz, and Málaga also stop at the smaller **San Bernardo** station a few minutes from Santa Justa, which is connected to downtown by tram. Hourly *cercanías* trains connect both stations (about a 4-minute trip). For tips on arrival at Santa Justa, see "Arrival in Sevilla," earlier.

Train Tickets: For schedules and tickets, visit the Renfe Travel Center, at the train station (daily 8:00-22:00, take a number and wait). Many travel agencies in Sevilla also sell train tickets; look for a train sticker in agency windows. Train info: +34 912 320 320, www.renfe.com.

From Sevilla by AVE Train to Madrid: The AVE express train is expensive but fast (2.5 hours to Madrid; hourly departures 7:00-23:00). Departures between 16:00 and 19:00 can book up far in advance, and surprise holidays and long weekends can totally jam up trains—reserve as far ahead as possible.

From Sevilla by Train to Córdoba: There are three options for this journey: slow and cheap regional, *media distancia* trains (7/day, 1.5 hours); fast and cheap regional high-speed **Avant** (or Alvia) trains (hourly, 45 minutes, requires reservation); and fast and expensive **AVE** trains (almost hourly, 45 minutes, requires reservation). Unless you must be on a particular departure, there's no reason to pay more for AVE; Avant trains are just as quick and a third the price. However, promotional fares for the AVE can be as cheap as regional trains when booked in advance. (If you have a rail pass, you still must buy a reservation; Avant reservations are about half the cost as for AVE.)

Other Trains from Sevilla to: Málaga (hourly, 45 minutes on AVE; 7/day, 2 hours on Avant; 5/day, 2.5 hours on slower regional trains), **Ronda** (4/day, 3 hours, transfer in Bobadilla or Córdoba), **Granada** (6/day, 2.5 hours), **Jerez** (nearly hourly, 1.25 hours), **Toledo** (hourly, 4 hours, transfer in Madrid), **Barcelona** (2/day direct, more with transfer in Madrid, 5.5 hours), **Algeciras** (3/day, 5-6 hours, transfer at Antequera or Bobadilla—bus is better). There are no direct trains to **Lisbon,** Portugal, so you'll have to take AVE to Madrid, then overnight to Lisbon; buses or a direct flight to Lisbon are far better (see below).

BY BUS

Sevilla has two bus stations: The El Prado de San Sebastián station, near Plaza de España, primarily serves regional destinations; and the Plaza de Armas station, farther north (past the bullring), handles most long-distance buses. Go to the TI for the latest schedules.

From El Prado de San Sebastián station to Andalucía and the South Coast: Regional buses are operated by Comes (www.tgcomes.es), Damas (www.damas-sa.es), and Autocares Valenzuela (www.grupovalenzuela.com). Connections to **Jerez** are frequent, as many southbound buses head there first (7/day, 1.5 hours, run by all three companies; note that train is also possible—see earlier). Damas runs buses to some of Andalucía's hill towns, including **Ronda** (7/day, 2.5 hours, fewer on weekends) and **Arcos** (2/day, 2 hours; more departures possible with transfer in Jerez). For Spain's South Coast, a Comes bus departs Sevilla four times a day and heads for **Tarifa** (3 hours, but not timed well for taking a ferry to Tangier that same day—best to overnight in Tarifa), then **Algeciras** (3-4 hours), and ends at **La Línea/Gibraltar** (4.5 hours). However, if **Algeciras** is your goal, Autocares Valenzuela has a much faster direct connection (7/day, fewer on weekends, 2.5 hours). There is one bus a day from this station to **Granada** (3 hours); the rest depart from the Plaza de Armas station.

From Plaza de Armas station to: Madrid (9/day, 6 hours, www.socibus.es), **Córdoba** (7/day, 2 hours), **Granada** (7/day, 3 hours), **Málaga** (7/day direct, 3 hours), **Nerja** (2/day, 5 hours), **Barcelona** (2/day, 16.5 hours, including one overnight bus).

By Bus to Portugal: The cheapest way to get to **Lisbon** is by bus (3/day, departures at 7:00, 8:00, and 23:59, 7 hours, leaves from both Sevilla bus stations, www.alsa.es). The midnight departure continues past Lisbon to **Coimbra** (arriving 10:30) and **Porto** (arriving 13:00). Sevilla also has direct bus service to **Lagos,** on the Algarve (5/day in summer, 2/day off-season, 5.5 hours, buy ticket a day or two in advance May-Oct, www.damas-sa.es). The bus departs from Sevilla's Plaza de Armas bus station and arrives at the Lagos bus station. If you'd like to visit Tavira on the way to Lagos, purchase a bus ticket to Tavira (3-hour trip), have lunch there, then take the train to Lagos.

ROUTE TIPS FOR DRIVERS

Sevilla to Arcos (55 miles/88 km): The remote hill towns of Andalucía are a joy to tour by car with Michelin map 578 or any other good map. Drivers can follow signs to *Cádiz* on the fast toll expressway (blue signs, E-5, AP-4); the toll-free N-IV is curvy and dangerous. About halfway to Jerez, at Las Cabezas de San Juan, take A-371 to Villamartín. From there, circle scenically (and clockwise) through the thick of the Pueblos Blancos—Zahara and Grazalema—to Arcos.

It's about two hours from Sevilla to Zahara. You'll find decent but winding roads and sparse traffic. It gets worse (but very scenic) if you take the tortuous series of switchbacks over the 4,500-foot summit of Puerto de Las Palomas (Pigeons Pass, climb to the viewpoint) on the direct but difficult road (CA-9104) from Zahara to Grazalema (you'll see several hiking trailheads into Sierra de Grazalema Natural Park).

Another scenic option through the park from Grazalema to Arcos is the road (A-372) that goes up over Puerto del Boyar

(Boyar Pass), past the pretty little valley town of Benamahoma, and down to El Bosque.

To skirt the super-twisty roads within the park while passing through a few more hill towns, the road from Ronda to El Gastor, Setenil (cave houses and great olive oil), and Olvera is another picturesque alternative.

GRANADA

For a time, as a thriving Islamic city-state, Granada was the grandest city in Spain. But after the tumult that came with the change from Moorish to Christian rule, it lost its power and settled into a long slumber. Today, Granada seems to specialize in evocative history and good living. Settle down in the old center and explore monuments of the Moorish civilization and its conquest. Taste the treats of a North African-flavored culture that survives here today.

Compared to other Spanish cities its size, Granada is delightfully cosmopolitan—it's worked hard to accept a range of cultures, and you'll see far more ethnic restaurants here than elsewhere in Andalucía. Its large student population (including many students from abroad) also lends it a youthful zest. The Grenadine people are serious about hospitality and have earned a reputation among travelers for being particularly friendly and eager to help you enjoy their historic city.

Granada's magnificent Alhambra palace/fortress was the last stronghold of the Moorish kingdom in Spain. The city's exotically tangled Moorish quarter, the Albayzín, invites exploration. From its viewpoints, romantics can enjoy the sunset and evening views of the grand, floodlit Alhambra.

After visiting the Alhambra and then seeing a blind beggar, a Spanish poet wrote, "Give him a coin, for there is nothing worse in this life than to be blind in Granada." This city has much to see, yet it reveals itself in unpredictable ways; it takes a poet to sort through and assemble the jumbled shards of Granada. Peer through the intricate lattice of a Moorish window. Hear water burbling unseen among the labyrinthine hedges of the Generalife's gardens. Listen to a flute trilling deep in the swirl of alleys around the cathedral. Don't be blind in Granada—open all your senses.

PLANNING YOUR TIME

You could conceivably hit Granada's highlights in one very busy day, sandwiched between two overnights. With a more relaxed itinerary, Granada is worth two days and two nights. You can easily connect to Granada by direct flight from Barcelona, then continue to other destinations by train or bus.

Note that it's critical to reserve a ticket for the Alhambra well in advance (see "Alhambra Tour," later). In the summer, do what you can to avoid the brutal heat of the early afternoon. Start early, take a break somewhere cool, and stay out late.

Granada in One Day

With just one full day here, fit in the top sights by following this intense plan: In the morning, take my self-guided walk of the old town (visiting the cathedral and Royal Chapel). After a quick lunch, spend the afternoon at the Alhambra (reservation essential). From the Alhambra, take minibus #C32 (or a taxi) into the Albayzín quarter to the San Nicolás viewpoint for sunset, then find the right place for a suitably late dinner.

Granada in Two Days

Day 1: Stroll the Alcaicería market streets and follow my self-guided tour of the old town, including a visit to the cathedral and its Royal Chapel. Enjoy the vibe at Plaza Nueva, the town's main square. Wander up into the Albayzín Moorish quarter, stopping by a funky teahouse along the way. End your day at the San Nicolás viewpoint—the golden hour before sunset is best, when the Alhambra seems to glow with its own light.

Day 2: Follow my self-guided tour of the Alhambra; you'll see the elaborate and many-roomed Palacios Nazaríes, the Renaissance Palace of Charles V, the refreshing Generalife and its gardens, and more.

On any **evening,** tapa-hop for dinner (consider Gayle's Granada Tapas Tours) or splurge on fine dining at a *carmen*. When the evening cools down, join the paseo. Take in a *zambra* dance in the Sacromonte district. Relax in an Arab bath (Hammam al Andalus) or a *tetería* (tea shop), or both. Slow down and smell the incense.

Orientation to Granada

Modern Granada sprawls (235,000 people), but its main sights are all within a 20-minute walk of Plaza Nueva, where dogs wag their tails to the rhythm of modern hippies and street musicians. Most of my recommended hotels are within a few blocks of Plaza Nueva. Make this the hub of your Granada visit.

Plaza Nueva sits between two hills: On one side is the great Moorish palace, the Alhambra, and on the other is the best-preserved Moorish quarter in Spain, the Albayzín. To the southwest are the cathedral, Royal Chapel, and Alcaicería (Moorish market), where the city's two main drags—Gran Vía de Colón (often just called "Gran Vía") and Calle Reyes Católicos—lead away into the modern city.

TOURIST INFORMATION

The Granada TI is inside City Hall on Plaza del Carmen, a short walk from the cathedral (Mon-Sat 9:00-18:00, Sun until 14:00, longer hours in summer, +34 958 248 280, http://en.granadatur.com). Another TI, tucked away just above Plaza Nueva near the Santa Ana Church, covers Granada and all of Andalucía. This TI also posts all of Granada's bus departures (Mon-Fri 9:00-19:30, Sat-Sun 9:30-15:00, +34 958 575 202).

Sightseeing Pass: The €40 **Granada Card** may get you an Alhambra reservation when the main Alhambra website is sold out. It includes admission to the Alhambra ("Alhambra General" ticket; see "Alhambra Tour," later), entry to the main sights in town (the cathedral, Royal Chapel, Carthusian Monastery), plus bus rides and a few other admissions and discounts—and it's good for five days. It can be purchased online three months in advance (http://en.granadatur.com/granada-card).

ARRIVAL IN GRANADA

By Train: Granada's modest train station is connected to the center by a €6 taxi ride, frequent buses, or a 30-minute walk down Avenida de la Constitución and Gran Vía. The train station does not have luggage storage.

Taxis wait out front. It's a two-minute walk to reach the bus stop: Exiting the train station, walk straight ahead up tree-lined Avenida Andaluces (following the Metro tracks). At the first major intersection, find a covered bus stop to the right on Avenida de la Constitución. Buy a ticket from a machine at the stop or purchase a Credibús pass (see "Getting Around Granada," later). Bus #4, #8, #11 and #33 head down Avenida de la Constitución to Gran Vía and stop at the cathedral (Catedral)—three blocks from Plaza

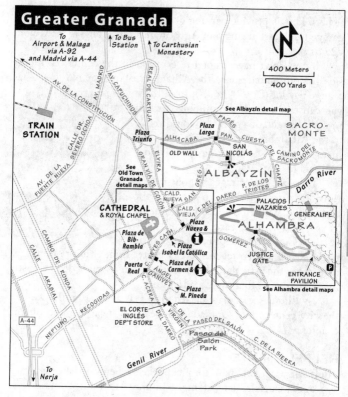

Greater Granada

Nueva and most of my recommended hotels (stops are shown on monitors).

By Bus: Located on the city outskirts, Granada's bus station *(estación de autobuses)* has a good and cheap cafeteria, ATMs, luggage lockers, and a privately run tourist agency masquerading as an official TI. All of these services are downstairs, where you exit the buses.

Upstairs is the main arrivals hall with ticket windows, ticket machines, and a helpful information counter in the main hall that hands out printed schedules. All buses are operated by Alsa (www.alsa.es). To get from the bus station to the city center, it's either a 10-minute taxi ride (€8) or a 25-minute ride on bus #33 (€1.40, pay driver). For Plaza Nueva, get off on Gran Vía at the Catedral stop (check monitors).

By Car: Driving in Granada's historic center is restricted to buses, taxis, and tourists with hotel reservations. If you have a reservation, simply drive past the sign and make sure your hotel registers you with the local traffic police (this is routine for them, but if they don't do it within 48 hours, you'll be stuck with a steep ticket). Hotels provide parking or have a deal with a central-zone garage (such as Parking San Agustín, just off Gran Vía del Colón, €25/day).

If you don't have a hotel reservation in the center, park outside the prohibited zone. The Alhambra, above the old town, has a huge pay lot (€19/24 hours); from there you can walk, catch the minibus, or taxi into the center. If you're driving directly to the Alhambra, you can easily avoid the historic center (see "Getting There" under "Alhambra Tour," later).

There are also garages just outside the restricted zone: the Triunfo garage to the east (€20/day, Avenida de la Constitución 5) or the Neptune garage to the south (Centro Comercial Neptuno, €17/day, on Calle Neptuno). To reach the city center from either parking garage, catch the articulated #4 bus nearby (on Avenida de la Constitución) and get off at the Catedral stop.

By Plane: Granada's relaxed airport is about 10 miles west of the city center. See "Granada Connections" near the end of this chapter.

HELPFUL HINTS

Theft Alert: Be on guard for pickpockets wherever there's a crowd and especially late at night in the Albayzín. Your biggest threat is being conned while enjoying drinks and music in Sacromonte. Pushy women, usually hanging out near the cathedral and Alcaicería, may accost you with sprigs of rosemary, then demand payment for fortune-telling services—just say, *"No, gracias."*

Festivals: From late June to early July, the popular **International Festival of Music and Dance** offers classical music, ballet, flamenco, and zarzuela (light opera) nightly in the Alhambra and other historic venues at reasonable prices (visit TI or ticket office in the Corral del Carbón for schedule, www. granadafestival.org).

Bookstore: You'll find the **Alhambra Bookstore** at Calle Reyes Católicos 40—for location, see the "Granada Old Town Walk" map, later. Other branches are at the entrance pavilion of the Alhambra and inside the Palace of Charles V (+34 958 227 846, www.alhambratienda.es).

Laundry: La Colada is closest to my recommended hotels north of Plaza Nueva (daily 10:30-21:30, self-service, Calle de Elvira 85, mobile +34 637 834 997). **TLavo** will pick up and deliver laundry to your hotel—have your hotel help with the phone call (Mon-Sat 10:00-15:00 & 17:00-20:00, closed Sun, Calle Real de Cartuja 67, +34 958 279 659, www.lavanderiatlavo.es).

Travel Agency: Mega-chain El Corte Inglés sells plane, train, and bus tickets (Mon-Sat 10:00-21:30, closed Sun, ticket desk in basement level near supermarket, Carrera de la Virgen 20, +34 958 223 240).

Goodbye to Singlehood: Famed for its fun tapas and cheap beer, Granada is inundated on weekend evenings with Hen and Stag parties (called "goodbye to singlehood" parties here). The city can seem busier at midnight than at noon as crazily dressed brides and grooms prowl the streets with gangs of friends looking for fun.

GETTING AROUND GRANADA

With cheap taxis, frisky minibuses, good city buses, and nearly all points of interest an easy walk from Plaza Nueva, you'll get around Granada easily.

Tickets for minibuses and city buses cost €1.40 per ride (buy from curbside machines or driver; must use machine for bus #4 tickets). For schedules and routes, see TransportesRober.com.

Credibús cards save you money if you'll be riding often—or, since they're shareable, if you're part of a group (can be loaded with €5, €10, or €20). To get a €5 card—likely all you'll need—ask for *"un bono de cinco."* These are valid on all buses and include transfers if made within 45 minutes.

By Minibus: Handy little made-for-tourists red minibuses cover the city center; they depart every few minutes from Plaza Nueva, Plaza Isabel La Católica, and Gran Vía (Catedral stop) until late in the evening. For locations of bus stops in the city center, see the "Granada Old Town Walk" map, later.

Bus #C30 is the best for a trip up to the Alhambra, departing 30 yards uphill from Plaza Isabel La Católica, with stops at the Alhambra entrance pavilion and the Justice Gate (Puerta de la Justicia), among others (every 5-7 minutes, 7:00-23:00).

Bus #C31 departs from Plaza Nueva and circles counterclockwise around the Albayzín quarter, navigating the narrow one-way lanes (every 8-10 minutes, 7:00-23:00).

Bus #C32 connects the Alhambra to the Albayzín quarter and goes through the city center. For the Alhambra, catch it from the same spot as #C30 listed above (every 20-30 minutes, 7:00-23:00).

Bus #C34 runs from Plaza Nueva to Sacromonte (every 20 minutes, 8:00-22:00).

Tours in Granada

Hop-On, Hop-Off Tourist Train

For a relaxing and scenic loop through the old town, the touristy hop-on, hop-off train can be time and money well spent (€8/24 hours, daily 9:30-23:00, Nov-March until 19:30, leaves every 20 minutes, includes Alhambra and Albayzín quarter, recorded English narration—use your own earbuds or buy onboard, www. granada.city-tour.com).

Walking Tours

Cicerone offers informative and spirited two-hour city tours describing the fitful and fascinating changes the city underwent over 500 years ago as it morphed from a Moorish capital to a Christian one. The tour doesn't enter any actual sights, but it weaves together bits of the Moorish heritage that survive around the cathedral and in the Albayzín. Tours are usually in both English and Spanish daily at 10:30; reservations are encouraged but not required (€29, RS%—show this book; basic Granada tours leave from Calle San Jerónimo 10, +34 958 561 810, mobile +34 607 691 676, www. ciceronegranada.com). They also offer small group tours of the Alhambra that include an entry time to Palacios Nazaríes (price based on size of group, ideally reserve at least 1-2 months ahead).

"Free" (Tip-Based) Walking Tours

Students who've memorized a script lead entertaining walks through the historic town center. While you won't get the quality of a licensed guide, the price is right: Just show up, have fun, and tip what you like. With competing advertising umbrellas and enthusiastic welcomes, groups offering these tours daily in English gather at Plaza Nueva and at Plaza Isabel La Católica. Some popular tours are **Feel the City** (www.feelthecitytours.com), **Follow Me Granada** (www.followmegranada.com), **Free Tour Granada** (www.freetour.com/granada), and **Walk in Granada** (www. walkingranada.com).

Local Guides

Margarita Ortiz de Landazuri (mobile +34 687 361 988, www. alhambratours.com) and **Miguel Ángel** (mobile +34 617 565 711, miguelangelalhambratours@gmail.com) are good English-speaking, licensed private guides with lots of experience and a passion for teaching. In addition to the Alhambra, they give tours of Sacromonte, the Albaycín, and other parts of Granada. Guide rates are standard (€130/3 hours, €260/day).

Olive Oil Tour

This company helps you explore Granada's countryside while sampling local olive oil. Choose between a three-hour tour that departs

Granada at a Glance

▲▲▲**Alhambra** The last and finest Moorish palace in Iberia, highlighting the splendor of that civilization in the 13th and 14th centuries. **Hours:** Daily 8:30-20:00 (mid-Oct-March until 18:00); also Tue-Sat for nighttime visits (Fri-Sat only in off-season). See page 109.

▲▲**Royal Chapel** Lavish 16th-century chapel with the tombs of Queen Isabel and King Ferdinand. **Hours:** Mon-Sat 10:15-18:30, Sun 11:00-18:00. See page 126.

▲▲**San Nicolás Viewpoint** Breathtaking vista over the Alhambra and the Albayzín—best at sunset. See page 133.

▲**Granada Cathedral** The second-largest cathedral in Spain, with a fine Renaissance interior. **Hours:** Mon-Sat 10:00-18:30, Sun 15:00-17:45. See page 130.

▲**Exploring the Albayzín Walk** Spain's best old Moorish quarter. See page 136.

▲**Great Mosque of Granada** Islamic house of worship featuring a minaret with a live call to prayer and a courtyard with commanding views. **Hours:** Daily 11:00-21:00, shorter hours in winter. See page 136.

GRANADA

in the morning or afternoon (€43) or add a wine tasting and light tapas (€58). Tours are in English and depart from a central meeting point in the city (reserve ahead, +34 958 559 643, mobile +34 651 147 504, www.oliveoiltour.com).

Gayle's Granada Tapas Tours

Having lived in Granada since 1996, Scottish-born Gayle Mackie knows where to find the best food. She and her team take small groups off the beaten path to characteristic tapas bars, providing cuisine tips and fascinating insights into Granada. The various routes offer a moveable feast (amounting to a filling meal) with good wine and craft beer (2.5 hours, €40-60/person, tours for 2-8 people, private tours available, daily at 20:00, some days also at 13:00, mobile +34 619 444 984, www.granadatapastours.com).

Granada Old Town Walk

This short self-guided walk covers all the essential old town sights. Along the way, we'll see vivid evidence of the dramatic Moorish-to-Christian transition brought about by the Reconquista—the

Granada Old Town Walk

Walk
1 Corral del Carbón
2 Alcaicería
3 Plaza de Bib-Rambla
4 Granada Cathedral
5 Royal Chapel Square
6 Plaza Isabel La Católica
   (Bus to Alhambra)
7 Plaza Nueva
8 To Paseo de los Tristes
   & Hammam El Bañuelo

Other
9 Alhambra Bookstore
10 Gran Vía Cathedral Bus
   Stop (from Train & Bus Stations)
11 Gran Vía del Colón Bus Stop
   (to Train & Bus Stations)
12 Plaza Nueva Bus Stop
   (to Albayzín & Sacromonte)

long and ultimately successful battle to retake Spain from the Muslim Moors and reestablish Christian rule.

• *Start at Corral del Carbón, near Plaza del Carmen.*

1 Corral del Carbón

A caravanserai (of Silk Road fame) was a protected place for merchants to rest their animals, spend the night, get a bite to eat, and spin yarns. This Moorish structure, the only surviving caravanserai of Granada's original 14, is just a block from the Alcaicería silk market (the next stop on this walk). Stepping through the grand horseshoe-arch entry, you'll find a courtyard with 14th-century Moorish brickwork surrounding a fountain. This plain yet elegant structure evokes the times when traders gathered here with exotic goods and swapped tales from across the Muslim world.

It's a common mistake to think of the Muslim Moors as somehow not Spanish. They lived here for seven centuries and were just as "indigenous" as the Romans, Goths, and Celts. While the Moors were Muslim,

they were no more connected to Arabia than they were to France.

After the Reconquista, this space was used as a storehouse for coal (hence "del Carbón"). These days it houses offices where you can buy tickets for musical events, a handy public WC (to the right as you enter), and sometimes an Alhambra tourist info office.

• *From the caravanserai, exit straight ahead down Puente del Carbón to the big street named Calle Reyes Católicos. The street covers the Darro River, which once ran openly here, spanned by a series of bridges. Today, the modern commercial center is to your left.*

Cross here and continue one block farther to the horseshoe-shaped gate marked Alcaicería. *Notice the pedestrian street, Zacatín, just before you reach the gate. It paralleled the Darro River in the 19th century; today it's a favorite paseo destination, busy each evening with strollers. Pass through the Alcaicería gate and walk 20 yards into the old market to the first intersection at Calle Ermita.*

❼ Alcaicería

Originally an Arab souk (bazaar) and silk market, this warren of narrow streets is known as the Alcaicería (al-kai-thay-REE-ah).

Offering precious silver, spices, and silk, the market had 10 armed gates and its own guards. Silk was huge in Moorish times, and silkworm-friendly mulberry trees flourished in the countryside. It was such an important product that the sultans controlled and guarded it by constructing this fine, fortified market. After the Reconquista, the Christians realized this market was good for business and didn't mess with it. Later, the more zealous Philip II had it shut down. A terrible fire in 1850 destroyed what

was left. Today's Alcaicería is an "authentic fake"—rebuilt in the late 1800s as a tourist attraction to complement the romantic image of Granada popularized by the writings of Washington Irving.

Explore the mesh of tiny shopping lanes: overpriced trinkets, popcorn machines, balloon vendors, leather goods spread out on streets, kids playing soccer, barking dogs, dogged shoe-shine boys, and the whirring grind of bicycle-powered knife sharpeners. You'll invariably meet obnoxious and persistent women pushing their green rosemary sprigs on innocents in order to extort money. Be strong.

• *Turn left down Calle Ermita. After 50 yards, you'll leave the market via another fortified gate and enter a big square crowded with outdoor restaurants. Skirt around the tables to the Neptune fountain, which marks the center of the...*

❸ Plaza de Bib-Rambla

This exuberant square, just two blocks behind the cathedral (from the fountain you can see its blocky bell tower peeking above the big orange building) was once the center of Moorish Granada. Although Moorish rule of Spain lasted 700 years, it declined in its final centuries under weak leadership—even while Christian forces grew more determined. As Muslims fled south from reconquered lands, they flooded into Granada, then held by the last remnants of the Moorish kingdom. By 1400, Granada had an estimated 100,000 people—huge for medieval Europe. This was the main square, the focal point for markets and festivals, but it was much smaller then, hemmed in by the jam-packed city.

Under Christian rule, the Moors who remained were initially tolerated (as they were considered good for business), and this area became their ghetto. Then, with the Inquisition (which peaked under Philip II, c. 1550), ideology trumped pragmatism, and Muslims and Jews were evicted or forced to convert—and some were executed. The elegant square you see today was built, and built big. In-your-face Catholic processions started here. To assert Christian rule, all the trappings of Christian power were layered upon what had been the trappings of Moorish power. Between here and the cathedral were the Christian University (the big orange building) and the adjacent archbishop's palace.

Today Plaza de Bib-Rambla is good for coffee or a meal amid the color and fragrance of flower stalls and the burbling of its Neptune-topped fountain. It remains a multigenerational hangout, where it seems everyone is enjoying a peaceful retirement.

With Neptune facing you, leave the plaza by the left corner (along Calle Pescadería) to reach a smaller, similarly lively square—little Plaza Pescadería, where families spill out to enjoy its many restaurants. For a quick snack, drop into tiny **Cunini Pescadería**—just beyond its namesake restaurant—for a takeaway bite of *pescaito frito*—fried fish.

• *Backtrack from Cunini Pescadería and leave the plaza to the left, on Calle Marqués de Gerona; straight ahead you'll see a small square fronting a very big church.*

❹ Granada Cathedral (Catedral de Granada)

Wow, the cathedral facade just screams triumph. That's partly because its design is based on a triumphal arch, built over a destroyed mosque. Five hundred yards away, there was once open space outside the city wall with good soil for a foundation. But the Christian conquerors said, "No way." Instead, they destroyed the mosque and built their cathedral right here on difficult, sandy soil. This was the place where the people of Granada had traditionally worshipped—and now they would worship as Christians.

Building of the church started in the early 1500s and didn't finish until the early 1700s. It began with a Gothic foundation but over two centuries the design evolved: The interior layout is mostly Renaissance, its last altars are Neoclassical, and its facade, finished by hometown artist Alonso Cano (1601-1667), is Baroque. Accentuating the power of the Roman Catholic Church, the emphasis here is on Mary rather than Christ. The facade declares *Ave Maria*. (This was Counter-Reformation time, and the Church was threatened by Protestant Christians. Mary was also more palatable to Muslim converts, as she is revered in the Quran.)

• *To tour the cathedral now, you can enter here (the interior is described in more detail on page 130). You'll exit on the far side, near the big street called Gran Vía de Colón.*

If you're skipping the cathedral interior for now, circle around the building to the right, keeping the church on your left, until you reach the small square facing the Royal Chapel.

❺ Royal Chapel Square

This square was once ringed by important Moorish buildings: a hammam (public bath), a caravanserai (Days Inn), the silk market, the leading mosque, and a madrassa (school).

With Christian rule, the **Palacio de la Madraza** (its facade painted in 3-D Baroque style with faux gray stonework) became

Granada's first City Hall. Five hundred years ago, this was a Quranic school. If you pay to enter (€2, daily 10:30-20:00) you'll get a ground-floor peek at an ornate-as-the-Alhambra mini prayer room and mihrab; upstairs, a modern university lecture room boasts a circa 1500 Mudejar interlocking wood ceiling, finely painted and circled by a script celebrating the Christian conquest.

Also on this square is the entrance to the Royal Chapel, where the coffins of Ferdinand and Isabel were moved in 1521 from the Alhambra (for details on visiting the chapel, see page 126).

• *Continue up the cobbled, stepped lane to Gran Vía. Turn right and walk toward the big square just ahead (near where minibuses to the Alhambra stop), across the busy Calles Reyes Católicos.*

❻ Plaza Isabel La Católica

Granada's two grand boulevards, Gran Vía and Calle Reyes Católicos, meet here at Plaza Isabel La Católica. Above the fountain, a beautiful statue shows Columbus unfurling a long contract with Isabel. It lists the terms of the explorer's MCCCCLXXXXII voyage: "For as much as you, Columbus, are going by our command to discover and subdue some Islands and Continents in the ocean...." Two reliefs below the figures show the big events in Granada of 1492: Isabel and Ferdinand accepting Columbus' proposal, and a stirring battle scene (which never happened) at the Alhambra walls.

Isabel may have been driven by her desire to spread Catholicism, but Spain's interest was in finding a maritime trade route to the Far East and its spices (Ottoman Turks had cut off the traditional overland route). Columbus himself was driven by his desire for money. As a reward for adding territory to Spain's Catholic empire, Isabel promised Columbus the ranks of Admiral of the Oceans and Governor of the New World. To sweeten the pot, she tossed in one-eighth of all the riches he brought home. Isabel died thinking that Columbus had found India or China. Columbus died poor and disillusioned.

Look back at the fine buildings flanking the start of Gran Vía. With the arrival of cars and the modern age, the people of Granada wanted a Parisian-style boulevard. In the early 20th century, they mercilessly cut through the old town and created Gran Vía and its French-style buildings—in the process destroying everything in its path, including many historic convents. Elegant facades—like the two circa-1910 Paris-inspired buildings facing the square—once ornamented the entire Gran Vía. Now, turn 180 degrees to see the 1970s aesthetic: ugly.

Calle Reyes Católicos, named for the "Catholic Monarchs" Ferdinand and Isabel, leads from this square downhill to the busy intersection called Puerta Real. From there, Acera del Darro takes you through modern Granada to the river, passing the huge El Corte Inglés department store and lots of modern commerce. This area erupts with locals out strolling each night. For one of the best Granada paseos, wander the streets here around 19:00.

• *Follow Calle Reyes Católicos uphill for a couple of blocks until you reach...*

❼ Plaza Nueva

Plaza Nueva is dominated at the far end by the regional Palace of Justice (grand Baroque facade with green Andalusian flag). The fountain is capped by a stylized pomegranate—the symbol of the city, always open and fertile. The main action here is the comings and goings of the busy little shuttle buses serving the Albayzín. The local hippie community, nicknamed the *pies negros* (black feet) for obvious reasons, hangs out here and on Calle de Elvira. They squat—with their dogs and guitars—in abandoned caves above those the Roma (Gypsies) occupy in Sacromonte. Many are the children of rich Spanish families from the north, hell-bent on disappointing their high-achieving parents.

• *Our tour continues with a stroll up Carrera del Darro. Leave Plaza Nueva opposite from where you entered, on the little lane that runs alongside the Darro River. This is particularly enjoyable in the cool of the evening.*

❽ Paseo de los Tristes

This stretch of road is also called Paseo de los Tristes—"Walk of the Sad Ones." It was once the route of funeral processions to the cemetery at the edge of town. As you leave Plaza Nueva, notice the small Church of Santa Ana on your right. This was originally a mosque—the church tower replaced a minaret. Notice the ceramic brickwork. This is Mudejar art by Moorish craftsmen, whose techniques were later employed by Christians.

Follow Carrera del Darro along the Darro River, which flows around the base of the Alhambra. Six miles upstream, part of the

Darro is diverted to provide water for the Alhambra's many fountains—a remarkable feat of Moorish engineering in 1238.

After passing two small, picturesque bridges, the road widens slightly for a bus stop. Here you'll see the broken nub of a once-grand 11th-century bridge that led to the Alhambra. Notice two slits in the column: One held an iron portcullis to keep bad guys from entering the town via the river. The second held a solid door that was lowered to dam up water, then released to flush out the riverbed and keep it clean.

• Across from the remains of the bridge is the brick facade of our last stop, the stark but evocative ruins of an Arab bath.

Hammam El Bañuelo (Arab Baths)

In Moorish times, hammams were a big part of the community (working-class homes didn't have bathrooms). Baths were strictly segregated and were more than places to wash: These were social meeting points where business was done. In Christian times it was assumed that conspiracies brewed in these baths—therefore, only a few of them survive. This place gives you the chance to explore one of the best-preserved examples of an 11th-century Arab public bath in Spain.

Cost and Hours: €5, covered by Dobla de Oro card (described under "Alhambra Tour," later); daily 9:00-14:30 & 17:00-20:30, mid-Sept-March 10:00-17:00; Carrera del Darro 31, www.alhambra-patronato.es.

Visiting the Baths: Upon entering, you pass through the foyer and into the cold room, the warm room (where services like massage were offered), and finally the hot, or steam, room. Beyond that, you can see the oven that generated the heat, which flowed under the hypocaust-style floor tiles (the ones closest to the oven were the hottest). The romantic little holes in the ceiling once had stained-glass louvers that attendants opened and closed with sticks to regulate the heat and steaminess. Whereas Romans soaked in their pools, Muslims just doused. Rather than being totally immersed, people scooped and splashed water over themselves. Imagine attendants stoking the fires under the metal boiler...while people in towels and wooden slippers (to protect their feet from the heated floors) enjoyed all the spa services you can imagine as beams of light slashed through the mist.

This was a great social mixer. As all were naked, class distinctions disappeared—elites learned the latest from commoners. Mothers found matches for their kids. A popular Muslim phrase sums up the attraction of the baths: "This is where anyone would spend their last coin."

• Just across from the baths is a stop for minibus #C31 and #C32—the easy way to head up to the **Albayzín.** Otherwise, continue straight *ahead. On your right is the* **Church of San Pedro,** *the parish church of Sacromonte's Roma community (across from the Mudejar Art Museum). Within its rich interior is an ornate oxcart used to carry the host on the annual pilgrimage to Rocío, a town near the Portuguese border. Just past this, on your left, is* **Santa Catalina de Zafra,** *a convent of cloistered nuns (they worship behind a screen that divides the church's rich interior in half).*

This walk ends at **Paseo de los Tristes**—*with its bar and restaurant tables spilling out under the floodlit Alhambra. From here, the road arcs up to the Albayzín and into Sacromonte. If you've worked up a hunger, you can backtrack a few blocks to Calle de Gloria, where the* **Convento de San Bernardo** *sells cookies and monastic wine. Look for the* Venta de Dulces *sign on the corner; goods are sold from behind a lazy Susan.*

GRANADA

Alhambra Tour

The last and greatest Moorish palace, the Alhambra, is one of Europe's top sights and worth ▲▲▲. Attracting 8,000 visitors a day, it's the reason most tourists come to Granada. Nowhere else does the splendor of Moorish civilization shine so beautifully.

The last Moorish stronghold in Europe is really a symbol of retreat. As the Christian Reconquista gradually moved south, taking Córdoba (1237) and Sevilla (1248), displaced Muslims relocated to Granada, home of the Nasrids—the last Islamic kingdom in Spain. The Nasrids themselves would fall in 1492, but until that time Granada flourished as an intellectual and artistic center.

As you tour their grand palace, remember that while much of Europe slumbered through the Dark Ages, here Moorish magnificence blossomed—ornate stucco, plaster "stalactites," colors galore, scalloped windows framing Granada views, exuberant gardens, and water, water everywhere. Water—so rare and precious in most of the Islamic world—was the purest symbol of life to the Moors. The Alhambra is decorated with water: standing still, cascading, masking secret conversations, and drip-dropping playfully.

The Alhambra consists of four sights clustered together atop a hill, all covered by the following self-guided tour:

Palacios Nazaríes: Exquisite Moorish palace, the Alhambra's must-see sight (ticket required).

Palace of Charles V: Christian Renaissance palace plopped on top of the Alhambra after the Reconquista, with the fine Alhambra Museum inside (free to enter).

Generalife Palace and Gardens: Small summer palace with fragrant, lovely manicured gardens (ticket required).

Alcazaba Fort: Empty but evocative old fort with tower and views (ticket required).

ALHAMBRA TICKETS IN A NUTSHELL

To ensure you'll see the Palacios Nazaríes, the highlight of the Alhambra, book an "Alhambra General" ticket in advance (includes the Palacios Nazaríes, Alcazaba, and Generalife Palace and its gardens). Demand far exceeds the supply of about 8,000 tickets per day, so buy as far in advance as possible (tickets available one year ahead—but keep in mind that they're nonrefundable and cannot be changed). Tickets covering just the Generalife and Alcazaba are more readily available—but you'll miss the Palacios Nazaríes.

When booking tickets online, be prepared to enter the passport number of each visitor in your group; each person will be required to show their passport when entering the sight.

Ticketing options for the Alhambra change frequently; confirm details at https://tickets.alhambra-patronato.es/.

GETTING THERE

There are two entrances to the sprawling Alhambra: the Justice Gate, near the Palacios Nazaríes, and the entrance pavilion, 400 yards farther along at the top of the complex. If you've booked With tickets in hand, you can go directly to the Justice Gate. You have four options for getting there:

On Foot: From Plaza Nueva, it's a 20-minutes hike. Leave the plaza going up Cuesta de Gomérez. Keep going straight—you'll see the Alhambra high on your left. You'll soon reach the Justice Gate, which leads to the Palacios Nazaríes.

By Bus: Just uphill from Plaza de Isabel La Católica, catch the #C30 or #C32 minibus, marked *Alhambra*. Stops include *Generalife* (entrance pavilion/ticket office and gardens), *Charles V,* and *Justice Gate.* See "The Alhambra" map on page 113 for stop locations.

By Taxi: It's a €6 ride from Plaza Nueva.

By Car: If you have a car in town, do not use it to go to the Alhambra. But if you're coming from outside the city, you can drive here without passing through Granada's historic center. From the freeway, take the exit marked *Alhambra*. Signs lead you to a public parking lot, located near the entrance pavilion (€2.70/hour). Overnight and multiday parking is available (€19/24 hours, guarded at night). Leave the same way you came in.

PLANNING YOUR TIME

Alhambra General tickets come with a 30-minute time slot for admission to the Palacios Nazaríes (first entry to palaces at 8:30, last entry one hour before closing). You must enter the Palacios Nazaríes within the 30-minute window, but once inside, you can linger as long as you like. You can see the other Alhambra sights any time during that single day.

Don't miss your appointed time. Ticket checkers at the Palacios Nazaríes are strict. If you're seeing the Generalife Palace and its gardens first, allow at least 15 minutes to walk to the Palacios Nazaríes.

Although you can see the sights in any order, to minimize walking, a good plan is to see the three sights at the lower end first: Start with the Palace of Charles V and the Alcazaba fort, then visit Palacios Nazaríes. When you finish touring the palace, leave through the Partal Gardens, then take a pleasant 15-minute gradual uphill stroll to the Generalife and its gardens.

If you have a long wait for your Palacios Nazaríes appointment, you could do the gardens first, then head down to the other three. Or you can kill time luxuriously on the breezy view terrace of the parador bar within the Alhambra wall.

ORIENTATION TO THE ALHAMBRA

Cost: There are many ticket options for the Alhambra: Be sure to purchase a ticket that includes the Palacios Nazaríes.

- **Alhambra General:** €15, covers the Palacios Nazaríes, Alcazaba fort, and Generalife Palace and its gardens.
- **Gardens, Generalife, and Alcazaba:** €7.50, covers daytime admission to almost everything—but not Palacios Nazaríes.
- **Night Visit to Palacios Nazaríes:** €8.50, nighttime-only visit to the Palacios Nazaríes.
- **Night Visit to Gardens and Generalife:** €5.50, nighttime-only visit to the Generalife Palace and its gardens.
- **Alhambra Experiences:** €15, nighttime visit to Palacios Nazaríes, then next-morning entry to the Alcazaba, Generalife, and its gardens.
- **Dobla de Oro General:** €21, valid 3 days, includes Alhambra General ticket (with a timed-entry to Palacios Nazaríes) and several smaller Nasrid sights.
- **Dobla de Oro at Night:** €16, valid 3 days, includes a nighttime-only visit to Palacios Nazaríes and Nasrid sights.
- **Children's and Discounted Tickets:** Children under 12 are free, but still need a reservation booked online in their name.

Hours: The entire Alhambra complex is open daily 8:30-20:00 (mid-Oct-March until 18:00). Last entry is one hour before closing.

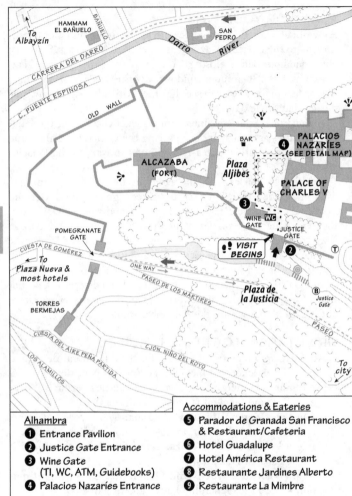

Alhambra
1. Entrance Pavilion
2. Justice Gate Entrance
3. Wine Gate
(TI, WC, ATM, Guidebooks)
4. Palacios Nazaríes Entrance

Accommodations & Eateries
5. Parador de Granada San Francisco & Restaurant/Cafeteria
6. Hotel Guadalupe
7. Hotel América Restaurant
8. Restaurante Jardines Alberto
9. Restaurante La Mimbre

Evening Hours: The Palacios Nazaríes and the Generalife are open and nicely lit some evenings (Tue-Sat 22:00-23:30; mid-Oct-March Fri-Sat 20:00-21:30). Note that night tickets include the palace or the Generalife, but not both (as you have only 90 minutes inside). These tickets are not timed-entry, and it's extremely crowded when the doors open; you must enter no later than one hour before closing.

Information: Visitor info +34 958 027 971, ticket help line +34 858 889 002, https://tickets.alhambra-patronato.es/.

Reservations: Buy tickets online. Select a ticket, choose a date, then select an entry time for Palacios Nazaríes (you'll have a 30-minute window to enter). When asked for a "document

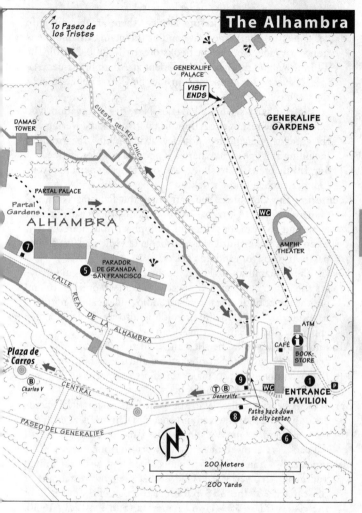

The Alhambra

To Paseo de los Tristes

GENERALIFE PALACE

VISIT ENDS

GENERALIFE GARDENS

DAMAS TOWER

CUESTA DEL REY CHICO

PARTAL PALACE

Partal Gardens

ALHAMBRA

WC

AMPHI-THEATER

PARADOR DE GRANADA SAN FRANCISCO

CALLE REAL DE LA ALHAMBRA

ATM

CAFÉ

BOOK-STORE

Plaza de Carros

Charles V

CENTRAL

PASEO DEL GENERALIFE

Generalife

Paths back down to city center

WC

ENTRANCE PAVILION

GRANADA

N

200 Meters

200 Yards

number," use your passport number. Print the ticket or store it on your phone. Tickets are released in intervals throughout the year (at 12 months out, 3 months out, and 1 month out). If tickets appear sold out for a particular date three months in advance, for example, check again one month ahead.

Without Reservations: If you are unable to get a reservation for the Palacios Nazaríes, you can **ask your hotel** to book a ticket for you when you reserve your room, or buy a **Granada Card** sightseeing pass—it may score you a reservation even when the main Alhambra website is sold out; see "Tourist Information" at the beginning of this chapter.

For **in-person ticketing advice**, there are helpful info desks next to the Wine Gate and at the main Alhambra entrance pavilion, close to the bookstore (daily, 8:00-20:00). The TI in town and most hotels are adept at Alhambra issues. An info desk sometimes operates inside the Corral del Carbón in the town center.

If you can't secure a Palacios Nazaríes reservation, you can **enjoy the rest of the Alhambra** with a ticket covering just the gardens, Generalife, and Alcazaba. Walking the grounds, including the Palace of Charles V and the parador, is free.

Getting In: Be prepared to show passports for each person in your group, matched to their tickets.

Reentering the Complex: You can enter the Palacios Nazaríes, Generalife, and Alcazaba just once, but otherwise you may come and go from the Alhambra complex throughout the day. Keep your ticket until the end of your visit, and have your passport ready for random checks.

Tours: The Alhambra's excellent €6 interactive audioguide covers the entire complex (can be reserved ahead online). Rental booths are at both entrances and audioguides can be returned to either location. The audioguide is also available as a free app, downloadable from the Alhambra website.

Alhambra Guidebook: The slick and colorful *Alhambra and Generalife in Focus* is sold at bookstores and shops but not inside the Alhambra (€11; to make the most of your visit, buy and read it before you tour the sight).

Services: A service center, with bag check (free for ticket holders only), WCs, and water and snack machines, is at each entrance. There are no WCs inside the Palacios Nazaríes. Small daypacks are allowed but must be worn in front.

Eating: Within the Alhambra walls, food options are limited and generally overpriced. Choose between the restaurant or the cafeteria at the **$$$ parador;** the peaceful ambience of the courtyard at **$$$ Hotel América** (Sun-Fri 12:30-16:30, closed Sat); a small **$ bar-café kiosk** in front of the Alcazaba fort (basic sandwiches and snacks); and **vending machines** (at the WC) next to the Wine Gate, near the Palace of Charles V. You're welcome to bring a **picnic** as long as you eat it outside ticketed areas.

For better-value (but still touristy) options, head to the area around the entrance pavilion at the top of the complex, where there's a strip of handy eateries.

$$$ Restaurante Jardines Alberto, across from the entrance pavilion, has a nice courtyard and offers a charming setting (daily 12:00-23:30, off-season until 18:00; Paseo de la

Sabica 1, +34 958 221 661, climb the stairs from the street). The breezy **$$$ Restaurante La Mimbre** offers shade and a break from the crowds. They also serve breakfast (daily 9:30-23:00, Paseo del Generalife 18, +34 958 222 276).

City Tour from the Alhambra: The hop-on, hop-off tourist train leaves from the top of the Alhambra, offering a convenient hour-long sightseeing tour on the way back to town instead of walking (see "Tours in Granada," earlier.)

◐ SELF-GUIDED TOUR

This tour assumes that you'll visit the Alhambra sights from the bottom of the complex to the top. The first three sights cluster at the bottom end, while the Generalife and its gardens are about a 15-minute walk away, at the top.

GRANADA

▲▲Palace of Charles V

While it's only natural for a conquering king to build his own palace over that of his foe, Holy Roman Emperor Charles V (who

ruled as Charles I over Spain) respected the splendid Moorish palace. And so, to make his mark, he built a modern Renaissance palace for official functions and used the existing Palacios Nazaríes as a royal residence. With a unique circle-within-a-square design by Pedro Machuca, a pupil of Michelangelo, this is Spain's most impressive Renaissance building. Stand in the circular courtyard surrounded by mottled marble columns, then climb the stairs. Perhaps Charles' palace was designed to have a dome, but it was never finished—his son, Philip II, abandoned it to build El Escorial, his own, much more massive palace outside Madrid (the final and most austere example of Spanish Renaissance architecture). Even without a dome, acoustics are perfect in the center—stand in the middle and sing your best aria. The palace doubles as a venue for the popular International Festival of Music and Dance.

▲Alhambra Museum

On the ground floor of the Palace of Charles V, this museum (Museo de la Alhambra) shows off some of the Alhambra's best surviving Moorish art. Its well-described artifacts—including tiles, characteristic green, blue, and black pottery, lion fountains, and a beautiful carved-wood door—are beautifully displayed (free, Wed-Sat 8:30-20:00, Sun and Tue until 14:30, shorter hours off-season, closed Mon year-round). The **Fine Arts Museum** (Museo de Bellas Artes, upstairs, free) has Christian-era paintings and statues and is of little interest to most.

• *From the front of the Palace of Charles V, the Alcazaba is the towering brick structure across a moat, straight ahead.*

Alcazaba

This fort—the original "red castle" ("Alhambra")—is the oldest and most ruined part of the complex, offering exercise and fine city views. What you see is from the mid-13th century, but there was probably a fort here in Roman times. Once upon a time, this tower defended a medina (town) of 2,000 Muslims living within the Alhambra walls. It's a huge, sprawling complex—wind your

way through passages and courtyards, over uneven terrain, to reach the biggest tower at the tip of the complex. Then climb stairs steeply up to the very top. From there (looking north), find Plaza Nueva and the San Nicolás viewpoint in the Albayzín. To the south are the Sierra Nevada Mountains. Notice the tower's four flags: the blue of the European Union, the green and white of Andalucía, the red and yellow of Spain, and the red and green of Granada.

Speaking of flags, imagine that day in 1492 when the Christian cross and the flags of Aragon and Castile were raised on this tower, and (according to a probably fanciful legend) the fleeing Moorish king Boabdil (Abu Abdullah, in Arabic) looked back and wept. His mom chewed him out, saying, "You weep like a woman for what you couldn't defend like a man." With this defeat, more than seven centuries of Muslim rule in Spain came to an end. Much later, Napoleon stationed his troops at the Alhambra, contributing substantially to its ruin.

• *If you're going from the Alcazaba to Palacios Nazaríes, backtrack toward the Palace of Charles V and join the line (to the left, behind the palace) during the 30-minute entry time stamped on your ticket.*

▲▲▲Palacios Nazaríes

Crowds crush into the jewel of the Alhambra at the start of each 30-minute entry interval. If your entry time is particularly crowded, consider lingering at the start to let things quiet down. Once inside, relax. You're no longer under any time constraints. You'll walk through three basic sections: royal offices, ceremonial rooms, and private quarters. Built mostly in the 14th century, this palace offers your best possible look at the refined, elegant Moorish civili-

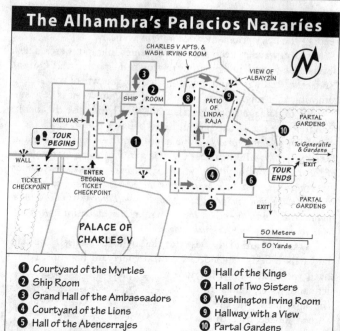

The Alhambra's Palacios Nazaríes

CHARLES V APTS. &
WASH. IRVING ROOM

VIEW OF
ALBAYZÍN

SHIP
ROOM

PATIO
OF
LINDA-
RAJA

MEXUAR→

PARTAL
GARDENS

TOUR
BEGINS

To Generalife
& Gardens

WALL

EXIT

TICKET
CHECKPOINT

ENTER
SECOND
TICKET
CHECKPOINT

TOUR
ENDS

EXIT

PARTAL
GARDENS

PALACE OF
CHARLES V

50 Meters

50 Yards

❶ Courtyard of the Myrtles
❷ Ship Room
❸ Grand Hall of the Ambassadors
❹ Courtyard of the Lions
❺ Hall of the Abencerrajes

❻ Hall of the Kings
❼ Hall of Two Sisters
❽ Washington Irving Room
❾ Hallway with a View
❿ Partal Gardens

GRANADA

zation of al-Andalus (the Arabic word for the Moorish-controlled Iberian Peninsula).

You'll visit rooms decorated from top to bottom with carved wood ceilings, stucco stalactites, ceramic tiles, molded-plaster

walls, and filigree windows. Open-air courtyards feature fountains with bubbling water, which give the palace a desert-oasis feel. A garden enlivened by lush vegetation and peaceful pools is the Quran's symbol of heaven. The palace is well-preserved and well restored, but the trick to fully appreciating it is to imagine it furnished and filled with Moorish life: Sultans with hookah pipes lounging on pillows upon Persian carpets, heavy curtains on the windows, and ivory-studded wooden furniture. The whole place was painted with bright colors, many suggested by the Quran—blue (heaven), green (oasis), red (blood), and gold (wealth). Throughout the palace, walls, ceilings, vases, carpets, and tiles were covered with decorative patterns and calligraphy, mostly poems and verses of praise from the Quran and from local poets.

Much of what is known about the Alhambra is known simply from reading the inscriptions that decorate its walls.

As you wander, keep the palace themes in mind: water, a near absence of figural images (they're frowned upon in the Quran), "stalactite" ceilings—and few signs telling you where you are. As tempting as it might be to touch the stucco, don't—it is very susceptible to damage from the oils from your hand. Use this book's map to locate the essential stops listed below.

• *Begin by walking through a few administrative rooms (the mexuar, the council of the wise men, where scribes were busy doing the office work of the state bureaucracy) with a stunning Mecca-oriented prayer room (the oratorio, with a niche on the right facing Mecca, and lacy windows filling it with light and great views) and a small courtyard with a round fountain. Eventually you hit the big rectangular courtyard with a fishpond lined by two myrtle-bush hedges.*

❶ Courtyard of the Myrtles (Patio de Arrayanes): The standard palace design included a central courtyard like this. Moors

loved their patios—with a garden and water, under the sky. The apartments of the sultan's women looked over this courtyard: two apartments for wives on either side (four was the maximum allowed), and a dorm for the concubines at the far end (a man could have "as many concubines as he could maintain with dignity"). In accordance with medieval Moorish mores, women rarely ventured outside the home, so they stayed in touch with nature in courtyards like the Courtyard of the Myrtles—named for the fragrant myrtle hedges that add to the courtyard's charm. Notice the wooden screens ("jalousies" erected by jealous husbands) that allowed the cloistered women to look out without being clearly seen. The upstairs was likely for winter use, and the cooler ground level was probably used in summer.

• *Head left from the entry through gigantic wooden doors into the long narrow antechamber called the...*

❷ Ship Room (Sala de la Barca): It's understandable that many think the Ship Room is named for the upside-down-hull shape of its fine cedar ceiling. But the name is actually derived from the Arab word *baraka*, meaning "divine blessing and luck." (President Obama's first name came from the same Arabic root word.) As you passed through this room, blessings and luck are exactly what you'd need—because in the next room, you'd be face-to-face with the sultan.

• *Oh, it's your turn. Enter the ornate throne room.*

❸ Grand Hall of the Ambassadors (Gran Salón de los Embajadores): The palace's largest room, also known as the Salón de Comares, functioned as the throne room. It was here that the sultan, seated on a throne opposite the

entrance, received foreign emissaries. Ogle the room—a perfect cube—from top to bottom. Made from 8,017 pieces inlaid like a giant jigsaw puzzle, the star-studded, domed wooden ceiling suggests the complexity of Allah's infinite universe. Wooden stalactites form the cornice, running around the entire base of the ceiling. The stucco walls, even without their original paint and gilding, are still glorious. The filigree windows once held stained glass and had heavy drapes to block out the heat. Some precious 16th-century tiles survive in the center of the floor.

A visitor here would have stepped from the glaring Courtyard of the Myrtles into this dim, cool, incense-filled world to meet the silhouetted sultan. Imagine the alcoves functioning busily as workstations, and the light at sunrise or sunset, rich and warm, filling the room.

Let your eyes trace the finely carved Arabic script. Muslims avoided making images of living creatures—that was God's work. But they could carve decorative religious messages. One phrase—"only Allah is victorious"—is repeated 9,000 times throughout the palace. Find the character for "Allah": It looks like a cursive W with a nose on its left side, with a vertical line to the right. The swoopy toboggan blades underneath are a kind of artistic punctuation used to set off one phrase.

In 1492, two historic events likely took place in this room. Culminating a 700-year-long struggle, the Reconquista was completed here as the last Moorish king, Boabdil, signed the terms of his surrender before eventually going into exile in Morocco.

And it was here that Columbus made one of his final pitches to Isabel and Ferdinand to finance a sea voyage to the Far East. Imagine the scene: The king, the queen, and the greatest minds from the University of Salamanca gathered here while Columbus produced maps and pie charts to make his case that he could sail west to reach the east. Ferdinand and the professors laughed and called Columbus mad—not because they thought the world was flat (most educated people knew otherwise), but because they thought Columbus had underestimated the size of the globe, and thus the length and cost of the journey.

GRANADA

But Isabel said, *"Sí, señor."* Columbus fell to his knees (promising to pack light, wear a money belt, and use a good guidebook).

Opposite the Ship Room entrance, photographers pause for a picture-perfect view of the tower reflected in the Courtyard of the Myrtles pool. This was the original palace entrance (before the Palace of Charles V was built).

• *Continue deeper into the palace, to a courtyard where, 600 years ago, only the royal family and their servants could enter. It's the much-photographed...*

❹ **Courtyard of the Lions** (Patio de los Leones): This delightful courtyard is named for the famous fountain at its center with its ring of 12 marble lions—

originals from the 14th century. Conquering Christians disassembled the fountain to see how it worked, rendering it nonfunctional; it finally flowed again in 2012. From the center of the courtyard, four channels carry water outward—figuratively to the corners of the earth and literally to various more private apartments of the royal family. The arched gallery that surrounds the courtyard is supported by 124 perfectly balanced columns. The craftsmanship is first-class. For example, the lead fittings between the precut sections of the columns allow things to flex during earthquakes, preventing destruction.

Six hundred years ago, the Muslim Moors could read the Quranic poetry that ornaments this court, and they could understand the symbolism of this lush, enclosed garden, considered the embodiment of paradise or truth. ("How beautiful is this garden / where the flowers of Earth rival the stars of Heaven. / What can compare with this alabaster fountain, gushing crystal-clear water? / Nothing except the fullest moon, pouring light from an unclouded sky.") They appreciated this part of the palace even more than we do today.

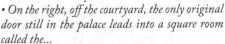

• *On the right, off the courtyard, the only original door still in the palace leads into a square room called the...*

❺ **Hall of the Abencerrajes** (Sala de los Abencerrajes): This was the sultan's living room, with an exquisite ceiling based on the eight-sided Muslim star.

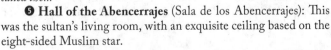

Islamic Art

Rather than making paintings and statues, Islamic artists expressed themselves with beautiful but functional objects. Ceramics (most of them blue and white, or green and white), carpets, glazed tile panels, stucco-work ceilings, and glass tableware are covered with complex patterns. The intricate interweaving, repetition, and unending lines suggest the complex, infinite nature of God, known to Muslims as Allah.

You'll see few pictures of humans, since Islamic doctrine holds that the creation of living beings is God's work alone. However, secular art by Muslims for their homes and palaces was not bound by this restriction; you'll get an occasional glimpse of realistic art featuring men and women enjoying a garden paradise, a symbol of the Muslim heaven.

Look for floral patterns (twining vines, flowers, and arabesques) and geometric designs (stars and diamonds). The decorative motifs (Arabic script, patterns, flowers, shells, and so on) that repeat countless times throughout the palace were made by pressing wet plaster into molds. The most common pattern is calligraphy—elaborate lettering of an inscription in Arabic, the language of the Quran. A quote from the Quran on a vase or lamp combines the power of the message with the beauty of the calligraphy.

The name of the room comes from a bloody event that's said to have occurred here in the 16th century. According to legend, the father of Boabdil invited members of the North African Abencerraje family to a banquet—and then promptly massacred them to thwart a threat to his dynasty. He is said to have stacked 36 Abencerraje heads in the pool, under the sumptuous honeycombed stucco ceiling in this hall.

• *At the end of the court opposite where you entered is the...*

❻ **Hall of the Kings** (Sala de los Reyes): This hall is famous for its paintings on the goat-leather ceiling depicting scenes of the sultan and his family. The center room's group portrait shows the first 10 of the Alhambra's 22 sultans. The scene is a fantasy, since these people lived over a span of many generations. The two end rooms display scenes of princely pastimes, such as hunting and shooting skeet. In a palace otherwise devoid of figures, these depictions offer a rare look at royal life in the palace.

• *Continue around the lion fountain. Before entering the next room, you'll pass doors leading right and left to a 14th-century WC plumbed by running water and stairs up to the harem. Next is the...*

❼ **Hall of Two Sisters** (Sala de Dos Hermanas): The Sala de Dos Hermanas—nicknamed for the giant twin slabs of white marble on the floor flanking the fountain—has another oh-wow stucco ceiling lit by clerestory windows. This is another royal reception hall, with alcoves for private use and a fountain. Running water helped cool and humidify the room but also added elegance and extravagance, as running water was a luxury most could only dream of.

The room features geometric patterns and stylized Arabic script quoting verses from the Quran. If the inlaid color tiles look "Escher-esque," you've got it backward: Escher is Alhambra-esque. M. C. Escher was inspired by these very patterns on his visit. Study the geometry of the patterns—they remind us of the Moorish expertise in math. The sitting room (farthest from the entry) has low windows, because Moorish people sat on the floor. Some rare stained glass survives in the ceiling. From here the sultana enjoyed a grand view of the medieval city (before a 16th-century wing blocked the view).

• *That's about it for the palace. From here, we enter the later, 16th-century section, and wander past the domed roofs of the old baths down a hallway to a pair of rooms decorated with mahogany ceilings. Marked with a large plaque is the...*

❽ **Washington Irving Room:** While living in Spain in 1829, Washington Irving stayed in the Alhambra, and he wrote *Tales of the Alhambra* in this room. It was a romantic time, when the palace was home to Roma and donkeys. His "tales" rekindled interest in the Alhambra, causing it to be recognized as a national treasure. A plaque on the wall thanks Irving, who later served as the US ambassador to Spain (1842-1846). Here's a quote from Irving's *The Alhambra by Moonlight:* "On such heavenly nights I would sit for hours at my window inhaling the sweetness of the garden, and musing on the checkered fortunes of those whose history was dimly shadowed out in the elegant memorials around."

• *As you leave, stop at the open-air...*

❾ **Hallway with a View:** Here you'll enjoy the best-in-the-palace view of the labyrinthine Albayzín—the old Moorish town on the opposite hillside. Find the famous San Nicolás viewpoint (below where the white San Nicolás church tower breaks the horizon—see the crowds of tourists taking pictures of you). Green patches are the gardens of *carmenes* (old noble farms, many that

are now romantic restaurants). Below is the river and the Paseo de los Tristes (with its square filled with inviting restaurants). Creeping into the mountains on the right are the Roma neighborhoods of Sacromonte. Still circling old Granada is the Moorish wall (built in the 1400s to protect the city's population, swollen by Muslim refugees driven south by the Reconquista).

The Patio de Lindaraja (with its garden of maze-like hedges) marks the end of the palace visit. Before exiting, you can detour right into the "Secrets Room"—a domed brick room of the former baths with fun acoustics. Whisper into a corner, and your friend—with an ear to the wall—can hear you in the opposite corner. Try talking in the exact center.

• *Step outside into...*

❿ The Partal Gardens (El Partal): The Partal Gardens are built upon the ruins of the Partal Palace. Imagine a palace like the one you just toured, built around this reflecting pond. A fragment of it still stands—once the living quarters—on the cooler north side. Its Mecca-facing oratory (the small building a few steps above the pool) survives. The Alhambra was the site of seven different palaces in 150 years. You have toured parts of just two or three.

• *Leaving the palace, climb a few stairs, continue through the gardens, and follow signs directing you left to the Generalife (or right to the Alcazaba and the rest of the Alhambra grounds, if you haven't already visited them).*

The path to the Generalife and its gardens is a delightful 15-minute stroll through lesser (but still pleasant) gardens, along a row of fortified towers—just follow signs for Generalife. *Just before reaching the Generalife, you'll cross over a bridge and look down on the dusty lane called Cuesta del Rey Chico (a handy shortcut for returning to town later).*

▲▲Generalife Palace and Gardens

The sultan's vegetable and fruit orchards, and the summer palace retreat called the Generalife (heh-neh-rah-LEE-fay), were outside the protection of the Alhambra wall; today, they're a short hike uphill past the entrance pavilion. The thousand-or-so residents of the Alhambra enjoyed the fresh fruit and veggies grown here. But most important, this little palace provided the sultan with a cool and quiet summer escape.

Follow the simple one-way path through the sprawling gardens. You'll catch glimpses of a sleek, modern outdoor theater, built in the 1950s. It continues to be an important concert venue for Granada.

From the head of the theater, signs will lead you through manicured hedges, along delightful ponds, and past flowing fountains to the sultan's small summer palace.

Before arriving at the bright white palace, pass through the

The Alhambra Grounds

As you wander the grounds, remember that the Alhambra was once a city of a thousand people fortified by a 1.5-mile rampart and 30 towers. The zone within the walls was a **medina,** an urban town. The path from the entrance pavilion along the garden-like Calle Real de la Alhambra to the palace passes through the ruins of the medina (destroyed by the French in 1812). This path traces the south wall, with its towers. In the distance are the snow-capped Sierra Nevada peaks—the highest mountains in Iberia. While you need a ticket to visit the highlights of the Alhambra, the medina—with the Palace of Charles V, a church, a line of shops showing off traditional woodworking techniques, and the fancy Alhambra parador—is wide open and free to everyone.

It's especially fun to snoop around the historic **Parador de Granada San Francisco,** which—as a national monument—is open to the public. Once a Moorish palace within the Alhambra, it was later converted into a Franciscan monastery, with a historic claim to fame: Its church is where the Catholic Monarchs (Ferdinand and Isabel) chose to be buried. For a peek, step in through the front door leading to a small garden area and reception. Continue

dismounting room (imagine dismounting onto the helpful stone ledge, and letting your horse drink from the trough here). Enter the most accurately re-created Arabian garden in Andalucía.

Here in the retreat of the Moorish kings, this garden is the closest thing on earth to the Quran's description of heaven. It was planted more than 600 years ago—that's remarkable longevity for a European garden. While there were originally only eight water jets, most of the details in today's garden closely match those lovingly described in old poems. The flowers, herbs, aromas, and water are exquisite...even for a sultan. Up the Darro River, the royal aqueduct diverted a life-giving stream of water into the Alhambra. It was channeled through this extra-long decorative fountain to irrigate the bigger garden outside, straight to see the burial place, located in the open-air ruins of the church (passing the reception-desk area and a delightful former cloister; the history is described in English). The slab on the ground near the altar—a surviving bit from the mosque that was here before the church—marks the place where the king and queen rested until 1521 (when they were moved to the Royal Chapel downtown). Now a hotel, the parador has a restaurant and terrace café—with lush views of the Generalife—open to all.

The medina's main road deadended at the **Wine Gate** (Puerta del Vino), which protected the fortress. When you pass through the Wine Gate, you enter a courtyard that was originally a moat, then a reservoir (in Christian times). The well—now encased in a bar-kiosk—is still a place for cold drinks.

You can exit down to the city from the Wine Gate via the Justice Gate, immediately below. From there you'll walk past a Renaissance fountain and pass through the **Pomegranate Gate** (Puerta de las Granadas) into the modern city, close to Plaza Nueva.

then along an aqueduct into the Alhambra for its thirsty residents. And though the splashing fountains are a delight, they are a 19th-century addition. The Moors liked a peaceful pond instead.

At the end of the pond, you enter the sultan's tiny three-room summer retreat. From the last room, climb 10 steps into the upper Renaissance gardens (c. 1600). The ancient tree rising over the pond inspired Washington Irving, who wrote that this must be the "only surviving witness to the wonders of that age of al-Andalus."

Climbing up and going through the turnstile, you enter the Romantic 19th-century garden. Your visit to the Alhambra is complete, and you've earned your reward. "Surely Allah will make those who believe and do good deeds enter gardens beneath which rivers flow; they shall be adorned therein with bracelets of gold and pearls, and their garments therein shall be of silk" (Quran 22.23).

• *From here you have two options: If you're exhausted, just head to the right and follow* salida *signs toward the gardens' exit (next to the Alhambra's entrance pavilion). The #C30 and #C32 minibuses return from here to Plaza Isabel La Católica.*

But if you want a little more exercise (and views), turn left at the sign for "continuación de la visita," and take the half-mile loop up and around to see the staircase called Escalera del Agua, whose banisters double as little water canals. From the top, you'll have a chance to enter the "Romantic Viewpoint"—climb up the stairs for a top-floor view over the gardens (pleasant enough, but less impressive than other views at the Alhambra). Then hike back down through the garden and follow salida signs, *through the long oleander trellis tunnel, to the exit.*

There are two direct and **scenic routes to town.** *One is the easily overlooked Cuesta del Rey Chico pathway. It starts under the two stone arches not far from the entrance pavilion, by Restaurante La Mimbre and the minibus stop—a sign just past the restaurant entrance will confirm you're on the right path. You'll walk downhill on a peaceful, cobbled lane scented with lavender and rock rose, beneath the Alhambra ramparts and past the sultan's horse lane leading up to the Generalife. In 15 minutes you're back in town at Paseo de los Tristes, where you can stroll along a level road to Plaza Nueva or continue walking into the Albayzín district (walking downhill on this trail from the Alhambra, you can't get lost).*

The other route is the shortest and most common: a straight walk along the main road and the base of the fortress wall until you reach a fountain on the left. Follow the shady canopy of trees down, down, down until reaching Cuesta de Gomérez and Plaza Nueva.

GRANADA

More Sights in Granada

IN THE OLD TOWN
▲▲Royal Chapel (Capilla Real)

Without a doubt Granada's top Christian sight, this lavish chapel in the old town holds the dreams—and bodies—of Queen Isabel and King Ferdinand. The Catholic Monarchs were all about the Reconquista. Their marriage united the Aragon and Castile kingdoms, allowing an acceleration of the Christian and Spanish push south. In its last 10 years, the Reconquista snowballed. Symbolic of Ferdinand and Isabel's eventual victory, Granada—the last Moorish capital—was their chosen burial place. This chapel, while smaller and less architecturally striking than Granada's cathedral, is far more historically significant.

Cost and Hours: €5, includes audioguide, Mon-Sat 10:15-18:30, Sun 11:00-18:00; entrance on Calle Oficios, just off Gran Vía del Colón—go through iron gate; +34 958 227 848, www.capillarealgranada.com.

Visiting the Chapel: In the lobby, before you enter the chapel, notice the **painting of Boabdil** (on the black horse) giving the key of Granada to the conquering King Ferdinand. Boabdil wanted to fall to his knees, but the Spanish king, who had great respect for his Moorish foe, embraced him instead. They fought a long and noble war (for instance, respectfully returning the bodies of dead soldiers). Ferdinand is in red, and Isabel is behind him wearing a crown. The painting is flanked by **glass-enclosed exhibits** comparing wood sculptures of the four royal family members buried here with their marble tomb sculptures (their faces are too high up to see clearly inside the chapel).

Isabel decided to make Granada the capital of Spain (and burial place for Spanish royalty) for three reasons: 1) With the conquest of this city, Christianity had finally overcome Islam in Europe; 2) her marriage with Ferdinand, followed by the conquest of Granada, had marked the beginning of a united Spain; and 3) in Granada, she agreed to sponsor Columbus.

Step into the **chapel.** The light and lacy silver-filigree style is Plateresque Gothic, named for and inspired by the fine silverwork of the Moors. The chapel's interior was originally austere, with fancy touches added later by Ferdinand and Isabel's grandson, Holy Roman Emperor Charles V. Five hundred years ago, this must have been the most splendid space imaginable. Because of its speedy completion (1506-1521), the Gothic architecture is unusually harmonious.

In front of the main altar, the **four royal tombs** are Renaissance-style. Carved in Italy in 1521 from Carrara marble, they were sent by ship to Spain.

The faces—based on death masks—are considered accurate. **Ferdinand** and **Isabel** are the lower, and humbler, of the two couples. (Isabel fans attribute the bigger dent she puts in the pillow to the weight of her larger brain.) Isabel's contemporaries described the queen as being of medium height, with auburn hair and blue eyes, and possessing a serious, modest, and gentle personality. (Compare Ferdinand and Isabel's tomb statues with the painted and gilded wood statues of them kneeling in prayer, flanking the altarpiece.)

Philip the Fair and **Juana the Mad** (who succeeded Ferdinand and Isabel) lie on the left. Philip was so "Fair" that it drove the insanely jealous Juana "Mad." Philip died young, and Juana, crazy like a fox, used her "grief" over his death to forestall a second marriage, thereby ensuring that their son Charles would inherit the throne. Charles was a key figure in European history, as his coronation merged the Holy Roman Empire (Philip the Fair's Habsburg domain) with Juana's Spanish empire. Charles V ruled a

GRANADA

vast empire stretching from Holland to Sicily, and from Bohemia to Bolivia (1519-1556; you can see his palace within the Alhambra complex). Today's Spaniards reflect that while the momentous marriage created their country, it also sucked them into centuries of European squabbling, eventually leaving Spain impoverished.

Granada lost power and importance when Philip II, the son of Charles V, built his El Escorial palace outside Madrid, establishing that city as the single capital of a single Spain. This coincided with the beginning of Spain's decline, as the country squandered its vast wealth trying to maintain an impossibly huge empire. Spain's rulers were defending the romantic, quixotic dream of a Catholic empire—ruled by one divinely ordained Catholic monarch—against an irrepressible tide of nationalism and Protestantism that was sweeping across the vast Habsburg holdings in Central and Eastern Europe. Spain's relatively poor modern history can be blamed, in part, on its people's stubborn unwillingness to accept the end of this old-regime notion. Even Franco borrowed symbols from the Catholic Monarchs to legitimize his dictatorship and keep the 500-year-old legacy alive.

Look at the intricate **carving** on the Renaissance tombs. Dating from around 1520, it's a humanistic statement, with these healthy, organic, realistic figures rising out of the Gothic age. Charles V thought the existing chapel wasn't dazzling enough to honor his grandparents' importance, so he funded decorative touches like the iron screen and the fine 16th-century copy of the Rogier van der Weyden painting *The Deposition* (to the left after passing through the screen). Immediately to the right of the painting, with the hardest-working altar boys in Christendom holding up gilded Corinthian columns, is a chapel with a locked-away relic (an arm) of John the Baptist.

From the feet of the marble tombs, step downstairs to see the actual **coffins.** They are plain. Ferdinand and Isabel were originally buried in the Franciscan monastery up at the Alhambra (in what is today the parador). You're standing in front of the two people who created Spain. The fifth coffin (on right, marked *Príncipe Miguel*) belongs to a young Prince Michael, who would have been king of a united Spain and Portugal. (A sad—but too-long—story...)

The **high altar** is one of the finest Renaissance works in Spain. It's dedicated to two Johns: the Baptist and the Evangelist. In the center you can see the Baptist and the Evangelist chatting as if over tapas—an appropriately humanistic scene. Scenes from the Baptist's life are on the left: John beheaded after Salomé's fine dancing, and (below) John baptizing Jesus. Scenes from the Evangelist's life are on the right: John's martyrdom (a failed attempt to boil him alive in oil), and, below, John on Patmos (where he may have written the last book of the Bible, Revelation). John is talking to the eagle that, according to tradition, flew him to heaven. Flanking both Johns, statues of Ferdinand and Isabel kneel in prayer. A colorful series of reliefs at the bottom level recalls the Christian conquest of the Moors (left to right): a robed processional figure, Boabdil with army and key to Alhambra, Moors expelled from Alhambra, conversion of Muslims by tonsured monks (two panels, right of altar table), and another robed figure.

A finely carved Plateresque arch, with the gilded royal initials *F* and *Y*, leads from the chapel into the sacristy/treasury/museum, where you'll see a small glass pyramid. This holds Queen Isabel's silver crown ringed with pomegranates (symbolizing Granada), her scepter, and King Ferdi-

nand's sword. Do a counterclockwise spin around the room to see it all, starting to the right of the entry arch. There you'll see the devout Isabel's prayer book, in which she followed the Mass. The book and its sturdy box date from 1496. According to legend, the fancy box on the other side of the door is supposedly the one that Isabel filled with jewels and gave to bankers as collateral for the cash to pay Columbus. In the corner (also behind glass) is the ornate silver-and-gold cross that Cardinal Mendoza, staunch supporter of Queen Isabel, carried into the Alhambra on that historic day in 1492—and used as the centerpiece for the first Christian Mass in the conquered fortress. Below the cross is Isabel's simple rosary, belt, and other personal items. She embraced Franciscan teaching, gave most of her jewels to the Church and, for a queen, lived quite austerely.

Next, the big silver-and-gold silk tapestry is the altar banner for the mobile campaign chapel of Ferdinand and Isabel, who always traveled with their army. In the case to its left, you'll see the original Christian army flags raised over the Alhambra in 1492.

The next zone of this grand hall holds the first great **art collection** established by a woman. Queen Isabel amassed more than 200 important paintings. After Napoleon occupied Granada (from 1808 until 1812), only 31 remained. Even so, this is an exquisite collection, all on wood, featuring works by Sandro Botticelli, Pietro Perugino, the Flemish master Hans Memling, and some less-famous Spanish masters. (Find the paintings by Perugino and Botticelli ahead on the left.)

Finally, at the end of the room are two **carved sculptures** of Ferdinand and Isabel, the originals from the high altar. Charles V considered these primitive (I disagree) and replaced them with the ones you saw earlier.

To reach the cathedral (described next), exit the treasury behind Isabel, and walk around the block to the right.

▲Granada Cathedral (Catedral de Granada)

Granada's cathedral is the second-largest church in the country (after Sevilla's) and one of the few to exhibit Renaissance features. Its 200-year-long construction saw it begin as a Gothic church, then laid out using Renaissance elements, before being decorated in Baroque style.

Cost and Hours: €5, includes audioguide, Mon-Sat 10:00-18:30, Sun 15:00-17:45, +34 958 222 959, www.catedraldegranada. com.

Visiting the Cathedral: Enter the church from Plaza de las Pasiegas. Before exploring the interior, step into the cathedral's little **museum** (tucked into the corner behind the ticket counter). Filling the ground floor of the big bell tower, it's worth seeking out for two pieces of art: a Gothic, hexagonal-shaped monstrance with a Renaissance-era base given to the cathedral by Isabel, and a beautiful sculpture of San Pablo (Paul, with a flowing beard, carved in wood and painted)—a self-portrait by hometown great Alonso Cano.

Leave the museum and stand in the back of the **nave** for an overview. Survey the church. It's huge. It was designed to be the national church when Granada was the capital of a newly reconquered-from-the-Muslims Spain. High above the main altar are square niches originally intended for the burial of Charles V and his family. But King Philip II changed focus and abandoned Granada for El Escorial, so the niches are now plugged with saintly paintings. High above under the stained glass are seven scenes from the life of Mary (by Alonso Cano).

The cathedral's cool, spacious **interior** is mostly Renaissance—a refreshing break from the closed-in, dark Gothic of so many Spanish churches. In a move that was modern back in the 18th century, the wooden walls of the choir (which dominates the center of most Spanish churches) were taken out so that common people could see as well as hear Mass. At about the same time, a bishop ordered the interior painted with lime (for hygienic reasons, during a time of disease). The people liked it, and it stayed white.

Notice the two rear chapels (sand-colored, on right and left); they're Neoclassical in style and a far cry from the Gothic beginnings of the church. As you explore, remember that the abundance of Marys is all part of the Counter-Reformation. Most of the side chapels are decorated in Baroque style.

As you walk to the front for a closer look at the **altar,** take a small detour to the scale model of the entire complex (left of pews). Examine the cathedral's immensity. The Royal Chapel (right side) is shaped like a small church would be, complete with mini transepts and fitting perfectly into the corner of the cathedral. Resume your walk to the altar, passing two fine Baroque organs with horizontal trumpet pipes, unique to Spain.

Standing before the altar, notice the abundance of gold leaf. It's from Spain's Darro River, which originally attracted Romans here for its gold. As this is a seat of the local bishop, there's a fine wooden bishop's throne on the right.

Between the pairs of Corinthian columns on both sides of the altar are **sculptures** with a strong parenting theme: Inside the thick, round frames at the top are busts of Adam and Eve, from whom came mankind. Around them are the four gold-covered evangelists, who—with the New Testament—brought the Good News of salvation to believers. Completing the big parenting picture (under Adam and Eve) are Ferdinand and Isabel, kneeling in prayer, who brought Catholicism to the land. Their complex coat of arms (beneath each respective statue) celebrates how their marriage united two influential kingdoms to create imperial Spain.

To your right is the ornate carved-stone Gothic door to the **Royal Chapel** (described earlier), with 15th-century decorations that predate the cathedral. The chapel holds the most important historic relics in town—the tombs of the Catholic Monarchs. And, because the chapel and cathedral are run by two different religious orders, this door is always closed and there are separate admission fees for each. In the chapel, immediately to the left of the door, is a politically incorrect version of St. James the Moor-Slayer, with his sword raised high and an armored Moor trampled under his horse's hooves.

The chapel to the right of the door features a painting by Cano—but the frame itself is a masterpiece. Cano carved the wooden frame, gilded it, painted over the gold leaf, and scratched through where he wanted the gold to show.

Strolling behind the altar, look for the **giant music sheets:** They're mostly 16th-century Gregorian chants. Notice the sliding C clef. Rather than a fixed G or F clef, the monks knew that this clef—which could be located wherever it worked best on the staff—marked middle C, and they chanted to notes relative to that. Go ahead—try singing a few verses of the Latin.

Step to the center to view the high altar from the rear. The giant four-sided swiveling music rack held these huge sheets, allowing monks to sign in unison in the days before printed hymnals. Look up at the paintings in the dome: Church fathers plugging the planned royal tombs and, above those, the Cano scenes of Mary's life.

The **sacristy** (between the exit and the St. James altarpiece, in the right corner)—filled with closets and drawers for the robes and garments necessary for the high Church pageantry—is worth a look. It's lush and wide open; its gilded ceilings, mirrors, and wooden cabinets give it a light, airy feel. Two grandfather clocks made in London (one with Asian motifs) ensured that everyone got dressed on time. The highlight of this room is another work by Cano—a small, delicate painted wood statue of the *Immaculate Conception*, under the Crucifixion.

Exit the cathedral through its little **shop** (with a nicely curated selection of religious and secular souvenirs). If you walk straight out, you'll come directly to Gran Vía and the stop for minibus #C32 for the Albayzín (to walk to the Albayzín, head left up Gran Vía for two blocks, then turn right on Calle Cárcel Baja). But first, for a fun detour, make a quick left into the little lane immediately upon exiting the cathedral—you'll be just steps from Medievo, a fine purveyor of bulk spices and teas.

Hammam al Andalus (Arab Baths)

For an intimate and subdued experience, consider some serious relaxation at these Arab baths, where you can enjoy three different-temperature pools and a steam room.

Cost and Hours: €38 for 1.5-hour soak in the baths (more if you add a massage), open daily 10:00-24:00, appointments scheduled every even-numbered hour, coed with mandatory swimsuits, quiet atmosphere encouraged, free lockers and towels available, no loaner swimsuits but you can buy one, just off Plaza Nueva—follow signs a few doors down from the TI to Santa Ana 16, paid reservation required—ask about cancellation policy, +34 958 229 978, www.hammamalandalus.com.

▲▲Paseo Without the Tourists

While Granada's old town is great for strolling, it's also fun to just be in workaday Granada with everyday locals. A five-minute walk from Plaza Nueva gets you into a delightful urban slice of Andalucía. To enjoy an evening paseo without tourists, start with a tapas crawl along any of the streets beyond Plaza del Carmen (see "Beyond Plaza del Carmen" under "Eating in Granada," later), then stroll down Carrera de la Virgen, off Plaza del Campillo, where there's always something cultural going on. Carrera de la Virgen leads gracefully down to the Paseo del Salón riverbank park, passing the El Corte Inglés department store.

THE ALBAYZÍN

Spain's best old Moorish quarter, with countless colorful corners, flowery patios, and shady lanes, is worth ▲. While the city center of Granada feels more or less like many other pleasant Spanish cities, the Albayzín is unique. You can't say you've really seen Granada until you've at least strolled a few of its twisty lanes. Climb high to the San Nicolás church for the best view of the Alhambra (see "To San Nicolás on Foot," below). Then, to really get to know this neighborhood, wander through its evocative back streets (following my "Exploring the Albayzín Walk," later).

▲▲San Nicolás Viewpoint (Mirador de San Nicolás)

This popular spot, looking across to the Alhambra from the edge of the Albayzín, is one of Europe's most romantic viewpoints. To best

enjoy it, be here at sunset, when the Alhambra glows red and Álbayzín seniors share the benches with lovers, hippies, and tourists. For an overpriced drink with the same million-euro view, step into the bar at the recommended El Huerto de Juan Ranas (restaurant just below the viewpoint and to the left, at Calle de Atarazana 8). Order a drink, tip the Roma musicians who perform here, settle in, and consider it a concert. For more advice on drinking and dining with a view, see "Eating in Granada," later.

Getting There: Ride the bus, hike up, or take a taxi (about €5—ride up and explore downhill). The handy Albayzín **minibuses #C31** and **#C32** make a loop through the quarter, getting you scenically and sweatlessly to the San Nicolás viewpoint. Buses depart about every 10 minutes from the Cathedral/Gran Vía or Plaza Nueva.

To San Nicolás on Foot: It's a steep but fascinating 30-minute walk up (see route on the "Albayzín Neighborhood" map). Start from the west end of Plaza Nueva on Calle de Elvira. When you see a tiny signal light,

GRANADA

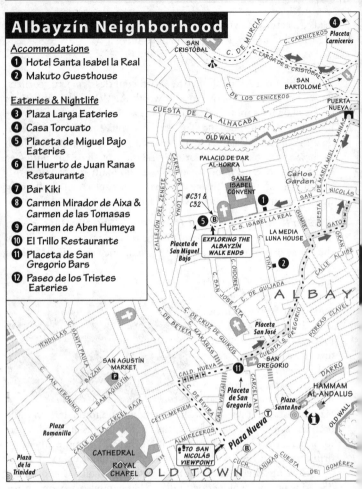

Albayzín Neighborhood

Accommodations

❶ Hotel Santa Isabel la Real
❷ Makuto Guesthouse

Eateries & Nightlife

❸ Plaza Larga Eateries
❹ Casa Torcuato
❺ Placeta de Miguel Bajo Eateries
❻ El Huerto de Juan Ranas Restaurante
❼ Bar Kiki
❽ Carmen Mirador de Aixa & Carmen de las Tomasas
❾ Carmen de Aben Humeya
❿ El Trillo Restaurante
⓫ Placeta de San Gregorio Bars
⓬ Paseo de los Tristes Eateries

GRANADA

turn uphill (90 degrees, right) on Calle Calderería Nueva. Follow this stepped street—a virtual tunnel of hippie souvenirs leading to a stretch of Moroccan eateries and pastry shops, vendors of imported North African goods, halal butchers, and inviting *teterías* (Moorish tearooms). Ahead is the tiny square and Church of San Gregorio.

Placeta de San Gregorio, the tiny junction at the top of Calle Calderería Nueva, has a special hang-loose character. If you're not in a hurry, grab a rickety seat here at Bar las Cuevas, under the classic church facade with potted plants and a commotion of tiled roofs. Enjoy the steady stream of people flowing by. Another fine perch a few steps higher up is Taverna 22, great for a Reserva 1925 (Granada's best craft beer), *vermut de la casa,* or a sweet sherry *(jerez).*

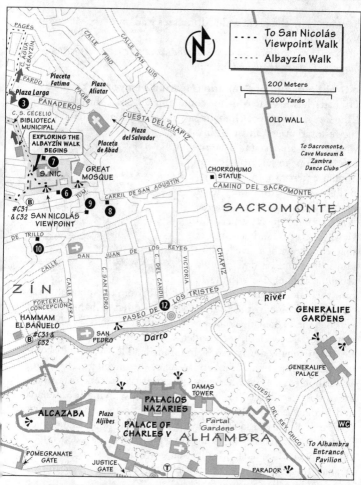

The **Church of San Gregorio** is the domain of a small group of Franciscan sisters. Step inside for a moment of tranquility and holiness in the midst of this lively town. One of the sisters, dressed in glorious white, kneels at the altar in prayer all day, every day.

Continue your climb up Cuesta de San Gregorio. When you reach the big brick tower of a Moorish-style house, **La Media Luna** (with tall palm trees and a keyhole-style doorway), stop for a photo and a breather, then follow the wall, continuing uphill. At the T-intersection (with the painted black cats on the wall), turn right on Aljibe del Gato. A bit farther on, take the first left onto the stepped Cuesta de María de la Miel. Keep going up, up, up. Take the first right, on Camino Nuevo de San Nicolás, then walk to the street that curves up left. Continue up the curve, and soon you'll see feet hanging from the plaza wall. More steps lead up to the viewpoint. Whew! You made it!

• *Just next to the San Nicolás viewpoint (to your left as you face the Alhambra) is the striking and inviting...*

▲Great Mosque of Granada (Mezquita Mayor de Granada)

Granada has a vital Muslim community. Local Muslims write, "The Great Mosque of Granada signals, after a hiatus of 500 years,

the restoration of a missing link with a rich and fecund Islamic contribution to all spheres of human enterprise and activity." Built in 2003 (with money from the local community and Islamic Arab nations), it has a peaceful view courtyard and a minaret that comes with a live call to prayer five times a day (printed schedule inside). It's stirring to hear the muezzin proclaim "God is Great" from the minaret. Visitors are welcome in the courtyard, which offers Alhambra views without the hedonistic ambience of the more famous San Nicolás viewpoint. Take a look at the video showing the mosque in action.

While many tourists come to Granada to learn about its complex cultural history, not all are aware of the ongoing relevance of its Islamic past. Today, five centuries after the Reconquista, there are almost 2 million Muslims in Spain. Those living in Granada and Andalucía are as Iberian as any modern Spaniard, as were their forbears. When you look out at the Alhambra from the mosque's garden, you are witnessing something built not by outsiders but by the people of Granada, who in that era were Muslim and spoke Arabic. This mosque is an acknowledgment of Islam's great importance to Granada's cultural fabric.

Cost and Hours: Free, daily 11:00-21:00, shorter hours in winter, +34 958 202 526, www.mezquitadegranada.com.

• *From the San Nicolás viewpoint and the Great Mosque, you're poised to begin my...*

▲Exploring the Albayzín Walk

This little stroll connects two Albayzín viewpoints, the well-known San Nicolás *mirador* and the less-visited San Cristóbal. In the 20 or 30 minutes it takes to complete the walk, you'll see why this hilltop neighborhood is recognized even by the people of Granada as a world apart. To trace the route, see the "Albayzín Neighborhood" map.

Each of the 20 churches in this district sits on a spot once occupied by a mosque. When the Reconquista first arrived in Granada,

Christians and Muslims attempted to coexist. But within a short time, the Christian Spaniards forced Muslims to convert and then expelled them altogether. By 1570 all but a remnant of Granada's Muslim community had been eliminated. What remained, though, was this neighborhood, the oldest part of Granada, with its narrow, cobbled streets and Moorish-style homes called *carmenes*. These large, walled houses with private gardens survive today in the form of the characteristic *carmen* restaurants so popular with visitors.

○ Self-Guided Walk: From the San Nicolás viewpoint, turn your back to the Alhambra and walk north (passing the Church of San Nicolás on your right and, farther on, the Biblioteca Municipal on your left). The small lane Callejón San Cecilio leads past a white brick arch (on your right)—now a chapel built into the old Moorish wall. You're walking by the scant remains of the pre-Alhambra fortress of Granada.

At the end of the lane, step down to the right through the 11th-century "New Gate" (Puerta Nueva—older than the Alhambra) and into **Plaza Larga.** You're now in the heart of the Albayzín. In medieval times, this tiny square (called "long," because back then it was) served as the local marketplace. It still is a busy market each morning. Casa Pasteles, at the near end of the square, serves good coffee and cakes.

From Plaza Larga, walk up **Calle Agua de Albayzín** (as you face Casa Pasteles, it's to your right). The street, named for the public baths that used to line it, shows evidence of the Moorish plumbing system: gutters. Back when many of Europe's streets were filled with muck, Granada had gutters with drains leading to clay and lead pipes.

At the top of the street, take a left and then another left onto Calle Principal de San Bartolomé, leading you to the **San Bartolomé Church.** This Mudejar church, built on top of a mosque, has a well next to the entrance. Unfortunately, it was one of the many churches set on fire during the Spanish Civil War, and the inside is completely empty.

Now cross the small plaza and continue straight ahead. Take a right onto Calle Larga de San Cristóbal; where the lane ends, look left to see the **San Cristóbal viewpoint.** Lesser known than the San Nicolás viewpoint, this *mirador* presents a great historical view of the Albayzín.

Gazing outward, notice the impressive **old wall** in the middle distance, first built by the Iberians in the 6th century BC, and later modified and strengthened by the Romans, Visigoths, and Moors. Behind the wall (and a white fence) is where the initial Roman citadel lay. In the 1200s, as the Nasrid dynasty was under heavy pressure from the Christian kingdoms, it was decided to build a better fortified palace on the hill behind the citadel: the Alhambra.

GRANADA

GRANADA

Safety in the Albayzín

While this charming Moorish district is certainly safe by day, it can be edgy after dark. Most of the area is fine to wander,

though many streets are poorly lit, and the maze of lanes can make it easy to get lost and wind up somewhere you don't want to be. Some nervous travelers choose to avoid the neighborhood entirely after dark, but I recommend venturing into the Albayzín to enjoy its restaurants, ideal sunset views, and charming ambience. Just exercise normal precautions: Leave your valuables at your hotel, stick to better-lit streets, and take a minibus or taxi home if you're unsure of your route. Violent crime is rare, but pickpocketing is common.

Now notice the white palace farther to the right, behind the old wall. This is the 15th-century **Palacio de Dar al-Horra,** named after its owner, Aixa la-Horra, who was the mother of Boabdil, the last emir of Granada. (We'll go by this palace later in our walk.) The highest mountain in the Iberian Peninsula is named for Aixa's husband, Sultan Muley Hacén (Abu al-Hasan Ali); legend says he is buried there. You can see the peak, Mulhacén (11,413 feet), from where you stand; it's a pyramid-shaped mountain and usually covered in snow.

From the viewpoint, backtrack to Calle Larga de San Cristóbal and follow it straight ahead to Plaza Larga. From here, walk back through the **Puerta Nueva** gate and down Placeta de las Minas (which becomes Cuesta de María de la Miel) to Camino Nuevo de San Nicolás. Turn right, and you'll soon come to the **Santa Isabel Convent,** where you can buy sweets from the nuns (daily 9:00-18:30). If you need more sustenance, **Placeta de San Miguel Bajo,** just beyond the convent, has options for a meal or a refreshing snack (see "Eating in Granada," later). If you have energy left, a visit to the nearby Palacio de Dar al-Horra (€5, covered by Alhambra Dobla de Oro ticket) is worthwhile for those interested in Spanish-Islamic architecture.

When you are ready to return to the town center, catch minibus #C31 or #C32 from Placeta de San Miguel Bajo, or walk downhill for 10 minutes to Plaza Nueva.

SACROMONTE

The Sacromonte district is home to Granada's thriving Roma community. Marking the entrance to Sacromonte is a statue of Chorrohumo (literally, "exudes smoke," and a play on the slang word for "thief": *chorro*). He was a Roma from Granada, popular in the 1950s for guiding people around the city.

While the neighboring Albayzín is a sprawling zone blanketing a hilltop, Sacromonte is much smaller—very compact and very steep. Most houses are burrowed into the cliff wall. Sacromonte has one main street: Camino del Sacromonte, which is lined with caves primed for tourists and restaurants ready to fight over the bill. (Don't come here expecting to get a deal on anything.) Intriguing lanes run above and below this main drag—a steep hike above Camino del Sacromonte is the cliff-hanging, parallel secondary street, Vereda de Enmedio, which is less touristy, with an authentically residential vibe.

Cave Museum of Sacromonte
(Museo Cuevas del Sacromonte)

This hilltop complex, also known as the Center for the Interpretation of Sacromonte (Centro de Interpretación del Sacromonte), is

a kind of open-air folk museum about Granada's unique Roma cave-dwelling tradition (though it doesn't have much on the people themselves). Getting there is a bit of a slog for what you'll see—but if you can combine your visit with one of their summertime flamenco and/or classical guitar concerts, it may be worth your while (see museum website for offerings).

The exhibits (with adequate, if not insightful, English descriptions) are spread through a series of whitewashed caves along a ridge, with spectacular views to the Alhambra. As you stroll from cave to cave, you'll see displays on the native habitat (rocks, flora, and fauna); crafts (basket-weaving, pottery making, metalworking, and weaving); and lifestyles (including a look into a typical home and kitchen). There's also an exhibit about other cave-dwelling cultures from around the "troglodyte world," and one about Sacromonte's vital role in the development of Granada's brand of flamenco. As you wander, imagine this in the 1950s, when it was still a bustling community of Roma cave-dwellers.

Cost and Hours: €5, daily 10:00-20:00, off-season

until 18:00, Barranco de los Negros, +34 958 215 120, www. sacromontegranada.com.

Getting There: You can ride minibus #C34 from Plaza Nueva (ask driver, *"¿Museo cuevas?"*; departs every 20 minutes) or take a taxi; the bus gives you elevated views. Get off next to the big Venta El Gallo restaurant, along the main road (several *zambra* performance caves line up along here, too—see next). From here, it's a steep 10-minute hike past cave dwellings up to the top of the hill— follow the signs.

Zambra Dance

A long flamenco tradition exists in Granada, and the Roma of Sacromonte are credited with developing this city's unique flavor of the Andalusian art form. Sacromonte is a good place to see *zambra*, a flamenco variation in which the singer also dances. A half-dozen cave-bars offering *zambra* in the evenings line Sacromonte's main drag. Hotels are happy to book you a seat and arrange the included transfer. Experiencing flamenco in a Roma cave is like seeing art in situ.

Two well-established venues are **Zambra Cueva de la Rocío** (€30, includes a drink and bus ride from and to your hotel, €23 without transport, daily show at 22:00, 1 hour, Camino del Sacromonte 70, +34 958 227-129, www.cuevalarocio.es) and **María la Canastera,** an intimate venue where the Duke of Windsor and actor Yul Brynner came to watch *zambra* (€29, includes drink and bus from hotel, €24 without transport, daily show at 22:00, 1 hour, Camino del Sacromonte 89, +34 958 121 183, www. marialacanastera.com). The biggest operation here is the restaurant **Venta El Gallo,** which has performances of more straightforward flamenco (not specifically *zambra*, €33 includes drink and bus from hotel, €26 without transport, daily shows at 21:00 and 22:30, dinner possible beforehand on outdoor terrace, Barranco de los Negros 5, +34 958 228 476, www.ventaelgallo.com). Or consider the summer performances at the Cave Museum (explained earlier).

If you don't want to venture to Sacromonte, try **Casa del Arte Flamenco,** which performs one-hour shows just off Plaza Nueva (€20, €3 discount for booking online; at 18:00, 19:30, and 21:00; Cuesta de Gomérez 11, +34 958 565 767, www. casadelarteflamenco.com).

NEAR GRANADA

Carthusian Monastery (Monasterio de la Cartuja)

A mile north of town on the way to Madrid, this monastery was built by Carthusian monks between the 16th and 18th centuries. Its unassuming sandstone exterior hides an interior that looks as if it were squirted from a can of whipped cream. La Cartuja is

Granada's Roma (Gypsies)

Both the English word "Gypsy" and its Spanish counterpart, *gitano,* come from the word "Egypt"—from where Europeans once believed these nomadic people originated. Today the preferred term is "Roma," since "Gypsy" has acquired negative connotations (though for clarity's sake, I've used both terms throughout this book).

After migrating from India in the 14th century, the Roma people settled mostly in the Muslim-occupied lands in southern Europe (such as the Balkan Peninsula, then controlled by the Ottoman Turks). Under medieval Muslims, the Roma enjoyed relative tolerance. They were traditionally good with crafts, animals, and blacksmithing.

The first Roma arrived in Granada in the 15th century—and they've remained tight-knit ever since. Today 50,000 Roma call Granada home, many of them in the district called Sacromonte. In most of Spain, Roma are more assimilated into the general population, but Sacromonte has a large, distinct Roma community.

Spaniards, who generally consider themselves to be tolerant, claim that in maintaining such a tight community, the Roma segregate themselves. The Roma call Spaniards *payos* ("whites"). Recent mixing of Roma and *payos* has given birth to the term *gallipavo* (rooster-duck), although who's who depends upon whom you ask.

The Roma challenge is nothing new. Five hundred years ago Queen Isabel issued a proclamation urging the "Gypsies" of her realm to pick and follow a religion, abandon their nomadic ways and settle down, get an honest job, and cease fortune-telling.

The stereotype holds that all Roma are thieves. And sure, some of them are. But others are honest citizens, trying to make their way in the world just like anyone else. Because of the high incidence of petty theft in Granada, it's wise to be cautious when dealing with a Roma person—but it's also important to keep an open mind.

sometimes called the "Christian Alhambra" for its elaborate white Baroque stucco work. In the rooms just off the cloister, notice the gruesome paintings of martyrs placidly meeting their grisly fates.

Cost and Hours: €5, Sun-Fri 10:00-20:00, Sat-Sun 10:00-13:00 & 15:00-20:00, shorter hours Nov-March, +34 958 161 932, www.cartujadegranada.com.

Getting There: While you can catch bus #8, it's easiest to just hop a taxi.

Sleeping in Granada

In July and August, when Granada's streets are littered with sunstroke victims, rooms are plentiful and prices soft. In the crowded months of April, May, September, and October, prices can spike up. Most places offer breakfast for an additional charge.

If you're traveling by car, see "Arrival in Granada" at the beginning of this chapter for driving and parking information.

ON OR NEAR PLAZA NUEVA

Each of these (except the hostel) is professional, plenty comfortable, and perfectly located within a 5- to 10-minute walk of Plaza Nueva.

$$$ Hotel Casa 1800 Granada sets the bar for affordable class. Its 25 rooms face the beautiful, airy courtyard of a 17th-century mansion in the lower part of the Albayzín (just steps above Plaza Nueva). Tidy, friendly, and well-run, it has a free, 24-hour refreshments bar and complimentary tea each afternoon (pricier rooms not much different except for the Alhambra views and patios, air-con, elevator, Benalúa 11, +34 958 210 700, www.hotelcasa1800granada.com, info.granada@hotelcasa1800).

$$ Casa del Capitel Nazarí, just off the church end of Plaza Nueva, is a restored 16th-century Renaissance manor with 23 tastefully down-to-earth rooms that are intimate, bright, and spacious, most facing a courtyard that hosts art exhibits (RS%, some view rooms, afternoon tea/coffee, air-con, elevator, loaner laptop, pay parking, Cuesta Aceituneros 6, +34 958 215 260, www.hotelcasacapitel.com, info@hotelcasacapitel.com). Their connected annex, **$$$ Mariana Pineda,** has five exquisitely decorated rooms in a former palace.

$$ Hotel Monjas del Carmen is a modern hotel with a friendly staff and bright clean rooms. It's nicely located just a few steps off Plaza Nueva (Plaza de los Cuchilleros 13, elevator, pay parking, +34 958 101 619, www.hotelmonjasdelcarmen.com, hotelmonjasdelcarmen@amchoteles.com).

$$ Hotel Anacapri is a bright, cool marble oasis with 53 vibrantly colored rooms and a comfortable lounge (family rooms, air-con, elevator, pay parking, 2 blocks toward Gran Vía from Plaza Nueva at Calle Joaquín Costa 7, just a block from cathedral bus stop, +34 958 227 477, www.hotelanacapri.com, reservas@hotelanacapri.com).

$ Hotel Inglaterra, with 36 basic rooms, is a little rough around the edges and feels institutional but is in an ideal location. Exterior rooms come with some noise from the popular bars below (air-con, elevator to third floor only, pay parking, Cetti Merien 6,

+34 958 221 559, www.hotelinglaterragranada.com, info@hotel-inglaterra.es).

¢ **Oasis Hostel Granada** offers a communal terrace, the scent of fried food, and lots of backpacker bonding, including daily tours and activities on request. It's just a block above the lively Moorish-flavored tourist drag (includes welcome drink with direct booking, pay parking, at the top end of Placeta Correo Viejo at #3, +34 958 215 848, www.oasisgranada.com, granada@hostelsoasis.com).

CHEAP SLEEPS ON CUESTA DE GOMÉREZ

These lodgings, all inexpensive and some ramshackle, are on this street leading from Plaza Nueva up to the Alhambra. Sprinkled among the knickknack stores are the storefront workshops of several guitar makers who are renowned for their handcrafted instruments.

$$ Hotel Puerta de las Granadas rents 36 crisp, clean rooms with a modern vibe. It has a courtyard, a terrace with an Alhambra view, and a handy location (RS%, air-con, family rooms, elevator, pay parking, Cuesta de Gomérez 14, +34 958 216 230, www.hotelpuertadelasgranadas.com, reservas@hotelpuertadelasgranadas.com).

$ Pensión Landazuri is run by friendly English-speaking Matilde Landazuri, her son Manolo, and daughters Margarita and Elisa. Their characteristic old house has 15 rooms—ask for a recently renovated one. It boasts hardworking, helpful management and a great roof garden with a splendid Alhambra view (family rooms, no elevator or air-con, pay parking, Cuesta de Gomérez 24, +34 958 221 406, www.pensionlandazuri.com, info@pensionlandazuri.com). The Landazuris also run a good, cheap café open for breakfast and lunch, next door.

$ Pensión Al Fin is located just up the street from Pensión Landazuri and run by the same family. Its five high-ceilinged rooms, with antique wooden beams and marble columns, are colorful and stylish, with Cuban flair. A glass floor in the lobby lets you peer into a well from an ancient house (some rooms with balconies, pay parking, reception at Pensión Landazuri, Cuesta de Gomérez 31, +34 958 228 172, www.pensionalfin.com, info@pensionalfin.com).

¢ **Hostal Navarro Ramos** is a small cheapie, renting seven quiet, clean rooms (5 with private baths) facing away from the street (no elevator, Cuesta de Gomérez 21, +34 958 250 555, www.pensionnavarroramos.com, info@pensionnavarroramos.com, Carmen).

¢ **Hostal Austria** rents 15 basic and clean rooms (family rooms, air-con, Cuesta de Gomérez 4, +34 958 227 075, www.pensionaustria.com, pensionaustria@pensionaustria.com).

Granada's Hotels & Restaurants

GRANADA

Accommodations

1. Hotel Casa 1800 Granada
2. Casa del Capitel Nazarí
3. Hotel Monjas del Carmen
4. Hotel Anacapri
5. Hotel Inglaterra
6. Oasis Hostel Granada
7. Hotel Puerta de las Granadas
8. Pensión Landazuri & Cafetería
9. Pensión Al Fin
10. Hostal Navarro Ramos
11. Hostal Austria
12. Hotel Los Tilos
13. To Hotel Reina Cristina, Hostals Casa de Reyes & Rodri; Pensión Zurita

Eateries & Tapas Bars

14. Bodegas Castañeda
15. Restaurante Carmela
16. La Cueva de 1900
17. Arrayanes
18. Los Diamantes
19. Café Bernina
20. Papas Elvira
21. Los Italianos Ice Cream
22. Supermarket
23. Mercado San Agustín
24. La Botillería
25. Taberna La Tana, Bar Los Diamantes II & Taberna de JAM
26. Café Fútbol & La Esquinita de Javi
27. Restaurante Chikito
28. Calle Calderería Nueva Eateries
29. Placeta de San Gregoria Eateries

NEAR THE CATHEDRAL

$ Hotel Los Tilos offers 30 comfortable, business-like rooms (some with balconies) on the charming traffic-free Plaza de Bib-Rambla. Guests are welcome to use the fourth-floor terrace with views of the cathedral and the Alhambra (RS%—free breakfast if you book direct, family rooms, air-con, pay parking, Plaza de Bib-Rambla 4, +34 958 266 712, www.hotellostilos.com, clientes@ hotellostilos.com, friendly José María).

On or near Plaza de la Trinidad

The charming, parklike square called Plaza de la Trinidad, just a short walk west of the cathedral area (Pescadería and Bib-Rambla squares), is home to several good accommodations.

$$ Hotel Reina Cristina has 55 quiet, homey rooms a few steps off Plaza de la Trinidad. Check out the great Mudejar ceiling at the top of the stairwell. The famous Spanish poet Federico García Lorca hid out in this house before being captured and executed by the Guardia Civil during the Spanish Civil War (includes breakfast, cheaper rate without breakfast, air-con, elevator, pay parking, near Plaza de la Trinidad at Tablas 4, +34 958 253 211, www.hotelreinacristina.com, clientes@hotelreinacristina.com).

$$ Hostal Casa de Reyes, run with class by Manolo and Carmen, has 18 well-appointed rooms in two buildings a block off the square. The public areas and rooms are flamboyantly decorated with medieval flair—colorful tiles, wood-carved life-sized figures, and swords (home-cooked dinner available—book in advance, air-con, elevator in one building only, pay parking, Laurel de las Tablas 17, +34 958 295 029, www.hostalcasadereyes.com, info@ hostallimagranada.eu).

$ Hostal Rodri, run by Manolo's brother José, has 10 similarly good rooms a few doors down that feel new and classy for their price range. Take in the sun on an "L"-shaped terrace (air-con, elevator, pay parking, Laurel de las Tablas 9, +34 958 288 043, www. hostalrodri.com, info@hostalrodri.com).

$ Pensión Zurita, well-run by personable Francisco and Loli, faces Plaza de la Trinidad. Twelve of the 14 rooms have modern, in-room baths and small exterior balconies. Even with double-pane windows, some rooms may come with night noise from cafés below (air-con, kitchen nook available for guest use, pay parking, Plaza de la Trinidad 7, +34 958 275-020, mobile +34 685 843 745, www. pensionzurita.es, pensionzurita@gmail.com).

IN THE ALBAYZÍN

For locations, see the "Albayzín Neighborhood" map on page 134.

$$$ Hotel Santa Isabel la Real, a handsome 16th-century edifice, has 11 rooms ringing a charming courtyard. Each room is a bit different; basic rooms look to the patio, while pricier rooms have better exterior views. The owners' antiques accentuate the Moorish ambience (breakfast included, air-con, elevator, pay parking, midway between San Nicolás viewpoint and Placeta de San Miguel Bajo on Calle Santa Isabel la Real, minibuses #C31 and #C32 stop nearby, +34 958 294 658, www.hotelsantaisabellareal.com, info@hotelsantaisabellareal.com).

¢ Makuto Guesthouse, a hostel tucked deep in the Albayzín, feels like a commune you can pay to join for a couple of days. With 39 beds in eight compact rooms clustered around a lush garden courtyard that's made for hanging out—including several hammock-and-lounge-sofa "hang-out zones"—it exudes a young, easygoing Albayzín vibe (private rooms available, includes breakfast, communal kitchen, Calle Tiña 18, +34 958 805 876, www.makutohostel.com, info@makutohostel.com). From the minibus stop on Calle Santa Isabel la Real, it's a long block down Calle Tiña and on the left.

IN AND NEAR THE ALHAMBRA

To stay on the Alhambra grounds, choose between a famous, overpriced parador and a practical and economical hotel above the parking lot. Both are a half-mile up the hill from Plaza Nueva (see "The Alhambra" map on page 113 for locations).

$$$$ Parador de Granada San Francisco offers 40 designer rooms in a former Moorish palace that was later transformed into a 15th-century Franciscan monastery. It's considered Spain's premier parador—and that's saying something (air-con, free parking, Calle Real de la Alhambra, +34 958 221 440, www.parador.es, granada@parador.es). You must book months ahead to spend the night in this lavishly located, stodgy, and historic palace. Any peasant, however, can drop in for a coffee, drink, snack, or meal. For more about the building's history, see "The Alhambra Grounds" sidebar earlier in this chapter.

$ Hotel Guadalupe, big and modern with 58 sleek rooms, is quietly and conveniently located overlooking the Alhambra parking lot. While it's a 30-minute hike above the town, many—especially drivers—find this to be a practical option (air-con, elevator, special parking rate in Alhambra lot, Paseo de la Sabica 30, +34 958 225 730, www.hotelguadalupe.es, info@hotelguadalupe.es).

Eating in Granada

Restaurants generally serve lunch from 13:00 to 16:00 and dinner from 20:00 until very late (remember, Spaniards don't start dinner until about 21:00). Granada's bars pride themselves on serving a small tapas plate free with any beverage—a tradition that's dying out in most of Spain. Save on your food expenses by doing a tapas crawl, and claim your "right" to a free tapa with every drink. Order your drink and wait for the free tapa before ordering food (if you order food too soon, you likely won't get the freebie). Avoid the touristy Calle Navas, right off Plaza del Carmen.

For more budget-eating thrills, buy picnic supplies near Plaza Nueva, and schlep them up into the Albayzín. This makes for a great cheap date at the San Nicolás viewpoint or on one of the scattered squares and lookout points.

In search of an edible memory? A local specialty, *tortilla de Sacromonte*, is a spicy omelet with lamb's brain and other organs. *Berenjenas fritas* (fried eggplant) and *habas con jamón* (small green fava beans cooked with cured ham) are worth seeking out. *Tinto de verano*—a red-wine spritzer with lemon and ice—is refreshing on a hot evening. For tips on eating near the Alhambra, see "Orientation to the Alhambra," earlier.

IN THE ALBAYZÍN

The food scene in the Albayzín can be a mixed bag. Part of the charm of the quarter is the lazy ambience on its squares. My two favorites are Plaza Larga and Placeta de Miguel Bajo. To find a particular square, ask any local, or follow my directions using the "Albayzín Neighborhood" map, earlier in this chapter. If dining late, take a taxi back to your hotel; Albayzín back streets can be poorly lit and confusing to follow.

Plaza Larga is extremely characteristic, with tapas bar tables spilling out onto the square, a morning market, and a much-loved pastry shop. A few blocks beyond Plaza Larga, **$$ Casa Torcuato** is a hardworking eatery serving creative food in a smart upstairs dining room. Or grab a table on the little square out front or in the downstairs bar. They serve a good fixed-price lunch, plates of fresh fish, and prizewinning, *salmorejo*-style gazpacho (closed Sun night and Wed, Calle Pagés 31, +34 958 288 148). Minibus #C34 stops a block away from the restaurant (or take a €5 taxi from Plaza Nueva).

Placeta de Miguel Bajo, the farthest hike into the Albayzín, boasts a spirited local scene—kids kicking soccer balls, old-timers warming benches, and women gossiping under the facade of a humble church. It's circled by a half-dozen inviting little bars

GRANADA

and restaurants—each very competitive with cheap lunch deals. In the evening, the most serious restaurant is **$ Bar Lara** with nice traditional plates, salads, paellas, and fish (closed Wed, Placeta de Miguel Bajo 4, +34 958 209 466). This square is a nice spot to end your Albayzín visit, as there's a viewpoint overlooking the modern city a block beyond the square. Minibus #C31 or #C32 rumbles by every few minutes, ready to zip you back to Plaza Nueva. Or just walk 10 minutes downhill.

Near the San Nicolás Viewpoint

This area is thoroughly touristy, so don't expect any local hangouts.

$$$ El Huerto de Juan Ranas Restaurante is a stuffy restaurant below a popular rooftop bar. Packed with a commotion of people taking selfies, sipping cocktails, and paying too much for tapas, it's immediately below the San Nicolás viewpoint and has amazing Alhambra views (daily 11:30-24:00, Calle de Atarazana 8, +34 958 286 925).

$$ Bar Kiki, a laid-back and popular bar-restaurant, is on an unpretentious square with no view but plenty of people-watching. They serve simple dishes outside on rickety tables and plastic chairs. Try their tasty fried eggplant (Thu-Tue 9:00-24:00, closed Wed, just behind viewpoint at Plaza de San Nicolás 9, +34 958 276 715).

Romantic *Carmenes*

For dinner in a dressy setting and a dreamy Alhambra view, consider dining in a *carmen*, a typical Albayzín house with a garden (buzz to get in). Long ago, wealthy families built these walled mansions with terraced gardens on the hillside. Today, the gardens of many of these *carmenes* host dining tables and romantic restaurants.

$$$ Carmen Mirador de Aixa is small and elegant. You'll pay a little more, but the food is exquisitely presented and the view is worth the price. Try the codfish or ox (Tue-Sat 20:00-23:00, also open for lunch Wed-Sun 13:30-15:30, closed Mon; next to Carmen de las Tomasas at Carril de San Agustín 2, +34 958 223 616, www.miradordeaixa.com).

$$$ Carmen de las Tomasas serves thoughtfully presented gourmet Andalusian cuisine with killer views on three terraces. The service is friendly if slightly formal (Tue-Sat 20:30-24:00, closed Sun-Mon; off-season also open for lunch, closed Mon; reservations required, Carril de San Agustín 4, +34 958 224 108, www.lastomasas.com, Joaquín).

$$ Carmen de Aben Humeya, with outdoor-only seating, is another smart option (daily 12:00-16:00 & 19:00-23:00, reservations required, Cuesta de las Tomasas 12, +34 958 228 345, www. abenhumeya.com).

$$ El Trillo Restaurante is homey, without pretense or big groups. Most tables are in a tranquil garden (with trees but no view); several choice tables upstairs have good Alhambra views. When it's cold, meals are served in their vintage dining room. The menu of modern Mediterranean and Spanish dishes is fun and creative, often with a surprising twist (daily 13:00-16:00 & 19:00-23:30, when reserving ask for garden or terrace; tricky to find—three levels below San Nicolás viewpoint, Calle Aljibe de Trillo 3, +34 958 225 182, www.restaurante-eltrillo.com).

Nightlife

For evening views, try the outdoor bars on **Paseo de los Tristes,** on a terrace over the river gorge: it's like a stage set, with the floodlit Alhambra high above and a happy crowd of locals. While there's no serious restaurant here, the scene is a winner. It's a simple, level, five-minute walk from Plaza Nueva.

NEAR PLAZA NUEVA

For people-watching, consider the many restaurants on Plaza Nueva or Plaza de Bib-Rambla. For locations, see the "Granada's Hotels & Restaurants" map, earlier in this section.

$$ Bodegas Castañeda, just a block off Plaza Nueva, has the right mix of lively, central, and cheap. When it's crowded, you need to power your way to the bar to order. When it's quiet, you can order at the bar and grab a little table (same prices). Consider their *tablas combinadas*—variety plates of cheese, meat, and *ahumados* (smoked fish)—and tasty *croquetas de jamón* (breaded and fried béchamel sauce with cured ham). Order a glass of gazpacho. The big kegs tempt you with local vermouths, and wine comes with a free tapa (daily 11:30-16:30 & 19:00-24:00, Calle Almireceros 1, +34 958 215 464). They've expanded with extra tables across the alley (where you can enjoy service and a bit of sanity as you dine), but don't be confused by the neighboring, similar "Antigua Bodega Castañeda" restaurant (run by a relative and not as good).

$$ Restaurante Carmela, with a sloppy ambience, is respected for its creative tapas, best enjoyed family-style. You can eat on the outside terrace or take a table in the modern interior (daily 8:00-24:00, just up from Plaza Isabel La Católica at Calle Colcha 13, +34 958 225 794).

$$ La Cueva de 1900, a family-friendly chain on the main drag, is appreciated for its simple dishes and quality ingredients. Though it lacks character, it's reliable and low stress. They're proud of their homemade hams, sausages, and cheeses—sold in 100-gram lots and served on grease-proof paper (daily 8:00-23:00, Calle Reyes Católicos 42, +34 958 229 327).

$ Cafetería Landazuri, connected to the recommended Pensión Landazuri, is a smart option for travelers walking down from the Alhambra and anyone who wants quality food at a bargain basement price. Manolo cooks to order; his individual-sized *tortilla española* and salads are good and filling (daily 7:00-16:00, Cuesta de Gomérez 24, +34 958 221 406).

$$ Arrayanes is a good Moroccan restaurant a world apart from my other listings. Brothers Mostafa and Ibrahím treat guests like old friends and will help you choose among the many salads, the *briwat* (chicken-and-cinnamon pastry appetizer), the *pastela* (first-course version of *briwat*), the couscous, or *tajin* dishes. The homemade lemonade with mint pairs well with everything (daily 13:30-16:30 & 19:30-23:30, two locations, just off of Calle Caldererería Nueva—from Church of San Gregorio, walk one block and take first right, uphill to Cuesta Marañas 4 and 7, +34 958 228 401).

$$ Los Diamantes is a modern, packed, high-energy local favorite for fresh seafood (free tapa with drink, only *raciones* and half-*raciones* on the menu, same price for picnic-bench seating or bar, daily 12:00-24:00, facing Plaza Nueva at #13, +34 958 075 313).

$ Café Bernina is a hardworking, bright and basic diner serving locals since 1930. It feels like a café/bakery (but with plenty of alcohol) and serves hearty salads, sandwiches, and muffins; tapas are served only at the bar. Indoor dining prices are lower than on the terrace. It's great for breakfast (daily 7:30-24:00, air-con, Almireceros 4—just behind Puerta & Bernina, facing Gran Vía but 30 yards off the big street opposite cathedral; +34 958 050 908).

Nightlife: For a happening scene, check out the bars on and around **Calle de Elvira.**

Cheap To-Go Options

A strip of dirt-cheap eateries (including pizza and kebab shops) lines the bottom end of Plaza Nueva. Some have stools, or get your food to go and enjoy it on a sunny plaza bench on the square.

$ Papas Elvira is a popular hole-in-the-wall with fast, cheap food from Morocco and Spain (daily until 24:00, Calle de Elvira 9).

Ice Cream: Italian-run and teeming with locals, popular **Los Italianos** serves ice cream, *horchata* (*chufa*-nut drink), and shakes. For something special, try their *cassata,* a slice (not scoop) of Neapolitan with frozen fruit in a cone. Their photo menu is helpful (daily 9:00-24:00, shorter hours and sometimes closed off-season, across the street from cathedral and Royal Chapel at Gran Vía 4, +34 958 224 034).

Supermarket: Covirán Supermercado is a handy option near Plaza Nueva and the cathedral (daily 10:00-23:30, Calle de Elvira 52).

Markets: Though heavy on fresh fish and meat, **Mercado San**

Agustín also sells fruits and veggies. If nothing else, it's as refreshingly cool as a meat locker (Mon-Sat 9:00-15:00, closed Sun, very quiet on Mon, a block north of cathedral and a half-block off Gran Vía on Calle Cristo San Agustín). Tucked away in the back of the market is a very cheap and colorful little eatery: **Cafetería San Agustín.** They make their own *churros* and give a small tapa free with each drink (menu on wall). If you are waiting for the cathedral or Royal Chapel to open, kill time in the market.

BEYOND PLAZA DEL CARMEN
Tapas Bars

Granada is a wonderland of happening little tapas bars. As the scene changes from night to night, it's best to simply wander and see what appeals. You'll be amazed at how the vibe changes when you venture just five minutes from the historic and touristic center. From Plaza del Carmen, wander through the gauntlet of touristy places along Calle Navas. Calle Navas eventually becomes Calle Virgen del Rosario, with a cluster of fun tapas spots. Consider these places (all within a block of each other):

$$ La Botillería is more relaxed than the standard tapas bar. It has a dressy zone (with nicer tables but the same menu) along with a fun bar scene and tables on a quiet little square. They serve good salads, tasty pork cheeks, and wine by the glass (daily 12:00-24:00, Calle Varela 10, +34 958 224 928).

$$ Taberna La Tana is a tight, intensely Andalusian place with tiny tables and people hanging out in the street. It's well known for its fine tapas, wine, and classic *raciones* (daily 13:00-16:30 & 20:30-24:00, Placeta del Agua 3, +34 958 225 248).

$$ Bar Los Diamantes II is famous for its seafood and happy energy. The menu is easy, prices are great, and locals appreciate fish fried in fresh olive oil. Portions can be huge; prices are the same at the bar, tables, and terrace. The seating in back feels like a fish-and-chips joint. I'd go for the *surtido de pescado* with five kinds of fish (daily 13:00-16:00 & 20:00-23:00, Calle Rosario 12, mobile +34 619 787 828).

$$ Taberna de JAM (pronounced "hahm") is a play on the word *jamón* and the initials of the renowned owner/*cortador* (one who cuts ham)—José Angel Muñoz. The extensive menu with traditional and innovative dishes is worthwhile, but this is *the* place for a plate of exquisite *jamón* matched with red wine—try sharing the *cata vertical* (tasting menu with four types of ham). They have a modern bar area and restaurant, as well as fine seating on the leafy square with a fountain...where prices jump a bit (Mon-Sat 9:00-16:00 & 20:00-24:00, closed Sun; at the top of Calle Virgen del Rosario at Plaza los Campos 1, +34 958 225 770).

$$ Café Fútbol is an old-school classic with an Art Deco vibe, serving basic Spanish dishes. It's the best place in town to finish your pub crawl (or start your day) with a dessert of chocolate and *churros;* a *media-ración* is plenty for two (daily 7:00-24:00, Plaza de Mariana Pineda 6, +34 958 226 662). It's just two blocks away (to the southwest) from a great local paseo street, Carrera de la Virgen, leading to the river (see "Paseo Without the Tourists," on page 132).

Restaurants for Full Meals

$$ Restaurante Chikito, a venerable classic on a leafy square at the top of a strolling boulevard, serves big plates *(para compartir)* designed to split. Its conservative local clientele appreciates the traditional Spanish cuisine and good prices; Sinatra would enjoy its tapas bar. Originally owned by an Argentine soccer star (see celebrity photos on the walls), it's enthusiastic about its meat. You can dine in the dressy, white-tablecloth interior or on the square (Thu-Tue 12:30-16:30 & 20:00-23:30, closed Wed, Plaza del Campillo 9, +34 958 223 364).

$$ La Esquinita de Javi has a "crank-out-the-fresh-seafood" formula and is run by the same family as Diamantes (listed earlier), but it's more like a normal sit-down restaurant. It has a family-friendly conviviality and an easy menu served in a well-lit, spacious interior and at pleasant tables on the square—where you'll pay more (Tue-Sat 13:00-16:00 & 20:30-23:00, Sun 13:00-16:00, closed Mon, two locations on Plaza Mariana Pineda, the better one is adjacent to Café Fútbol on downhill side, +34 958 049 142).

Granada Connections

BY PLANE

Granada's airport—Federico García Lorca Granada-Jaén Airport—provides fast connections to Spain's big cities. Iberia and low-cost carrier Vueling offer several direct flights daily to Madrid and Barcelona (code: GRX, +34 913 211 000, www.aena.es, select "F.G.L. Granada-Jaén"). Especially for Barcelona, flying is smart (1.5-hour trip versus 6-14 hours by train or bus).

To get between the airport and downtown, you can take a taxi (€35) or the much cheaper airport bus, timed to leave from directly outside the terminal when flights arrive and depart (€3, 16/day, 45 minutes to/from the Cathedral bus stop at the end of Gran Vía).

BY TRAIN OR BUS

From Granada by Train to: Madrid (3/day, 3.5 hours), **Toledo** (3/day, 4.5 hours, transfer in Madrid), **Málaga** (6/day, 1.5-3 hours, 1 transfer—bus is better), **Ronda** (3/day, 2.5 hours), **Barcelona** (3/day, 1 direct, 2 with change in Madrid, 6-7.5 hours—consider flying instead), **Córdoba** (4-7/day, 1.5 hours), **Sevilla** (6/day, 2.5 hours). Train info: +34 912 320 320, www.renfe.com.

From Granada by Bus to: Nerja (7/day, 2-3 hours), **Sevilla** (7/day to Plaza de Armas station, 2/day to El Prado station, 3 hours), **Córdoba** (8/day, 2.5-4 hours); **Madrid** (hourly, 5-6 hours; most to Estación Sur, a few to Avenida de América, 2 direct to T4 Barajas Airport), **Málaga** (hourly, 1.5-2 hours, several direct to Málaga airport, change here to continue to La Línea de la Concepción/ Gibraltar), **Algeciras** (4/

day, 4-5.5 hours), **Barcelona** (4/day, 14 hours). To reach **Ronda,** change in Antequera; to reach **Tarifa,** change in Algeciras or Málaga. Bus info: Alsa (www.alsa.es).

If there's a long line at the ticket windows, you can use the machines (press the flag for English)—but these only sell tickets for some major routes (such as Málaga).

GRANADA

CÓRDOBA

Straddling a sharp bend of the Guadalquivir River, Córdoba has a glorious Roman and Moorish past, once serving as a regional capital for both empires. It's home to Europe's best Islamic sight after Granada's Alhambra: the Mezquita, a splendid and remarkably well-preserved mosque that dates from AD 784. When you step inside the mosque, which is magical in its grandeur, you can imagine Córdoba as the center of a thriving and sophisticated culture. During the Dark Ages, when much of Europe was barbaric and illiterate, Córdoba was a haven of enlightened thought—famous for religious tolerance, artistic expression, and dedication to philosophy and the sciences. To this day, you'll still hear the Muslim call to prayer in Córdoba.

Beyond the magnificent Mezquita, the city of Córdoba has two sides: the touristy maze of old town streets immediately surrounding the giant main attraction (lined with trinket shops, hotels, and restaurants); and the workaday but interesting modern city (centered on Plaza de las Tendillas). In between are the side lanes of the Jewish Quarter, humming with history. Just a quick walk takes you from a commercialized vibe into real-life Córdoba.

PLANNING YOUR TIME

Ideally, Córdoba is worth two nights and a day. Don't rush the magnificent Mezquita, but also consider sticking around to experience the city's other pleasures: wander the evocative Jewish Quarter, enjoy the tapas scene, and explore the modern part of town.

However, if you're tight on time, it's possible to do Córdoba more quickly—especially since it's conveniently located on the AVE bullet-train line (and because, frankly, Córdoba has fewer

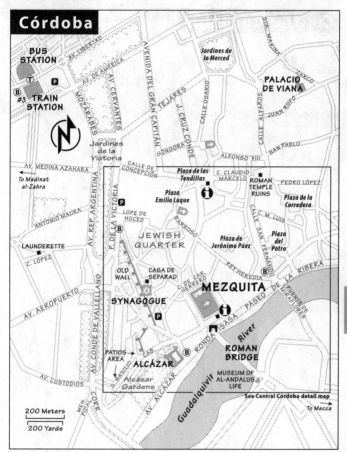

Córdoba

BUS STATION

#3 TRAIN STATION

Jardines de la Victoria

AV. MEDINA AZAHARA

To Madinat al-Zahra

LAUNDERETTE

C. LÓPEZ

AV. AEROPUERTO

200 Meters
200 Yards

AV. LIBERTAD

AV. DE AMÉRICA

AV. DE CERVANTES

MOZÁRABES

AVENIDA DEL GRAN CAPITAN

TEJARES

J. CRUZ CONDE

GÓNGORA

ALFONSO XIII

CALLE DE CONCEPCIÓN

AV. REP. ARGENTINA

ANTONIO MAURA

P. DE LA VICTORIA

LOPE DE HOCES

AV. CONDE DE VALLELLANO

OLD WALL

SYNAGOGUE

JEWISH QUARTER

CASA DE SEFARAD

C. DE CAR. HERRERO

AV. CUSTODIOS

PATIOS AREA

P. BASILIO

ALCÁZAR

Alcázar Gardens

AV. ALCÁZAR

MEN. PIDAL

Jardines de la Merced

PALACIO DE VIANA

ZARCO

CALLE ALFAROS

JUAN RUFO

SAN PABLO

STA. MARINA

CALLE OSARIO

CLAUDIO MARCELO

Plaza de las Tendillas

C. CLAUDIO MARCELO

ROMAN TEMPLE RUINS

PEDRO LÓPEZ

Plaza de la Corredera

Plaza Emilio Luque

BARROSO

Plaza de Jerónimo Páez

C. M. LUIS

C. SAN FERNANDO

Plaza del Potro

REY HEREDIA

MEZQUITA

PASEO DE LA RIBERA

ISASA

RONDA

PASEO DE MIRAFLORES

PUENTE DE

River

ROMAN BRIDGE

Guadalquivir

MUSEUM OF AL-ANDALUS LIFE

See Central Córdoba detail map

To Mecca

CÓRDOBA

major sights than the other two big Andalusian cities, Sevilla and Granada). To see Córdoba as an efficient stopover between Madrid and Sevilla (or as a side trip from Sevilla—frequent trains, 45-minute trip), focus on the Mezquita: taxi from the station, spend one hour there, explore the old town for an hour or two...and then get on your way.

Orientation to Córdoba

Córdoba's big draw is the mosque-turned-cathedral called the Mezquita (meth-KEE-tah). Most of the town's major sights are nearby, including the Alcázar, a former royal castle. And though the town seems to ignore its marshy Guadalquivir River (a prime bird-watching area), the riverbank sports a Renaissance triumphal arch next to a stout "Roman Bridge." The bridge leads to the town's

Central Córdoba

To Train &
Bus Stations

C. CONDE

Plaza de
San Nicolás

#3 &
Madinat
al-Zahra

Plaza
Emilio
Luque

Jardines
de la Victoria

Calle Lope de Hoces

Plaza de
la Trinidad

JEWISH

QUARTER

Plaza del
Neyra

To Madinat
al-Zahra

PUERTA DE
ALMODÓVAR
GATE

Glorieta
Media Luna

SYNAGOGUE

CASA DE
SEFARAD

BULLFIGHTING
MUSEUM

Plaza
Judá
Levi

Plaza
Maim.

Plaza de la
Constitución

OLD WALL

AVERROES
STATUE

Plaza
Campo de los
Santos Mártires

ROYAL
STABLES

ALCÁZAR

Alcázar
Gardens

PATIOS AREA

CÓRDOBA

200 Meters
200 Yards

Sights

1. Calleja de las Flores
2. Casa de Sefarad
3. Synagogue
4. Artisan Market
5. Puerta de Almodóvar Gate
6. Seneca Statue
7. Maimonides Statue
8. Averroes Statue
9. Bullfighting Museum
10. Baths of the Caliphate Alcázar
11. Museo Julio Romero de Torres
12. Caballerizas Reales

CÓRDOBA

old fortified gate (which houses a museum on Moorish culture, the Museum of al-Andalus Life). The Mezquita is buried in the characteristic medieval town. Around that stretches the Jewish Quarter, then the modern city—with some striking Art Deco buildings at Plaza de las Tendillas and more modern architecture lining Avenida del Gran Capitán.

TOURIST INFORMATION

Córdoba has a helpful TI at Plaza de las Tendillas (daily 9:00-14:00 & 17:00-19:15, +34 957 471 577, https://turismodecordoba.org). Another option is the Visitor Center near the Mezquita, covering both Córdoba and the Andalucía region (Mon-Fri 9:00-19:00, Sat-Sun 9:30-14:30, free WCs in basement along with a few ruins and a reproduction of how the Moorish city of "Qurtuba" looked 1,000 years ago, Plaza del Triunfo, +34 957 499 900, same website as the TI).

ARRIVAL IN CÓRDOBA

By Train or Bus: Córdoba's train station is located on Avenida de América. The modern glass-and-steel station has ATMs, restaurants, shops, an information counter, car rental agencies, and a small lounge for first-class passengers of the high-speed AVE train line. Taxis and local buses are just outside, to the left as you come up the escalators from the platforms.

The bus station is across the street from the train station (on the north side of Avenida Vía Augusta). There's no luggage storage at the train station, but the bus station has lockers (next to ticket booth #11, look for *Consigna/Locker* sign and buy token at machine, lockers are around the corner). More car rental agencies are located here.

To get to the old town, hop a **taxi** (€8 to the Mezquita) or catch **bus** #3 (stop is west of the train and bus stations, directly facing front of the taxi line, near archaeological ruins of Palatium Maximiani, buy €1.30 ticket on board, ask driver for *"mezquita,"* get off at Calle San Fernando, and take Calle del Portillo, following the twists and turns—and occasional signs—to the Mezquita).

It's about a 25-minute **walk** from either station to the old town. To walk from the train station to the Mezquita, turn left onto Avenida de América, then right through the pleasantly manicured Jardines de la Victoria park. Near the end of the park, on the left, you'll see a section of the old city walls. The Puerta de Almodóvar gate and a statue of Seneca mark the start of Calle de Cairuán (sometimes signposted as Kairuán)—follow this street downhill, with the wall still on your left, until you reach Plaza Campo de los Santos Mártires. Then head left, past the Alcázar, down Calle

Amador de los Rios, which leads directly to the Mezquita and the river.

By Car: The easiest way to enter the city center from Madrid or Sevilla on A-4/E-5 is to follow signs for *Córdoba sur* and *Plaza de Andalucía,* following palm-tree-lined A-431 (a.k.a. Avenida del Corregidor). Unless your hotel offers parking, avoid driving near the Mezquita. Instead, head for public parking: half a mile after crossing the Guadalquivir River, veer right onto Paseo de la Victoria, then look for a blue parking sign on the left (just before Calle Concepción) and a ramp down to an underground lot. To reach the bus and train stations (with car rental agencies), continue north on Paseo de la Victoria.

HELPFUL HINTS

Closed Days: The Alcázar, Madinat al-Zahra, Bullfighting Museum, Museo Julio Romero de Torres, Palacio de Viana, and Synagogue are closed on Monday.

Laundry: Solymar Tintoreria has self-service machines (Mon-Fri 9:30-13:30 & 17:00-20:30, Sat 9:30-13:30 only, closed Sun, Calle Maestro Priego López 2, +34 957 233 818).

Local Guides: Isabel Martínez Richter is a charming archaeologist who loves to make the city come to life for curious Americans (weekdays €140/3 hours, €170 on weekends and holidays, mobile +34 669 369 645, isabmr@gmail.com). **Ángel Lucena** is a good teacher and a joy to be with (€100/3 hours, mobile +34 607 898 079, lucenaangel@hotmail.com).

Hop-On, Hop-Off Bus: A 24-hour ticket is good for a "panoramic" circuit that stops at the train/bus station and generally in places you won't want to see; an "intimate" *microbús* route that stops at the Alcázar, Mezquita, Plaza de las Tendillas, Palacio de Viana, and elsewhere; and two one-hour walking tours of the Jewish Quarter/San Basilio neighborhood and the central shopping area around Plaza de las Tendillas (€20, purchase ticket at orange City Expert booth in train station or pay driver; buses depart about every 30 minutes 9:30-21:00, until 18:00 off-season; www.city-sightseeing.com).

Sights in Córdoba

MEZQUITA

Worth ▲▲▲, this massive former mosque—now with a 16th-century church rising up from the middle—was once the center of Western Islam and the heart of a cultural capital that rivaled Baghdad and Constantinople. A wonder of the medieval world, it's remarkably well-preserved, giving today's visitors a chance to soak up the ambience of Islamic Córdoba in its 10th-century prime.

Mezquita

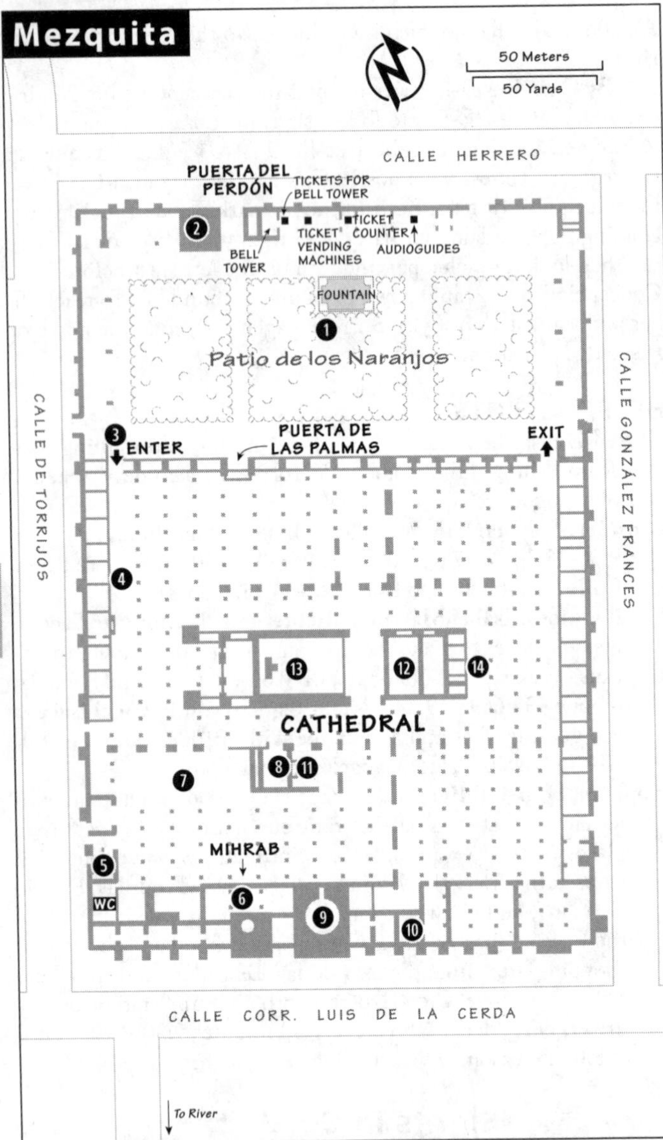

CÓRDOBA

50 Meters
50 Yards

CALLE HERRERO

PUERTA DEL PERDÓN

TICKETS FOR BELL TOWER

TICKET VENDING MACHINES

BELL TOWER

TICKET COUNTER

AUDIOGUIDES

❷

FOUNTAIN

❶

Patio de los Naranjos

CALLE DE TORRIJOS

CALLE GONZÁLEZ FRANCES

❸ ENTER

PUERTA DE LAS PALMAS

EXIT

❹

⓭ **⓬** **⓮**

CATHEDRAL

❼ **❽** **⓫**

❺ MIHRAB

WC **❻** **❾** **❿**

CALLE CORR. LUIS DE LA CERDA

To River

❶ Patio de los Naranjos
❷ Bell Tower/Minaret
❸ Entrance
❹ Visigothic Mosaic
❺ Visigothic Ruins
❻ Mihrab
❼ Villaviciosa Chapel
❽ Royal Chapel
❾ Treasury
❿ Stonemason Marks
⓫ Chapel of the Conversion of St. Paul
⓬ Altar
⓭ Choir
⓮ Gothic Vaulting

Cost: €11, ticket kiosk and machines inside the Patio de los Naranjos, Mon-Sat free entry 8:30-9:30 (because they don't want to charge a fee to attend the 9:30 Mass; no access to altar, choir, or treasury during free entry period), detailed but dry audioguide-€4.

Hours: Mon-Sat 8:30-19:00, Sun 8:30-11:30 & 15:00-19:00; Nov-Feb closes daily at 18:00; Christian altar accessible only after 11:00 unless you attend Mass; usually less crowded after 15:00. During religious holidays, particularly Holy Week, the Mezquita may close to sightseers at certain times of day—check the online events calendar before you go. You can also enjoy the Mezquita on a sound-and-light tour on most summer evenings (described under "Entertainment in Córdoba," later).

Information: +34 957 470 512, www.mezquita-catedraldecordoba.es.

Bell Tower Climb: €2, limited to 20 people every half-hour, daily 9:30-18:30, until 17:30 in winter. Reserve a time for your climb when you buy your ticket. Inside you'll see a few remnants of the original minaret that became the base structure for the bell tower, and as you climb, you'll have progressively better views of the mosque-cathedral and the city itself.

Planning Your Visit: Usually one hour is enough to visit the interior of the Mezquita. If you plan to climb the bell tower, save it for last.

◑ Self-Guided Tour

Before entering the patio, take in the exterior of the Mezquita. The mosque's massive footprint is clear when you survey its sprawling walls from outside. At 600 feet by 400 feet, it dominates the higgledy-piggledy medieval town that surrounds it.

❶ Patio de los Naranjos

The Mezquita's big, welcoming courtyard is free to enter. When this was a mosque, the Muslim faithful would gather in this courtyard to perform ablution—ritual washing before prayer, as directed by Muslim law. The courtyard walls display many of the former mosque's carved and painted ceiling panels and beams, which date from the 10th century. The rows of orange trees were added as a continuation of the columns in the prayer hall.

❷ Bell Tower/Minaret

Gaze up through the trees for views of the bell tower (c. 1600), built over the remains of the original Muslim minaret. For four centuries, five times a day, a singing cleric (the muezzin) would ride a donkey up the ramp of the minaret, then call to all Muslims in earshot that it was time to face Mecca and pray.

• *Buy your ticket (and, if you wish, rent an audioguide at a separate kiosk to the right). During regular hours, enter the building by passing through the keyhole gate at the far-right corner (pick up an English map-brochure as you enter). During the free entry period, enter through the Puerta de las Palmas.*

❸ Entrance

Walking into the former mosque from the patio, you pass from an orchard of orange trees into a forest of delicate columns (erected here in the eighth century). The more than 800 red-and-blue columns are topped with double arches—a round Romanesque arch above a Visigothic horse-shoe arch—made from alternating red brick and white stone. The columns and capitals (built of marble, granite, and alabaster) were recycled from ancient Roman ruins and conquered Visigothic churches. (Golden Age Arabs excelled at absorbing both the technology and the building materials of the peoples they conquered—no surprise, considering the culture's nomadic roots.) The columns seem to recede to infinity, as if reflecting the immensity and complexity of Allah's creation.

Although it's a vast room, the low ceilings and dense columns create an intimate and reverent atmosphere. The original mosque was brighter, before Christians renovated the place for their use and closed in the arched entrances from the patio and street. The giant cathedral sits in the center of the mosque. We'll visit it after exploring the mosque.

• *From either entrance, count five columns into the building and look for two small walls. Between them, find a glass floor covering a section of mosaic floor below. Look in.*

❹ Visigothic Mosaic

The mosque stands on the site of the early-Christian Church of San Vicente, built during the Visigothic period (sixth century). Peering down, you can see a mosaic that remains from that original church. This is important to Catholic locals, as it proves there was a church here before the mosque—thereby giving credence to those who see the modern-day church on this spot as a return to the site's original purpose, rather than a violation of the mosque.

• *Continue ahead to the wall opposite the entrance, where you'll find more...*

❺ Visigothic Ruins

On display in the corner are rare bits of carved stone from that same sixth-century church. (Most other stonework here had been scrubbed of its Christian symbolism by Muslims seeking to reuse them for the mosque.) Prince Abd al-Rahman bought the church from his Christian subjects before leveling it to build his mosque. From here, pan to the right to take in the sheer vastness of the mosque. (A hidden WC and drinking fountain are in the corner.)

• *Walk to your left until you come to the mosque's focal point, the...*

❻ Mihrab

The equivalent of a church's high altar, this was the focus of the mosque and remains a highlight of the Mezquita today. Picture the original mosque at prayer time, with a dirt floor covered by a patchwork of big carpets. More than 20,000 people could pray at once here. Imagine the multitude kneeling in prayer, facing the mihrab, rocking forward to touch their heads to the ground, and saying, *"Allahu Akbar, la ilaha illa Allah, Muhammad rasul Allah"*—"Allah is great, there is no God but Allah, and Muhammad is his prophet."

The mihrab, a feature in all mosques, is a decorated niche—in this case, more like a small room with a golden-arch entrance. During a service, the imam (prayer leader) would stand here to read scripture and give sermons. He spoke loudly into the niche, his back to the assembled crowd, and the architecture worked to amplify his voice so all could hear. Built in the mid-10th century by al-Hakam II, the exquisite room reflects the wealth of Córdoba in its prime. Three thousand pounds of shimmering multicolored glass-and-enamel cubes panel the walls and domes in mosaics designed by Byzantine craftsmen, depicting flowers and quotes from the Quran. Gape up.

Islamic Córdoba (756-1236): Medieval Europe's Cultural Capital

After political rivals slaughtered his family in 750, the 20-year-old Umayyad prince Abd al-Rahman fled the royal palace at Damascus, headed west across North Africa, and went undercover among the Berber tribesmen of Morocco. For six years he avoided assassination while building a power base amongst his fellow Arab expatriates and the local Muslim Berbers. As an heir to the title of "caliph" (a civil and religious leader), he sailed north and claimed Moorish Spain as his own, exerting his power by decapitating his enemies and sending their salted heads to the rival caliph in Baghdad. This split in Islam was somewhat like the papal schism that stirred up medieval Christian Europe, when the Church split into factions over who was the rightful pope.

Thus began an Islamic flowering in southern Spain under the Umayyads. They dominated Sevilla and Granada, ruling the independent state of "al-Andalus," with their capital at Córdoba.

By the year 950—when the rest of Europe was mired in poverty, ignorance, and superstition—Córdoba was Europe's greatest city, rivaling Constantinople and Baghdad. It had well over 100,000 people (Paris had a third that many), with hundreds of mosques, palaces, and public baths. The streets were paved and lit at night with oil lamps, and running water was piped in from the outskirts of the city. Medieval visitors marveled at the size and luxury of its mosque (the Mezquita), a symbol that the Umayyads of Spain were the equals of the caliphs of Baghdad.

This Golden Age was marked by a remarkable spirit of tolerance and cooperation in this region among the three great monotheistic religions: Islam, Judaism, and Christianity. As a proudly Andalusian guide once explained to me, "Umayyad al-Andalus was not one country with three cultures. It was one culture with

Overhead rises a colorful, starry dome with skylights and interlocking lobe-shaped arches.

• *Now turn around so that you're facing away from the mihrab. Ahead of you, and a bit to the left, is a roped-off open area. Gaze into the first chapel built within the mosque after the Christian Reconquista.*

❼ Villaviciosa Chapel

In 1236, Saint-King Ferdinand III conquered the city and turned the mosque into a church. The higher ceiling allowed for clerestory windows and more light, which were key to making it feel more church-like. Still, the locals continued to

three religions...its people shared the same food, dress, art, music, and language. Different religious rituals within the community were practiced in private. But clearly, Muslims ruled. No church spire could be taller than a minaret, and while the call to prayer rang out five times daily, there was no ringing of church bells."

The university rang with voices in Arabic, Hebrew, and Latin, sharing their knowledge of medicine, law, literature, and *al-jibra*. The city fell under the enlightened spell of the ancient Greeks, and Córdoba's 70 libraries bulged with translated manuscripts of Plato and Aristotle, works that would later inspire medieval Christians.

Ruling over the Golden Age were two energetic leaders—Abd al-Rahman III (912-961) and al-Hakam II (961-976)—who conquered territory, expanded the Mezquita, and boldly proclaimed themselves caliphs.

Córdoba's Y1K crisis brought civil wars that toppled the caliph (1031), splintering al-Andalus into several kingdoms. Córdoba came under the control of the Almoravids (Berbers from North Africa), who were less sophisticated than the Arab-based Umayyads. Then a wave of even stricter Islam swept through Spain, bringing the Almohads to power (1147) and driving Córdoba's best and brightest into exile. The city's glory days were over, and Sevilla and Granada replaced Córdoba as the center of Iberian Islam. On June 29, 1236, Christians conquered the city. That morning Muslims said their last prayers in the great mosque. That afternoon, the Christians set up their portable road altar and celebrated the church's first Mass. Córdoba's days as a political and cultural superpower were over.

CÓRDOBA

call it "la Mezquita," and left the structure virtually unchanged (70 percent of the original mosque structure survives to this day). Sixteen columns were removed and replaced by Gothic arches to make this first chapel. It feels as if the church architects appreciated the opportunity to incorporate the sublime architecture of the preexisting mosque into their church. Notice how the floor was once almost entirely covered with the tombs of nobles and big shots eager to make this their final resting place.

• *Immediately to your right (as you face the main entrance of the Mezquita), you'll see the...*

❽ Royal Chapel

The chapel—designed for the tombs of two Christian kings of Castile, Fernando IV and Alfonso XI—is completely closed off. Peek through the windows here or wander to the right side for the best views. While it was never open to the public, the tall, well-preserved Mudejar walls and dome are easily visible. Notice the elaborate stucco and tile work. The lavish Arabic-style decor dates from the 1370s, done by Muslim artisans after the Reconquista of the city. The floor is above your head to accommodate tombs buried beneath it. The fact that a Christian king chose to be buried in a tomb so clearly Moorish in design indicates the mutual respect between the cultures (before the Inquisition changed all that). The remains of both Castilian kings were moved to another Córdoba church in the 1700s, so it remains a mystery why this chapel is still closed to visitors.

• *Return to the mihrab, then go through the big, pink marble door to your immediate left, which leads into the Baroque...*

❾ Treasury (Tesoro)

The treasury is filled with display cases of religious artifacts and the enormous monstrance that is paraded through the streets of Córdoba each Corpus Christi, 60 days after Easter (notice the handles).

The monstrance was an attempt by 16th-century Christians to create something exquisite enough to merit being the holder of the Holy Communion wafer. As they believed the wafer actually was the body of Christ, this trumped any relics. The monstrance is designed to direct your gaze to heaven. While the bottom is silver-plated 18th-century Baroque, the top is late Gothic—solid silver with gold plating courtesy of 16th-century conquistadors. Gaze up at an equally spectacular ceiling.

The big canvas nearest the entrance shows Saint-King Ferdinand III, who conquered Córdoba in 1236, accepting the keys to the city's fortified gate from the vanquished Muslims. The victory ended a six-month siege and resulted in a negotiated settlement: The losers' lives were spared, providing they evacuated. Most went to Granada, which remained Muslim for another 250 years. The same day, the Spaniards celebrated Mass in a makeshift chapel right here in the great mosque.

The black-and-white marble tomb at the entrance opposite Ferdinand III belongs to Fray Pedro de Salazar y Toledo. After studies in Salamanca, Salazar had the honor of being the main preacher to two Spanish kings, Philip IV and Charles II. In 1686, he was named cardinal by Pope Innocent XI, but his local claim to fame is as founder of one of the first public hospitals in Córdoba, in use today as the School of Philosophy for the local university.

Among the other Catholic treasures, don't miss the ivory crucifix (next room, body carved from one tusk, arms carefully fitted on) from 1665. Get close to study Jesus' mouth—it's incredibly realistic. The artist? No one knows.

• *Just outside the treasury exit, a glass case holds casts that show many...*

⑩ Stonemason Marks

These casts bear the marks and signatures left by those who cut them to build the original Visigothic church and later, the mosque. Try to locate the actual ones on nearby columns. (I went five for six.) This part of the mosque has the best light for photography, thanks to skylights put in by 18th-century Christians.

The mosque grew over several centuries under a series of rulers. Remarkably, each ruler kept to the original vision—rows and rows of multicolored columns topped by double arches. Then came the Christians.

⑪ Chapel of the Conversion of St. Paul

Sharing a back wall with the Royal Chapel, the church ceded this space for the burial of Pedro Muñiz de Godoy—Grand Master of the Order of Santiago who fought several battles for Castile against the Portuguese in the 1300s. Godoy's descendants recently spent a fortune to painstakingly clean and restore the chapel, which drips with gold and 17th-century sculpture. The chapel is likely by the same architect as the choir you are about to see.

• *Find the towering church in the center of the mosque and step in.*

⑫ Altar

Rising up in the middle of the forest of columns is the bright, restored cathedral, oriented with its altar at the east end, per Christian tradition. Gazing up at the rich, golden decoration, it's easy to forget that you were in a former mosque just seconds ago. While the mosque is about 30 feet high, the cathedral's space soars 130 feet up. Look at the glorious ceiling.

In 1523 Córdoba's bishop proposed building this grand church in the Mezquita's center. The town council opposed it, but Charles V (called Charles I in Spain) ordered it done. If that seems like a travesty to you, consider what some locals will point out: Though it would have been quicker and less expensive for the Christian builders to destroy the mosque entirely, they respected its beauty and built their church into it instead.

As you take in the styles of these two great places of worship, ponder how they reflect the differences between Catholic and Islamic aesthetics and psychology: horizontal versus vertical, intimate versus powerful, fear-inspiring versus loving, dark versus bright, simple versus elaborate, feeling close to God versus feeling small before God.

The basic structure is late Gothic, with fancy Isabelline-style columns. The nave's towering Renaissance arches and dome emphasize the triumph of Christianity over Islam in Córdoba. The twin pulpits feature a marble bull, eagle, angel, and lion—symbols of the four evangelists. The modern *cátedra* (the seat of the bishop) is made of Carrara marble.

While churches and mosques normally both face east (to Jerusalem or Mecca), this space holds worship areas aimed 90 degrees from each other, since the mihrab faces south. Perhaps it's because from here you have to travel south (via Gibraltar) to get to Mecca. Or maybe it's because this mosque was designed by the Umayyad branch of Islam, whose ancestral home was Damascus—from where Mecca lies to the south.

• *Facing the high altar is a big, finely decorated wooden enclosure.*

⓭ Choir

The Baroque-era choir stalls were added much later—made in 1750 of New World mahogany. While cluttering up a previously open Gothic space, the choir is considered one of the masterpieces of 18th-century Andalusian Baroque. Each of the 109 stalls (108 plus the throne of the bishop) features a scene from the Bible: Mary's life on one side facing Jesus' life on the other. The lower chairs feature carved reliefs of the 49 martyrs of Córdoba (from Roman, Visigothic, and Moorish times), each with a palm frond symbolizing martyrdom and the scene of their death in the background.

The medieval church strayed from the inclusiveness taught by Jesus: choirs (which were standard throughout Spain) were for clerics (canons, priests, and the bishop). The pews in the nave were for nobles. And the peasants listened in from outside. (Lay people didn't understand what they were hearing anyway, as Mass was held in Latin until the 1960s.) Those days are long over. Today, a public Mass is said—in Spanish—right here most mornings (Mon-Sat at 9:30, Sun at 12:00 and 13:30).

• *Before leaving, walk to the back of the altar to admire the* ⓮ *Gothic vaulting mingled with Moorish arches—a combination found nowhere else in the world.*

NEAR THE MEZQUITA

These sights are all within a few minutes' walk of the Mezquita.

On and near the River

Just downhill from the Mezquita is the Guadalquivir River, which flows on to Sevilla and eventually out to the Atlantic. While silted up today, it was once navigable from here. The town now seems to turn its back

on the Guadalquivir, but the arch next to the Roman Bridge (with its ancient foundation surviving) and the fortified gate on the far bank (now housing a museum, described later) evoke a day when the river was key to the city's existence.

Triumphal Arch and Plague Monument

The unfinished Renaissance arch was designed to give King Philip II a royal welcome, but he arrived before its completion—so the job was canceled. ("Very Andalusian," according to a local friend.) The adjacent monument with the single column is an 18th-century plague monument dedicated to St. Raphael (who was in charge of protecting the region's population from its main scourges: plague, hunger, and floods).

Roman Bridge

The ancient bridge sits on its first-century-AD foundations and retains its 16th-century arches. It was the first bridge built over this river and established Córdoba as a strategic place. As European bridges go, it's a poor stepchild (its pedestrian walkway was unimaginatively redone in 2009), but Cordovans still stroll here nightly. Walk across the bridge for a fine view of the city—especially the huge mosque with its cathedral busting through the center. You'll be steps away from the museum described next.

▲Museum of al-Andalus Life and Calahorra Tower (Museo Vivo de al-Andalus)

This museum fills the fortified gate (built in the 14th century to protect the Christian city) at the far side of the Roman Bridge. Its worthy mission—to explain the thriving Muslim Moorish culture of 9th- to 12th-century Córdoba and al-Andalus—is undermined by its obligatory but clumsy audioguide system. You'll don a headset and wander through simple displays as the gauzy commentary lets you sit at the feet of the great poets and poke into Moorish living rooms. The scale models of the Alhambra and the Mezquita are fun, as are the dollhouse tableaus showing life in the market, mosque, university, and baths. It's worth the climb up to the rooftop terrace for the best panoramic view of Córdoba.

Cost and Hours: €4.50, includes one-hour audio tour; daily 10:00-14:00 & 16:30-20:30, Oct-April 10:00-18:00; Torre de la Calahorra, +34 957 293 929, www.torrecalahorra.es.

Jewish Córdoba

Córdoba's Jewish Quarter dates from the late Middle Ages, after Muslim rule and during the Christian era. These days, little evidence of that time remains. For a sense of the neighborhood in its thriving heyday, first visit the Casa de Sefarad, then the synagogue located a few steps away. For a pretty picture, find **Calleja de**

CÓRDOBA

Córdoba's Jewish Quarter: A 10-Point Scavenger Hunt

Whereas most of the area around the Mezquita is commercial and touristy, the neighborhood to the east seems somehow almost untouched by tourism and the modern world (as you leave the Mezquita, turn right and exit the orange-grove patio, then wander into the lanes immediately behind Hotel Mezquita). To catch a whiff of Córdoba as it was before the onslaught of tourism and the affluence of the 21st century, explore this district. Just meander and observe. Here are a few characteristics to look for:

1. **Narrow streets.** Skinny streets make sense in hot climates, as they provide much-appreciated shade. The ones in this area are remnants from the old Moorish bazaar, crammed in to fit within the protective city walls.

2. **Thick, whitewashed walls.** Both features serve as a kind of natural air-conditioning—and the chalk ingredient in the whitewash "bugs" bugs.

3. **Colorful doors and windows.** In this famously white city, what little color there is—mostly added in modern times—helps counter the boring whitewash.

4. **Iron grilles.** Historically, these were more artistic, but modern ones are more practical. Their continued presence is a reminder of the persistent gap through the ages between rich and poor. The wooden latticework covering many windows is a holdover from days when women, held to extreme standards of modesty, wanted to be able to see out while still keeping their privacy.

5. **Stone bumpers on corners.** These protected buildings against reckless drivers. Scavenged secondhand ancient Roman pillars worked well.

6. **Scuff guards.** Made of harder materials, these guards sit at the base of the whitewashed walls—and, from the looks of it, are serving their purpose.

7. **Riverstone cobbles.** These stones were cheap and local, and provided drains down the middle of a lane. They were flanked by smooth stones that stayed dry for walking (and now aid the rolling suitcases of modern-day tourists).

8. **Pretty patios.** Cordovans are proud of their patios. Walk up to the inner iron gates of the wide-open front doors and peek in (see "Patios" sidebar, later).

9. **Remnants of old towers from minarets.** Muslim Córdoba peaked in the 10th century with an estimated 600,000 people, which meant lots of neighborhood mosques.

10. **A real neighborhood.** People really live here. There are no tacky shops, and just about the only tourist is...you.

las Flores (a.k.a. "Blossom Lane"). This narrow flower-bedecked street frames the cathedral's bell tower as it hovers in the distance (the view is a favorite for local guidebook covers).

Casa de Sefarad

Set inside a restored 14th-century home directly across from the synagogue, this museum brings to life Córdoba's rich Jewish past. Exhibits in the rooms around a central patio recount Spanish Jewish history, focusing on themes such as domestic life, Jewish celebrations and holidays, and Sephardic musical traditions. Upstairs is an interpretive exhibit about the synagogue, along with rooms dedicated to the philosopher Maimonides and the Inquisition. Along with running this small museum, the Casa de Sefarad is a cultural center for Sephardic Jewish heritage (Sephardic Jews are those from Spain or Portugal). They teach courses, offer a library, and promote an appreciation of Córdoba's Jewish past.

Cost and Hours: €4, daily 10:00-19:00, opens and closes one hour later in winter, 30-minute guided tours in English by request if guide is available, across from synagogue at corner of Calle de los Judíos and Calle Averroes, +34 957 421 404, www.casadesefarad. es.

Concerts: The Casa de Sefarad hosts occasional concerts—acoustic, Sephardic, Andalusian, and flamenco—on its patio (€15, usually at 19:00, confirm schedule).

Synagogue (Sinagoga)

This small yet beautifully preserved synagogue was built between 1314 and 1315 and was in use right up until the final expulsion of the Jews from Spain in 1492.

Cost and Hours: Free, Tue-Sat 9:00-21:00, Sun and summers until 15:00, closed Mon year-round; Calle de los Judíos 20, +34 957 202 928, www.turismodecordoba.org/synagogue.

Visiting the Synagogue: The synagogue was built by Mudejar craftsmen during a period of religious tolerance after the Christian Reconquista of Córdoba (1236). During Muslim times, Córdoba's sizable Jewish community was welcomed in the city, though its members paid substantial taxes—money that enlarged the Mezquita and generated goodwill. That goodwill came in handy when Córdoba's era of prosperity and mutual respect ended with the arrival of the intolerant Almohad Berbers. Christians and Jews were repressed, and brilliant minds—such as the phi-

losopher Maimonides, whose statue sits nearby—fled for their own safety.

Its relatively small dimensions lead historians to believe this was a private or family synagogue. It's one of only three medieval synagogues that still stand in Spain (and the only one in Andalucía). That it survived at all is due to its having been successively converted into a church (look for the cross painted into a niche), a hospital, and a shoemakers' guild. The building's original purpose was only rediscovered in the late 19th century.

Rich Mudejar decorations of intertwined flowers and arabesques plaster the walls. The inscriptions in the main room are nearly all from the Bible's Book of Psalms (in Hebrew, with translations posted on each wall). On the east wall (the symbolic direction of Jerusalem), find the niche for the Ark, which held the scrolls of the Torah (the Jewish scriptures). The upstairs gallery was reserved for women.

Artisan Market (Zoco Municipal)

This charming series of courtyards off Calle de los Judíos was the first craft market in Spain. More than a dozen studios cluster around the pretty patios, where artists work in leather, glass, textiles, mosaics, and pottery. Their products—tiles, notecards, jewelry, leather bracelets, and bags—are sold in the associated retail shop.

Cost and Hours: Free to enter, daily 10:00-20:00, Calle de los Judíos s/n, +34 957 204 033, www.artesaniadecordoba.com.

City Walls

Built upon the foundation of Córdoba's Roman walls, these fortifications date mostly from the 12th century. While the city stretched beyond the walls in Moorish times, these fortifications protected its political, religious, and commercial center. Of the seven original gates, the Puerta de Almodóvar (near the synagogue) is best-preserved today. Along this wall, you'll find statues honoring Córdoba's great thinkers.

Statues of Seneca, Maimonides, and Averroes

Among Córdoba's deepest-thinking residents were a Roman philosopher forced to commit suicide, and a Jew and a Muslim who were both driven out during the wave of intolerance after the fall of the Umayyad caliphate. (Seneca is right outside the Puerta de Almodóvar; Maimonides is 30 yards downhill from the synagogue; Averroes is outside the old wall, where Cairuán and Doctor Fleming streets meet.)

Lucius Annaeus Seneca the Younger (c. 3 BC-AD 65) was born into a wealthy Cordovan family, but was drawn to Rome early in life. He received schooling in Stoicism and made a name for himself in oration, writing, law, and politics. Exiled to Corsica by Emperor Claudius, a remarkable reversal brought him into the role of trusted advisor to Emperor Nero, but eventually Nero accused Seneca of plotting against him and demanded Seneca kill himself. In true Stoic fashion, Seneca complied with this request in AD 65, leaving behind a written legacy that includes nine plays, hundreds of essays, and numerous philosophical works that influenced the likes of Calvin, Montaigne, and Rousseau.

Moses Maimonides (1135-1204), "the Jewish Aquinas," was born in Córdoba and raised on both Jewish scripture and the philosophy of Aristotle. Like many tolerant Cordovans, he saw no conflict between the two. An influential Talmudic scholar, astronomer, and medical doctor, Maimonides left his biggest mark as the author of *The Guide for the Perplexed*, in which he asserted that secular knowledge and religious faith could

go hand-in-hand (thereby inspiring the philosophy of St. Thomas Aquinas). In 1148, Córdoba was transformed when the fundamentalist Almohads assumed power, and young Maimonides and his family were driven out. Today tourists, Jewish scholars, and fans of Aquinas rub the statue's foot in the hope that some of Maimonides' genius and wisdom will rub off on them.

The story of **Averroes** (1126-1198) is a near match of Maimonides', except that Averroes was a Muslim lawyer, not a Jewish physician. He became the medieval world's number-one authority on Aristotle, also influencing Aquinas. Averroes' biting tract *The Incoherence of the Incoherence* attacked narrow-mindedness, asserting that secular philosophy (for the elite) and religious faith (for the masses) both led to truth. The Almohads banished him from the city and burned his books, ending four centuries of Cordovan enlightenment.

Bullfighting Museum (Museo Taurino Córdoba)

This museum, in a beautiful old palatial home of brick arcades and patios, examines Córdoba's bullfighting tradition. The introductory video provides a romanticized rundown of the sport (ask for the English version). Displays explore the landscape where bulls are bred and raised, and pay tribute to great bullfighters of the past (and their remarkably tiny waistlines) and to the tempo and aesthetics of the bullfight. It's high-tech, spacious, and merits a visit if you're interested in learning about an important local tradition. But if you've already seen the bullfight museums in Ronda or Sevilla, give this one a pass.

Cost and Hours: €4; Tue-Fri 8:30-20:45, Sat until 16:30, Sun until 14:30, shorter hours in summer, closed Mon year-round; Plaza de Maimonides s/n, +34 957 201 056, www.museotaurinodecordoba.es.

Alcázar (Alcázar de los Reyes Cristianos)

Tourists line up to visit Córdoba's overrated fortress, the "Castle of the Christian Monarchs," which sits strategically next to the Guadalquivir River. (I think they confuse it with the much more worthy Alcázar in Sevilla.) Upon entering, look to the right to see a big, beautiful garden rich with flowers and fountains. To the left is a modern-feeling, unimpressive fort. While it was built along the Roman walls in Visigothic times, constant reuse and recycling has left it sparse and barren (with the exception of a few interesting Roman mosaics on the walls). Crowds squeeze up and down the congested spiral staircases of "Las Torres" for meager views. Ferdinand and Isabel donated the castle to the Inquisition in 1482, and it became central to the church's effort to discover "false converts to Christianity"—mostly Jews who had decided not to flee Spain in 1492.

Cost and Hours: €4.50; Tue-Fri 8:30-20:45, Sat until 16:30, Sun until 14:30, shorter hours in summer, closed Mon year-round; +34 957 420 151. On Fridays and Saturdays, you're likely to see people celebrating civil weddings here.

Baths of the Caliphate Alcázar (Baños del Alcázar Califal)

The scant but evocative remains of these 10th-century royal baths are all that's left from the caliph's palace complex. They date from a time when the city had hundreds of baths to serve a population of several hundred thousand. The exhibit teaches about Arabic baths in general and the caliph's in particular. A 10-minute video (normally in Spanish, English on request) tells the story well.

Cost and Hours: €2.50, open same hours as Alcázar, on Plaza Campo de los Santos Mártires, just outside the wall—near the Alcázar, mobile +34 608 158 893.

AWAY FROM THE MEZQUITA
Plaza de las Tendillas

While most tourists leave Córdoba having seen only the Mezquita and the cute medieval quarter that surrounds it, the modern city offers a good peek at urban Andalucía. For the best glimpse of this area, browse Plaza de las Tendillas and the surrounding streets. The square, with an Art Deco charm, mixes slice-of-life scenes and touristic eateries. On the hour, a clock here chimes the chords of flamenco guitarist Juan Serrano—a Cordovan classic since 1961.

Characteristic cafés and shops abound. For example, **$ Café La Gloria,** proudly run by Rocío, provides an earthy Art Nouveau experience. Located just down the street from Plaza de las Tendillas, it has an unassuming entrance, but a sumptuous interior. Carved floral designs wind around the bar, mixing with *feria* posters and bullfighting memories. Pop in for a beer or coffee with the locals (daily 8:00-24:00, quiet after lunch crowd clears out, Calle Claudio Marcelo 15—for location see "Hotels & Restaurants in Central Córdoba" map, later, +34 957 477 780).

Roman Temple (Templo Romano)

The remains of this first-century Roman temple, a few minutes' walk from Plaza de las Tendillas, were discovered in the 1950s during a remodeling of City Hall. Today, you can stroll by the site for a free view of the towering columns and base of what was a massive temple in its day. It's particularly striking at night when illuminated (Calle Capitulares).

▲Museo Julio Romero de Torres

A city rich in mystical monuments and colorful patios, Córdoba has produced several fine artists during its long history. Well-to-do Julio Romero de Torres began painting at the age of 10 in 1884, under the tutelage of his father who was also a painter and director of the city's fine-arts museum. Early works resembled those of fellow Impressionists like Joaquín Sorolla, but in the 1920s, inspired by his passion for (or obsession with) flamenco, Julio developed a distinct style. He crafted soulful portraits of the dreamy-eyed, melancholic gaze of the women he loved to paint. After he died in 1930, his family donated many works to the city government and this museum opened one year later. Stroll through six small rooms and discover the sumptuous spirit of Córdoba through this captivating artist's eyes.

Cost and Hours: €4.50; Tue-Fri 8:30-19:30, Sat until 16:30, Sun until 14:30, shorter hours in summer, closed Mon year-round; Plaza del Potro 1, +34 957 470 356, www.museojulioromero.cordoba.es.

Palacio de Viana

Decidedly off the beaten path, this former palatial estate is a 25-minute walk northeast from the cluster of sights near the Mezquita. The complex's many renovations over its 500-year history are a case study in changing tastes. A guided tour whisks you through each room of an

Patios

In Córdoba, patios are taken seriously—even to the point of competition. In the first half of every May, the city hosts a fiercely fought contest, the Concurso Popular de Patios Cordobeses, to pick the city's most picturesque.

Patios, a common feature of houses throughout Andalucía, have a long history here. The Romans used them to cool off, and the Moors added lush, decorative touches. The patio functioned as a quiet outdoor living room, an oasis from the heat. Inside elaborate ironwork gates, roses, geraniums, and jasmine spill down whitewashed walls, while fountains play and caged birds sing. Some patios are owned by individuals, some are communal courtyards for several homes, and some grace public buildings like museums or convents.

Today homeowners take pride in these mini paradises, and have no problem sharing them with tourists. Keep an eye out for square metal signs that indicate historic homes. As you wander Córdoba's back streets, pop your head into any wooden door that's open. The proud owners (who keep inner gates locked) enjoy showing off their picture-perfect patios.

A concentration of patio-contest award-winners runs along Calle de San Basilio and Calle Martín Roa, just across from the Alcázar gardens. Seven of these winners have banded together to open their patios to the public for a single entry fee (€10; Mon and Wed-Sat 10:00-14:00 & 17:00-20:00, Sun 10:00-14:00, patios closed Tue; get tickets at office on Calle de San Basilio 14, mobile +34 654 530 377, www.patiosdesanbasilio.com). Many other nearby patios are free to visit.

exuberant 16th-century estate, while an English handout trudges through the dates and origin of each important piece. But the house is best enjoyed by ignoring the guide and gasping at the massive collection of—for lack of a better word—stuff. Decorative-art fans will have a field day. If your interests run more to flowers, skip the house and buy a "patio" ticket: 12 connecting garden patios, each with a different theme, sprawl around and throughout the residence. It's no Alhambra, but if you won't see the gardens in Granada, these are a wee taste of the Andalusian style.

Cost and Hours: House-€10, patios only-€6; Tue-Sat 10:00-19:00, Sun until 15:00, shorter hours in summer, closed Mon year-round, last entry one hour before closing; Plaza Don Gome 2—for location see "Córdoba" map on page 155, +34 957 496 741, www.palaciodeviana.com.

NEAR CÓRDOBA
Madinat al-Zahra (Medina Azahara)

Five miles northwest of Córdoba, this once-fabulous palace of the caliph was completely forgotten until excavations of its ruins began in the early 20th century.

Extensively planned, with an orderly design, Madinat al-Zahra was meant to symbolize and project a new discipline on an increasingly unstable Moorish empire in Spain. It failed. Only 75 years later, the city was looted and destroyed. Today, the site is mostly underwhelming—a jigsaw puzzle waiting to be reassembled by patient archaeologists. Check at the TI before committing to a trip, as the most interesting sections of the site may be closed for restoration.

Cost and Hours: €1.50; April-mid-June Tue-Thu 9:00-19:00, Fri-Sat until 22:00; mid-June-mid-Sept Tue-Sat 9:00-15:00 & 19:00-24:00; off-season Tue-Sat 9:00-18:00; Sun 9:00-15:00 and closed Mon year-round; +34 957 104 933, www.museosdeandalucia.es.

Getting There: Madinat al-Zahra is located on a back road five miles from Córdoba. By **car,** head to Avenida de Medina Azahara (one block south of the train station), following signs for *A-431;* the site is well-signed from the highway. The TI runs a **shuttle bus** that leaves several times a day and returns 2.5 hours later (€9, buy ticket at any TI; runs year-round Tue-Sat at 10:15, 11:00, and 15:00 plus extra Sat bus at 13:45, Sun at 10:15, 11:00, and 11:45; confirm current bus schedule at TI, informative English booklet). Catch the shuttle on Paseo de la Victoria at either of two stops shared with the Bus Turístico route (see the "Central Córdoba" map, earlier). You can also take a **taxi**—your driver will wait for three hours as you explore the site, then drive you back into town. Have your hotel call to reserve (Radio Taxi Córdoba, €30 for up to 4 people, +34 957 764 444).

Visiting Madinat al-Zahra: Built in AD 929 as a power center to replace Córdoba, Madinat al-Zahra was both a palace and an entirely new capital city—the "City of the Flower"—covering nearly half a square mile (only about 10 percent has been uncovered).

Excavations of the upper terrace have uncovered stables

and servants' quarters. Farther downhill, the house of a
high-ranking official has been
partially reconstructed. At the
lowest level, you'll come to the
remains of the mosque—placed
at a diagonal, facing true east.
The highlight of the visit is an
elaborate reconstruction of the
caliph's throne room, captur-
ing a moody world of horseshoe

arches and delicate stucco. Legendary accounts say the palace
featured waterfall walls, lions in cages, and—in the center of the
throne room—a basin filled with mercury, reflecting the colorful
walls. The effect likely humbled anyone fortunate enough to see
the caliph.

Entertainment in Córdoba

Caballerizas Reales de Córdoba

This equestrian show at the royal stables (just beyond the Alcázar)
combines an artful demonstration of different riding styles with
flamenco dance. If you're not going to Jerez to see the show at the
Royal Andalusian School of Equestrian Art, this is a fun and convenient alternative (€16.50; one-hour shows Wed-Sat at 21:00 or
21:30; mid-Sept-mid-April at 19:30, no shows Sun-Tue; outside in
summer, inside in winter, +34 957 497 843, www.cordobaecuestre.
com). During the day, you can tour the stables and vintage carriages (Mon 10:00-13:30, Tue-Sat 10:00-13:30 & 16:00-18:30,
Sun 10:00-13:00, longer hours in summer, Caballerizas Reales 1).

Flamenco

While flamenco is better in nearby Sevilla, you can see it in Córdoba, too. **Tablao Flamenco Cardenal** is the city's most popular
and awarded show, with 120 seats in a beautifully decorated private
patio. They also offer a preshow dinner with typical dishes from
Córdoba (€23, includes one drink, dinner for €11 extra, 1.5-hour
shows Mon-Thu at 20:15, Fri-Sat at 21:00, no shows Sun, confirm
schedule online, Buen Pastor 2—for location, see the "Hotels &
Restaurants in Central Córdoba" map, later, mobile +34 691 217
922, www.tablaocardenal.es).

El Alma de Córdoba

To experience "the soul of Córdoba"—or at least the Mezquita by
night—you can take this pricey one-hour audio tour, joining about
80 people to be shepherded around the complex listening via headset to an obviously Christian-produced sound-and-light show (€18,

March-Oct Mon-Sat, off-season Fri-Sat only, 1-2 shows a night, hours vary according to sunset; book at Mezquita or online; www.catedraldecordoba.es).

Sleeping in Córdoba

NEAR THE MEZQUITA

These are all within a five-minute stroll of the Mezquita.

$$$$ Balcón de Córdoba is an elegant little boutique hotel buried in the old town, just steps away from the Mezquita. With a compassionate staff, 10 stylish rooms, charming public spaces, plenty of attention to detail, and a magnificent rooftop terrace, it's a lot of luxury for the price. It feels both new and steeped in tradition. Look for the original architectural features of the 14th-century convent that once occupied this space. The restaurant serves wonderful cuisine, enhanced by evening views of the Mezquita from the terrace (includes breakfast, air-con, pay parking, restaurant open daily 13:00-15:00 & 19:00-23:00, Calle Encarnación 8, +34 957 498 478, www.balcondecordoba.com, reservas@balcondecordoba.com).

$$ La Llave de la Judería is a nine-room jewel box of an inn, featuring plush furniture, elegant and traditional decor, and attentive service. Quiet and romantic, it's tucked in the old quarter just far enough away from the tourist storm, yet still handy for sightseeing (terrace with Mezquita view, air-con, midway between Puerta de Almodóvar and the Mezquita at Calle Romero 38, +34 957 294 808, www.lallavedelajuderia.es, info@lallavedelajuderia.es). Charming Alberto and staff make you feel right at home.

$$ El Patio de la Costurera offers a uniquely Cordovan experience: sleeping in one of the city's prize-winning patios. Araceli and her sister rent four homey and colorful apartments, each with a kitchenette. While some noise might come from patio visitors during the day, the neighborhood is quiet at night and close to several recommended restaurants (air-con, Calle de San Basilio 40, mobile +34 654 530 377, www.elpatiodelacosturera.com, info@elpatiodelacosturera.com).

$$ Hotel Mezquita, just across from the Mezquita, rents 32 modern and comfortable rooms (10 with Mezquita views). The grand entrance lobby elegantly recycles an upper-class mansion (air-con, elevator, Plaza Santa Catalina 1, +34 957 475 585, www.hotelmezquita.comrecepcion@hotelmezquita.com).

$ Hotel Albucasis, at the edge of the tourist zone, features 15 basic, clean rooms, all of which face tranquil interior patios. The staff is friendly and accommodating, and the setting is cozy (air-con, elevator, pay parking, Buen Pastor 11, +34 957 478 625, www.hotelalbucasi.com, hotelalbucasis@hotmail.com).

$ Hotel González, with many of its 30 basic rooms facing a cool and peaceful patio, is humble but very sleepable. It's clean and well run, with a good location and price. Streetside rooms come with a bit of noise at night (air-con, elevator, Calle de los Manríquez 3, +34 957 479 819, www.hotelgonzalez.com, recepcion@hotelgonzalez.com).

¢ Al-Katre Backpacker is a fun 40-bed hostel run in a casual, homey way by three women. Its rooms (each with shared bathrooms) gather around a cool courtyard, and its terrace feels a world away (Calle Martínez Rucker 14, +34 957 487 539, www.alkatre.com, alkatre@alkatre.com).

IN THE MODERN CITY

While still within easy walking distance of the Mezquita, these places are outside of the main tourist zone—not buried in all that tangled medieval cuteness.

$$ Hotel Córdoba Centro sits at a good crossroads between the historic center around the Mezquita and the modern part of the city. Most of its 27 simple but comfortable rooms are interior, assuring a solid night's sleep, while nine rooms face the pedestrian street and coffee shop below (air-con, elevator, Jesús y María 8, +34 957 497 850, www.hotel-cordobacentro.es, reservas@hotel-cordobacentro.es).

$ Hotel Califa, a modern 65-room business-class hotel belonging to the NH chain, sits on a quiet street a block off busy Paseo Victoria, on the edge of the jumbled old quarter. Still close enough to the sights, it has a beautiful patio courtyard, and its slick, minimalist rooms can be a great value if you get a deal (air-con, elevator, pay parking, Lope de Hoces 14, +34 957 299 400, www.nh-hotels.com, nhcalifa@nh-hotels.com).

$ Hotel Boston, with 39 rooms, is a decent budget bet if you want a reliable, basic hotel away from the touristy Mezquita zone. It's a taste of workaday Córdoba (air-con, elevator, Calle Málaga 2, just off Plaza de las Tendillas, +34 957 474 176, www.hotel-boston.com, info@hotel-boston.com).

¢ Funky Córdoba Hostel rents 40 beds in a great neighborhood (private rooms available, air-con, terrace, kitchen, laundry facility, right by Plaza del Potro bus stop—take #3 from station—at Calle Lucano 12, +34 957 492 966, funkycordoba@funkyhostels.es).

Eating in Córdoba

Córdoba has a reputation among Spaniards as a great dining town, with options ranging from obvious touristy bars in the old center to enticing, locals-only hangouts a few blocks away. Specialties include *salmorejo*, Córdoba's version of gazpacho. It's creamier, with more bread and olive oil and generally served with pieces of ham and hard-boiled egg on top. Look for winners of the city's yearly oxtail stew *(rabo de toro)* contest and find your favorite. Most places serve white wines from the nearby Montilla-Moriles region; these *finos* are slightly less dry but more aromatic than the sherry produced in Jerez de la Frontera. Ask for a *fino fresquito* (chilled) and you'll fit right in.

NEAR THE MEZQUITA

Touristy options abound near the Mezquita. By walking a couple of blocks north or east of the Mezquita, you'll find plenty of cheap, accessible places offering a better value.

$$ Bodegas Mezquita is one of the touristy places, but it's easy and handy—a good bet for a bright, air-conditioned place near the mosque. They have a good *menú del día*, or you can order from their menu of tapas, half-*raciones*, and *raciones* (daily 12:30-23:30, one block above the Mezquita patio at Calle Céspedes 12, +34 957 490 004). They have another location also near the Mezquita, at Calle Corregidor Luis de la Cerda 73.

$ Bar Santos, facing the Mezquita, supplies the giant *tortilla de patatas* (potato omelette) that you see locals happily munching on the steps of the mosque. Their "fast" food is served to-go in disposable containers. A hearty tortilla and a beer make for a very cheap meal; add a *salmorejo* and it feels complete (daily 10:00-24:00, Calle Magistral González Francés 3, +34 957 893 220).

BARRIO SAN BASILIO

This delightful little quarter outside the town wall, just a couple of minutes' walk west of the Mezquita and behind the royal stables, is famous for its patios. It's traffic-free, quaint as can be, and feels perfectly Cordovan without the crush of tourists around the Mezquita.

$$ La Posada del Caballo Andaluz is a fresh, modern restaurant with tables delightfully scattered around a courtyard (no bar area). Enjoy tasty traditional Cordovan cuisine at great prices while sitting amid flowers and under the stars (daily 12:30-16:30 & 20:00-23:30, Calle de San Basilio 16, +34 957 290 374).

$$ Mesón San Basilio, just across the street, is the longtime neighborhood favorite, with no tourists and no pretense. Although there's no outside seating, it still offers a certain patio ambience, with a view of the kitchen action and lots of fish and meat dishes (classic fixed-priced meal, lunch special weekdays, Mon-Sat 13:00-16:00 & 20:00-24:00, Sun 20:00-24:00, Calle de San Basilio 19, +34 957 297 007).

$ Bodega San Basilio, around the corner, is rougher around the edges, serving rustic tapas and good meals to workaday crowds.

CÓRDOBA

Hotels & Restaurants in Central Córdoba

CÓRDOBA

Accommodations

1. Balcón de Córdoba
2. La Llave de la Judería
3. El Patio de la Costurera
4. Hotel Mezquita
5. Hotel Albucasis
6. Hotel González
7. Al-Katre Backpacker Hostel
8. Hotel Córdoba Centro
9. Hotel Califa
10. Hotel Boston
11. To Funky Córdoba Hostel

Eateries & Other

12. Bodegas Mezquita (2)
13. Bar Santos
14. La Posada del Caballo Andaluz
15. Mesón San Basilio
16. Bodega San Basilio
17. Taberna Restaurante Casa Rubio
18. Taberna Casa Salinas
19. Restaurante El Choto
20. El Churrasco Restaurante
21. Casa Mazal
22. Bodega Guzmán
23. To Bodegas Campos
24. Macsura Gastrotaberna
25. Taberna Salinas
26. To Taberna San Miguel (Casa el Pisto)
27. Taberna La Cazuela de la Espartería
28. La Llave
29. Tablao Flamenco Cardenal
30. Café La Gloria
31. Grocery (3)

To Train & Bus Stations

#3 & Madinat al-Zahra

Plaza de San Nicolás

Plaza Emilio Luque

C. CONDE

AV. DE LA REPÚBLICA ARGENTINA

200 Meters
200 Yards

Jardines de la Victoria

PASEO DE LA VICTORIA

CALLE DE EDUARDO DATO

CALLE PÉREZ DE CASTRO

DUQUE DE F. NÚÑEZ

C. SAN FELIPE

ARGOTE

C. SAN PEDRO

CALLE LOPE DE HOCES

Plaza de la Trinidad

JEWISH QUARTER

Plaza del Neyra

LEIVA

BUEN PASTOR

CALLE TEJÓN Y MARÍN

CALLE SÁNCHEZ DE FERIA

FERNÁNDEZ RUANO

To Madinat al-Zahra

PUERTA DE ALMODÓVAR GATE

C. ALMANZOR

CALLE JUDÍOS

SYNAGOGUE

CASA DE SEFARAD

SAL. ROMERO

BULLFIGHTING MUSEUM

AV. DEL DOCTOR FLEMING

Plaza Maim.

Plaza Judá Leví

CARD.

C. TOMÁS CONDE

MANRIQUE

AVENIDA DEL CONDE DE VALLELLANO

CALLE DOCTOR BARRAQUER

OLD WALL

AVERROES STATUE

AV. DE DR. FLEMING

Plaza Campo de los Santos Mártires

CALLE DE LAS CABALLERIZAS REALES

ROYAL STABLES

PATIOS AREA

CALLE DE SAN BASILIO

MARTÍN DE ROA

CALLE DE ENMEDIO

CALLE POSTRERA

ALCÁZAR

Alcázar Gardens

AVENIDA DEL

The bullfight decor gives the place a crusty character—and you won't find a word of English here (Wed-Mon 13:00-16:30 & 20:00-23:30, closed Tue, on the corner of Calle de Enmedio and small street leading to Calle de San Basilio at #29, +34 957 297 832).

Groceries: A **Super Alcoop** is at Calle Dr. Barraquer 12 (Mon-Fri 9:00-21:00, Sat until 14:00, closed Sun).

BETWEEN PUERTA DE ALMODÓVAR AND THE JEWISH QUARTER

The evocative Puerta de Almodóvar gate connects a parklike scene outside the wall with the delightfully jumbled Jewish Quarter just inside it, where cafés and restaurants take advantage of the neighborhood's pools, shady trees, and dramatic face of the wall. The first two recommendations are immediately inside the gate; the others are on or near Calle de los Judíos, which runs south from there.

$$ Taberna Restaurante Casa Rubio serves reliably good traditional dishes with smart, prompt service and several zones to choose from: a few sidewalk tables, with classic people-watching; inside, with a timeless interior and lively banter; or on the rooftop, with dressy white tablecloths and a view of the old wall (daily 13:00-16:00 & 19:30-23:00, Puerta de Almodóvar 5, +34 957 420 853).

$$ Taberna Casa Salinas, from the same people who run the highly recommended Taberna Salinas in the modern city, is a more basic place with a fine reputation for quality food at a good price (Thu-Tue 12:30-15:45 & 20:30-23:45 except closed Sun at lunch, closed all day Wed; near gate at Puerta de Almodóvar 2, +34 957 480 135).

$$$ Restaurante El Choto is a bright, formal, and dressy steak house buried deep in the Jewish Quarter. With a small leafy patio, it's touristy yet intimate, serving well-presented international dishes with an emphasis on grilled meat. The favorite is kid goat with garlic—*choto al ajillo* (Mon-Sat 12:30-24:00, Sun until 17:00, closed Mon in summer, reservations smart, Calle Almanzor 10, +34 957 760 115, www.restauranteelchotocordoba.es).

$$$ El Churrasco Restaurante is a charmingly old-fashioned place, where longtime patrons are greeted by name. The specialty is grilled meat and seafood, cooked simply and deliciously over oak-charcoal braziers in the open kitchen. It's a fun place for tapas in the bar or a meal under the glass roof of the dining room (daily 13:00-16:00 & 20:30-23:30, Calle Romero 16, +34 957 290 819).

$$ Casa Mazal, run by the nearby Casa de Sefarad Jewish cultural center, serves contemporary Jewish cuisine. Small dining rooms sprawl around the charming medieval courtyard of a former house. With a seasonal menu that includes several vegetarian options, it offers a welcome dose of variety from the typical Spanish standards (daily 12:00-16:00 & 19:00 until late, Calle Tomás Conde 3, +34 957 246 304).

$ Bodega Guzmán could hardly care less about attracting tourists. This bristly, dark holdover from a long-gone age proudly displays the heads of brave-but-unlucky bulls, while serving cold, very basic tapas to locals who burst into song when they feel the flamenco groove. Notice how everyone seems to be on a first-name basis with the waiters. It may feel like a drinks-only place, but they do serve rustic tapas and *raciones* (ask for the list in English). Choose a table or belly up to the bar and try a glass of local white wine, either dry *(blanco seco)* or sweet *(blanco dulce)*. If it's grape juice you want, ask for *mosto* (Fri-Wed 12:00-16:00 & 20:00-23:30, closed Thu, Calle de los Judíos 7, +34 957 290 960).

JUST EAST OF THE MEZQUITA ZONE

$$$ Bodegas Campos, my favorite place in town, is a historic and venerable eatery, attracting so many locals it comes with its own garage. It's worth the 10-minute walk from the tourist zone. They have a stuffy and expensive formal restaurant upstairs, but I'd eat in the more relaxed and affordable tavern on the ground floor. The service is great, portions are large, and the menu is inviting. Experiment—you can't go wrong. House specialties are bull-tail stew *(rabo de toro*—rich, tasty, and a good splurge) and anything with *pisto,* the local ratatouille-like vegetable stew. Don't leave without exploring the sprawling complex, which fills 14 old houses that have been connected to create a network of dining rooms and patios, small and large. The place is a virtual town history museum: Look for the wine barrels signed by celebrities and VIPs, the old refectory from a convent, and a huge collection of classic, original *feria* posters and great photos (daily 13:00-16:00 & 20:30-23:00; reservations smart, Calle de Lineros 32, +34 957 497 500, www.bodegascampos.com).

$$ Macsura Gastrotaberna serves beautifully presented international dishes for anyone who might need a break from *jamón*—think Asian-Spanish fusion. Choose between bright and white inside seating or watch the locals go by on a triangular patio outside (daily 11:30-23:30, Calle Cardenal González, +34 957 486 004).

IN THE MODERN CITY

These places are worth the 10- to 15-minute walk from the main tourist zone—walking here, you feel a world apart from the touristy scene. Combine a meal here with a paseo through the Plaza de las Tendillas area to get a good look at modern Córdoba. If Taberna

Salinas is full, as is likely, there are plenty of characteristic bars nearby in the lanes around Plaza de la Corredera.

$$ Taberna Salinas seems like a movie set designed to give you the classic Córdoba scene. Though all the seating is indoors, it's still pleasantly patio-esque and popular with locals for its traditional cuisine and exuberant bustle. The seating fills a big courtyard and sprawls through several smaller, semiprivate rooms. The fun menu features a slew of enticing *raciones* (spinach with chickpeas is a house specialty). Study what locals are eating before ordering. There's no drink menu—just beer, *fino,* or inexpensive wine. If there's a line (as there often is later in the evening), leave your name and throw yourself into the adjacent tapas-bar mosh pit for a drink (Mon-Sat 12:30-16:00 & 20:00-23:30, closed Sun and Aug; from Plaza de las Tendillas walk 3 blocks to the Roman Temple, then go 1 more block and turn right to Tundidores 3; +34 957 482 950).

$$ Taberna San Miguel is nicknamed "Casa el Pisto" for its famous vegetable stew *(pisto).* Well-respected, it's packed with locals who appreciate regional cuisine, a good value, and a place with a long Cordovan history. There's great seating in its charming interior or on the lively square (tapas at bar only, daily 12:00-16:00 & 20:00-24:00, closed Aug, 2 blocks north of Plaza de las Tendillas at Plaza San Miguel 1, +34 957 470 166).

$$ Taberna La Cazuela de la Espartería offers traditional Andalusian and Cordovan recipes, featuring dishes baked in *cazuelas* (ceramic dishes), such as *berenjenas de barro* (a kind of eggplant lasagna). The specialties pair nicely with the restaurant's numerous Spanish wines. Eat in the rustic dining room or enjoy their tapas and *raciones* at barrel tables in the bar or outdoors. Be sure to check out the "Las Tavernas" room upstairs, with striking bullfighter photos (Mon-Sat 13:00-16:15 & 20:00-24:00, Sun 13:30-16:30, Calle Rodríguez Marin 16, +34 957 488 952).

$ La Llave is a welcome break from heavy Spanish foods, serving up organic, seasonal dishes and the occasional traditional favorites like *salmorejo.* Eat inside the hip and chic Tiffany-blue café or cobble together a takeout meal. Choose from vegetarian dishes, cheeses and dips sold by weight, sodas, or wine on tap listed by grape (daily 10:00-22:00, near the Roman columns at the corner of Calle Rodríguez Marin and Calle Tundidores 1, +34 957 392 819).

Groceries: Día has a large branch near Plaza de las Tendillas (Mon-Sat 9:00-21:30, closed Sun, Sevilla 6). **Carrefour Express** is between Plaza de la Corredera and the Roman Temple ruins (daily 9:00-22:00, Calle Rodríguez Marín 13).

Córdoba Connections

From Córdoba by Train: Córdoba is on the slick **AVE** train line (reservations required), making it an easy stopover between **Madrid** (almost hourly, 2 hours) and **Sevilla** (45 minutes). The **Avant** train connects Córdoba to Sevilla just as fast for a lower price (hourly, 45 minutes). The slow *media distancia* train to Sevilla takes about twice as long, but doesn't require a reservation and is even cheaper (7/day, 1.5 hours).

Other trains go to **Barcelona** (6/day direct, 5 hours, many more with transfer in Madrid), **Granada** (4-7/day, 1.5 hours), **Ronda** (2/day direct on Altaria, 2 hours), **Jerez** (8/day, 2 hours, transfer in Sevilla), **Málaga** (fast and cheap Avant train, 6/day, 1 hour; fast and expensive AVE train, 11/day, 1 hour), and **Algeciras** (1/day direct, 4 hours, or connect to the bus in Málaga, 4 hours). Train info: +34 912 320 320, www.renfe.com.

By Bus to: Granada (8/day, 2.5-4 hours, Alsa), **Sevilla** (7/day, 2 hours, Alsa), **Madrid** (8/day, 5 hours, Socibus), **Nerja** (3/day, 4.5 hours, Alsa), **Málaga** (5-6/day, 2-3.5 hours, Alsa). You can check all schedules at www.estacionautobusescordoba.es. Bus info: Alsa, www.alsa.es; Socibus, www.socibusventas.es.

CÓRDOBA

ANDALUCÍA'S WHITE HILL TOWNS

Arcos de la Frontera • Ronda • Zahara and Grazalema • Jerez de la Frontera

Just as the American image of Germany is Bavaria, the Yankee dream of Spain is Andalucía. This is the home of bullfights, flamenco, gazpacho, pristine whitewashed hill towns, and glamorous Mediterranean resorts. The big cities of Andalucía (Granada, Sevilla, and Córdoba) and the south coast (Costa del Sol) are covered in separate chapters. This chapter explores Andalucía's hill-town highlights.

The Route of the White Hill Towns (Ruta de los Pueblos Blancos), Andalucía's charm bracelet of cute villages perched in the sierras, gives you wonderfully untouched Spanish culture. The most substantial and entertaining home base is Ronda, which stuns visitors with its breathtaking setting—straddling a gorge that thrusts deep into the Andalusian bedrock. Ronda's venerable old bullring, smattering of enjoyable sights, and thriving tapas scene round out its charms. Or, for something quieter and more exotic, spend a night in the romantic queen of the white towns, Arcos de la Frontera. (Towns with "de la Frontera" in their names were established on the front line of the centuries-long fight to recapture Spain from the Muslims, who were slowly pushed back into Africa.) Smaller hill towns, such as Zahara and Grazalema, offer plenty of beauty. As a whole, the hill towns—no longer strategic, no longer on any frontier—are now just passing time peacefully. Except for the cruise groups that wash in from Costa del Sol resorts like the tide, these towns feel a bit bypassed and mysterious.

West of the hill towns, the city of Jerez de la Frontera—teeming with traffic and lacking in charm—is worth a peek for its famous dancing horses and a glass of sherry on a bodega tour.

To study ahead, visit www.andalucia.com for information on festivals, museums, nightlife, and sports in the region.

PLANNING YOUR TIME

On a three-week vacation in Spain, Andalucía's hill towns are worth at least two nights and one day—or more. Ronda (bigger and with more going on) or Arcos (smaller and sleepier) make the best home bases. Ronda is closer to the Costa del Sol. Arcos is closer to Jerez, and conveniently situated halfway between Sevilla and Tarifa.

Ronda can keep you busy for an entire day. Arcos can be experienced in an evening. You could spend a day hopping from town to town in the more remote interior (including Grazalema and Zahara). See Jerez on your way in or out.

Unlike most hill towns, Arcos, Jerez, and Ronda are conveniently reached by public transportation: They have bus connections with surrounding towns, and Ronda is on a train line.

Spring and fall are high season throughout this area. In summer you'll encounter intense heat, but empty hotels, lower prices, and no crowds.

Arcos de la Frontera

Arcos smothers its long, narrow hilltop and tumbles down the back of the ridge like the train of a wedding dress. It's larger than most other Andalusian hill towns, but equally atmospheric. The old center is a labyrinthine wonderland, a photographer's feast. Viewpoint-hop through town. Feel the wind funnel through the narrow streets as cars inch around tight corners. Join the kids' soccer game on the churchyard patio. Enjoy the moonlit view from the main square.

Though it tries, Arcos is low energy. It doesn't have much to offer other than its basic whitewashed self. The locally produced English guidebook on Arcos waxes poetic and at length about very little. You can arrive late and leave early and still see it all.

Orientation to Arcos

Arcos consists of two parts: the fairy-tale old town on top of the hill and the more commercial lower, or new, town. The **main TI** is on the skinny one-way road leading up into the old town (Mon-Sat 9:30-14:00 & 15:00-19:30, Sun 10:00-14:00; Cuesta de Belén 5, +34 956 702 264, www.turismoarcos.com). A model there shows Arcos (in Latin, *Arx Arcis*—"high fortress") as it was in 1264 when the Christian Reconquista forces retook it from the Moors. On the

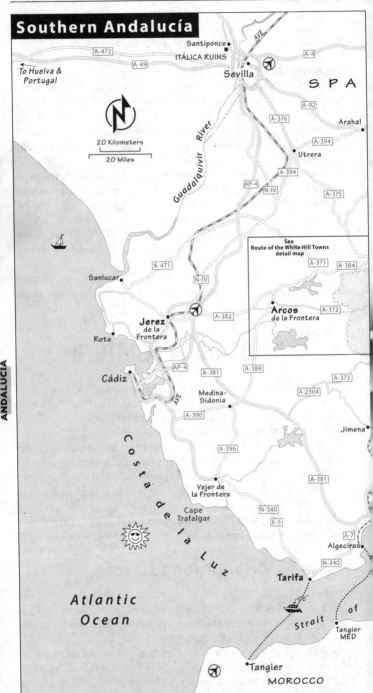

Southern Andalucía

To Huelva & Portugal

A-472

A-49

Santiponce
ITÁLICA RUINS

AVE

Sevilla

A-4

S P A

20 Kilometers

20 Miles

A-376

A-92

Arahal

A-394

Utrera

Guadalquivir River

A-394

AP-4

N-IV

A-375

A-471

N-IV

See
Route of the White Hill Towns
detail map

A-371

A-384

Sanlucar

Arcos
de la Frontera

A-372

Jerez
de la Frontera

A-382

A-389

Rota

A-373

AP-4

A-381

A-2304

Cádiz

AVE

Medina-
Sidonia

Jimena

A-390

A-396

A-381

Vejer de
la Frontera

Cape
Trafalgar

N-340

E-5

A-7

Algeciras

Costa de la Luz

N-340

Tarifa

Atlantic
Ocean

Strait   of

Tangier
MED

Tangier

MOROCCO

ANDALUCÍA

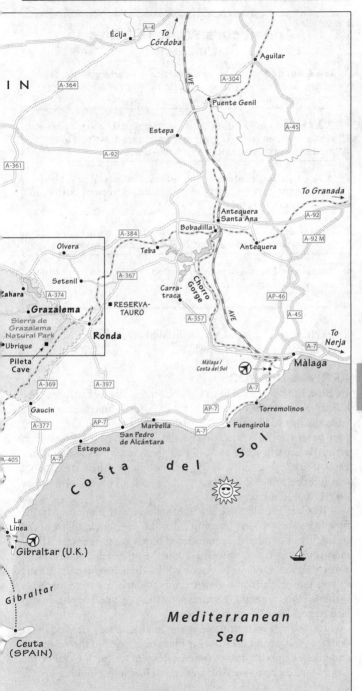

ANDALUCÍA

Andalucía's White Hill Towns at a Glance

▲▲▲**Ronda** Midsize town dramatically overhanging a deep gorge, and home to Spain's oldest bullring, with nearby prehistoric paintings at Pileta Cave.

▲▲**Arcos de la Frontera** Queen of the Andalusian hill towns, with a cliff-perched old town that meanders down to a vibrant modern center; well suited as a home base.

▲**Jerez de la Frontera** Proud equestrian mecca and birthplace of sherry, with plenty of opportunities to enjoy both in a relatively urban setting.

Zahara de la Sierra Tiny whitewashed village scenically set between a rocky Moorish castle and a turquoise reservoir.

Grazalema Bright-white town nestled in the green hills of the Sierra de Grazalema Natural Park.

---

floors above the TI is a skippable local history museum (sparse exhibits described only in Spanish).

ARRIVAL IN ARCOS

By Bus: The bus station is on Calle Corregidores, at the foot of the hill. To get up to the old town, catch the **shuttle bus** marked *Centro* from the bus stalls behind the station. Tell the driver the name of your hotel and he'll bring you to the closest stop (€1, pay driver, generally departs at :15 and :45 past the hour, runs roughly Mon-Fri 7:45-21:15, Sat until 14:15, none on Sun). Alternately, hop a taxi (€5 fixed rate; if none are waiting, call +34 956 704 640), or hike 15 uphill minutes.

By Car: The old town is a tight squeeze with a one-way traffic flow from west to east (coming from the east, circle south under town). The TI and my recommended hotels are in the west. If you miss your target, you must drive out the other end, double back, and try again. Driving in Arcos is like threading needles (many drivers pull in their side-view mirrors to buy a few extra precious inches). Turns are tight, parking is frustrating, and congestion can lead to long jams.

It's less stressful to park in the modern Paseo de Andalucía underground pay lot (€15/day) at Plaza de España in the new town and hike 15 uphill minutes to the old town. Or catch a taxi or the *Centro* shuttle bus—see "By Bus" above (as you're looking uphill,

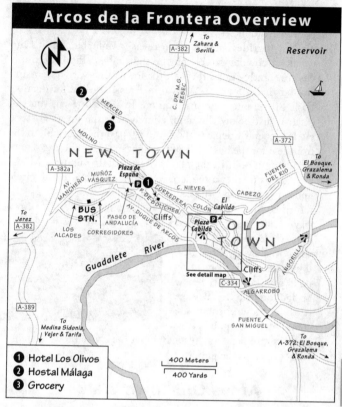

Arcos de la Frontera Overview

To Zahara & Sevilla — A-382

Reservoir

C. DR. M.G. RESEC.

MERCED

MOLINO

NEW TOWN

A-382a

MUÑOZ VÁSQUEZ

Plaza de España

A-372

PUENTE DEL RÍO

To El Bosque, Grazalema & Ronda

AV. MANCHEÑO

CORREDERA

C. NIEVES

P. DE BOLICHES

COLÓN

CABEZO

El Cabildo

BUS STN.

To Jerez A-382

PASEO DE ANDALUCÍA

AV. DUQUE DE ARCOS

Cliffs

Plaza Cabildo

OLD TOWN

LOS ALCADES

CORREGIDORES

ANGORILLA

Guadalete River

See detail map

Cliffs

C-334

ALGARROBO

A-389

To Medina Sidonia, Vejer & Tarifa

PUENTE SAN MIGUEL

To A-372: El Bosque, Grazalema & Ronda

❶ Hotel Los Olivos
❷ Hostal Málaga
❸ Grocery

400 Meters
400 Yards

ANDALUCÍA

the bus stop is to the right of the traffic circle). Many hotels offer discounts at this lot; inquire when booking your room.

Small cars capable of threading the narrow streets of the old town can park in the main square at the top of the hill (Plaza del Cabildo). Buy a ticket from the machine (€0.70/hour, 2-hour maximum, only necessary Mon-Fri 9:00-14:00 & 17:00-21:00 and Sat 9:00-14:00—confirm times on machine). Hotel guests parking here overnight must obtain a €5 dashboard pass from their hotelier; daytime parking charges still apply.

HELPFUL HINTS

Money: There are no ATMs in the old town. You'll find several ATMs in the new town along Calle Corredera and near the Paseo de Andalucía underground parking lot.

Groceries: You'll find smaller stores with a basic selection of groceries in the old town or close to the TI. For a bigger grocery store head to the **Mercadona** in the new town (Mon-Sat

9:00-20:00, closed Sun, Avenida San Juan Bautista de la Salle, www.mercadona.es).

Shuttle Bus Joyride: The old town is easily walkable, but it's fun to take a circular ramble on the shuttle bus. The little mini-bus constantly circles through the town's one-way system and around the valley (see "Arrival in Arcos," earlier, for details). For a 30-minute tour, just hop on. In the old town, you can catch it just below the main church near the mystical stone circle (generally departs at :20 and :50 past the hour). Sit in the front seat for the best view of the tight squeezes and the school kids hanging out in the plazas. After passing under a Moorish gate, you enter a modern residential neighborhood, circle under the eroding cliff, and return to the old town by way of the bus station and Plaza de España.

Views: For drivers, the best town overlook is from a tiny park just beyond the new bridge on the El Bosque road. In town, there are some fine viewpoints (for instance, from the main square), but the church towers are no longer open to the public.

Arcos Old Town Walk

This self-guided walk will introduce you to virtually everything worth seeing in Arcos. (Avoid this walk during the hot midday siesta.)

• Start at the top of the hill, in the main square dominated by the church.

Plaza del Cabildo

Stand at the viewpoint opposite the church on the town's main square. Survey the square, which in the old days doubled as a bullring. On your right is the parador, a former palace of the governor. It flies three flags: green for Andalucía, red-and-yellow for Spain, and blue-and-yellow for the European Union. On your left is City Hall, below the 11th-century Moorish castle where Ferdinand and Isabel held Reconquista strategy meetings (castle privately owned and closed to the public).

Now belly up to the railing and look down at the dramatic view. The people of

Arcos de la Frontera

OLD TOWN

To Plaza de España, Parking & Bus Station

To Bus Stn.

CASTLE (NOT OPEN)

SANTA MARIA

Plaza Cabildo

VIEWPOINT

CLOISTERED NUNS

BELÉN ARTÍSTICO

Plaza Boticas

PALACE

EL JUAN DE CUENCA

GALERIA

SAN PEDRO

GARDEN

MIRADOR

Cliffs

Río Guadalete

100 Meters
100 Yards

C-334

To A-372: El Bosque, Grazalema & Ronda

Accommodations
1. Parador de Arcos de la Frontera
2. Hotel El Convento
3. La Casa Grande
4. Casa Mirador San Pedro & Taberna San Pedro
5. Rincón de las Nieves
6. Hostal & Bar San Marcos

Eateries & Nightlife
7. Mesón Los Murales
8. Taberna Jóvenes Flamencos
9. Bar La Cárcel
10. Alcaraván
11. Lalola

ANDALUCÍA

Arcos boast that only they see the backs of the birds as they fly. Ponder the parador's erosion concerns (it lost part of its lounge in the 1990s when it dropped right off), the orderly orange groves, and the fine views toward the southernmost part of Spain. The city council considered building an underground parking lot to clear up the square, but nixed it because of the land's fragility. You're 300 feet above the Guadalete River.

• *Looming over the square is the...*

Church of Santa María

After Arcos was retaken from the Moors in the 13th century, this church was built atop a mosque. Notice the church's fine but chopped-off bell tower. The old one fell in the earthquake of 1755 (famous for destroying Lisbon). The replacement was intended to be the tallest in Andalucía after Sevilla's, but money ran out. It looks like someone lives on an upper floor. Someone does—the church guardian resides there.

Cost and Hours: €2, €3 combo-ticket includes Church of San Pedro, Mon-Fri 10:00-13:00 & 15:30-18:30, Sat 10:00-14:00, shorter hours in winter, closed Sun and Jan-Feb.

Visiting the Church: Buy a ticket and step inside, where you can see they've packed a lot of decoration into a small space. Work

your way between the pews to examine the beautifully carved choir. Its organ was built in 1789 with that many pipes. At the very front of the church, the nice Renaissance high altar, carved in wood, covers up a Muslim prayer niche that survived from the older mosque. The altar shows God with a globe in his hand (on top), and scenes from the life of Jesus (on the right) and Mary (left). To the left of the altar is a fine surviving 14th-century Andalusian Gothic fresco.

Continue circling the church and notice the elaborate chapels. Although most of the architecture is Gothic, the chapels are decorated in the Baroque and Rococo styles that were popular when the post-earthquake remodel began. The ornate statues are used in Holy Week processions. Sniff out the "incorruptible body" (miraculously never rotting) of St. Felix—a third-century martyr (directly across from the entry). Felix may be nicknamed "the incorruptible," but take a close look at his knee. He's no longer skin and bones...just bones and the fine silver mesh that once covered his skin. Rome sent his body here in 1764, after recognizing this church as the most important in Arcos. In the back of the church, near a huge fresco of St. Christopher (carrying his staff and Baby Jesus), is a gnarly Easter candle from 1767.

• *Back outside, circle clockwise around the church and examine the church exterior.*

Down four steps, find the third-century Roman votive altar with a carving of the palm tree of life directly in front of you. Though the Romans didn't build this high in the mountains, they did have a town and temple at the foot of Arcos. This carved stone was discovered in the foundation of the original Moorish mosque, which stood here before the first church was built. This has long been considered a fertility stone (women would come here to help with pregnancy).

Head down a few more steps and come to the main entrance (west portal) of the church (always closed). This is a good example of Plateresque Gothic—Spain's last and most ornate kind of Gothic.

In the pavement, notice the 15th-century magic circle with 12 red and 12 white stones—the white ones have various "constellations" marked (though they don't resemble any of today's star charts). When a child would come to the church to be baptized, the parents stopped here first for a good Christian exorcism. The exorcist would stand inside the protective circle and cleanse the baby of any evil spirits. While locals no longer do this (and a modern rain drain now marks the center), many Sufi Muslims still come here in a kind of pilgrimage every November. (Down a few more steps, you can catch the public minibus for a circular joyride through Arcos; see "Helpful Hints," earlier.)

Go down the next few stairs to the street and circle right. Peer down the next narrow path to the left called Cuesta de las Monjas.

The security grille (over the window above) protected cloistered nuns when this building was a convent. Look at the arches that prop up the houses downhill; all over town, arches support earthquake-damaged structures.

Continue straight under the **flying buttresses.** Notice the scratches of innumerable car mirrors on each wall (and be glad you're walking). The buttresses were built to shore up the church when it was damaged by an earthquake in 1699. (Thanks to these supports, most of the church survived the bigger earthquake of 1755.)

• *Now make your way...*

From Santa María to the Church of San Pedro

Completing your circle around the Church of Santa María (huffing back uphill), turn left under more arches built to repair earthquake damage and walk east down the bright, white Calle Escribanos ("Street of the Scribes"). Although it changes names, you'll basically follow this lane until you come to the town's second big church (San Pedro).

After a block, you hit Plaza Boticas. On your right is the last remaining **convent** in Arcos. Notice the no-nunsense, spiky window grilles high above, with tiny peepholes in the latticework for the cloistered nuns to see through. If you're hungry, check out the list and photos of the treats the nuns provide. Then step into the lobby under the fine portico to find their one-way mirror and a spinning cupboard that hides the nuns from view. Push the buzzer,

ANDALUCÍA

and one of the eight sisters (several are from Kenya and speak English well) will spin out some boxes of excellent, freshly baked cookies—made from pine nuts, peanuts, almonds, and other nuts—for you to consider (€7-8, open daily but not reliably 8:30-14:30 & 17:00-19:00; be careful—if you stand big and tall to block out the light, you might see the sister through the glass). If you ask for *magdalenas,* bags of cupcakes will swing around (€3.50). These are traditional goodies made from natural ingredients. Buy some treats to support their church work, and give them to kids as you complete your walk.

• *As you exit the convent, turn right and go right again down Calle Boticas.*

Be on the lookout for ancient columns tucked into building corners. All over town, these columns—many actually Roman, appropriated from their original ancient settlement at the foot of the hill—were put up to protect buildings from reckless donkey carts (and tourists in rental cars).

As you continue straight, notice that the walls are scooped out on either side of the windows. These are a reminder of the days when women stayed inside but wanted the best possible view of any action in the streets. These "window ears" also enabled boys in a more modest age to lean inconspicuously against the wall to chat up eligible young ladies.

Across from the old chapel facade ahead, find the **Palace del Mayorazgo,** which houses the Association of San Miguel. Duck right, past a bar, into one of the oldest courtyards in town—you can still see the graceful Neo-Gothic lines of this noble home from 1850. Enjoy any art exhibits and the garden. The bar is a club for retired men—always busy when a bullfight's on TV or during card games. The guys are friendly, and drinks are cheap. You're welcome to flip on the light and explore the old-town photos in the back room.

• *Just beyond, facing the elegant front door of that noble house, is Arcos' second church...*

Church of San Pedro

Enter through the small door to the left of the main entrance (€2, €3 combo-ticket includes Church of Santa María, same hours as Church of Santa María). You know it's the Church of San Pedro because San Pedro, mother of God, is the centerpiece of the facade. Let me explain. It really is the town's second church, having had an extended battle with Santa María for papal recognition as the leading church in Arcos. When the pope finally favored Santa María (he declared it a minor basilica in 1993), San Pedro's parishioners changed their prayers. Rather than honoring "María," they wouldn't even say her name. They prayed "San Pedro, mother

of God." Like Santa María, it's a Gothic structure, filled with Baroque decor (including a stunning organ covered with cherubs), many Holy Week procession statues, and humble English descriptions. Santa María may have won papal recognition, but this church has more relic skeletons in glass caskets (flanking both sides of the main altar are St. Fructuoso and St. Víctor, martyrs from the third century AD). The music stand in the choir illustrates how the entire chorus can sing from just four hymnals.

• *Back outside, explore...*

Back Lanes, Artisan Workshops, and Courtyards

In the cool of the evening, the tiny square in front of the church—about the only flat piece of pavement around—serves as the old-town soccer field for neighborhood kids. Until a few years ago, this church also had a resident bellman—notice the cozy balcony halfway up. He was a basket-maker and a colorful character, famous for bringing a donkey into his quarters that grew too big to get back out. Finally, he had no choice but to kill and eat the donkey.

Twenty yards beyond the church, step into the humble **Galería de Arte San Pedro,** featuring artisans in action and their reasonably priced paintings, engravings, and pottery (Mon-Fri 10:00-21:00, Sat-Sun until 19:00, shorter hours in winter).

Crossing behind the church to the next lane, signs direct you to a **mirador**—a tiny square 100 yards downhill that affords a commanding view of Arcos. The reservoir you see to the northeast of town is used for water sports in the summertime. Looking south, among the rolling fields you'll see a power plant that local residents protested—to no avail—based on environmental concerns. Wind-driven generators blink along the horizon at night. Relax on a bench and take in this spectacular view.

• *Return to the Church of San Pedro, then circle down and right along Calle Maldonado as we head back toward the main square.*

Just below San Pedro's is a delightful little **Andalusian garden** (formal Arabic style, with aromatic plants such as jasmine, rose, and lavender, and water in the center). About 100 yards farther along on Maldonado (on the right after the dip), peek into the **Belén Artístico,** a little cave-like museum, which highlights a popular Spanish tradition of setting up a Nativity scene during Christmas using miniature figures (free but donations accepted, generally Mon-Sat 10:30-13:30, closed Sun).

ANDALUCÍA

• *This street eventually leads you back to Plaza Boticas (and those clois-tered nuns selling cookies).*

The lanes that run steeply down behind Plaza Boticas and the Church of Santa María offer both exercise and a chance to see into **Arcos' lovely courtyards.** The lane called Higinio Capote is par-ticularly picturesque with its many geraniums. Peek discreetly into the private patios. These wonderful, cool-tiled courtyards filled with plants, pools, furniture, and happy family activities are typical of Arcos. Except in the mansions, these patios are generally shared by several families. Originally, each courtyard served as a catch-ment system, funneling rainwater to a drain in the middle, which filled the well. You can still see tiny wells in wall niches with now-decorative pulleys for the bucket.

Nightlife in Arcos

Arcos is a quiet town. When I ask locals about nightlife, they say, "We sleep." But you'll find a tiny pulse of nocturnal energy here and there. The newer part of Arcos has a modern charm. In the cool of the evening, all generations enjoy life out around Plaza de España (15-minute walk from the old town).

The old town is pretty quiet after hours. But the fun little bar, **Taberna San Pedro** (next to the Church of San Pedro), seems to be spoiling for a party. It's a tiny, cozy joint with typical tapas, a proud selection of wines from Cádiz, and a mishmash of paintings, mata-dor photos, and *fútbol* banners (closed Tue). And **Lalola** (down the hill, past the TI at Corredera 11) is great for drinks, tapas, and "Flamenquito" Fridays with a guitarist and *cajón* player.

Sleeping in Arcos

Hotels in Arcos consider April, May, August, September, and Oc-tober to be high season. Note that some hotels double their rates during the motorbike races in nearby Jerez de la Frontera (usually April or May) and during Holy Week before Easter.

IN THE OLD TOWN

Drivers should obtain a parking pass from their hotel to park over-night on the main square. (The pass does not exempt you from daytime rates.) Otherwise, park in the Paseo de Andalucía lot at Plaza de España in the new town and walk or catch a taxi or the shuttle bus up to the old town (see "Arrival in Arcos," earlier).

$$$ Parador de Arcos de la Frontera is royally located, with 23 elegant and reasonably priced rooms (eight have balconies). The terraces offer splendid views of the town and the valley below (air-con, elevator, Plaza del Cabildo, +34 956 700 500, www.parador. es, arcos@parador.es).

$$ Hotel El Convento, deep in the old town just beyond the parador, is the best value in town. Run by a hardworking family and their wonderful staff, this cozy hotel offers 13 delicately romantic rooms—all with great views, most with balconies. In 1998 I enjoyed a big party here with most of Arcos' big shots as they dedicated a fine room with a grand-view balcony to "Rick Steves, Periodista Turístico." Guess where I sleep when in Arcos... (RS%, communal terrace, usually closed Nov-Feb, Maldonado 2, +34 956 702 333, www.hotelelconvento.es, reservas@hotelelconvento.es).

$$ La Casa Grande is a lovingly appointed *Better Homes and Moroccan Tiles* kind of place that rents eight rooms with big-view windows. As in a lavish yet authentic old-style inn, you're free to enjoy its fine view terrace and homey library, or have a traditional breakfast (extra) on the atrium-like patio. They also offer massage services (family rooms, air-con, Wi-Fi in public areas only, Maldonado 10, +34 956 703 930, www.lacasagrande.net, info@ lacasagrande.net, Elena).

$$ Casa Mirador San Pedro, in the shadow of the Church of San Pedro, has seven rustically cozy rooms and a whimsical rooftop terrace with great Arcos views. The windows are single pane, but the street noise quiets down in the evening (apartment available, air-con, El Juan de Cuenca 2—around the corner from Taberna San Pedro, mobile +34 635 189 005, miradorjuandecuenca@hotmail.com).

$ Rincón de las Nieves, with simple Andalusian charm, has a cool inner courtyard filled with plants and ceramics surrounded by three rooms. Two rooms have their own outdoor terraces with obstructed views, and all have high ceilings and access to the rooftop terrace (the highest in town) with nearly 360-degree views (air-con, Boticas 10, also rents an apartment, +34 956 701 528, mobile +34 656 886 256, www.rincondelasnieves.com, rincondelasnieves@ gmail.com, Paqui).

¢ Hostal San Marcos, above a neat little bar in the heart of the old town, offers four air-conditioned rooms and a great sun terrace with views of the reservoir (air-con, Marqués de Torresoto 6, best to reserve by phone at +34 956 105 429, mobile +34 675 459 106, www.hostalsanmarcosdearcos.com, reservas@elpatio-arcos. com, José Luis speaks some English).

IN THE NEW TOWN

See the "Arcos de la Frontera Overview" map, earlier, for these new town accommodations.

$$ Hotel Los Olivos is a bright, cool, and airy place with 19 rooms, an impressive courtyard, roof garden, generous public spaces, bar, view, friendly folks, and easy pay parking. The four view rooms can be a bit noisy in the afternoon, but—with double-pane windows—are usually fine at night (RS%, includes breakfast, Paseo de Boliches 30, +34 956 700 811, www.hotel-losolivos.es, reservas@hotel-losolivos.es, Raquel, Marta, and Miguel Ángel).

¢ Hostal Málaga is surprisingly nice and a very good value if for some reason you want to stay on the big road at the Jerez edge of town. Nestled on a quiet lane between truck stops off A-393, it offers 17 clean, attractive rooms and a breezy two-level terrace (air-con, easy parking, Avenida Ponce de León 5, +34 956 702 010, www.hostalmalaga.com, hostalmalaga@hotmail.com, Josefa and son Alejandro speak a *leetle* English).

Eating in Arcos

VIEW DINING

$$$ The **Parador** (described earlier, under "Sleeping in Arcos") has a formal restaurant and a cafeteria with a cliff-edge setting. Its tapas and *raciones* are reasonably priced, and even just a drink and a snack on the million-dollar-view terrace at sunset is a nice experience (daily 13:00-16:00 & 20:00-23:00, shorter hours off-season, on main square, +34 956 700 500).

CHEAPER EATING IN THE OLD TOWN

Several decent, rustic bar-restaurants are in the old town, within a block or two of the main square and church. Most serve tapas and *raciones* both at the bar and at their tables.

$$ Mesón Los Murales serves tasty, affordable tapas, *raciones*, and fixed-price meals in their simple bar or at tables in the square outside (Fri-Wed 10:00-24:00, closed Thu, Plaza Boticas 1, mobile +34 678 064 163).

$$ Taberna Jóvenes Flamencos offers a fun and accessible menu and is high-energy for Arcos. Try their specialties—*abajao*, an egg-and-asparagus dish, and *perolitos*, an egg scramble in a mini pan (Thu-Tue 12:00-24:00, closed Wed, Calle Dean Espinosa 11, mobile +34 657 133 552).

$$ Bar La Cárcel ("The Prison"), across the street, celebrates seafood and local meats (Tue-Sun 12:00-24:00, closed Mon, Calle Dean Espinosa 18, +34 956 700 410).

$$ Alcaraván, run by the same owners as La Cárcel, tries to be a bit trendier yet *típico*. A funky and fun ambience fills its medieval vault in the castle's former dungeon. This place attracts French and German tourists who give it a cooler vibe (Wed-Sun 12:00-17:00 & 18:00-23:00, closed Mon-Tue, Calle Nueva 1, +34 956 907 293).

$$ Bar San Marcos is a tiny, homey bar with five tables and an easy-to-understand menu offering hearty, simple home cooking (Sun-Mon 9:00-16:30, Tue-Sat 8:00-24:00, Marqués de Torresoto 6, +34 956 700 721).

Arcos Connections

BY BUS

Leaving Arcos by bus can be frustrating—buses generally leave late, the schedule information boards are often inaccurate, and the ticket window usually isn't open (luckily, you can buy tickets on-board). Buses run less frequently on weekends. The closest train station to Arcos is Jerez.

Two bus companies—Damas and Comes—share the Arcos bus station. If your Spanish is good, you can call the Jerez offices for departure times—otherwise ask your hotelier or the TI for help. To find out about the Arcos-Jerez schedule, make it clear you're coming from Arcos (Damas, www.damas-sa.es; Comes, www.tgcomes.es). Also try Movelia.es for bus schedules and routes.

From Arcos by Bus to: Jerez (hourly, 40 minutes, Damas), **Ronda** (2/day, 2 hours, Comes), **Sevilla** (1-2/day, 2 hours, more departures with transfer in Jerez, Damas).

ROUTE TIPS FOR DRIVERS

Arcos to Sevilla (55 miles/90 km): The trip to **Sevilla** takes about 1.5 hours if you pay €7 for the toll road that starts near Jerez. To continue to **southern Portugal,** follow the freeway to Sevilla, and skirt the city by turning west on the SE-30 ring road in the direction of Huelva. It's a straight shot from there on A-49/E-1.

Arcos to Tarifa (80 miles/130 km): If you're going to Tarifa, take the tiny A-389 road at the Jerez edge of Arcos toward Paterna and Medina Sidonia, where you'll pick up A-381 to Algeciras, then on to Tarifa. Another option is to continue through Medina Sidonia to Vejer on A-396, from where you can cut south to Tarifa.

Ronda

With more than 34,000 people, Ronda is one of the largest white hill towns. It's also one of the most spectacular, thanks to its gorge-straddling setting.

Approaching the town from the train or bus station, it seems flat...until you reach the New Bridge and realize that it's clinging to the walls of a canyon. During Moorish times, this was a tight fortified town of 9,000—a bastion second only to Granada during the last years of Moorish rule in southern Spain. (It fell to Christian forces only in 1485—seven years before Granada.) The cliffside setting, while practical back then, today is simply dramatic, and that "old town" is now home to only 1,000 people.

Ronda's main attractions are its gorge-spanning bridges, the oldest bullring in Spain, and an intriguing old town. Spaniards know Ronda as the cradle of modern bullfighting and the romantic home of 19th-century *bandoleros* (bandits). But the real joy of Ronda these days lies in exploring its back streets and taking in its beautiful balconies, exuberant flowerpots, wispy gardens, and panoramic views. Walking the streets, you feel a strong local pride and a community where everyone seems to know everyone.

While day-trippers from cruise ships and the touristy Costa del Sol clog Ronda's streets during the day, locals retake the town in the early evening, making nights peaceful. Since it's served by train and bus, Ronda makes a relaxing break for nondrivers traveling between Granada, Sevilla, and Córdoba. Drivers can use Ronda as a convenient base from which to explore many of the other *pueblos blancos*.

Orientation to Ronda

Ronda's breathtaking ravine divides the town's labyrinthine Moorish quarter and its new, noisier, and more sprawling Mercadillo quarter. A massive-yet-graceful 18th-century bridge connects these two neighborhoods. Most things of touristic importance (TI, hotels, bullring) are clustered within a few blocks of the bridge. The paseo (early evening stroll) happens in the new town, on Ronda's major pedestrian and shopping street, Carrera Espinel.

TOURIST INFORMATION

Ronda's hardworking TI, across the square from the bullring, covers not only the town but all of Andalucía. It gives out good, free maps of the town, Andalusia's roads, Granada, Sevilla, and the Route of the White Towns. The TI also organizes a creative array of activities such as tours, concerts, and walks, all described in helpful lists (Mon-Fri 10:00-19:00, Sat until 17:00, Sun until

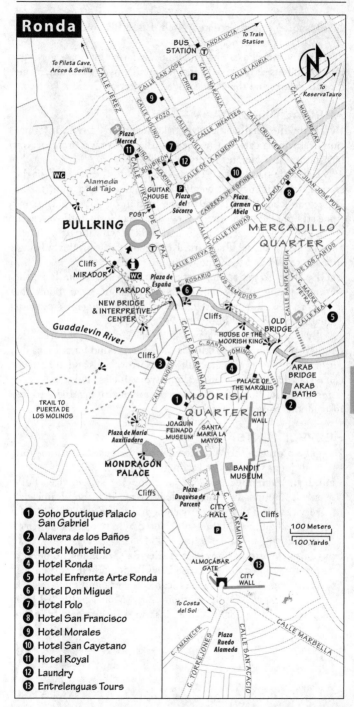

Ronda

To Pileta Cave, Arcos & Sevilla

To Train Station

To ReservaTauro

BUS STATION

CALLE ANDALUCIA

CALLE JEREZ

CALLE SAN JOSE

CALLE CHICA

CALLE NARANJA

CALLE LAURIA

CALLE MONTEROS

CALLE CRUZ VERDE

CALLE INFANTES

CALLE SEVILLA

CALLE MOLINO

POZO

9

Plaza Merced

11

7

SOBIRON

NIÑO MARINA

CALLE VIRGEN DE LA PAZ

GUITAR HOUSE

12

CALLE DE LA ALMENDRA

10

CARRERA DE ESPINEL

Plaza Carmen Abela

C. JUAN JOSE PUYA

C. MARIA CABRERA

8

WC

Alameda del Tajo

Plaza del Socorro

P

POST

MERCADILLO QUARTER

CALLE SANTA CECILIA

C. DE LOS CANTOS

C. MADRE PEÑA

CALLE TIENDAS

BULLRING

Cliffs

MIRADOR

i

WC

PARADOR

Plaza de España

6

C. ROSARIO

CALLE NUEVA

CALLE VIRGEN DE LOS REMEDIOS

CALLE REAL

5

NEW BRIDGE & INTERPRETIVE CENTER

Guadalevín River

Cliffs

Cliffs

OLD BRIDGE

HOUSE OF THE MOORISH KING

3

CALLE TENORIO

C. SANTO DOMINGO

4

CALLE ARMIÑAN

PALACE OF THE MARQUIS

ARAB BRIDGE

ARAB BATHS

2

TRAIL TO PUERTA DE LOS MOLINOS

Plaza de María Auxiliadora

1

MOORISH QUARTER

CITY WALL

JOAQUÍN PEINADO MUSEUM

SANTA MARÍA LA MAYOR

MONDRAGÓN PALACE

BANDIT MUSEUM

Cliffs

Plaza Duquesa de Parcent

CITY HALL

P

C. DE ARMIÑAN

Cliffs

100 Meters

100 Yards

ALMOCÁBAR GATE

CITY WALL

13

To Costa del Sol

Plaza Ruedo Alameda

C. AMANECER

C. TORREJONES

CALLE SAN ACACIO

CALLE MARBELLA

ANDALUCÍA

1 Soho Boutique Palacio San Gabriel
2 Alavera de los Baños
3 Hotel Montelirio
4 Hotel Ronda
5 Hotel Enfrente Arte Ronda
6 Hotel Don Miguel
7 Hotel Polo
8 Hotel San Francisco
9 Hotel Morales
10 Hotel San Cayetano
11 Hotel Royal
12 Laundry
13 Entrelenguas Tours

14:30, shorter hours Oct-late March, Paseo Blas Infante, +34 952 187 119, www.turismoderonda.es).

Sightseeing Pass: The €8 **Bono Turístico** city pass gets you into four sights—the Arab Baths, Joaquín Peinado Museum, Mondragón Palace, and the New Bridge Interpretive Center.

ARRIVAL IN RONDA

By Train: The small station has ticket windows, a train information desk, and a café, but no lockers (there's storage at the nearby bus station; see "Helpful Hints," below).

From the station, it's a 15-minute **walk** to the center: Exit the station, turn right onto Avenida de Andalucía, and walk to the large roundabout (you'll see the bus station on your right). Continue straight down the street (now called San José) until you reach its end at Calle Jerez. Turn left and walk downhill past a church and the Alameda del Tajo park. Keep going, passing the bullring, to reach the TI and the famous bridge.

By Bus: To get to the center from the bus station, leave the station walking to the right of the roundabout, then follow the directions for train travelers described above. Baggage storage is available (see "Helpful Hints" below).

By Car: Street parking away from the center is often free. The handiest place for paid parking is the underground lot at Plaza del Socorro (one block from the bullring). Narrow lanes and tight turns can be challenging for even medium-size vehicles, and some access is restricted for nonresidents. Be sure to get driving and parking instructions from your hotel.

HELPFUL HINTS

Baggage Storage: The WC attendant at the bus station can store your luggage in a locked room (daily 8:30-20:00).

Laundry: HigienSec has one machine for self-service. Full-service options can include delivery to your hotel (same-day service if you drop off early enough; Mon-Fri 10:00-14:00 & 17:00-20:30, Sat 10:00-14:00, closed Sun, two blocks north of the bullring at Calle Molino 6, +34 952 875 249).

Souvenirs: Worth a browse is **Taller de Grabados Somera,** a printmaking studio near the New Bridge. Their inexpensive, charming prints of Ronda's iconic scenery and famous bulls are hand-pulled right in their shop (Mon-Fri 10:00-19:00, Sat-Sun 10:30-18:00, Calle Rosario 4, just across from the parador).

Tours in Ronda

Walking Tours

Many local guides work in conjunction with the TI to offer two-hour guided city walks (€10-20 for afternoon visits). Reserve and pay at the TI.

Entrelenguas is a cultural center in Ronda that offers much more than Spanish-language lessons. Alex, Mar, and Javier guide visitors around Ronda, focusing on monuments (€55) or cultural immersion and local businesses (€75). They can do wine tastings on request (€35) or even put together a cooking class for a small group (Calle Espíritu Santo 9, +34 951 083 862, www.entrelenguas.es).

Local Guide

Energetic and knowledgeable **Antonio Jesús Naranjo** will take you on a two-hour walking tour of the city's sights (€125, reserve early, mobile +34 639 073 763, www.guiaoficialderonda.com).

Sights and Experiences in Ronda

IN THE NEW TOWN
Alameda del Tajo Park

One block away from the bullring, the town's main park is a great breezy place for a picnic lunch, people-watching, a snooze in the shade, or practicing your Spanish with seniors from the nearby old-folks' home. Don't miss letting loose a few butterflies in your stomach at its tiny view terrace. It overlooks the scenic Serranía de Ronda mountains—and a drop of nearly 200 meters...straight down.

ANDALUCÍA

▲▲Bullring (Real Maestranza de Caballería de Ronda)

Ronda is the birthplace of modern bullfighting, and this was the first great Spanish bullring. Philip II initiated bullfighting as war training for knights in the 16th century. Back then, there were two kinds of bullfighting: the type with noble knights on horseback, and the coarser, man-versus-beast entertainment for the commoners (with no rules...much like when WWF wrestlers

bring out the folding chairs). Ronda practically worships Francisco Romero, who melded the noble and chaotic kinds of bullfighting with rules to establish modern bullfighting right here in the early 1700s. He introduced the scarlet cape, held unfurled with a stick.

His son Juan further developed the ritual (local aficionados would never call it a "sport"—you'll read newspaper coverage of fights not on the sports pages but in the culture section), and his grandson Pedro was one of the first great matadors (killing nearly 6,000 bulls in his career).

Ronda's bullring and museum rivals Sevilla's as Spain's most interesting. To tour the ring, stables, chapel, and museum, buy a ticket at the back of the bullring.

Cost and Hours: €8, daily 10:00-20:00, March and Oct until 19:00, Nov-Feb until 18:00, +34 952 874 132, www.rmcr.org.

Tours: The excellent €1.50 audioguide describes everything and is essential to fully enjoy your visit (drop it at the gift shop as you leave).

Bullfights: Bullfights are scheduled only for the first weekend of September during the *feria* (fair). Whereas every other *feria* in Andalucía celebrates a patron saint, the Ronda fair glorifies legendary bullfighter Pedro Romero. (As these fights are so limited and sell out immediately, Sevilla and Madrid are more practical places for a tourist to see a bullfight.)

◯ Self-Guided Tour: I'd visit in this order. Disobey *exit* signs and enter directly to the right to see the bullfighters' **chapel.** Before going into the ring, every matador would stop here to pray to Mary for safety—and hope to see her again.

• *Just beyond the chapel are the doors to the museum exhibits filling two long hallways: horse gear on the left, and the story of bullfighting on the right, all with English translations.*

The **horse gear exhibit** makes the connection with bullfighting and the equestrian upper class. As throughout Europe, "chivalry" began as a code among the sophisticated, horse-riding gentry. (In Spanish, the word for "gentleman" is the same as the word for "horseman"—*caballero*.)

Return to the hallway behind the chapel for the **history exhibit.** It's a shrine to bullfighting and the historic Romero family. First it traces the long history of bullfighting, going all the way back to the ancient Minoans on Crete. Historically, there were only two arenas built solely for bullfighting: in Ronda and Sevilla. Elsewhere, bullfights were held in town squares—you'll see a painting of Madrid's Plaza Mayor filled with spectators for a bullfight. (For this reason, to this day, even a purpose-built bullring is generally called *plaza de toros*—"square of bulls.") You'll also see stuffed bull heads, photos, "suits of light" worn by bullfighters, and capes (bulls are colorblind, but the traditional red cape was designed to disguise all the blood). One section explains some of the big "dynasties" of fighters. At the end of the hall are historical posters from Ronda's bullfights (all originals except the Picasso). Running along the left wall are various examples of artwork glorifying bullfighting, including original Goya engravings.

• *Exit at the far end of the bullfighting history exhibit into the arena.*

Here's your chance to play *toro*, surrounded by 5,000 empty seats. The two-tiered **arena** was built in 1785—on the 300th anniversary of the defeat of the Moors in Ronda. As you leave the museum and walk out on the sand, look ahead to see the ornamental columns and painted doorway marking the royal box where the king and dignitaries sit (over the gate where the bull

enters). Opposite the VIP box is the place for the band (marked *música*), which, in the case of a small town like Ronda, is most likely a high school band. Notice the 136 classy columns, creating a kind of 18th-century theater. Lovers of the "art" of bullfighting will explain that the event is much more than the actual killing of the bull. It celebrates noble heritage and Andalusian horse culture.

• *Just beyond the arena are more parts of the complex. Find the open gate beneath the VIP seats.*

Walk through the bulls' entry into the bullpen and the **stables.** There are six bulls per fight (plus two backups) and three matadors. Before the fight, the bulls are penned up in this bovine death row, and ropes and pulleys safely open the right door at the right time. Climb the skinny staircase and find the indoor arena *(picadero)* and see Spanish thoroughbred horses training from the **Equestrian School** of the Real Maestranza (often during weekdays). Explore the spectators' seating before exiting through the gift shop.

• *From the bullring you can walk out to the **Mirador de Ronda** viewpoint and along the cliffside walkway to the New Bridge.*

▲▲▲The Gorge and New Bridge (Puente Nuevo)

The ravine, called El Tajo—over 300 feet deep and just about 200 feet wide—divides Ronda into the whitewashed old city (Moorish Quarter) and the new town (El Mercadillo) that was built after the Christian reconquest in 1485. The New Bridge mightily spans the gorge. A different bridge was built here in 1735, but it fell after six years. This one was built from 1751 to 1793. Look down from the bridge viewpoint. Spit.

ANDALUCÍA

You can see the foundations of the original bridge and a super view of the New Bridge from the walkway between the gorge and the parador—the town's former town hall-turned-hotel—which overlooks the gorge and bridge from the new-town side.

From the new-town side of the bridge (just outside the parador), you'll see the entrance to the **New Bridge Interpretive Center,** where you can pay to climb down and enter the structure of the bridge itself (€2; Mon-Fri 10:00-19:00, Sat-Sun until 15:00, closes earlier off-season). Inside the empty-feeling hall are modest audiovisual displays about the bridge's construction and the famous visitors to Ronda—worth a quick look only if you have the Bono Turístico pass. The views of the bridge and gorge from the outside are far more thrilling than anything you'll find within.

IN THE OLD TOWN
▲Church of Santa María la Mayor (Iglesia de Santa María)

This church (built from the 15th to the 17th century) has a fine Mudejar bell tower and shares a parklike square with orange trees and City Hall. It was built on and around the remains of Moorish Ronda's main mosque (which was itself built on the site of an ancient Roman temple to Julius Caesar). With a pleasantly eclectic interior that features some art with unusually modern flair, and a good audioguide to explain it all, it's worth a visit.

Cost and Hours: €4.50, daily April-Sept 10:00-20:00, closed Sun 13:00-14:00 for Mass, may close earlier off-season, includes audioguide, Plaza Duquesa de Parcent in the old town.

Visiting the Church: In the room where you purchase your ticket, look for the rare surviving door to the Moorish mosque (that's a mirror; look back at the actual door). The mihrab faced not Mecca, but Gibraltar—where you'd travel to get to Mecca. Partially destroyed by an earthquake, the church was reconstructed with the fusion (or confusion) of Moorish, Gothic, Renaissance, and Baroque styles you see today.

Inside the church, marvel at the magnificent Baroque **Altar del Sagrario** with a statue of the Immaculate Conception in the center. The smaller altar (adjacent on the right) is a good example of Churrigueresque architecture, a kind of Spanish Rococo in which the decoration consumes the architecture—notice that you can hardly make out the souped-up columns. Its fancy decor provides a frame for the artistic highlight of the town, the Dolorosa ("Virgin of the Ultimate Sorrow"). The big fresco of St. Christopher with Baby Jesus on his shoulders (left, above the door where you entered) shows the patron saint both of Ronda and of travelers.

In the center of the church is an elaborately carved **choir** with a series of modern reliefs depicting scenes from the life of the Virgin

Mary. Similar to the Via Crucis (Way of the Cross), this is the Via Lucis (Way of the Light), with 14 stations focusing on the Resurrection and its aftermath (such as #13—the Immaculate Conception, and #14—Mary's assumption into heaven) that serve as a worship aid to devout Catholics. The centerpiece is an ethereal Mary as the light of the world (with the moon, stars, and sun around her).

Head to the left around the choir, noticing the bright **paintings** along the wall by French artist Raymonde Pagegie. He gave sacred scenes a fresh twist—like the Last Supper attended by female servants, or (opposite) the scene of Judgment Day, when the four horsemen of the apocalypse pause to adore the Lamb of God.

The **treasury** (at the far-right corner, with your back to the choir) displays vestments that look curiously like matadors' brocaded outfits—appropriate for this bullfight-crazy town. Before exiting the treasury, find a spiral staircase. Climb the 73 steps to a U-shaped **terrace** around the church's rooftop. Survey the entire deck (ducking under the buttresses) for great views. The highlight is actually inside: Find a tiny door that leads to a breathtaking perch high above the elaborate main altar. (Imagine walking around this ledge before there was the railing.)

Mondragón Palace City Museum (Palacio de Mondragón)

This beautiful, originally Moorish building was erected in the 14th century and is the legendary (but not actual) residence of Moorish kings. The building was first restored in the 16th century (notice the Mudejar tiled courtyard), and its facade dates only from the 18th century. Upstairs is Ronda's Municipal Museum, focusing on prehistory and geology. Wander through its many kid-friendly rooms. Peruse the exhibits on Neolithic toolmaking and early metallurgy (like a seventh-century BC mold for making a sword from molten metal), and brief descriptions of local Roman history. If you plan to visit the Pileta Cave (see "Sights near Ronda," later), find the panels that describe the cave's formation and shape. Linger in the two small gardens with wonderful panoramic views.

ANDALUCÍA

Cost and Hours: €3.50; Mon-Fri 10:00-19:00, Sat-Sun until 15:00, closes earlier off-season; on Plaza Mondragón, +34 952 870 818.

Nearby: Leaving the palace, wander left a few short blocks to the nearby Plaza de María Auxiliadora for more views and a look at the two rare *pinsapos* (resembling extra-large Christmas trees) in the middle of the park; this part of Andalucía is the only region in Europe where these ancient trees still grow.

Plaza de María Auxiliadora leads to **the best Ronda view at sunset** from a viewpoint where windmills once stood. Photographers go crazy reproducing the most famous postcard view of Ronda—the entirety of the New Bridge. Look for the tiled *Puerta de los Molinos* sign and head down, down, down. This pathway is not for the faint of heart, and a bad idea in the heat of the afternoon sun. Wait until just before sunset for the best light and cooler temperatures.

Bandit Museum (Museo del Bandolero)

This tiny museum, while not as intriguing as it sounds, has an interesting assembly of *bandolero* photos, guns, clothing, knickknacks, and old documents and newspaper clippings. The Jesse Jameses and Billy el Niño of Andalucía called this remote area home. One brand of romantic bandits fought Napoleon's army—often more effectively than the regular Spanish troops. The exhibits profile specific *bandoleros* and display books (from comics to pulp fiction) that helped romanticize these heroes of Spain's "Old West." The museum is a bit of a tourist trap—with every available space packed full of memorabilia, and a well-stocked gift shop—but helpful English descriptions make it a fun stop. A free 20-minute movie about *bandoleros* plays only in Spanish.

Cost and Hours: €4, daily 11:00-20:30, Oct-April until 19:00, across main street below Church of Santa María la Mayor at Calle Armiñán 65, +34 952 877 785, www.museobandolero.com.

▲Joaquín Peinado Museum (Museo Joaquín Peinado)

Housed in an old palace, this fresh museum features an overview of the life's work of Joaquín Peinado (1898-1975), a Ronda native and pal of Picasso. Because Franco killed creativity in Spain for much of the last century, nearly all of Peinado's creative work was done in Paris. His style evolved through the big "isms" of the 20th century, ranging from Expressionism to Cubism, and even to eroticism. Peinado's works follow the major trends of his time—understandable, as he was friends with one of the art world's biggest

talents. The short movie that kicks off the display is only in Spanish, though there are good English explanations throughout the museum. Find a famous Cubist version of Don Quixote upstairs and a few Picasso pieces downstairs. It's an interesting modern art experience with no crowds, and fun to be exposed to a lesser-known but very talented artist in his hometown.

Cost and Hours: €4, Mon-Fri 10:00-17:00, Sat until 15:00, closed Sun, Plaza del Gigante, +34 952 871 585, www.museojoaquinpeinado.com.

▲Walk Through Old Town to Bottom of Gorge

From the New Bridge you can descend down Cuesta de Santo Domingo (cross the bridge from the new town into the old, and take the first left just beyond the former Dominican convent, once the headquarters of the Inquisition in Ronda) into a world of white-washed houses, tiny grilled balconies, and winding lanes—the old town. (Be ready for lots of ups and downs—this is not a flat walk.)

A couple of blocks steeply downhill (on the left), you'll see the **House of the Moorish King** (Casa del Rey Moro). It was never home to a king; it was given its fictitious name by the grandson of President McKinley, who once lived here. Although the house is closed and its once-fine belle époque garden is overgrown, it does offer visitors entry to the **"Mine,"** an exhausting series of 280 slick, dark, and narrow stairs (like climbing down and then up a 20-story building) leading to the floor of the gorge. The Moors cut this zig-zag staircase into the wall of the gorge in the 14th century to access water when under siege, then used Spanish slaves to haul water up to the thirsty town (€5, daily 10:00-20:00).

Fifty yards downhill from the garden is the **Palace of the Marquis of Salvatierra** (Palacio del Marqués de Salvatierra, closed to public). As part of the "distribution" of spoils following the Reconquista here in 1485, the Spanish king gave the land for this grand house to the Salvatierra family (who live here to this day). The facade is rich in colonial symbolism from Spanish America—note the pre-Columbian-looking characters (four Peruvian Indians) flanking the balcony above the door and below the family coat of arms.

Just below the palace, stop to enjoy the view terrace. Look below. There are two old bridges, with the Arab Baths just to the right.

Twenty steps farther down, you'll pass through the Philip V gate, for centuries the main gate to the fortified city of Ronda.

ANDALUCÍA

Continuing downhill, you come to the **Old Bridge** (Puente Viejo), rebuilt in 1616 upon the ruins of an Arabic bridge. Enjoy the views from the bridge (but don't cross it yet—we'll do that after visiting the baths below). Then continue down the old stairs past a small, Moorish-inspired electric substation. Swing around the little chapel at the bottom of the staircase to look back up to the highly fortified Moorish city walls. A few steps ahead is the oldest bridge in Ronda, the Arab Bridge (a.k.a. the San Miguel Bridge). For centuries, this was the main gate to the fortified city. In Moorish times, you'd purify both your body and your soul here before entering the city, so just outside the gate was a little mosque (now the chapel) and the Arab Baths.

The **Arab Baths** (Baños Árabes), worth ▲, are evocative ruins that warrant a quick look. They were located half underground to maintain the temperature and served by a donkey-powered water tower. You can still see the top of the shaft (30 yards beyond the bath rooftops, near a cypress tree, connected to the baths by an aqueduct). Water was hoisted from the river below to the aqueduct by ceramic containers that were attached to a belt powered by a donkey walking in circles. Inside the baths, two of the original eight columns scavenged from the Roman ruins still support brick vaulting (€3.50, free Tue 15:00-19:00; generally open Mon-Fri 10:00-19:00, Sat-Sun until 15:00; shorter

hours off-season). A delightful 10-minute video brings the entire complex to life—Spanish and English versions run alternately. Ask about the next English showing as you go in.

From here, hike back to the new town along the other side of the gorge: Climb back up to the Old Bridge, cross it, and take the brick stairs immediately on the left, which lead scenically along the gorge through the Jardines de Cuenca park. Leave the park going left and then uphill on Calle Virgen de los Remedios to the recommended Bar El Lechuguita. Stop for a much-deserved break here, then continue down Calle Rosario to return to the New Bridge.

▲▲Concert at Ronda Guitar House

Local Spanish guitar artist Paco Seco performs a 45-minute solo concert in a 50-seat theater in the back of his shop nearly every night at 19:00. It's an intimate affair with Paco describing his three guitars (historic, classical, and flamenco) and the pieces he performs. Travelers who show this guidebook get a free glass of Ronda wine to enjoy during the show (be sure to ask, as Paco's wife Lucy is happy to provide this to Rick Steves travelers). Seating is first-come, first-seated (Lucy puts your name on the chair). Buy tickets in person, by phone, or from the TI. The Ronda Guitar House is a half-block from the city park at Calle Mariano Soubiron 4 (concert-€15, shop open 10:00-21:00, closed in July, +34 951 916 843, www.rondaguitarhouse.com).

Sights near Ronda

▲Pileta Cave (Cueva de la Pileta)

The Pileta Cave, set in a dramatic, rocky limestone ridge at the eastern edge of Sierra de Grazalema Natural Park, offers Spain's most intimate look at Neolithic and Paleolithic paintings that are more than 30,000 years old. Farmer José Bullón and his family live down the hill from the cave—which was discovered by Bullón's grandfather in 1905. The caves are open only to escorted groups, as guides (speaking English and Spanish) take up to 25 visitors at a time deep into the mountain. Because the number of cave visitors is strictly limited, Pileta's rare paintings are among the best-preserved in the world.

Cost and Hours: €10; tours run year-round Mon-Fri at 11:30, 13:00, and 16:00; Sat-Sun at 11:00, 12:00, 13:00, 16:00, and 17:00; also at 18:00 daily April-early Oct; €3 interpretive map, €10 guidebook; mobile +34 666 741 775 (phone answered 10:00-13:00), www.cuevadelapileta.org.

Reservations and Getting In: Call at least a day ahead, then arrive at least 15 minutes before your reserved time. Budget in a 10-minute steep hike to the ticket booth from the parking lot.

Getting There: Pileta Cave is 14 miles from Ronda, past the town of Benaoján, at the end of an access road. It's particularly handy if you're driving between Ronda and Grazalema.

From Ronda, you can get to the cave by taxi—it's about a half-hour drive on twisty roads—and have the driver wait (€70 round-trip). If you're driving, it's easy: Leave Ronda through the new part of town and take A-374 towards Sevilla. After a few miles, exit left toward Benaoján on MA-7401. Go through Benaoján (MA-7401 changes names to MA-8400), then take a sharp left onto MA-8401 and follow signs (reading *Cueva de la Pileta*) to the cave. Leave nothing of value visible in your car.

Visiting the Cave: Arrive early and be flexible. Bring a sweater and sturdy shoes. You need a good sense of balance to take the tour. The 10-minute hike from the parking lot up a stone-stepped trail to the cave entrance is moderately steep. Inside the cave, it can be difficult to keep your footing on the slippery, uneven floor while being led single file, with only a lantern light illuminating the way.

As you walk the cool half-mile, your guide explains the black, ochre, and red drawings, which are more than 30,000 years old—that's five times as old as the Egyptian pyramids. Among other animals, you'll see horses, goats, cattle, and a rare giant fish, made from a mixture of clay and fat by finger-painting prehistoric people. Surprisingly, the plain-looking stick drawings in black are more recent than the discernible animal shapes. The 200-foot main hall is cavernous and feels almost sacred. Throughout the site, mineral monoliths look adorned in lace and drapery. Stalagmites and stalactites reach toward one another as they have for a million years or so in these caves, and some formations lend themselves to appropriate names like "The Organ" and "The Castle."

Eating near the Cave: Nearby, the lovely village of Montejaque (much nicer than Benaoján) has several good restaurants clustered around the central square.

▲ReservaTauro

As the birthplace of modern bullfighting, Ronda attracts plenty of *aficionados* and even bullfighters themselves. Rafael Tejada worked as an engineer for many years but eventually switched gears to train as a bullfighter. In 2011, he bought land in the nearby *serranía* to raise horses, cows, and stud bulls, and now welcomes visitors to experience his working farm. A visit here allows you to get up close and personal with bulls and horses, as well as try out some matador skills in a practice ring (no bulls, no worries...just the capes). The two-hour option lets you also help the herdsman in one of his daily tasks, such as feeding the free-range bulls, and concludes with local wine and tapas.

Cost and Hours: €28/person for 70 minutes, €40/person for 2 hours, €90/person for 2-3 hour private tour; daily 10:00-19:00, until 18:00 off-season; reservations recommended, +34 951 166 008, www.reservatauro.com.

Getting There: Drivers should leave Ronda through the new part of town and take A-367 (Carretera Ronda-Campillos) toward Campillos. After about 5.5 miles, turn right into a stone gate marked by a small black-and-white, arrow-shaped sign labeled *RESERVATAURO*. If you're visiting without a car, request a special taxi (€24) for round-trip transportation when you book your tour by phone or email.

Sleeping in and near Ronda

Ronda has plenty of reasonably priced, decent-value accommodations. It's crowded only during Holy Week (the week leading up to Easter) and the first week of September (for bullfighting season). Most of my recommendations are in the new town, a short stroll from the New Bridge and about a 10-minute walk from the train station. In cheaper places, ask for a room with a *ventana* (window) to avoid the few interior rooms. Breakfast is usually not included. If arriving by car, email your hotel for driving and parking instructions. For locations, see the "Ronda" map on page 205.

IN THE OLD TOWN

Clearly the best options in town, these hotels are worth reserving early. The first listing is right in the heart of the old town, while Alavera de los Baños is a steep 15- to 20-minute hike below, but still easily walkable to all the sights (if you're in good shape) and in a bucolic setting.

$$ Soho Boutique Palacio San Gabriel has 22 pleasant rooms, a kind staff, public rooms filled with art and books, a cozy wine cellar, and a fine garden terrace. It's a large 1736 labyrinth of a townhouse that's been converted into a characteristic hotel, marinated in history. If you're a cinephile, kick back in the charming TV room—with seats from Ronda's old theater and a collection of DVD classics—then head to the breakfast room to check out photos of big movie stars (and, ahem, a certain travel writer) who have stayed here (RS%, air-con, incognito elevator, Calle Marqués de Moctezuma 19 at Plaza del Gigante, +34 952 190 392, www.sohohoteles.com, palaciosangabriel@sohohoteles.com).

$$ Alavera de los Baños, a delightful oasis located next to ancient Moorish baths at the bottom of the hill, has nine comfortable rooms, two spacious suites, and big inviting public places, with appropriately Moorish decor. This hotel offers a swimming pool, a peaceful Arabic garden, and an eclectic aura of Mediterranean, Moorish, and modern decor. Enjoy the pastoral views of the vast countryside and the horses just beyond the garden (includes breakfast, some rooms have balconies, free parking, closed mid-Dec-Jan, steeply below the heart of town at Calle Molino de Alarcón 2, +34 952 879 143, www.alaveradelosbanos.com, hotel@alaveradelosbanos.com, well run by personable Christian and Inma).

$$$ Hotel Montelirio perches on the cliffs of the western side of the Moorish quarter with dramatic views of the valley and the new town. The former 17th-century palace of a count, it feels both traditional and plush with its 15 classically tasteful rooms (the view rooms are worth the splurge) and its elegant common areas (air-con, elevator, pool, sun deck, terrace dining, Tenorio 8, +34 952 873 855, www.hotelmontelirio.com, recepcion@hotelmontelirio.com).

$ Hotel Ronda provides an interesting mix of minimalist and traditional Spanish decor in this refurbished mansion, which is both quiet and homey. Although its five rooms are without views, the small, lovely rooftop deck overlooks the town (air-con, Ruedo

Doña Elvira 12, +34 952 872 232, www.hotelronda.net, reservas@ hotelronda.net, some English spoken by kind and gentle Sra. Nieves).

IN THE NEW TOWN

More convenient than charming (except the Hotel Enfrente Arte Ronda—in a class all its own), these hotels put you in the thriving new town.

$$ Hotel Enfrente Arte Ronda, on the edge of things a steep 10- to 15-minute walk below the heart of the new town, is relaxed and funky. The 12 rooms are spacious and exotically decorated, but dimly lit. It features a sprawling maze of public spaces with offbeat and repurposed decor, a peaceful bamboo garden, a game and reading room, small swimming pool, sauna, and terraces with sweeping countryside views. Guests can help themselves to free drinks from the self-service bar or have their feet nibbled for free by "Dr. Fish." This one-of-a-kind place is in all the guidebooks, so reserve early (includes buffet breakfast with home-baked bread, air-con, elevator, Calle Real 40, +34 952 879 088, www.enfrentearte.com, enfrentearte@gmail.com).

$$ Hotel Don Miguel, facing the gorge next to the bridge, can seem like staying in a cave, but it couldn't be more central. Of its 30 sparse but comfortable rooms, 20 have gorgeous views. Street rooms come with a little noise (air-con, elevator, pay parking a block away, Plaza de España 4, +34 952 877 722, www. hoteldonmiguelronda.com, reservas@dmiguel.com).

$ Hotel Polo is a boutique gem run by the Puya family in the heart of the new town. Each of its 36 bright and spacious rooms features a watercolor painted by Miguel Puya. Inviting common spaces like the social "Food Corner" and the vast rooftop terrace provide a tranquil respite and cool views (family rooms, air-con, elevator, honesty bar, pay parking, Padre Mariano Souvirón 8, +34 952 872 447, www.hotelpolo.net, reservas@hotelpolo.net).

$ Hotel San Francisco offers 27 small, nicely decorated rooms and rooftop terrace a block off the main pedestrian street in the town center. Their public cafeteria doubles as the breakfast room (family rooms available, air-con, elevator, pay parking, María Cabrera 20, +34 952 873 299, www.hotelsanfrancisco-ronda.com, recepcion@hotelsanfrancisco-ronda.com).

$ Hotel Morales has 18 simple but prim-and-proper rooms, and friendly Lola helps you feel right at home. Interior rooms can be a bit dark, so request to be streetside. There's little traffic at night (air-con, elevator, pay parking nearby, Sevilla 51, +34 952 871 538, www.hotelmorales.es, reservas@hotelmorales.es).

$ Hotel San Cayetano puts you in the heart of the evening paseo. With 22 basic, traditional Mediterranean rooms, it pro-

ANDALUCÍA

vides easy access to recommended restaurants on a pedestrian off-
shoot of the main drag (air-con, elevator, pay parking nearby, Sevilla 16, +34 952 161 212, www.hotelsancayetano.com, reservas@
hotelsancayetano.com).

¢ **Hotel Royal** has a dark reception hall but friendly staff and
29 clean, spacious, simple rooms—many on the main street that
runs between the bullring and bridge. Thick glass keeps out most of
the noise, while the tree-lined Alameda del Tajo park is just across
the way (air-con, pay parking, Calle Virgen de la Paz 42, +34 952
871 141, www.hotelroyalronda.es, reservas@hotelroyalronda.es).

IN THE COUNTRYSIDE NEAR PILETA CAVE

A good base for visiting Ronda and the Pileta Cave (as well as
Grazalema) is **$$ Cortijo las Piletas.** Nestled at the edge of Si-
erra de Grazalema Natural Park (just a 15-minute drive from
Ronda, with easy access from the main highway), this spacious
family-run country estate has eight rooms and plenty of opportuni-
ties for exploring the surrounding area (includes breakfast, din-
ner offered some days—book in advance, mobile +34 605 080 295,
www.cortijolaspiletas.com, info@cortijolaspiletas.com, Pablo and
Elisenda). Another countryside option is **$ Finca La Guzmana,**
run by Peter, an expat Brit. Six beautifully appointed pastel rooms
surround an open patio at this renovated estate house (includes
breakfast, mobile +34 600 006 305, www.laguzmana.com, info@
laguzmana.com). Both hotels offer bird-watching, swimming, and
hiking.

Eating in Ronda

Plaza del Socorro, a block in front of the bullring, is an energetic
scene, bustling with tourists and local families enjoying the square
and its restaurants. The pedestrian-only **Calle Nueva** is lined with
hardworking eateries. To enjoy a drink or a light meal with the best
view in town, consider the terraces of Hotel Don Miguel just under
the bridge.

Sweets: For coffee and pastries, locals like the elegant little
$ Confitería Daver, where they say "once you step inside...it's too
late" (café open daily 8:00-20:30, Calle Virgen de los Remedios 6).

Groceries: The **Día** supermarket is conveniently in the new
town (Mon-Sat 9:15-21:15, closed Sun, Calle Cruz Verde 18).
Maskom is two blocks from Alameda del Tajo park (daily 9:30-
21:30, Calle Molino 36).

TAPAS IN THE CITY CENTER

Ronda has a fine tapas scene. You won't get a free tapa with your
drink as in some other Spanish towns, but these bars have acces-

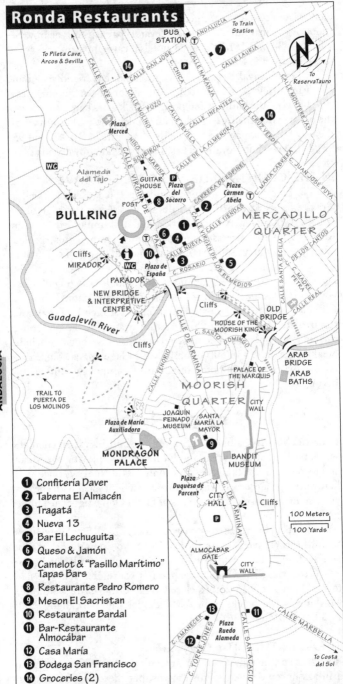

Ronda Restaurants

1. Confitería Daver
2. Taberna El Almacén
3. Tragatá
4. Nueva 13
5. Bar El Lechuguita
6. Queso & Jamón
7. Camelot & "Pasillo Marítimo" Tapas Bars
8. Restaurante Pedro Romero
9. Meson El Sacristan
10. Restaurante Bardal
11. Bar-Restaurante Almocábar
12. Casa María
13. Bodega San Francisco
14. Groceries (2)

sible tapas lists, and they serve bigger plates. Each of the following places could make a fine solo destination for a meal, but they're close enough that you can easily try more than one.

$$ Taberna El Almacén offers a modern take on traditional tapas from many Spanish regions in an industrial chic setting. Friendly, approachable staff can explain the day's specials that are *fuera de carta* (not listed on the menu). Even veggie haters rave over their *pisto*—a type of ratatouille where all ingredients are first cooked separately, then mixed together and served with a fried egg on the side. This is a good spot to try local wines as well (Tue-Sat 13:00-16:00 & 20:30-23:00, Sun 13:00-16:00, closed Mon, Calle Virgen de los Remedios 7, +34 951 489 818).

$$ Tragatá serves creative and tasty tapas in a stainless-steel minimalist bar. There's just a handful of tall tiny tables and some bar space inside, with patio seating on the pedestrian street (same menu), and an enticing blackboard of the day's specials. You'll pay more for it, but if you want to sample Andalusian gourmet (such as asparagus on a stick sprinkled with grated manchego cheese), this is the place to do it. Venture into their serious and pricier plates (daily 13:15-15:45 & 20:00-23:00, Calle Nueva 4, +34 952 877 209).

$$ Nueva 13, the latest entrant in the Calle Nueva tapa fest, serves up admirable and affordable *raciones*. Specials such as *rabo de toro* (bull's-tail stew) and *calamares* (squid) are listed on the giant blackboard inside. Locals love to hang out at the bar, and postcards from previous international visitors adorn the walls. Tables spill onto the pedestrian lane—those with tablecloths are for the full menu, and the rest are for the bar menu (Tue-Sat 12:00-16:00 & 19:00-23:00, Sun 12:00-16:00, closed Mon, Calle Nueva 13, +34 952 190 090).

$ Bar El Lechuguita, a traditional hit with locals, serves a long and tasty list of €1 tapas. Rip off a tapas inventory sheet, cross-reference it with the laminated English translation, and mark which ones you want. Be adventurous and don't miss the bar's namesake, *lechuguita* (#16, a wedge of lettuce with vinegar, garlic, and a secret ingredient). The order-form routine makes it easy to communicate and get exactly what you like, plus you know the exact price. This place is small—just a bar and some stand-up ledges along the wall, plus some rustic tables with stools outside. Ideally, be there when the doors open and grab a spot at the bar (Mon-Sat 13:00-15:00 & 20:15-23:30, closed Sun, Calle Virgen de los Remedios 35).

$ Queso & Jamón is my pick for quality *bocadillos* (sandwiches) with your choice of cheeses and hams. Brothers Antonio and Paco can also advise you on different cured meats, dairy products, oils, and marmalades for a customized foodie picnic (Plaza de España 1, +34 952 877 114).

ANDALUCÍA

NEAR THE BUS STATION

Away from the tourist crowds along Calle Salvador Carrasco, there's a strip of bustling tapas bars that locals call the *Pasillo Marítimo* (Maritime Corridor). Pop into any of them for typical Spanish and Andalusian shareable bar snacks and local conversation.

$$ Camelot goes a step beyond with their sleek interior and tasty, great-value seafood and meat dishes. *Ronderos* like to say it's "food from here for people from here" (Tue-Mon 12:00-16:00 & 20:00-23:00, closed Wed).

DINING IN THE CITY CENTER

Ronda is littered with upscale-seeming restaurants that toe the delicate line between a good dinner spot and a tourist trap.

$$$ Restaurante Pedro Romero, though touristy and overpriced, is a venerable institution in Ronda. It's named for Ronda's most famous son, the first great bullfighter. Assuming a shrine to bullfighting draped in *el toro* memorabilia doesn't ruin your appetite, rub elbows with the local bullfighters or dine with the likes (well, photographic likenesses) of Orson Welles, Ernest Hemingway, and Francisco Franco (daily 12:00-16:00 & 19:30-23:00, aircon, across from bullring at Calle Virgen de la Paz 18, +34 952 871 110).

$$$ Meson El Sacristan is a well-respected restaurant serving classical and innovative dishes with a focus on meat (many prepared in the wood-fired oven). Their 12-hour *rabo de toro* oxtail stew is a favorite. It's a good place to slow down—enjoy the helpful waiters and the rustic setting, either inside or on the quiet square. Their tasting menus are enticing, and the savory homemade *croquetas* are exceptional (Thu-Mon 11:30-23:00, Tue until 17:00, closed Wed and in extreme summer heat, reservations smart, Plaza Duquesa de Parcent 14, +34 952 875 684).

$$$$ Restaurante Bardal has the only Michelin star in town. Local-wonder chef Benito Gómez serves two tasting menus (16 tiny courses-€85, 20 courses-€100, wine extra). While almost comically fancy, this is a delicious experience featuring morsels based on local ingredients. Benito serves about 20 people each lunch and dinner, and all are treated like VIPs (Tue-Sat 12:00-16:30 & 20:00-23:30, closed Sun-Mon, reserve ahead, Calle José Aparicio 1, +34 951 489 828, www.restaurantebardal.com).

OUTSIDE THE ALMOCÁBAR GATE

To entirely leave the quaint old town and bustling city center with all of its tourists and grand gorge views, hike 10 minutes out to the far end of the old town, past City Hall, to a big workaday square that goes about life as if the world didn't exist outside Andalucía.

$$ Bar-Restaurante Almocábar is a favorite eatery for many

Ronda locals. Its restaurant—a cozy eight-table room with Moorish tiles and a window to the kitchen—serves up tasty, creative, well-presented meals from a menu that's well described in English (plus a handwritten list of the day's specials). Many opt for the good salads—rare in Spain. At the bar up front, choose from gourmet tapas like the *serranito* (a pork, roast pepper, and tomato mini sandwich) or you can order from the dining-room menu (Wed-Mon 13:00-16:00 & 19:30-23:00, closed Tue, reservations smart, Calle Ruedo Alameda 5, +34 952 875 977).

$$$ Casa María is a delightful, family-run place managed by Elias and Isabel, daughter Maria, and Lucero the dog. There's no menu—only the promise of a wonderful meal. Just sit down, and for €30 you'll be treated to a full home-cooked feast: salad, vegetables, fish, meat, and dessert. It's worth making a reservation for this adventure. In summer, their tables spill out onto the plaza (Wed-Mon 12:00-15:00 & 19:30-22:30, closed Tue, facing Plaza Ruedo Alameda at #27, +34 951 083 663).

$$ Bodega San Francisco is a rustic bar with homey restaurant seating upstairs and tables out front and on the square. They offer an accessible list of *raciones* and tapas, as well as serious plates and big splittable portions (long hours, closed Thu, same menu in bar and restaurant, Ruedo de Alameda 32, +34 952 878 162).

Ronda Connections

Some destinations are linked with Ronda by both bus and train. Direct bus service to other hill towns can be sparse (as few as one per day), and train service usually involves a transfer in Bobadilla. It's worth spending a few minutes in the bus or train station on arrival to compare schedules and plan your departure (or pick up timetables at the TI). Your options improve from major transportation hubs such as Málaga.

From Ronda by Bus to: Algeciras (1/day, 3 hours, Comes), **La Línea/Gibraltar** (no direct bus, transfer in Algeciras; Algeciras to La Línea/Gibraltar—2/hour, 45 minutes, buy ticket on bus, Comes), **Arcos** (2/day, 2 hours, Comes), **Grazalema** (2/day, 1 hour, Damas), **Zahara** (2/day, Mon-Fri only, 45 minutes, Comes), **Sevilla** (7/day, 2.5 hours, fewer on weekends, Damas; also see trains), **Málaga** (15/day Mon-Fri, 8-10/day Sat-Sun, 2 hours, Damas; access other Costa del Sol points from Málaga), **Marbella** (6/day, 1.5 hours, Avanza), **Nerja** (4 hours, transfer in Málaga; can take train or bus from Ronda to Málaga, bus is better). If traveling to **Córdoba**, it's easiest to take the train since there are no direct buses. Bus info: Damas (www.damas-sa.es), Avanza (www.avanzabus.com), and Comes (www.tgcomes.es).

By Train to: Algeciras (4/day, 2 hours), **Málaga** (1/day, 2.5

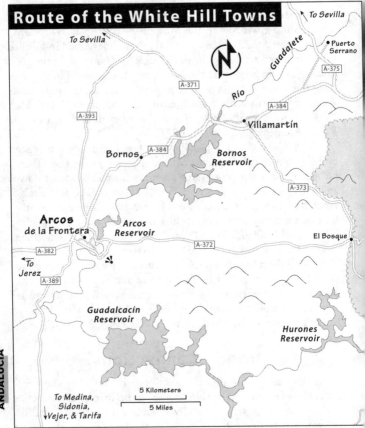

Route of the White Hill Towns

To Sevilla

To Sevilla

Guadalete

Puerto Serrano

A-375

A-371

Río

A-384

Villamartín

A-393

Bornos
A-384

Bornos Reservoir

A-373

Arcos de la Frontera

Arcos Reservoir

A-372

El Bosque

A-382

To Jerez

A-389

Guadalcacín Reservoir

Hurones Reservoir

5 Kilometers

5 Miles

To Medina, Sidonia, Vejer, & Tarifa

ANDALUCÍA

hours, 2 more with transfer in Bobadilla), **Sevilla** (4/day, 3 hours, transfer in Bobadilla, Córdoba, or Antequera), **Granada** (3/day, 2.5 hours), **Córdoba** (2/day direct, 2 hours; 2 more with transfer in Antequera, 2 hours), **Madrid** (2/day direct, 4 hours; more with transfer in Antequera). Any transfer is a snap and time-coordinated; with four trains arriving and departing simultaneously, double-check that you're jumping on the right one. Train info: +34 912 320 320, www.renfe.com.

ROUTE TIPS FOR DRIVERS

Ronda to the South Coast: Drivers who want to dip down to the coast from Ronda can catch A-397 and head over the mountains and down to San Pedro de Alcántara (about 30 miles/50 km). Many trucks use this route as well, so the going may be slow if following a convoy. The longer, winding A-369/A-377 route (about 50 miles/80 km) offers a scenic alternative to reach the coastal town of Estepona. You'll go through gorgeous countryside and a series of

whitewashed villages, but note that the A-377 stretch of this road (from Gaucín to the coast), while perfectly drivable, is in rough shape—expect to go slowly.

Zahara and Grazalema

There are plenty of interesting hill towns to explore. Public transportation is frustrating, so I'd do these towns only by car. Useful information on the area is rare. Fortunately, a good map, the tourist brochure (pick it up in Sevilla or Ronda), and a spirit of adventure work fine.

Along with Arcos, Zahara de la Sierra and Grazalema are my favorite white villages. While Grazalema is a better overnight stop, Zahara is a delight for those who want to hear only the sounds of the wind, birds, and elderly footsteps on ancient cobbles.

ZAHARA DE LA SIERRA

This tiny town in a tingly setting under a Moorish castle (worth ▲ and the climb) has a spectacular view over a turquoise reservoir. While the big church facing the town square is considered one of the richest in the area, the smaller church has the most-loved statue. The Virgin of Dolores is Zahara's answer to Sevilla's Virgin of Macarena (and is similarly paraded through town during Holy Week).

The **TI** is located in the main plaza (closed Mon, gift shop, Plaza del Rey 3, +34 956 123 114, www.zaharadelasierra.es). Upstairs from the TI are Spanish-only displays about the flora and fauna of nearby Sierra de Grazalema Natural Park. A map posted nearby shows the tour and trail system.

Drivers can park for free in the main plaza, or continue up the hill to the parking lot at the base of the castle, just past the recommended Hotel Arco de la Villa. It's one way up and one way down, so follow *salida* signs to depart. The street that connects both churches, Calle de San Juan, is lined with tapas bars and cafés.

Sights in Zahara: During Moorish times, Zahara lay within the fortified castle walls above today's town. It was considered the

gateway to Granada and a strategic stronghold for the Moors by the Christian forces of the Reconquista. Locals tell of the Spanish conquest of the Moors' castle (in 1482) as if it happened yesterday: After the Spanish failed several times to seize the castle, a clever Spanish soldier noticed that the Moorish sentinel would check if any attackers were hiding behind a particular section of the wall by tossing a rock and setting the pigeons in flight. If they flew, the sentinel figured there was no danger. One night a Spaniard hid there with a bag of pigeons and let them fly when the sentinel tossed his rock. Upon seeing the birds, the guard assumed he was clear to enjoy a snooze. The clever Spaniard then scaled the wall and opened the door to let in his troops, who conquered the castle. Ten years later Granada fell, the Muslims were back in Africa, and the Reconquista was complete.

Skip the church, but it's a fun climb up to the remains of the **castle** (free, tower always open). Start at the paved path across from the town's upper parking lot. It's a moderately steep 15-minute hike

ANDALUCÍA

past some Roman ruins and along a cactus-rimmed ridge to the top, where you can enter the tower. Use your phone's flashlight or feel along the stairway to reach the roof, and enjoy spectacular views from this almost impossibly high perch far above the town. As you pretend you're defending the tower, realize that what you see is quite different from what the Moors saw: the huge lake dominating the valley is a reservoir—before 1991, the valley had only a tiny stream.

Sleeping and Eating in Zahara: $ Hotel Arco de la Villa is the town's only real hotel (16 small modern rooms, Wi-Fi in common areas only, +34 956 123 230, www.tugasa.com, arco-de-la villa@tugasa.com). Its very good **$ restaurant** offers a reasonably priced *menú del día*, along with reservoir and mountain views.

GRAZALEMA

A beautiful postcard-pretty hill town, Grazalema offers a royal balcony for a memorable picnic, a square where you can watch old-timers playing cards, and plenty of quiet white-washed streets and shops to explore. Situated within Sierra de Grazalema Natural Park, Grazalema is graced with lots of scenery and greenery. Driving here from Ronda on A-372, you pass through a beautiful parklike grove of

cork trees. While the park is known as the rainiest place in Spain, it's often just covered in a foggy mist. If you want to sleep in a small Andalusian hill town, this is a good choice.

The bare-bones **TI** is located at the car park at the cliffside viewpoint, Plaza de los Asomaderos. When open, it's generally staffed with Spanish-only speakers who can give you a town map and not much else (closed Mon and some holidays, +34 956 132 052, better info online at www.grazalemaguide.com or http://turismograzalema.com). Enjoy the view, then wander into the town.

A tiny lane leads a block from the center rear of the square to Plaza de Andalucía (filled by the tables of a commotion of tapas bars). Shops sell the town's beautiful and famous handmade wool blankets and good-quality leather items from nearby Ubrique. A block farther uphill takes you to the main square with the church, Plaza de España. A coffee on the square here is a joy. Small lanes stretch from here into the rest of the town.

For outdoor gear and adventures, including hiking, caving,

ANDALUCÍA

Grazalema

CALLE DEL CHORRITO

CALLE E. GRAZALEMEÑOS

CALLE DEL PRADO

CALLE DEL TINTE ALTO

CALLE DE SEVILLA

CALLE NUEVA

CALLE DE LA TEJA

CALLE SANTA CLARA ❶

CALLE DE SAN DANIEL ❼

CALLE DEL CARMEN

CALLE DE SAN JOSE

CALLE DE JEREZ

CALLE DE LA TIERRA COLORADA

CALLE NUEVA

CALLE DE CORRALES PRIMEROS

To
Zahara,
El Bosque
& Arcos

A-372

CALLE DEL PIE DE PALO

CALLE DE LAS PARRAS

and canoeing, contact **Horizon** (summer Mon-Sat 9:00-14:00 & 17:00-20:00, closed Sun, shorter hours off-season, off Plaza de España at Calle las Piedras 1, +34 956 132 363, mobile +34 655 934 565, www.horizonaventura.com).

Sleeping in Grazalema: $ La Mejorana Guesthouse is your best bet—if you can manage to get one of its six rooms. This beautifully perched garden villa, with royal public rooms, overlooks the valley from the top of town (includes breakfast, pool, on tiny lane below Guardia Civil headquarters at Santa Clara 6, +34 956 132 527, mobile +34 649 613 272, www.lamejorana.net, info@lamejorana.net, Ana and Andrés can help with local hiking options).

$ Hotel Peñón Grande, named for a nearby mountain, is just off the main square and rents 16 comfortable business-class rooms (air-con, Plaza Pequeña 7, +34 956 132 434, www.hotelgrazalema.com, hotel@hotelgrazalema.com).

¢ Casa de Las Piedras, just a block from the main square, has 16 comfortable en suite double rooms with air-con. The beds feature the town's locally made wool blankets (RS% with 2-night minimum, Calle de las Piedras 32, +34 956 132 014, www.casadelaspiedras.es, reservas@casadelaspiedras.net, Caty and Rafi).

Accommodations
1 La Mejorana Guesthouse
2 Hotel Peñón Grande
3 Casa de Las Piedras

Eateries & Other
4 Plaza de Andalucía Eateries
5 El Torreón
6 Mesón El Simancón
7 Gastrobar La Maroma
8 Supermarket
9 Horizon Adventure Tours

ANDALUCÍA

They also rent nearby apartments that sleep 2-8 people; see details on their website.

Eating in Grazalema: Tiny Plaza de Andalucía has several good bars for tapas with umbrella-flecked tables spilling across the square, including **$$ Zulema** (big salads), **$ La Posadilla**, and **$ La Cidulia.** To pick up picnic supplies, head to the **Eroski** supermarket (Mon-Sat 9:00-14:00 & 17:00-21:00, closed Sun, on Calle las Piedras 12).

$$ El Torreón specializes in local cuisine such as lamb and game dishes, and also has many vegetarian options. Diners are warmed by the woodstove while deer heads keep watch (Thu-Tue 12:00-16:00 & 19:00-23:00, closed Wed, Calle Agua 44, +34 956 132 313).

$$ Mesón El Simancón serves well-presented cuisine typical of the region in a romantic setting. While a bit more expensive, it's considered the best restaurant in town (Wed-Mon 12:00-16:00 & 19:00-23:00, closed Tue, facing Plaza de los Asomaderos and the car park, +34 956 132 421).

$ Gastrobar La Maroma serves home-cooked regional specialties at affordable prices (Tue-Sat 12:00-16:00 & 19:30-22:30,

Sun 13:00-17:00, closed Mon, Calle Santa Clara, near La Mejorana Guesthouse, mobile +34 617 543 756, José & María).

Grazalema Connections: By Bus to Ronda (2/day, 45 minutes), **El Bosque** (1/day, 45 minutes). Bus service is provided by Damas (www.damas-sa.es).

Jerez de la Frontera

With more than 200,000 people, Jerez de la Frontera is your typical big-city mix of industry and dusty concrete suburbs, but it has a lively old center and two claims to touristic fame: horses and sherry. Jerez is ideal for a noontime visit on a weekday. See the famous horses, sip some sherry, wander through the old quarter, and swagger out. For the most efficient visit if arriving by bus or train, taxi from the train station right to the Royal Andalusian School for the equestrian performance, then walk around the corner to Sandeman's for the next English tour.

Orientation to Jerez

Thanks to its complicated medieval street plan, there is no easy way to feel oriented in Jerez—so ask for directions liberally.

The helpful **TI** is on Plaza del Arenal (Mon-Fri 9:00-15:00 & 16:30-18:30, Sat-Sun 9:30-14:30, +34 956 338 874, www. turismojerez.com).

ARRIVAL IN JEREZ
By Bus or Train: The bus and train stations are located side by side, near the Plaza del Minotauro (with enormous headless statue). Unfortunately, you can't store luggage at either one. You can stow bags for free in the Royal Andalusian School's *guardaropa* (coat room) if you attend their equestrian performance, but only for the duration of the show.

Cheap and easy **taxis** wait in front of the train station (€5 to TI; about €7 to the horses). Otherwise, it's a 20-minute **walk** from the stations to the center of town and the TI: Angle across the brick plaza (in front of the stations, with two black smokestacks) to find Calle Diego Fernández de Herrera. Follow this street for several blocks until you reach a little square (Plaza de las Angustias). Leave the square at the far left side down Calle Corredera. In a few minutes you'll arrive at Plaza del Arenal (ringed with palm trees, with a large fountain in the center); the TI is in the arcaded building across the plaza.

By Car from Arcos: Driving in Jerez can be frustrating. The

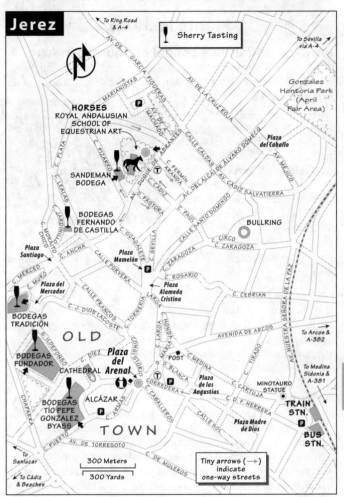

Jerez

♙ **Sherry Tasting**

To Ring Road & A-4

To Sevilla via A-4

AV. DE T. GARCÍA FIGUERAS

AV. DE LA CRUZ ROJA

Gonzalez Hontoria Park (April Fair Area)

MARIANISTAS

AV. DE J. MACHADO

CALLE CALDAS

AV. DEL ALCALDE ÁLVARO DOMECQ

Plaza del Caballo

HORSES
ROYAL ANDALUSIAN SCHOOL OF EQUESTRIAN ART

C. PIZARRO

C. PLAYA

C. LEALAS

DUQUE DE ABRANTES

C. FERMÍN ARANDA

C. CÁDIZ

AV. MÉXICO

AV. CÁDIZ SALVATIERRA

SANDEMAN BODEGA

C. PASTORA

BODEGAS FERNANDO DE CASTILLA

C. JARDINILLO

MORABITO CHICO

C. GUADALETE

C. PAUL

CALLE SANTO DOMINGO

BULLRING

Plaza Santiago

C. MERCED

C. ANCHA

Plaza Mamelón

C. SEVILLA

C. CIRCO

C. ZARAGOZA

C. MURO

CALLE PORVERA

C. ROSARIO

Plaza Alameda Cristina

Plaza del Mercador

CALLE FRANCOS

C. TORNERÍA

C. CEBRIAN

C. J. DIOS LACOSTE

C. LARGA

BODEGAS TRADICIÓN

S. ILDEFONSO

OLD

C. DIEZ

CONSISTORIO

C. MARÍA ANTONIA JESÚS

AVENIDA DE ARCOS

To Arcos & A-382

BODEGAS FUNDADOR

Plaza del **Arenal**

POST

C. MEDINA

C. TIRADO

AV. NUESTRA. SEÑORA DE LA PAZ

To Medina Sidonia & A-381

CATHEDRAL

D. BLANCA

Plaza de las Angustias

C. CARTUJA

MINOTAURO STATUE

ALCÁZAR

CORREDERA

C. CABALLEROS

C. D. F. HERRERA

TRAIN STN.

BODEGAS TÍO PEPE GONZALEZ BYASS

C. ARMAS

CALLE SOL

Plaza Madre de Dios

BUS STN.

CHAPARRA

C. PUERTO

TOWN

AV. DE TORRESOTO

C. DE MULEROS

To Sanlucar

To Cádiz & Beaches

300 Meters
300 Yards

Tiny arrows (→) indicate one-way streets

ANDALUCÍA

outskirts are filled with an almost endless series of roundabouts. Continuing straight through each one (you'll see a rail bridge) and follow traffic and signs to *Centro Ciudad*. The circuitous route will ultimately take you into Plaza Alameda Cristina; park in one of the many underground garages (at Plaza Alameda Cristina or Plaza Arenal, €2.20/hour) and catch a cab or walk. For street parking, blue-line zones require prepaid parking tickets on your dashboard (Mon-Fri 9:00-13:30 & 17:00-20:00, Sat 9:00-14:00, free on Sun and July-Aug afternoons).

Sights in Jerez

▲▲Royal Andalusian School of Equestrian Art

If you're into horses, a performance of the Royal Andalusian School of Equestrian Art (Fundación Real Escuela Andaluza del Arte Ecuestre) is a must. Even if you're not, this is art like you've never seen.

Getting There: From the bus or train stations to the horses, it's about a €9 **taxi** ride. Taxis wait at the exit of the school for the return trip. One-way streets mean there is only one way to arrive by **car:** Follow signs to *Real Escuela de Arte Ecuestre*. Expect to make at least one wrong turn, so allow a little extra time. You'll find plenty of free parking behind the school.

Equestrian Performances

This is an equestrian ballet with choreography, purely Spanish music, and costumes from the 19th century. The stern riders and their talented, obedient steeds prance, jump, hop on their hind legs, and do-si-do in time to the music, all to the delight of an arena filled with mostly tourists and local horse aficionados.

The riders cue the horses with subtle dressage commands, either verbally or with body movements. You'll see both purebred Spanish horses (of various colors, with long tails, calm personalities, and good jumping ability) and the larger mixed breeds (with short tails and a walking—not prancing—gait). The horses must be three years old before their three-year training begins, and most performing horses are male (stallions or geldings), since mixing the sexes brings problems.

The equestrian school is a university, open to all students in the EU, and with all coursework in Spanish. Although still a male-dominated activity, there have recently been a few female graduates. Tightly fitted mushroom hats are decorated with different stripes to show each rider's level. Professors often team with students and evaluate their performance during the show.

Cost and Hours: €21 general seating, €27 "preference" seating; 1.5-hour shows run at 12:00 Tue and Thu (March-July and Nov-Dec), Tue and Thu-Fri (Aug-Oct), and Thu (Jan-Feb), additional shows one Sat a month (twice in June-July); +34 956 922 580, best to purchase in advance online at www.realescuela.org. General seating is fine; some "preference" seats are too close for good overall views. The show explanations are in Spanish.

ANDALUCÍA

Training Sessions

The public can get a sneak preview at training sessions on nonperformance days. Sessions can be exciting or dull, depending on what the trainers are working on. Afterward, you can take a 1.5-hour guided tour of the stables, horses, multimedia and carriage museums, tack room, gardens, and horse health center. Sip sherry in the arena's bar to complete this Jerez experience.

Cost and Hours: €11, Mon 10:00-14:00 plus Wed and Fri Nov-July, last entry at 12:00, tours depart when a large enough group forms. A shorter €6.50 tour covers only the museums and saddlery.

▲▲Sherry Bodega Tours

Spain produces more than 10 million gallons per year of the fortified wine known as sherry. The name comes from English attempts to pronounce Jerez. Although sherry was traditionally the drink of England's aristocracy, today's producers have left the drawing-room vibe behind. Your tourist map of Jerez is speckled with *venencia* symbols, each representing a sherry bodega that offers tours and tasting. (*Venencias* are specially designed ladles for dipping inside the sherry barrel, breaking through the yeast layer, and getting to the good stuff.) For all the bodegas, it's smart to confirm tour times before you go, as schedules can be changeable.

Bodegas Tradición

Although founded in 1998, this winery continues family winemaking traditions that date back to 1650. Their guided tours do a remarkable job of explaining the sometimes difficult-to-understand method of producing sherry. Aficionados claim that their award-winning sherries are not to be missed. Art lovers will get an extra treat: a museum-worthy private collection of works by Murillo, Velázquez, El Greco, Zurburán, Goya, and many others.

Cost and Hours: €35 for 1.5-hour tour, includes 5 sherries, always available in English for up to 12 people; Sept-June Mon-Fri

Sherry

Spanish sherry is not just the sweet dessert wine sold in the States as sherry. In Spain, sherry is (most commonly) a chilled and very dry fortified white wine, often served with appetizers such as tapas, seafood, and cured meats.

British traders invented the sherry-making process as a way of transporting wines so they wouldn't go bad on a long sea voyage. Some of the most popular brands (such as Sandeman and Osbourne) were begun by Brits, and for years it was a foreigners' drink. But today, sherry is typically Spanish.

Sherry is made by blending wines from different grapes and vintages, all aged together. Start with a strong, acidic wine (from grapes that grow well in the hot, chalky soil around Jerez). Mature it in large vats until a yeast crust (*flor*) forms on the surface, protecting the wine from the air. Then fortify it with distilled alcohol.

Next comes sherry-making's distinct *solera* process. Pour the young fortified wine into the top barrel of a unique contraption—a stack of oak barrels called a *criadera*. Every year, one-third of the oldest sherry (in the barrels on the ground level) is bottled. To replace it, one-third of the sherry in the barrel above is poured in, and so on. This continues until the top barrel is one-third empty, waiting to be filled with the new year's vintage.

Fino is the most popular type of sherry (and the most different from Americans' expectations)—white, dry, and chilled. The best-selling commercial brand of *fino* is Tío Pepe; *manzanilla* is a regional variation of *fino,* as is *montilla* from Córdoba. Darker-colored and more complex varieties of sherry include *amontillado* and *oloroso.* And yes, Spain also produces the thick, sweet cream sherries served as dessert wines. A good raisin-y, syrupy-sweet variety is Pedro Ximénez (often marked just "PX"), made from sun-dried grapes of the same name.

9:00-17:00, Sat-Sun 10:00-14:00; July-Aug daily 8:00-15:00; reservations required, private tours available, Calle Cordobeses 3, +34 956 168 618, www.bodegastradicion.com.

Bodegas Rey Fernando de Castilla

Founded in the 1960s by a family with 200 years of winemaking experience, this *bodega* has become a powerhouse, focusing on producing amazing sherry, brandies, and vinegars. Of note are their Palo Cortado and Pedro Ximénez varieties.

Cost and Hours: €15 for tour and tasting; English tours

available Mon-Fri 10:00-14:00—reservations required; Jardini-llo 7, +34 956 182 454, www.fernandodecastilla.com, bodegas@ fernandodecastilla.com.

Sandeman

Just around the corner from the equestrian school is the vener-able Sandeman winery, founded in 1790 and the longtime drink of English royalty. This tour is the aficionado's choice for its knowl-edgeable guides and their quality explanations of the process. Each stage is explained in detail, with visual examples of *flor* (the yeast crust) in backlit barrels, graphs of how different blends are made, and a quick walk-through of the bottling plant. The finale is a chance to taste three varieties.

Cost and Hours: €10 regular sherries, €15 rare sherries, €10 adds tapas to the tasting, tour/tasting lasts 1-1.5 hours; English tours run Mon-Fri 3/day, fewer in winter, Sat by appointment only, closed Sun and all of Jan—check schedules online; reservations not required, Calle Pizarro 10, mobile +34 675 647 177, www.sandeman.com.

Tío Pepe González Byass

The makers of the famous Tío Pepe offer a tourist-friendly tour, with more pretense and less actual sherry-making on display (that's done in a new, enormous plant outside town). But the grand circle of sherry casks signed by a *Who's Who* of sherry drinkers is worth-while. Taste two sherries at the end of the 1.5-hour tour.

Cost and Hours: €16 for tour/tasting, €19 for light tapas lunch with tour; tours run Mon-Sat at 12:00, 13:00, 14:00, 16:00, and 17:00; Sun at 12:00, 13:00, and 14:00; Manuel María González 12, +34 956 357 016. Drivers can park in the underground Alameda Vieja lot at the skippable Alcázar (€2.10/hour).

Other Sherry Bodegas

You'll come across many other sherry bodegas in town, including **Fundador,** located near the cathedral. This bodega, founded by Pedro Domecq, is the oldest in Jerez and the birthplace of the city's brandy. Tastings here are generous (€12, €6 extra for cheese with tastings; Mon-Fri at 12:00, 14:00, and 16:00, also at 20:00 May-Sept, Sat at 12:00 only; Calle San Ildefonso 3, +34 956 151 552, www.grupoemperadorspain.com).

Jerez Connections

Jerez's bus station is shared by multiple bus companies, each with its own schedule. The big ones serving most southern Spain desti-nations are Damas (www.damas-sa.es), Comes (www.tgcomes.es), and Socibus (https://socibusventas.es). Shop around for the best departure time and most direct route. While here, clarify routes for any further bus travel you may be doing in Andalucía—especially if you're going through Arcos de la Frontera, where the ticket office is often closed. Also try Movelia.es for bus schedules and routes.

From Jerez by Bus to: Tarifa (1/day on Algeciras route, 2.5 hours, more frequent with transfer in Cádiz, Socibus), **Algeciras** (1/day, 2.5 hours, Socibus) **Arcos** (hourly, 40 minutes, Damas), **Ronda** (2/day, 2.5-3 hours), **La Línea/Gibraltar** (1/day, 2.5 hours), **Sevilla** (4/day, 1-1.5 hours), **Granada** (1/day, 4.5 hours).

By Train to: Sevilla (hourly, 1 hour), **Madrid** (5/day direct, 4 hours; nearly hourly with change in Sevilla, 4 hours), **Barcelona** (nearly hourly, 7-8 hours, all with change in Sevilla and/or Madrid). Train info: tel.+34 912 320 320, www.renfe.com.

Near the Hill Towns

If you're driving between Arcos and Tarifa, here are several sights to explore.

YEGUADA DE LA CARTUJA

This breeding farm, which raises Hispanic Arab horses according to traditions dating back to the 15th century, offers a 2-hour guided visit and show on Saturday at 11:00 (€23 for best seats in *tribuna* section, €17 for seats in the stands, Finca Fuente del Suero, Carretera Medina-El Portal, +34 956 162 809, www.yeguadacartuja. com). From Jerez, take the road to Medina Sidonia, then turn right in the direction of El Portal—you'll see a cement factory on your right. Drive for five minutes until you see the farm.

MEDINA SIDONIA

This town is as whitewashed as can be, surrounding its church and hill, which is topped with castle ruins. I never drive through here without a coffee break and a quick stroll. Signs to *centro urbano* route you through the middle to Plaza de España (lazy cafés, bakery, plenty of free parking just beyond the square out the gate). If it's lunchtime, consider buying a picnic, as all the necessary shops are nearby and the plaza benches afford a solid workaday view of a perfectly untouristy Andalusian town. According to its own TI, the town is "much appreciated for its vast gastronomy." Small lanes lead from the main square up to Plaza Iglesia Mayor, where you'll find the church and TI (+34 956 412 404, www.medinasidonia. com). At the church, an attendant will show you around for a tip. Even without giving a tip, you can climb yet another belfry for yet another vast Andalusian view. The castle ruins just aren't worth the trouble.

VEJER DE LA FRONTERA

Vejer, south of Jerez and just 30 miles north of Tarifa, will lure all but the very jaded off the highway. Vejer's strong Moorish roots give it a distinct Moroccan (or Greek Island) flavor—you know, black-clad women whitewashing their homes, and lanes that can't decide if they're roads or stairways. The town has no real sights—other than its remarkable views—and very little tourism, making it a pleasant stop. The TI is at Calle de los Remedios 2 (+34 956 451 736, www.turismovejer.es).

The coast near Vejer has a lonely feel, but its pretty, windswept beaches are popular with windsurfers and sand flies. The Battle of Trafalgar was fought just off Cabo de Trafalgar (only a nondescript lighthouse today). I drove the circle so you don't have to.

Sleeping in Vejer: A newcomer on Andalucía's tourist map, the old town of Vejer has just a few hotels. **$$ Hotel La Botica de Vejer** provides 13 comfortable rooms in what was once a local apothecary. Homey decor and view patios add to the charm (Calle Canalejas 13, near Plaza de España, +34 956 450 225, www.laboticadevejer.com). **$$ Hotel Convento San Francisco** is a poorman's parador with spacious rooms in a refurbished convent (Calle Plazuela, +34 956 451 001, www.tugasa.com), while **¢ Hostal La Posada** is family-run place in a modern apartment flat (Calle de los Remedios 21, +34 956 450 258, www.hostal-laposada.com, no English spoken).

SPAIN'S SOUTH COAST

Nerja • Gibraltar • Tarifa

Much of Spain's south coast is so bad, it's interesting. To northern Europeans, the sun is a drug, and this is their needle. Anything resembling a quaint fishing village has been bikini-strangled and Nivea-creamed. Oblivious to the concrete, pollution, ridiculous prices, and traffic jams, tourists lie on the beach like the local sardine skewers—cooking, rolling, and sweating under the sun. It's a fascinating study in human nature.

The most famous stretch of coast is the Costa del Sol, where human lemmings make the scene and coastal waters are so polluted that hotels are required to provide swimming pools. And where Europe's most popular beach isn't crowded by high-rise hotels, most of it's in a freeway chokehold. But the Costa del Sol has suffered in recent economic crises: Real estate, construction, and tourism power the economy, and when these are in decline, the effects are apparent. Crime and racial tensions rise as once-busy individuals are without work.

But the south coast holds a few gems. If you want a place to stay and play in the sun, unroll your beach towel at Nerja, the most appealing resort town on the coast.

And remember that you're surprisingly close to jolly olde England: The land of tea and scones, fish-and-chips, pubs, and bobbies awaits you—in Gibraltar. Though a British territory, Gibraltar has a unique cultural mix that makes it far more interesting than the anonymous resorts lining the coast.

Beyond "The Rock," the whitewashed port of Tarifa—the least-developed piece of Spain's generally overdeveloped southern coast—is a workaday town with a historic center, broad beaches, and good hotels and restaurants. Most important, Tarifa is the

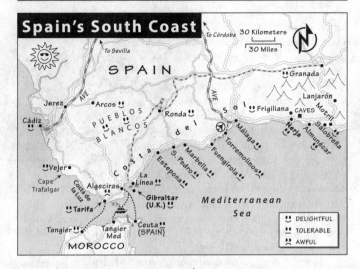

Spain's South Coast

To Córdoba

30 Kilometers

30 Miles

SPAIN

To Sevilla

Granada

Lanjarón

Jerez • Arcos Ronda Frigiliana CAVES Motril

Cádiz PUEBLOS Málaga Nerja Salobreña

BLANCOS Torremolinos Almuñécar

Vejer Fuengirola

Cape Marbella

Trafalgar S. Pedro

Algeciras Estepona

La Línea *Mediterranean*

Tarifa Gibraltar *Sea*

(U.K.)

Tangier Tangier Ceuta

Med (SPAIN)

MOROCCO

	DELIGHTFUL
	TOLERABLE
	AWFUL

perfect springboard for a quick trip to Tangier, Morocco (see next chapter).

These three places alone—Nerja, Gibraltar, and Tarifa—make Spain's south coast worth a trip.

PLANNING YOUR TIME

My negative opinions on the "Costa del Turismo" are valid for peak season (mid-July to mid-Sept). If you're there during a quieter time and you like the ambience of a beach resort, it can be a pleasant stop. Off-season it can be neutron-bomb quiet, with many hotels and restaurants closed until their clients return for the sun.

The whole 150 miles of coastline takes six hours by bus or three hours to drive with no traffic jams. You can resort-hop by bus across the entire Costa del Sol and reach Nerja for dinner. If you want to party on the beach, it can take as much time as it would to get to Mazatlán.

To day-trip to Tangier, Morocco, head for Tarifa.

Nerja

Despite cashing in on the fun-in-the-sun culture, Nerja (NEHR-hah) has kept much of its Old World charm. It has good beaches, a fun evening paseo (strolling scene) that culminates at the Balcony of Europe viewpoint, enough pastry shops and nightlife to keep you fed and entertained, and locals who get more excited about their many festivals than the tourists do.

Although Nerja's population swells from about 22,000 in win-

ter to about 90,000 in the summer, it's more of a year-round destination and a real town than many other resorts. Spaniards have a long tradition of vacationing here, and pensioners from northern Spain move here—enjoying long life spans, thanks in part to the low blood pressure that comes from a diet of fish and wine. While they could afford to travel elsewhere in summer, to escape the brutal heat of inland Spain many Spanish parents take turns with their kids in family condos on the south coast. Whoever stays home to work gets to "be Rodriguez" *(estar de Rodríguez)*, an idiom whose closest English equivalent is "when the cat's away, the mice will play."

For the average traveler coming from Madrid or Barcelona, walking Nerja's streets, where everyone seems to have all the time in the world, is a psychological adjustment—but that's why you're here.

Orientation to Nerja

The tourist center of Nerja is right along the water and crowds close to its famous bluff, the Balcony of Europe (Balcón de Europa). Fine strings of beaches flank the bluff, stretching in either direction. The old town is just inland from the Balcony, while the more modern section slopes up and away from the water.

Tourist Information: The helpful English-speaking TI has bus schedules, tips on beaches and side trips, and brochures for nearby destinations, such as the Caves of Nerja, Frigiliana, Málaga, and Ronda (generally Mon-Fri 10:00-14:00 & 16:30-20:00, Sat-Sun 10:00-13:45; longer evening hours in summer; 100 yards from the Balcony of Europe and a half-block inland from the big church, +34 952 521 531, http://turismo.nerja.es). They also stock the local newspaper *SUR in English*, and their free *Route on Walks* booklet describes good local walks.

ARRIVAL IN NERJA

By Bus: The Nerja station is just a bus stop with an info kiosk on Avenida de Pescia (Mon-Tue 6:00-20:15, Wed-Sun 7:00-12:15 & 14:45-19:00, schedules posted, Alsa, www.alsa.es). To travel from Nerja, buy tickets at the kiosk; if the kiosk is closed, buy them on the bus. If uncertain, ask which side of the street your bus departs from. Because many buses leave at the same times, arrive at least 15 minutes before departure to avoid having to elbow other tourists.

Costa del Sol History

Many Costa del Sol towns come in pairs: the famous beach town with little history, and its smaller yet much more historic partner established a few miles inland—safely out of reach of the Barbary pirate raids that plagued this coastline for centuries. Nerja is a good example of this pattern. Whereas it has almost no history and was just an insignificant fishing village until tourism hit, its more historic sister, Frigiliana, hides out in the nearby hills. The Barbary pirate raids were a constant threat. In fact, the Spanish slang for "the coast is clear" is *"no hay moros en la costa"* (there are no Moors on the coast).

Decadence and lots of skin on the beach are rather new here. During the time of the dictator Franco, the Catholic Church and the Spanish government made society very conservative. Beaches were generally gender segregated. When Raquel Welch starred in *Fathom,* a spy comedy filmed here in 1966, a babe in a bikini was pretty shocking.

Tourism is also a new thing in Nerja. Its first hotels (Balcón de Europa and Portofino) date from after World War II, but tourism didn't start picking up until the 1980s, when the phenomenal Spanish TV show *Verano Azul (Blue Summer)* was set here. This post-Franco program featured the until-then off-limits topics of sexual intimacy, marital problems, adolescence, and so on in a beach-town scene (imagine combining *All in the Family, Baywatch,* and *The Hills*). To this day, when Spaniards hear the word "Nerja," they think of this TV hit.

Despite the fame, development didn't really take off until about 2000, when the expressway finally and conveniently connected Nerja with the rest of Spain. (Granada is now just an easy hour away.) Thankfully, a building code prohibits any new buildings higher than three stories in the old town.

SOUTH COAST

By Car: To find the old-town center and the most central parking, follow *Balcón de Europa, Centro Urbano,* or *Centro Ciudad* signs, and then pull into the big underground municipal lot beneath the Plaza de España (which deposits you 200 yards from the Balcony of Europe; €2/hour, €22/24 hours). The enormous aboveground Parking Carabeo, just east of the Balcony, is slightly cheaper but exposed to brutal sun (€1.80/hour, €18/24 hours). The handiest free parking is about a 10-minute walk farther out, next to the bridge over the dry riverbed (near the town bus stop, just off N-340). Street parking in Nerja can be very tight. Blue lines mean it's metered (pay and display); white lines indicate it's generally free. If you do find a space, read signs carefully—on certain days of the month you're required to move your car. It's best to ask your hotelier if your street spot is OK.

Nerja

To Nerja Caves, Aqueduct,
Cantarriján Beach
& Granada

N-340

100 Meters
100 Yards

AVENIDA DE PESCIA

AV. PESCIA

N-340

To
Málaga

C. JOAQUIN HERRERA

BUS
INFO

WC

Plaza
Cantarero

CALLE A. BUENO

Plaza
Ermita

C. SAN MIGUEL

C. INGENIO

30

P
Free

Río Chillar

Parque
Verano
Azul

CALLE ANTONIO FERRANDIZ CHANQUETE

CALLE CHAPARIL

CALLE DE CASTILLA PEREZ

"TUTTI
FRUTTI"
AREA

MANUEL MARÍN

C. DIPUTACIÓN PROVINCIAL

24

30

32

32

5

CALLE ANT. MILLÓN

CALLE EL BARRIO

CALLE DE CHAPARIL

DOCTOR FERRÁN

C. MÁLAGA

To
El Playazo
Beach

La Torrecilla
Beach

Cliffs

SOUTH COAST

9

28

M. NÚÑEZ

CALLE DE LA PINTADA

CALLE COLÓN

CALLE ALFONSO XII

8

CALLE DE ANGUSTIAS

11

BRONCE

C. NUEVA

C. DE LA CRUZ

12

ANIMAS

NERJA
MUSEUM

Plaza
de
España

CALLE DE GRANADA

4

2

Plaza de
Cavana

C. CARMEN

EL
SALVADOR

23

Del Salón
Beach

CALLE DE ALMIRANTE FERNÁNDIZ

PAS. S. JUAN

CALLE DE

CALLE DE

31   26

17   27   14

15   7

GLORIA

CALLE LA PINTADA

13

29

10

30

POST

CALLE

Cliffs

6

1

Plaza Balcón
de Europa

BALCONY OF
EUROPE

19

18

16

Cliffs

Mediterranean   Sea

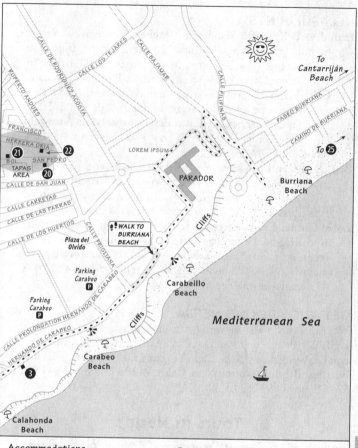

Accommodations

1. Hotel Balcón de Europa
2. Hotel Plaza Cavana
3. Hotel Carabeo
4. Hotel Mena Plaza
5. Hostal Don Peque
6. Hostal & Cafetería Marissal
7. Pensión Miguel
8. Hostal Dianes
9. Hostal Lorca

Eateries & Other

10. Anahí Café
11. Churros 4 Esquinas
12. Good Stuff Café
13. Oliva
14. Sevillano Restaurant & Bar Redondo #2
15. Bar Redondo #1
16. El Pulguilla Fish Bar & Restaurant
17. Los Barriles
18. Haveli
19. Coach & Horses Pub
20. El Chispa (Bar Dolores)
21. La Puntilla Bar Restaurante
22. La Taberna de Pepe
23. Cochran's Terrace Bar Restaurant
24. La Marina
25. To El Chiringuito de Ayo & Educare Aventura
26. Bar El Molino
27. El Burro Blanco
28. Bodega Los Bilbainos
29. El Valenciano Helados Ice Cream
30. Grocery (3)
31. Foodstore Andaluz
32. Launderette (2)

HELPFUL HINTS

Laundry: Full-service launderette **Bubbles Burbujas** is run by friendly Jo from England (same-day service if you drop off in the morning, no self-service, Mon-Fri 9:00-15:00, Sat 9:00-13:00, closed Sun; a few blocks north of Plaza de Cavana at Calle Manuel Marín 1, just off Calle Granada—look for Pasaje Granada pedestrian passage on left, mobile +34 665 539 256). For self-service, try **Lavandería Autoservicio Axarquia** on Calle Castilla Pérez (coins only—no change given, daily 8:00-21:00, +34 952 522 104).

British Media: For a taste of the British expat scene, pick up the monthly magazine *Street Wise* (www.streetwise.es) or tune in to Coastline Radio at 97.6 FM. To imagine being a retired Scandinavian here, pick up *Soltalk* (www.soltalk.com).

Local Guide: **Carmen Fernández** is an excellent licensed guide whose regional knowledge extends from tailored cityscapes to stunning natural areas around Nerja, Frigiliana, Antequera, and Málaga (€90/3 hours, €125/5 hours, mobile +34 610 038 437, mfeyus@gmail.com).

GETTING AROUND NERJA

You can easily **walk** anywhere you need to go. **Taxis** are widely available; you can find stands at Plaza Ermita and near the bus station on Avenida de Pescia. Expect to pay €5-15 (for example, €6 to Burriana Beach, €9 to the Nerja Caves, €12 to Frigiliana, +34 952 524 519 or +34 952 520 537).

Tours in Nerja

The little generic **Tourist Train** offers a 25-minute ramble through town, but there's not a lot to say or see (€4, daily 10:00-18:00 from Plaza Cavana, recorded multilanguage narrations).

For offbeat tours, try **Play Nerja,** which offers 1.5-hour town tours on Segway (€50), electric bike (€30), and foot (€20). Drop in to see what's on (small groups, generally English only, erratic departures, just off Plaza Cavana at Calle Iglesia 2, mobile +34 663 811 514, www.playnerja.com).

Educare Aventura offers kayak and paddleboard rental at Burriana Beach, either on your own (€15/2 hours) or with a guide (€24/2.5 hours). They also have 4x4 tours and hiking trips into the nearby Sierra de Tejeda and Sierra Nevada mountains (office located just behind the recommended Chiringuito de Ayo restaurant at Camino de Burriano 28, +34 952 039 026, www.educare-aventura.com).

Sights in Nerja

▲▲Balcony of Europe (Balcón de Europa)

The bluff, jutting happily into the sea, is completely pedestrianized. It's the center of Nerja's paseo and a magnet for street performers.

The mimes, music, and puppets can draw bigger crowds than the Balcony itself, which overlooks the Mediterranean, miles of coastline, and little coves below.

But this happy bluff was the site of a castle for a thousand years (from the ninth century until a big earthquake in 1884). The Nerja castle was part of a 16th-century lookout system. After the Christian Reconquista drove Muslim Moors into exile in 1492, pirate action from Muslim countries in North Africa picked up. Lookout towers were stationed within sight of one another all along the coast. Warnings were sent whenever pirates threatened (smoke by day, flames by night). To the east (left), if you look closely, you can see two towers breaking the horizon on the distant bluffs.

Later, a Spanish fort built here in the 16th century was destroyed by the English in the early 1800s to keep it from being captured by Napoleon. Its cannons tumbled into the sea, where they sat rusting for about a century. Two were salvaged, cleaned up, and placed here, pointing east and west. Study the beautifully aged metalwork.

Joining the promenade crowds is a cute statue of King Alfonso XII, reminding locals of this popular sovereign—the great-great-

grandfather of today's King Felipe VI—who came here after the devastating earthquake of 1884 (a huge number of locals died). He mobilized the local rich to dig out the community and put things back together. Standing on this promontory amid the ruins of the earthquake-devastated castle, he marveled at the view and coined its now-famous name, Balcón de Europa.

Walk beneath the Balcony for views of the scant remains (bricks and stones) of the ninth-century Moorish castle. Locals claim an underground passage connected the Moorish fortress

SOUTH COAST

with the mosque that existed where the Church of El Salvador stands today.

Church of El Salvador (Iglesia de El Salvador)

Just a block inland from the Balcony, this church was likely built on the ruins of a mosque (in around 1600). You can visit it briefly before the daily 19:00 Mass starts or possibly find it open during the afternoon (no set hours). Its wooden ceiling is Mudejar—made by Moorish artisans working in Christian times. The woodworking technique is similar to that featured in the Alhambra in Granada. Inlaid tiles depicting the stations of the cross ring the walls, and a modern mural of the Annunciation (by local artist Paco Hernandez) decorates the rear of the nave. In front, on the right, is a niche featuring Jesus with a young St. Isidoro, the patron saint of Madrid, Nerja, and farmers (sugarcane farming was the leading industry here before tourism hit). The towering tree in front of the church was brought here from Chile in 1885 and is a symbol of the city. From the porch of the church, look inland (left) to see City Hall, marked by four flags (Andalucía's is green for olive trees and white for the color of the houses in this part of Spain).

Nerja Museum (Museo de Nerja)

This museum, with modern exhibits well described in English, is a good option on a rainy day or if you've just had too much sun. It's run in association with the Nerja Caves (described under "Sights near Nerja"). Exhibits focus on the history of Nerja and the surrounding region, from prehistoric times through its sugar cane heritage. A highlight is the exhibit on the nearby Nerja Caves, including prehistoric tools, weapons, and a skeleton found there. Don't miss the 10-minute video (played constantly in the theater) that shows a Franco-era newsreel about the discovery of the caves in 1959 by farm boys looking for bats. They found prehistoric paintings that go back over 20,000 years.

Cost and Hours: €3, €13 combo-ticket with Nerja Caves; open daily 10:00-16:30, July-Aug until 19:00; Plaza de España 4, +34 952 527 224, www.cuevadenerja.es.

Town Strolls

Nerja was essentially destroyed after the 1884 earthquake—and at the time there was little here beyond the castle anyway. So there's not much to see in the town itself. However, a few of its main streets are worth a ramble. From the Balcony of Europe head inland. Consider first grabbing some ice cream at El Valenciano Helados, a local favorite. You could try the refreshing *chufa*-nut specialty drink called *horchata*.

A block farther beyond the *heladería*, the old town's three main streets come together. The oldest and most picturesque street,

Calle Hernando de Carabeo, heads off to your right (notice how buildings around here are wired on the outside). On the left, Calle Pintada heads inland. Its name means "the painted street," as it was spiffed up in 1885 for the king's visit. Today it's the town's best shopping street, especially the stretch below Calle de la Gloria. And between Calles Carabeo and Pintada runs Calle Almirante Ferrándiz, Nerja's restaurant row, which is particularly lively in the evenings.

BEACHES

The single best thing to do on a sunny day in Nerja is to hit the beach: swim, sunbathe, sip a drink, go for a hike along the rocky coves...or all of the above.

Many of Nerja's beaches are well equipped with bars and restaurants, free showers, and rentable lounge chairs and umbrellas (€4-5/person for chair and umbrella, same cost for 10 minutes or all day). Nearby restaurants rent beach furniture, and you're welcome to take drinks and snacks out to your spot. Spanish law requires all beaches to be open to the public. While there are some nude beaches (such  as Cantarriján, described later), keep in mind that in Europe, any beach can be topless. Watch out for red flags on the beach, which indicate when the seas are too rough for safe swimming (blue=safe, orange=caution, red=swimming prohibited). Keep a careful eye on your valuables—or better yet, leave them in the hotel.

During the summer, Spanish sun worshippers pack the beach from about 11:00 until around 13:30, when they move into the beach restaurants for relief from the brutal rays. The most typical Spanish beach cafés are called *chiringuitos*—shacks selling drinks and simple, cheap-but-good eats. Considering practically every beach has one, *chiringuitos* are a way of life along the coast. When Spaniards play on the *playa* they simply say "see you at the *chiringuito*" to meet friends for a beer and *espetos*—fish, usually sardines, skewered whole, stacked tepee style, and cooked over coal in large barbeque pits.

Beaches lie west and east of the Balcony of Europe. For each area, I've listed beaches from nearest to farthest. Even if you're not swimming or sunbathing, walking along these beaches (and the trails that connect them, if open) is a delightful pastime.

West of the Balcony of Europe

A pleasant series of beaches begin just beneath the Balcony of Europe and stretch on toward sunset. The first is a singular cove, while the next are accessed from the end of Calle Málaga, a five-minute walk through town, and are connected by a promenade and trails.

Del Salón Beach (Playa del Salón)

The sandiest (and most crowded) beach in Nerja is down the walkway to the right of Cafetería Marissal, just west of the Balcony of Europe (to the right as you look out to sea). For great drinks with a view, stop by the recommended Cochran's Terrace on the way down.

Playa la Torrecilla and Playa el Chucho

Farther west is another sandy beach, **Playa la Torrecilla,** crowded with sunbathers, shops, and restaurants. From here, a waterfront promenade brings you to the beach **Playa el Chucho,** popular with families for its shallow water.

El Playazo ("Big Beach")

A short hike west of Playa el Chucho, this beach is preferred by locals, as it's less developed than the more central ones (no showers, bring your own everything). It offers a couple of miles of wide-open spaces that allow for fine walks and a chance to "breathe in the beach."

East of the Balcony of Europe

An appealing walkway called the Paseo de los Carabineros once connected the enticing beaches east of the Balcony, but it's been closed for several years due to erosion and a lack of funds to restore it. For that reason, you'll walk through the modern town above the coast to reach the beaches east of the Balcony of Europe.

Calahonda Beach (Playa Calahonda)

Directly beneath the Balcony of Europe (to the left as you face the sea) is one of Nerja's most characteristic little patches of sun. This pebbly beach is full of fun pathways, crags, and crannies. To get to the beach from the Balcony, simply head down through the arch across from El Valenciano Helados ice cream stand...you'll be on the beach in seconds. Outside of July and August, this beach is relaxed and inviting.

Carabeo and Carabeillo Beaches (Playa Carabeo/Playa Carabeillo)

Tiny and barely developed, these two beaches are wedged into wee coves between the bustling Calahonda and Burriana beaches. For many, their lack of big restaurants and services is a deal-breaker. For others, it's a plus. To reach them, walk along Calle Hernando de Carabeo. The stairs down to Carabeo Beach are at a little view-point on the right (with a big wall map of the area). A bit farther along, a larger view plaza has stairs down to Carabeillo.

Burriana Beach (Playa de Burriana)

Nerja's leading beach is a 20-minute walk east from the Balcony of Europe. Big, bustling, crowded, and fun, it's understandably a top attraction. Burri-ana is ideal for families, with a grand promenade, paddleboats, kayaks, play-grounds, volleyball courts, and other entertainment options. The beach is also lined with a wide range of inviting cafés and restau-rants serving fresh seafood

and *espetos*. Recommended El Chiringuito de Ayo is a destination in itself for its legendary lunchtime paella feast. But consider also the fine eateries neighboring Ayo's.

Getting There: It's an easy walk or a €6 taxi ride. To walk, follow Calle Hernando de Carabeo to the viewpoint plaza above Carabeillo Beach. At the roundabout, go up the first street to the right (you'll see a no-entry sign for cars), jog left (up Calle Cóm-peta) alongside Nerja's boxy parador, then walk around the para-dor, following the signs for *Playa Burriana*. The path will curl right, then twist down a switchbacked path to the beach.

Cantarriján Beach (Playa del Cantarriján)

The only beach listed here not within easy walking distance of Nerja, this is the place if you're craving a more desolate beach (and have a car). Drive about four miles (15 minutes) east (toward Herradura) to the Cerro Gordo exit, and follow *Playa Cantarriján* signs (paved road, just before the tunnel). Park at the viewpoint and hike 30 minutes down to the beach (or, in summer, ride the shuttle bus). Down below, rocks and two restaurants separate two pristine beaches—one for people with bathing suits (or not); the other, more secluded, more strictly for nudists. As this beach is in a natural park and requires a long hike, it provides a fine—and rare—chance to experience the Costa del Sol in some isolation.

SIGHTS NEAR NERJA

The area around Nerja has its own charms, with caves, hiking, and the appealing whitewashed village of Frígiliana.

▲Nerja Caves (Cueva de Nerja)

These caves (2.5 miles east of Nerja), with an impressive array of stalactites and stalagmites, are a classic roadside attraction. The huge caverns, filled with backlit formations, are a big hit with cruise-ship groups and Spanish families—so it's best to go in the morning, when crowds are usually lighter. The visit involves a 45-minute audioguide tour, during which you'll climb deep into the mountain, up and down 400 dark stairs. At the end you reach the Hall of the Cataclysm, where you'll circle the world's largest stalactite column (certified by the *Guinness Book of World Records*). Someone figured out that it took one trillion drops to make the column. The caves, discovered in 1959, have hosted human beings for 30,000 years. If you're fascinated by what you see here, the museum in town has a good exhibit on the caves.

Cost and Hours: €11, €13 combo-ticket with Nerja Museum; daily 9:30-16:30, July-Aug until 19:00, timed entry on the hour and half-hour—book ahead online, last entry one hour before closing; guided tours and science-oriented or nighttime tours also available; easy pay parking, +34 952 529 520, www.cuevadenerja.es.

Getting There: To reach the caves, catch a bus across the street from Nerja's main bus stop (Alsa bus, €1.20, roughly hourly, 10-minute ride—get schedule from TI or the Nerja Museum, or check www.alsa.es). A taxi costs around €9 one-way. Drivers will find the caves well signed (exit 295 on A-7)—just follow the *Cueva de Nerja* signs right to the parking lot. As a little bonus, a footbridge behind the ticket window crosses over a free botanical garden before descending into the pleasant sea village of Maro.

Hiking Around Nerja

Europeans visiting the region for a longer stay generally use Nerja as a base from which to hike. The TI can describe a variety of hikes (ask for the free trails booklet). One of the most popular hikes, Rio Chillar, is a refreshing walk up a river (at first through a dry riverbed, and later up to your shins in water; 7 miles one-way, 2-3 hours total, access the riverbed from Calle de Joaquín Herrera, behind the bus station). Another, more demanding hike takes you to the 5,000-foot summit of El Cielo for the most memorable king-of-the-mountain feeling this region offers.

An easy, somewhat dull two-mile walk ends with a surprisingly impressive sight with an interesting history—the Eagle Aqueduct (Acueducto del Águila). Heading east from town, follow the green-and-white stone sidewalk all the way along Avenida de Pescia. Thirty minutes outside Nerja, you'll pass Capistrano Playa (above Burriana Beach), where you can enjoy views of the coastline, Nerja, and El Cielo in the distance. Half a mile later you'll see the ruins of a 19th-century sugar mill (on the left).

Shortly after the ruins, look for the *Cala Barranco del Maro* sign pointing to the right. Follow the path downhill past the Old Maro Bridge to the base of the aqueduct. Thirty-six arches support four levels; it was built in the 1870s to supply water to the ruined sugar mill you passed on the way here. Look for the double-headed eagle weathervane that gives the aqueduct its name. Bombed during Spain's civil war, the structure was restored in 2011. From here you can cross the Old Maro Bridge and continue on to Maro, a whitewashed, seaside, cliff-top village sitting just below the Nerja Caves (connected over N-340 by a pedestrian footbridge) and above two popular beaches. Alternately, backtrack to Nerja the way you came.

Nightlife in Nerja

Bar El Molino offers live Spanish folk singing nightly in a rustic cavern that's actually an old mill—the musicians perform where the mules once trod. It's touristy but fun (starts at 22:00 but pretty dead before 23:00, fewer shows off-season, no cover—just buy a drink, Calle San José 4). The local sweet white wine, *vino del terreno*—made up the hill in Frigiliana—is popular here (€3/glass).

El Burro Blanco is a touristy flamenco bar that's enjoyable and intimate, with shows nightly in the summer from 21:30. Keeping expectations pretty low, they advertise "The Best Flamenco Show in Nerja" (€15 admission includes a drink, four dancers, recorded music Sun-Thurs, live music Fri-Sat, off-season shows on Tue and Sat only at 20:00, on corner of Calle Pintada and Calle de la Gloria, www.flamencoennerja.com, mobile +34 615 153 961).

Bodega Los Bilbainos is a classic, dreary old dive—a favorite with local men and communists (tapas and drinks, Calle Alejandro Bueno 8).

For more nightlife, check out the pub bars and dance clubs on Antonio Millón and Plaza Tutti Frutti.

Sleeping in Nerja

The entire Costa del Sol is crowded during August and Easter Week, when prices are at their highest. Reserve in advance for peak season—basically mid-July through mid-September—which is prime time for Spanish families to hit the beaches. Any other time of year, Nerja has plenty of available comfy, easygoing low-rise resort-type hotels and rooms.

Compared to the pricier hotels, the better *hostales* are an excellent value. Hostal Don Peque and Pensión Miguel are within a few blocks of the Balcony of Europe.

SOUTH COAST

CLOSE TO THE BALCONY OF EUROPE

$$$$ Hotel Balcón de Europa is the most central place in town. It's right on the water and the square, with the prestigious address Balcón de Europa 1. It has 108 rooms with modern style, plus all the comforts—including a pool and an elevator down to the beach. It's popular with groups. All the suites have seaview balconies, and most regular rooms also come with views (air-con, elevator, gym, sauna, pay parking, +34 952 520 800, www.hotelbalconeuropa. com, reservas@hotelbalconeuropa.com).

$$$ Hotel Plaza Cavana, with 40 rooms, overlooks a plaza lily-padded with cafés. It feels a bit institutional, but if you'd like a central location, marble floors, modern furnishings, an elevator, and a small unheated rooftop swimming pool, dive in (RS%, breakfast included for Rick Steves readers, some view rooms, family rooms, air-con, mini fridge, elevator, pay parking, 2 blocks from Balcony of Europe at Plaza de Cavana 10, +34 952 524 000, www. hotelplazacavana.com, info@hotelplazacavana.com).

$$ Hotel Carabeo is a boutique hotel with seven classy rooms on the cliff east of downtown—less than a 10-minute walk away, but removed from the bustle of the Balcony of Europe (closed mid-Nov-mid-March, five view rooms, includes continental breakfast, air-con, Calle Hernando de Carabeo 34, +34 952 525 444, www. hotelcarabeo.com, info@hotelcarabeo.com).

$$ Hotel Mena Plaza is clean, bright, and friendly, offering 34 rooms on the lethargic Plaza de España right by the Nerja Museum. Some rooms have views and wide balconies (family room, air-con, elevator, pay parking, pool, rooftop terrace, +34 952 520 965, www.hotelmenaplaza.es, info@hotelmenaplaza.es).

$ Hostal Don Peque, an easy couple of blocks' walk from the Balcony of Europe, has 14 bright, colorful, and cheery rooms (eight with balconies—a few with sea views). Owners Roberto and Clara moved here from France and have infused the place with their personalities. They lend beach equipment, and their bar-terrace with a hot tub and views over rooftops and the sea is enticing (family room, breakfast April-Oct only, air-con, Calle Diputación 13, +34 952 521 318, mobile +34 640 778 988, www.hostaldonpeque.com, info@hostaldonpeque.com).

$ Hostal Marissal has an unbeatable location next door to the fancy Hotel Balcón de Europa, and 23 modern, spacious rooms with old-fashioned furniture and balconies (some overlooking the Balcony of Europe action). Their cafeteria and bar, run by helpful staff, make the Marissal even more welcoming (family room, some view rooms, apartment, double-paned windows, air-con, elevator, Balcón de Europa 3, reception at Cafetería Marissal—staffed mornings only in off-season but they'll send you a code to access your room, +34 952 520 199, www.hostalmarissal.com, reservas@hostalmarissal.com).

$ Pensión Miguel offers nine sunny and airy rooms in the heart of "Restaurant Row" (some street noise in front rooms). Breakfast is served on the pretty green terrace with mountain views. The owners—British expats Ian and Jane—are longtime Nerja devotees who will help make your stay a delight (family suite, no air-con but fans and fridges, laundry service, beach equipment, Calle Almirante Ferrándiz 31, +34 952 521 523, mobile +34 679 046 122, www.pensionmiguel.net, pensionmiguel@gmail.com).

$ Hostal Dianes is a simple place—there's no elevator, no breakfast, no balconies, or views—with 10 airy, old-fashioned rooms and a pleasant rooftop terrace. Its location, straddling the residential and nightlife districts, is close enough to the action but far enough away to provide a friendly welcome, good value, and a peaceful night's slumber (large family room, air-con, Calle Pintada 67, +34 952 528 116, www.hostaldianes.com, info@hostaldianes.com).

IN A RESIDENTIAL NEIGHBORHOOD

$ Hostal Lorca is located in a quiet residential area a five-minute walk from the center, three blocks from the bus stop, and close to a small, handy grocery store. Run by a friendly, energetic Dutch couple, Femma and Rick, this *hostal* has nine modern, comfortable rooms and an inviting backyard with a terrace and a small pool. You can use the microwave and take drinks (on the honor system) from the well-stocked fridge. This quiet, homey place is a winner (family room, no air-con but fans, look for a house with flags at Calle Méndez Núñez 20, +34 952 523 426, www.hostallorca.com, hostallorcanerja@gmail.com).

Eating in Nerja

There are three Nerjas: the private domain of the giant beachside hotels; the central zone, packed with fun-loving (and often tipsy) expats and tourists eating and drinking from trilingual menus; and the back streets, where local life goes on as if there were no tourists. The whole old town (around the Balcony of Europe) is busy with lively restaurants. And you're just a 10-minute taxi ride from the whitewashed hill town of Frigiliana, with several lovely restaurants tucked away in its back lanes and perched on its viewpoints.

To pick up picnic supplies, head to the **Mercadona** supermarket (Mon-Sat 9:00-21:00, closed Sun, inland from Plaza Ermita on Calle San Miguel). There's also a handy **Carrefour Express** closer to town (daily) and a **Coviran** supermarket right on Calle Almirante Ferrándiz (daily 9:30-21:00). For an interesting selection of imported foods, check out Frank and Marianne's **Foodstore Andaluz,** a Dutch-run grocery that stocks especially good chocolates and sweets (daily 10:00-20:00, Calle Pintada 46, mobile +34 681 327 841).

Breakfast: Many hotels here overcharge for breakfast. Don't hesitate to go elsewhere, as lots of places serve breakfast for more reasonable prices. For breakfast with a front-row view of the promenade action on the Balcony of Europe, head to one of the first two listed here.

$$ Cafetería Marissal (in the recommended *hostal* of the same name) features wicker seats under the palm trees (options include English breakfasts and a buffet, daily from 8:30).

$ Anahí Café serves tempting pastries and cheap breakfasts to early risers on a tiny balcony overlooking Calahonda Beach— they also sell picnic-perfect loaves of bread to go (daily 8:00-22:00, Calle Puerta del Mar 6, +34 952 521 457).

$ Churros 4 Esquinas is where the chef fries up hot *churros* to dip into a hot pudding-like chocolate drink (daily 7:00-23:00, *churros* 7:00-12:30 & 17:00-20:00, Calle Pintada 57, on the corner of Calle Angustias, mobile +34 626 126 564).

If you're up for a short hike before breakfast, a great target is the recommended **$ El Chiringuito de Ayo** on Burriana Beach (cash only).

At the **$ Good Stuff Café,** Adam makes savory quiches and pies, and Irene makes scones, brownies, carrot cake, banana bread, and Victoria sponge cake (Mon-Sat 9:00-20:00, closed Sun and August; Calle Castilla Perez 4, mobile +34 606 512 586).

ALONG RESTAURANT ROW

Strolling up Calle Almirante Ferrándiz (which some locals call "Cristo" at its far end), you'll find a good variety of eateries, albeit filled with tourists. The presence of expats means you'll find places serving food earlier in the evening than the Spanish norm.

$$$ Oliva feels like a premium restaurant on a cruise ship— white-tablecloth ambience and a gourmet twist on international fusion cuisine made from local products. It's tucked away through a courtyard off the Calle Pintada and has seating both inside and on a quiet back square (daily 13:00-16:00 & 19:00-23:00, Calle Pintada 7, +34 952 522 988).

$$ Sevillano Restaurant, an elegant fixture in a sea of high-energy tapas bars, serves the hungry on both sides of Calle de la Gloria. While they have a standard bar offering free tapas with each drink, for formal dining try the ground-floor dining room or the second-floor rooftop section on the uphill side (daily, Calle Gloria 15 and 17, +34 951 325 119).

$$ Bar Redondo, a sloppy place popular with locals and visitors alike, is a colorfully tiled *taparía* and watering hole. Bartend-ers work from within the completely round, marble-topped bar; if you can't find room there, grab a spot at a wine-barrel table on the street. Buy any drink and choose a free tapa from their enticing list of 25 options. Their bigger dishes, like the *ensalada redondo*, are worth considering. Their second venture, directly across the side-walk, serves seafood and keeps the same format: round bar and free tapas with your drink (daily 12:30-24:00, Calle de la Gloria 10, +34 952 523 344).

$$ El Pulguilla Fish Bar and Restaurant is a great, high-energy place for Spanish cuisine, fish, and tapas. Its two distinct zones (tapas bar up front and more formal restaurant out back) are jammed with enthusiastic locals and tourists. The lively no-non-sense stainless-steel tapas bar doubles as a local pickup joint later in the evening. Drinks come with a free small plate of clams, mus-sels, shrimp, chorizo sausage, or seafood salad. For a sit-down meal (same menu and cost), head all the way back to one of two gigantic terraces (one under a canopy and the other under the stars). Enjoy an exhibit of old black-and-white town photos as you pass through the middle room. Half-portions *(media-raciones)* are available for many items, allowing you to easily sample different dishes (Tue-Sun 12:30-15:45 & 19:00-23:30, closed Mon—"to give our clients a day off," Calle Almirante Ferrándiz 26, +34 952 521 384).

$$ Los Barriles is a family-run bar where Rafa, Carmen, and their son serve up drinks and a short, simple menu of *raciones*, in-cluding a fiery chorizo sausage. Your best bet is to order a drink and wait for the tapa that comes with it. Locals flock here and tourists are treated like locals (long hours, closed Sunday, Calle San José 2).

$$ Haveli, run by Amit and his Swedish wife, Eva, serves good Indian cuisine in a dressy first-floor dining room and on a sunny rooftop terrace. For more than three decades, it's been a hit with Brits, who know their Indian food (daily 19:00-24:00, Sat-Sun also open 13:00-15:00, closed Wed off-season, Calle Almi-rante Ferrándiz 44, +34 952 524 297).

$$ Coach & Horses Pub is a little bit of old England run by no-nonsense British expat Catherine—this is where to find bangers and mash. Although she serves the only real Irish steaks in town, she also caters to vegetarians, with daily specials that go beyond the usual omelet. In fine weather, enjoy the terrace seating (daily 10:30-15:00 & 18:30-late, Calle Almirante Ferrándiz 70, +34 952 520 071).

TAPAS BARS ON OR NEAR CALLE HERRERA ORIA

A 10-minute gentle uphill hike from the water takes you into the residential thick of things, where the sea views come thumbtacked

Britain's Home Away from Home

Particularly in the resorts around Málaga, many of the foreigners who settle in for long holidays are British—you'll find beans on your breakfast plate and Adele for Muzak. Spanish visitors complain that some restaurants have only English menus, and indeed, the typical expats here actually try *not* to integrate. I've heard locals say of the British, "If they could, they'd take the sun back home with them—but they can't, so they stay here." The Brits enjoy their English TV and radio stations, and many barely learn a word of Spanish. (Special school buses take their children to private English-language schools that connect with Britain's higher-education system.) For an insight into this British community, read the free local expat magazines.

to the walls, prices are lower, and locals fill the tables. These three tapas bars are within a block of one another. Each is a colorful local hangout with different energy levels on different nights. Survey all three before choosing one, or have a drink and tapa at each. These places offer table-service meals during normal dining hours, but the action is at the bar, which is generally open all day for tapas and drinks.

Remember that in Nerja, tapas are snack-size portions, generally not for sale but free with each drink. To turn them into more of a meal, ask for the menu and order a full-size *ración* or half-size *media-ración*. The half-portions are generally much bigger than you'd expect.

$ El Chispa (a.k.a. Bar Dolores) is big on seafood, which locals enjoy on an informal terrace adjacent to the bar (enter directly from the street). Their *tomate ajo* (garlic tomato) is tasty, and their piping-hot *berenjena* (fried and salted eggplant) is worth considering—try it topped with *miel de caña*, molasses-like sugarcane syrup. They serve huge portions—*media-raciones* are enough for two (daily, Calle San Pedro 12, +34 952 523 697).

$ La Puntilla Bar Restaurante fills the corner with a boisterous, tiled bar and a more formal restaurant with outdoor tables spilling onto the cobbles (show this book and get a free *digestivo*, daily 12:00-24:00, a block in front of Los Cuñaos at Calle Bolivia 1, +34 952 528 951).

$ La Taberna de Pepe is a family-run, sit-down restaurant (with a few outdoor tables), though it does have a small bar with tapas. The tight, cozy (almost cluttered) interior is decorated with old farm tools and crammed with happy eaters choosing from a short menu of well-executed seafood. It feels a cut above its neigh-

bors (Fri-Wed 12:15-16:00 & 19:00-24:00, closed Thu, Calle Herrera Oria 30, +34 952 522 195).

NEAR THE BALCONY OF EUROPE

$$ Cochran's Terrace Bar Restaurant, just behind Hostal Maris-
sal, serves mediocre meals in a wonderful seaview setting, over-
looking Del Salón Beach (daily 12:00-15:30 & 19:00-23:00). They
also offer breakfast from 8:30 to 10:30 and drinks all day.

$$ La Marina, away from the tourist zone, is a neighborhood
seafood joint bustling with locals and worth the walk. Their *gam-
bas* plate spills onto nearly every butcher-paper tablecloth in the
restaurant (daily 12:00-16:00 & 19:00-24:00, Calle Castilla Pérez
20, +34 952 521 299).

PAELLA FEAST ON BURRIANA BEACH

$ El Chiringuito de Ayo is famous for its character of an owner
and its beachside all-you-can-eat paella feast at lunchtime. For 30
years, Tito (a.k.a. Ayo, a Spanish term of endearment similar to
"grandfather") has been feeding locals. A lovable ponytailed bohe-
mian who promises to be here until he dies, Ayo is a very big personality. He's one of the five kids who discovered the Nerja Caves,
formerly a well-known athlete, and now someone who makes it a
point to hire hard-to-employ people as a community service. The
paella fires get stoked up at about noon and continue through mid-
to-late afternoon. Grab one of a hundred tables under the canopy
next to the rustic open-fire cooking zone and enjoy the beach setting in the shade with a jug of sangria. It's a 20-minute walk from
the Balcony of Europe, at the east end of Burriana Beach—look for
Ayo's rooftop pyramid (open daily "sun to sun" with a full menu,
paella served only in the afternoon, cash only, Playa de Burriana,
+34 952 522 289).

Breakfast at Ayo's: Consider arriving at Ayo's at 9:00. Locals
order the *tostada con aceite de oliva* (toast with olive oil and salt). Ayo
also serves toasted ham-and-cheese sandwiches and good coffee.

Nerja Connections

While there are some handy direct bus connections from Nerja to
major destinations, many others require a transfer in the town of
Málaga. The closest train station is in Málaga. Fortunately, connections between Nerja and Málaga are easy, and the train and
bus stations in Málaga are right next to each other (for more about
Málaga, see "Coastal Towns," later).

Almost all buses from Nerja are operated by Alsa (www.alsa.
es), except the local bus to Frigiliana, which is run by Grupo Fajardo (ask for schedule at TI).

From Nerja by Bus to: Málaga (1-2/hour, 1.5 hours), **Nerja Caves** (1/hour, 10 minutes), **Frigiliana** (about hourly, 15 minutes), **Granada** (7/day, 2-3 hours), **Córdoba** (3/day, 4.5 hours), **Sevilla** (2/day, 5 hours), **Algeciras** (1/day, 3.5 hours). To reach **Ronda, Gibraltar,** or **Tarifa,** you'll transfer in Málaga.

To Málaga Airport (about 40 miles west): Take a direct Alsa bus (2/day, 1.5 hours). Otherwise, catch a bus to the Málaga bus station, then take the local Line A express airport bus (also called L-75, 2/hour, 15 minutes, €3, buy ticket on board) or commuter train C1 (2-3/hour, 10 minutes, €1.80; Málaga's train station is a five-minute walk across the street from the bus station). A taxi from Nerja costs about €65, or ask your Nerja hotelier about airport shuttle transfers (code: AGP, +34 952 048 804).

ROUTE TIPS FOR DRIVERS

Nerja to Granada (60 miles, 95 km, 100 views): Drive east along the coast toward Motril or take the faster A-7, then head north to Granada on the slower N-323 or the quicker A-44. While scenic side trips may beckon, don't arrive late in Granada without a confirmed hotel reservation. See the Granada chapter ("Arrival in Granada/By Car") for tips on how to avoid getting a traffic ticket when driving into the city center.

Frigiliana

The picturesque whitewashed village of Frigiliana (free-hee-lee-AH-nah), only four miles inland from Nerja, makes for a wonderful side trip. A thousand feet above sea level, full of history, and feeling like it dropped in from the mountains of Morocco, it's a striking contrast to its beach resort sister.

Getting There: It's easy: Catch the hourly bus from the stop on Avenida de Pescia (Grupo Fajardo bus, €1, 15 minutes) or hop in a taxi (around €12 one-way).

Getting Oriented: Your landing pad is **Plaza del Ingenio,** a utilitarian hub dividing the old and the new towns. At this little square you'll find the bus stop, taxi stand, tourist train departure point (€3, 25 minutes), free WC, and start of my proposed guided old town walk (next). The TI is a 100-yard walk uphill, in the new town (daily 10:00-14:00, sometimes later; +34 952 534 261, www.turismofrigiliana.es). Pick up a map and the translations of the tiles you'll see displayed around town. The TI shares a building with the free **archaeological museum,** with artifacts and tools unearthed near Frigiliana (including the fifth-century BC skull of a 10-year-old child). Above the TI, situated on a bluff, is an old tower with a grand view.

Frigiliana has many characteristic and romantic little **restau-**

rants, some with commanding views. As the town is most charming in the evening, consider coming up for an early evening walk and dinner (ride the bus up and catch a cab home). Local specialties to try are *berenjenas con miel de caña* (fried eggplant with local cane syrup) and *tortillas de bacalao con miel de caña* (cod cakes with cane syrup).

FRIGILIANA OLD TOWN WALK

This 30-minute stroll—rated ▲▲—comes with lots of ups and downs, commanding views, and delightful back lanes. (It's easier to follow with the fine little town map from the TI. If hoping to catch a bus back to Nerja, note departure times before you start.)

Begin by climbing from Plaza del Ingenio up to the terrace in front of the factory *(ingenio)*—the blocky, un-whitewashed, double-smokestack building that dominates the town. Dating from the 16th century, this still produces molasses-like sugarcane syrup, *miel de caña* (factory closed to public).

From the left end of the factory terrace, hike up the steep street (Calle Real) past shops tempting you with local wine, cork products, and *miel de caña*. At the fork, stay right on the stepped lane (Calle Hernando el Darra) with its black-and-white pavement. At #10 (on the right), notice the tile in the wall—the first in a series of a dozen around town that describe, in poetic Spanish, the story of the 1568 Battle of Peñón.

A few steps before the top of the lane (at #26), turn right into a covered passageway. Climb 100 yards to a viewpoint on the right (above the romantic Garden Restaurant). The valley was once filled with sugarcane. But since the 1970s the cane has been replaced by avocado and mango trees.

Circle uphill and to the left. The street plan dates to medieval times, when the Moors tucked their village here, high in the hills away from coastal raiders. The whitewash dates to the 18th century, when a plague killed 40 percent of the population. To sterilize the town, everything was burned or slathered in lime to kill the germs. It turned out that the whitewash reflected the sun, keeping things cool. People liked it, and it remains to this day. While houses must be white, the trim is your choice. Enjoy the traffic-free tranquility, small restaurants, big views, and flowers.

Follow the lane straight over the crest of the hill and then down. Notice the distinctive, traditional door knockers, shaped like a woman's hand. Common in Morocco, these date back to Moorish times and are known as the "hand of Fatima"—the daughter of the Prophet Muhammad—and are intended to ward off evil.

Continuing scenically downhill, head left down the stepped and steep El Zacatin lane. This means "little souk," and you can imagine it in Moorish times bustling with shops.

El Zacatin ends at Calle Real. At the T-intersection, go a few steps to the right to the inviting café-lined plaza in front of the church.

The **Church of San Antonio of Padua** was built in 1679 and whitewashed in the 1700s to defend against that plague. Step inside. It does retain some of its original painted decor from 1679 at the top of two arches. Skulls (with bishop's miter and royal crown) are a reminder that death is the great equalizer. The second arch is colorfully dedicated to Virgin Mary with her "Ave Maria" logo under the crown. The wooden ceiling is Mudejar style (done by Moorish craftsmen after the Christian reconquest). Many of the altarpieces are floats that hit the streets for a procession each Semana Santa (Holy Week, leading up to Easter). In the left front chapel, notice the dozen masks—one for each of the apostles—worn during Semana Santa.

Leaving church, turn left and follow Calle Real (the only lane in the old town wide enough to fit a car) back to where you started.

Coastal Towns

Buses take five hours to make the Nerja-Gibraltar trip, including a transfer in Málaga, where you may have to change bus companies. Along the way, buses stop at each of the following towns (see map on page 239).

MÁLAGA

Málaga's busy airport is the gateway to the Costa del Sol, and taking a long layover in this seaside city may be worth your while. It has spruced itself up in recent years and deserves at the very least a lengthy stroll and visits to the two impressive museums.

Tourist Information: You can find a TI (Mon-Sat 10:00-14:00 & 16:00-20:00, Sun 10:00-13:00, shorter hours off-season) and information desk in the center of the train station (in front of tracks 1-8) or a larger office at the marina (daily 9:00-20:00, Plaza de la Marina 11, +34 951 926 020, www.malagaturismo.com).

Arrival in Málaga: The bus and train stations—a block apart at the western edge of the town center—both have pickpockets and lockers. You'll want to store your bags in the more modern lockers at the train station.

The easiest and fastest way to get from the airport to the city center is by train (€1.80, 10 minutes, get off at Málaga Centro Alameda). You can also take a taxi (about €15, 15 minutes) to the *casco viejo* (old town). The Line A express bus (also called L-75, €3, pay cash on bus, 15-20 minutes) takes you blocks from the cathedral—get off at Paseo del Parque–Plaza de la Marina, a long tree-lined plaza with florist stalls. From there wander into the old town's pedestrianized zone, which is easy to navigate thanks to signposts on almost every corner indicating tourist sights.

Sights in Málaga: The **Museo Picasso Málaga** holds over 200 paintings, sculptures, and ceramics spanning the artist's life and artistic styles. Pablo Picasso was born in Málaga and first discussed establishing a museum here in 1953. It finally opened 50 years later, thanks to a donation by the artist's daughter-in-law and grandson (€9, audioguide included; daily July-Aug 10:00-20:00, March-June & Sept-Oct until 19:00, Nov-Feb until 18:00; Calle San Agustín 8, a block away from the cathedral entrance; +34 952 127 600, www.museopicassomalaga.org).

For a look at Spanish art just prior to Picasso, visit the **Museo Carmen Thyssen Málaga,** which features 19th-century paintings with mostly Andalusian themes from the collection of Carmen Cervera. (A former Miss Spain, she's the widow of industrial tycoon Hans Heinrich von Thyssen-Bornemisza, whose famous art collection is housed in Madrid.) There are more than 250 works by Sorolla, Fortuny, Zuloaga, Zurbarán, and other Spanish artists exhibited in the restored 16th-century Palace of Villalón (€10, audioguide included; Tue-Sun 10:00-20:00, closed Mon; Plaza Carmen Thyssen/Calle Compañía 10; +34 902 303 131, www.carmenthyssenmalaga.org).

Málaga Connections: Málaga's big, airy, U-shaped **bus station,** on Paseo de los Tilos, has long rows of counters for the various bus companies. In the center of the building is a helpful info desk that can print out schedules for any destination and point you to the right ticket window (daily 7:00-22:00, tel.+34 952 350 061, www.estabus.emtsam.es). Flanking the information desk on either side are old-fashioned pay lockers (buy a token—*una ficha*—from the automat, access closed overnight). The station also has several basic eateries, newsstands, and WCs.

The slick, modern **train station** is just a five-minute walk away: Exit at the far corner of the bus station, cross the street, and enter the big shopping mall (with a food court upstairs) labeled *Estación María Zambrano*—walk a few minutes through the mall to the train station. Modern lockers are by the entrance to tracks 10-11 (security checkpoint), and car-rental offices are by the entrance to tracks 1-8. A TI kiosk is in the main hall, just before the shopping mall. To go from the train station to the bus station, enter the mall by the TI kiosk and follow signs to *estación de autobuses*.

SOUTH COAST

From Málaga by Bus to: Nerja (1-2/hour, 1.5 hours, Alsa), **Ronda** (15/day Mon-Fri, 8-10/day Sat-Sun, 2 hours, Damas; avoid slower Portillo buses), **Algeciras** (hourly, 2-3 hours, Portillo), **La Línea de Concepción/Gibraltar** (5/day, 3 hours, Portillo), **Tarifa** (2/day, 2.5-4 hours, Portillo), **Sevilla** (7/day direct plus 2/day from Málaga's airport, 2.5-4 hours, Alsa), **Granada** (hourly, 1.5-2 hours, Alsa), **Córdoba** (5-6/day, 2-3.5 hours, Alsa), **Madrid** (7/day, 6 hours, Interbus), **Marbella** (hourly, 1 hour, Portillo). Bus info: Alsa (www.alsa.es), Damas (www.damas-sa.es), Interbus (www.interbus.es), Portillo (http://portillo.avanzabus.com).

From Málaga by Train to: Ronda (1/day, 2 hours, 1 more with transfer in Bobadilla), **Algeciras** (3-4/day, 4 hours, transfer in Bobadilla—same as Ronda train, above), **Madrid** (hourly, 3 hours on AVE), **Córdoba** (6/day on Avant, 1 hour; more expensive but no faster on AVE: hourly, 1 hour), **Granada** (6/day, 1.5-3 hours, 1 transfer—bus is better), **Sevilla** (6/day, 2 hours on Avant; 5/day, 3 hours on slower regional trains), **Jerez** (3/day, 4.5 hours, transfer in Dos Hermanas), **Barcelona** (3/day direct on AVE, 6 hours; more with transfer). Train info: +34 912 320 320, www.renfe.com.

FUENGIROLA AND TORREMOLINOS

The most built-up part of the region, where those most determined to be envied settle down, is a bizarre world of Scandinavian package tours, flashing lights, pink flamenco, multilingual menus, and all-night happiness. Fuengirola is like a Spanish Mazatlán with a few older, less-pretentious budget hotels between the main drag and the beach. The water here is clean and the nightlife fun and easy. The once-idyllic Torremolinos has been strip-malled and parking-metered.

MARBELLA

This is the most polished and posh town on the Costa del Sol. High-priced boutiques, immaculate streets set with intricate pebble designs, and beautifully landscaped squares testify to Marbella's arrival on the world-class-resort scene. Have a *café con leche* on the beautiful Plaza de Naranjos in the old city's pedestrian section. Wander down to modern Marbella and the high-rise beachfront apartment buildings to walk along the wide promenade lined with restaurants. Check out the beach scene. Marbella is an easy stop on the Algeciras-Málaga bus route (as you exit the bus station, take a left to reach the center of town). You can also catch a handy direct bus here from the Málaga airport (€9.50, rough-

ly every 1-2 hours, fewer off-season, 45 minutes, http://portillo.
avanzabus.com).

SAN PEDRO DE ALCÁNTARA

This town's relatively undeveloped sandy beach is popular with
young travelers. San Pedro's neighbor, Puerto Banús, is "where the
world casts anchor." This luxurious, Monaco-esque jet-set port,
complete with casino, is a strange mix of Rolls-Royces, yuppies,
boutiques, rich Arabs, and budget browsers.

Gibraltar

One of the last bits of the empire on which the sun never set,
Gibraltar is an unusual
mix of Anglican propri-
ety, "God Save the Queen"
tattoos, English book-
stores, military memo-
ries, and tourist shops. It's
understandably famous
for its dramatic Rock of
Gibraltar, which rockets

improbably into the air from an otherwise flat terrain, dwarfing
everything around it. If the Rock didn't exist, some clever military
tactician would have tried to build it to keep an eye on the Strait
of Gibraltar.

Britain has controlled this highly strategic spit of land since
taking it by force in 1704, in the War of Spanish Succession. In
1779, while Britain was preoccupied with its troublesome overseas
colonies, Spain (later allied with France) declared war and tried
to retake Gibraltar; a series of 14 sieges became a way of life, and
the already-imposing natural features of the Rock were used for
defensive purposes. During World War II, the Rock was further
fortified and dug through with more and more strategic tunnels. In
the mid- to late-20th century, during the Franco period, tensions
ran high—and Britain's grasp on the Rock was tenuous.

Strolling Gibraltar, you can see that it was designed as a modern military town (which means it's not particularly charming). But
over the past 20 years the economy has gone from one dominated
by the military to one based on tourism (as, it seems, happens to
many empires). On summer days and weekends, the tiny colony is
inundated by holiday-goers, primarily the Spanish (who come here
for tax-free cigarettes and booze) and British (who want a change
in weather but not in culture). As more and more glitzy high-rise

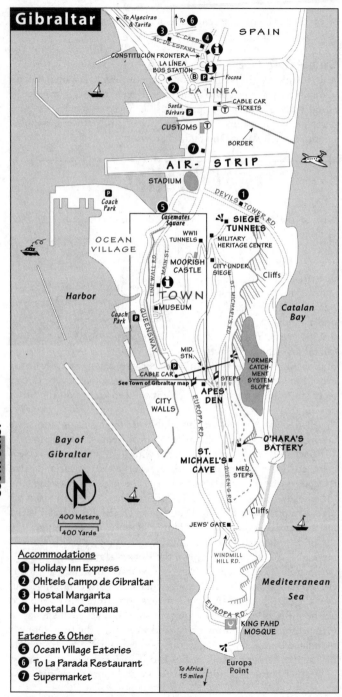

Gibraltar

To Algeciras & Tarifa

To **6**

SPAIN

3
C. CARB.
AV. DE ESPAÑA
4

CONSTITUCIÓN FRONTERA
LA LÍNEA
BUS STATION

B **P** *Focona*

2
LA LÍNEA

Santa
Bárbara **P**

CABLE CAR
TICKETS **T**

CUSTOMS **T**

BORDER

7

AIR- STRIP

STADIUM

Coach
Park **P**

DEVILS **1** TOWER RD.

5
Casemates
Square

SIEGE
TUNNELS

OCEAN
VILLAGE

WWII
TUNNELS

MILITARY
HERITAGE
CENTRE

MAIN ST.

LINE WALL RD.

MOORISH
CASTLE

CITY UNDER
SIEGE

Cliffs

Catalan
Bay

TOWN

Harbor

ST. MICHAEL'S RD.

■ MUSEUM

QUEENSWAY

Coach
Park **P**

P

MID.
STN.

FORMER
CATCH-
MENT
SYSTEM
SLOPE

CABLE CAR

STEPS

See Town of Gibraltar map

APES'
DEN

CITY
WALLS

EUROPA RD.

O'HARA'S
BATTERY

Bay of
Gibraltar

ST.
MICHAEL'S
CAVE

QUEEN'S RD.

MED.
STEPS

Cliffs

400 Meters
400 Yards

JEWS' GATE ■

WINDMILL
HILL RD.

Mediterranean
Sea

Accommodations
1 Holiday Inn Express
2 Oh!tels Campo de Gibraltar
3 Hostal Margarita
4 Hostal La Campana

Eateries & Other
5 Ocean Village Eateries
6 To La Parada Restaurant
7 Supermarket

EUROPA RD.

KING FAHD
MOSQUE

To Africa
15 miles

Europa
Point

SOUTH COAST

resorts squeeze between the stout fortresses and ramparts—as if trying to create a mini-Monaco—there's a sense that this is a town in transition.

Though it may be hard to imagine a community of 30,000 that feels like its own nation, real Gibraltarians, as you'll learn when you visit, are a proud bunch. They were evacuated during World War II, and it's said that after their return, a national spirit was forged. If you doubt that, be here on Gibraltar's national holiday— September 10—when everyone's decked out in red and white, the national colors.

Gibraltarians have a mixed and interesting heritage. Spaniards call them Llanitos (yah-NEE-tohs), meaning "flat" in Spanish, though the residents live on a rock. The locals—a fun-loving and tolerant mix of British, Spanish, and Moroccan, virtually all of whom speak the Queen's English—call their place "Gib."

From a traveler's perspective, Gibraltar—with its quirky combination of Brits, monkeys, and that breathtaking Rock—is an offbeat detour that adds some variety to a Spanish itinerary. If you're heading to Gibraltar from Spain (as you almost certainly are), be aware most Spaniards still aren't thrilled with this enclave of the Commonwealth on their sunny shores. They basically ignore the place—so, for example, if you're inquiring about bus schedules, don't ask how to get to Gibraltar, but rather to La Línea de la Concepción, the neighboring Spanish town. A passport is required to cross the border.

PLANNING YOUR TIME

Make Gibraltar a day trip (or just one overnight); rooms are expensive compared to Spain. Avoid visiting on a Sunday, when just about everything except the cable car is closed.

Before you walk across the border, decide whether you want to take the cable car to the top of the Rock or visit it via a private taxi tour, which you can book online or hire on the spot at a taxi stand just inside the border (see taxi tour under "Sights in Gibraltar," later). Skip the heavily advertised big-bus tour.

If you decide on the cable car, stop at the Gibraltarinfo window on the left before passport control, next to the La Línea taxi stand. If the cable car is running, buy tickets here and take the free shuttle directly to the cable-car station, where you can join the Fast Track line and avoid some of the wait. Ride to the peak for Gibraltar's ultimate top-of-the-rock view.

Then, either walk down—taking in the Apes' Den, siege tunnels, and other sights—or ride the cable car back into town. From the lower cable-car station, follow my self-guided town walk all the way back to Casemates Square. Spend your remaining free time in town before returning to Spain. Note that all the old walls and fortresses make Gibraltar tricky to navigate. Ask for directions: Locals speak English.

Tourists who stay overnight find Gibraltar a peaceful place in the evening, when the town can just be itself. No one's in a hurry. Families stroll, kids play, seniors window shop, and everyone chats...but the food is still not that great.

There's no reason to take a ferry from Gibraltar to visit Morocco—for many reasons, it's a better side trip from Tarifa (specifics covered on page 303).

Orientation to Gibraltar

Gibraltar is a narrow peninsula (three miles by one mile) jutting into the Mediterranean. Virtually the entire peninsula is domi-

nated by the steep-faced Rock itself. The locals live down below in the long, skinny town at the western base of the mountain (much of it on reclaimed land).

For tips on little differences between Gibraltar and Spain— from area codes to electricity— see "Helpful Hints," later.

Tourist Information: Gibraltar's main TI is at John Mackintosh Square, a 10-minute walk south of Casemates Square, near City Hall. Pick up a free map and—if it's windy—confirm that the cable car is running (Mon-Fri 9:00-16:30, Sat 9:30-15:30, Sun 10:00-13:00, +350 200 45000, www.visitgibraltar.gi). At the border, there's a TI window in the customs building (Mon-Fri 9:00-16:30, closed Sat-Sun, +350 200 50762).

ARRIVAL IN GIBRALTAR

No matter how you arrive, you'll need your passport to cross the border. These directions will get you as far as the border; from there, see "Getting from the Border into Town."

By Bus: Spain's La Línea de la Concepción bus station is a five-minute walk from the Gibraltar border. To reach the border, exit the station and bear left toward the Rock (you can't miss it). If you need to store your bags, you can do so at the Gibraltar Airport (see "Helpful Hints," later).

By Car: You don't need a car in Gibraltar. It's simpler to park in La Línea and just walk across the border.

Freeway signs in Spain say *Algeciras* and *La Línea*, often pretending that Gibraltar doesn't exist until you're very close. After taking the La Línea-Gibraltar exit off the main Costa del Sol road, your best bet is to follow signs for *Aduana de Gibraltar* (Gibraltar customs).

Spain vs. Gibraltar

Spain has been annoyed about Gibraltar ever since Great Britain nabbed this prime 2.5-square-mile territory in 1704 (during  the War of Spanish Succession) and was granted it through the Treaty of Utrecht in 1713. Although Spain long ago abandoned efforts to reassert its sovereignty by force, it still tries to make Gibraltarians see the error of their British ways. Over the years Spain has limited Gibraltar's air and sea connections, choked traffic at the three-quarter-mile border, and even messed with the local phone system in efforts to convince Britain to give back the Rock. Still, given the choice—which they got in referenda in 1967 and 2002—Gibraltar's residents steadfastly remain Queen Elizabeth's loyal subjects, voting overwhelmingly (99 percent in the last election) to continue as a self-governing British dependency. Brexit has raised new questions about the relationship, however, and it's possible Spain will again challenge Gibraltar's sovereignty.

The Santa Bárbara parking lot is closest to the border, with room for 650 cars. Ignore anyone who claims to be a cashier and only pay as you leave, at machines or the official booth (€2/hour, €10/day). If Santa Bárbara is full, try a bit farther away at either Parking La Línea or Parking Focona. La Línea's main square—Plaza de la Constitución—covers a huge underground parking garage; just look for the blue "*P*" signs (€18.20/day). The Focona underground lot is also handy (€2.40/hour, €16.50/day, on Avenida 20 de Abril, near the bus station). You'll also find blue-lined pay parking spots in this area (signs give time limits). From the square, it's a five-minute stroll to the border, where you can catch a bus or taxi into town (see "Getting from the Border into Town," next).

If you do drive into Gibraltar, customs checks at the border create a bottleneck. There's often a 30-minute wait during the morning rush hour into Gibraltar and during the evening rush hour back out. Once in Gibraltar, drive along the harbor side of the ramparts (on Queensway—but you'll see no street name). There are big parking lots here and at the cable-car terminal. Parking is generally free—if you can find a spot (it's tight during weekday working hours). By the way, while you'll still find English-style roundabouts, cars here stopped driving on the British side of the road in the 1920s.

Getting from the Border into Town

The "frontier" (as the border is called) is a chaotic hubbub of travel agencies, confused tourists, crafty pickpockets, and duty-free shops (you may see people standing in long lines, waiting to buy cheap cigarettes). The guards barely even look up as you flash your passport. Note that as soon as you cross the border, the currency changes from euros to pounds (see "Helpful Hints," next).

To reach downtown, you can walk (20 minutes), catch a bus, or take a taxi. To get into town by **foot,** walk straight across the runway (look left, right, and up), then head down Winston Churchill Avenue. Angle right at the second roundabout, then walk along the fortified Line Wall Road to Casemates Square.

From the border, you can ride **bus #5** (regular or London-style double-decker, runs every 15 minutes) three stops to Market Square (just outside Casemates Square) or stay on to Cathedral Square, at the center of town. From Market Square, Gibraltar city buses head to various points on the peninsula—a useful route for most tourists is bus #2, which goes to the cable-car station and Europa Point (Gibraltar's southernmost point). Border buses and city buses have different, nontransferable tickets (border bus-€2.10/£1.40 one-way, city bus-€2.40/£1.80 one-way or €3.30/£2.50 for an all-day ticket; drivers accept either currency and give change).

A **taxi** from the border is pricey (€9/£6 to the cable-car station). If you plan to join a taxi tour up to the Rock (see "Sights in Gibraltar," later), note that you can book one right at the border.

HELPFUL HINTS

Gibraltar Isn't Spain: Gibraltar, a British colony, uses different coins, currency (see below), and stamps than those used in Spain. Note that British holidays such as the Queen's (official) birthday (on a Saturday in June) and Bank Holidays are observed, along with local holidays such as Gibraltar's National Day (Sept 10).

Use Pounds, not Euros: Gibraltar uses the British pound sterling (£1 = about $1.30). Like other parts of the UK, Gibraltar mints its own Gibraltar-specific banknotes and coins featuring local landmarks, people, and historical events—offering a colorful history lesson. Gibraltar's pounds are not generally accepted in the UK, so try to use up your Gibraltar bills before you leave.

Merchants in Gibraltar also accept euros...but at an unfavorable exchange rate. You'll save money by hitting up an ATM and taking out what you'll need (look along Main Street). Before you leave, stop at an exchange desk and change back what you don't spend (at about a 5 percent loss), since Gibraltar currency is hard to change in Spain.

On a quick trip, don't bother drawing out cash; you can

buy things with your credit card or use euros (though you may get pounds back in change).

Phones: To dial a Gibraltar phone number, use country code 350 (United Kingdom) rather than 34 (Spain).

Hours: This may be the United Kingdom, but Gibraltar follows a siesta schedule, with some businesses closing from 13:00 to 15:00 on weekdays and shutting down at 14:00 on Saturdays until Monday morning.

Electricity: Gibraltar uses the British three-pronged plugs (not the European two-pronged ones). Your hotel may be able to loan you an adapter.

Baggage Storage: There's no luggage storage at the bus station, but there is a bag check at the Gibraltar Airport, which is right across the border (£3-6/item; go to airport info desk in departures hall).

John Mackintosh Hall: This is your classic British effort to provide a cozy community center. Without a hint of tourism, the upstairs library welcomes drop-ins to enjoy local newspapers and free Wi-Fi (Mon-Fri 9:30-19:30, closed Sat-Sun, 308 Main Street, +350 200 78000).

Activities: The **King's Bastion Leisure Centre** fills an old fortification (the namesake bastion) with a modern entertainment complex just outside Cathedral Square. On the ground floor is a huge bowling alley; upstairs are an ice-skating rink and a three-screen cinema (www.leisurecinemas.com). Rounding out the complex are bars, restaurants, discos, and lounges (daily 9:00-24:00, air-con, +350 200 44777, www.kingsbastion.gov.gi).

Monkey Alert: The monkeys, which congregate at the Apes' Den on the Rock, have gotten more aggressive over the years, spoiled by being fed by tourists. Keep your distance and don't feed them; it's best to have no food with you when you visit the Rock.

Gibraltar Walk

Gibraltar town is long and skinny, with one main street (called Main Street). Stroll the length of it from the cable-car station to Casemates Square, following this little self-guided walk. A good British pub and a room-temperature pint of beer await you at the end.

From the cable-car terminal, turn right (as you face the harbor) and head into town. Soon you'll come to the **Trafalgar cemetery,** a reminder of the colony's English military heritage; two of the seamen who died of wounds after the 1805 Battle of Trafalgar are buried here, and those who perished during the battle

Town of Gibraltar

Accommodations

1. O'Callaghan Eliott Hotel
2. To Hoilday Inn Express
3. Bristol Hotel

Eateries

4. The Clipper Pub
5. The Star Bar
6. The Living Room
7. Gauchos Steakhouse
8. All's Well Pub
9. Market Place & Produce Market
10. Supermarket
11. Marks & Spencer; Bon Bon Cash & Carry
12. The Waterfront & other eateries

Other

13. John Mackintosh Hall
14. Governor's Residence
15. Convent Guard Room
16. John & Yoko's Wedding Site
17. King's Bastion Leisure Centre

SOUTH COAST

To Airstrip & Border

To Siege Tunnels

MOORISH CASTLE

FISHMARKET LN.
SMITH DORRIEN AVE.
CORRAL RD.

Casemates Square

QUEENSWAY

RECLAMATION RD.

COOP.

PARLIAMENT LN.

IRISH TOWN
TUCKEY
MAIN ST.
ENGINEER LN.
BELL LN.

MARKET
CORNWALL'S
MABELL LN.

John Mackintosh Square

COLLEGE LN.
KING ST.

SYNAGOGUE

GIBRALTAR MUSEUM

Common-wealth Park

LIBRARY
GOVERNOR'S ST.
P. EDWARD'S RD.

Cathedral Square

GEORGE'S

GOV. LN.
MAIN ST.

LIME WALL ROAD
TOWN RANGE
PRINCE EDWARD'S RD.
FLAT BASTION RD.

QUEENSWAY

Queensway Quay & Marina

100 Meters
100 Yards

CHARLES V WALL

Trafalgar Cemetery

SOUTHPORT GATES

BOYD RD.

ROSIA RD.
EUROPA RD.

To Top of the Rock

CASTLE RD.
WILLIS'S RD.

To St. Michael's Cave

CABLE CAR STATION

Botanical Gardens

were consigned to the sea. (Of course, Lord Nelson was taken to London and buried in St. Paul's Cathedral.) Next you'll arrive at the **Charles V wall**—a reminder of Gibraltar's Spanish military heritage—built in 1540 by the Spanish to defend against marauding pirates. Gibraltar was controlled by Moors (711-1462), Spain (1462-1704), and then the British (since 1704). Passing through the Southport Gates, you'll see one of the many blue-and-white history plaques posted about town.

Heading into town, you pass the tax office, then **John Mackintosh Hall,** which has free Wi-Fi and a copy of today's *Gibraltar Chronicle* upstairs in its library. The *Chronicle* comes out Monday through Friday and has covered the local news since 1801. The Methodist church (which puts on a rousing karaoke-style service on Sunday afternoons) sponsors the recommended **Carpenter's Arms** tearoom.

The pedestrian portion of Main Street begins near the **governor's residence.** The British governor of Gibraltar took over a Franciscan convent, hence the name of the local White House: The Convent. The formally classic **Convent Guard Room,** facing the governor's residence, is good for photos.

Gibraltar's courthouse stands behind a **small tropical garden,** where John and Yoko got married back in 1969 (as the ballad goes, they "got married in Gibraltar near Spain"). Sean Connery did, too. Actually, many Brits like to get married here because weddings are cheap, fast (only 48 hours' notice required), and legally recognized as British.

Main Street now becomes a **shopping drag.** You'll notice lots of colorful price tags advertising tax-free booze, cigarettes, and sugar (highly taxed in Spain). Lladró porcelain, while made in Valencia, is popular here (because it's sold without the hefty Spanish VAT—Value-Added Tax). The Catholic cathedral retains a whiff of Arabia (as it was built on the remains of a mosque), while the big **Marks & Spencer department store** helps vacationing Brits feel at home.

Continue several more blocks through the bustling heart of Gibraltar. If you enjoy British products, this is your chance to stock up on Cadbury chocolates, digestive biscuits, wine gums, and Weetabix—but you'll pay a premium, since it's all "imported" from the UK.

The town (and this walk) ends at **Casemates Square.** While a lowbrow food circus today, it originated as a barracks and place for ammunition storage. When Franco closed the border with Spain in 1969, Gibraltar suffered a labor shortage, as Spanish guest workers could no longer commute into Gibraltar. The colony countered by inviting Moroccan workers to take their place—ending a nearly 500-year Moroccan absence, which began when the Moors fled in 1462. As a result, today's Moroccan community dates only from the 1970s. Whereas the previous Spanish labor force simply commuted in to work, the Moroccans needed apartments, so Gibraltar converted the Casemates barracks for that purpose. Cheap Spanish labor has crept back in, causing many locals to resent store clerks who can't speak proper English.

If you go through the triple arches at the end of the square, you'll reach the covered **produce market** and food stalls. Across the busy road a few minutes' walk farther is the well-marked entrance to the **Ocean Village** boardwalk and entertainment complex (described later, under "Eating in and near Gibraltar").

Sights in Gibraltar

IN TOWN
▲Gibraltar Museum

Built atop a Moorish bath, this museum tells the story of a chunk of land that has been fought over for centuries. Start with the cheerleading 15-minute video overview of the story of the Rock—a worthwhile prep for the artifacts (such as ancient Roman anchors made of lead) you'll see in the museum. Then wander through the remains of the 14th-century Moorish baths. Upstairs you'll see military memorabilia, a 15-foot-long model of the Rock (compare it with your map to see all the changes), wonderful century-old photos of old Gibraltar, paintings by local artists, and, in a cave-like room off the art gallery, a collection of prehistoric remains and artifacts. The famous skull of a Neanderthal woman found in Gibraltar is a copy (the original is in the British Museum in London). Unearthed in Forbes' Quarry (at the north end of the Rock) in 1848, this was the first Neanderthal skull ever discovered. No one realized its significance until a similar skull found years later in Germany's Neanderthal Valley was correctly identified—stealing the name, claim, and fame from Gibraltar.

Cost and Hours: £5, Mon-Fri 10:00-18:00, Sat until 14:00, closed Sun, on Bomb House Lane near the cathedral, www.gibmuseum.gi.

ON THE ROCK OF GIBRALTAR

The actual Rock of Gibraltar—specifically, the Upper Rock Nature Reserve—is the colony's best sight. Its main draws are the stupendous view from the very top and the temperamental resident monkeys you'll encounter on the way down. Other attractions include a hokey cave (St. Michael's), a glass "skywalk" and a suspension bridge, and the impressive Great Siege Tunnels drilled into the rock.

Visiting the Rock: You have two options for touring the Rock—take a taxi tour or ride the cable car.

The **taxi tour** includes entry to St. Michael's Cave and the Great Siege Tunnels, a couple of extra stops, and running commentary from your licensed cabbie/guide. Because the cable car doesn't get you very close to the cave and tunnels (and doesn't cover cave and tunnel admission), take the taxi tour if you'll be visiting these sights and don't want to walk.

The **cable car** takes you to the very top of the Rock (which the taxi tours don't). You can then take a long, steep, scenic walk down, connecting the various sights by foot as you stroll along paved lanes (it's a pleasant walk down).

There's no reason to take a big-bus tour (advertised and sold all over town) considering how fun and easy the taxi tours are. Private cars are not allowed high on the Rock.

Taxi Tour of the Rock

Minivans driven by cabbies trained and licensed to lead these 1.5-hour trips are standing by at the border and at various points in town (including Cathedral Square, John Mackintosh Square, Casemates Square, Trafalgar Cemetery, and near the cable-car station). They charge £31/person (likely 4-person minimum, includes nature reserve and sights ticket, +350 200 70027, www.

gibraltartaxiassociation.com). Taxi tours and big buses do the same 1.5-hour loop tour with four stops: a Mediterranean viewpoint (called the Pillar of Hercules), St. Michael's Cave (15-minute visit), a viewpoint near the top of the Rock where you can get up close to the monkeys, and the Great Siege Tunnels (20-minute visit). Buddy up with other travelers and share the cost.

Cable Car to the Summit

Buy your tickets for the six-minute cable-car ride at the Gibraltarinfo kiosk just before the border, at the cable-car station, or online at http://gibraltarinfo.gi/cable-car/. Tickets bought at the Gibraltarinfo kiosk or online include Fast Track entry as well as shuttle service to and from the border. The cable car won't run if it's windy or rainy; if the weather is questionable, ask at the Gibraltarinfo kiosk or the TI before heading to the station.

To take in all the sights, I recommend **hiking down** instead of taking the cable car back. Simply hiking down without visiting the sights is enjoyable, too. Approximate hiking times: from the top of the cable car to St. Michael's Cave—25 minutes; from the cave to the Apes' Den—20 minutes; from the Apes' Den to the Great Siege Tunnels—30 minutes; from the tunnels back into town, passing the Moorish Castle—20 minutes. Total walking time, from top to bottom: about 1.5 hours (on paved roads with almost no traffic), not including sightseeing. For hikers, I've connected the dots with directions later.

In winter (Nov-March), the cable car stops halfway down for those who want to get out, gawk at the monkeys, and take a later car down—but you'll probably see monkeys at the top anyway.

Cost: A one-way cable-car ticket up is £14. A round-trip ticket is £16, but you won't be able to leave the upper cable-car area. If you plan to ride up and walk down, you'll also need to buy a £13 "nature reserve" ticket (includes entry to all sights).

Hours: The cable car runs every 10-15 minutes, or continuously in busy times (daily from 9:30; April-Oct last ascent at 19:15, last descent at 19:45; Nov-March last ascent at 17:15, last descent at 17:45). Lines can be long if a cruise ship is in town.

Information: http://gibraltarinfo.gi/cable-car/.

Multimedia Guide/App: The included multimedia guide explains what you're seeing from the spectacular viewpoints up top (pick it up at the well-marked booth at the summit—must leave ID and return before leaving the summit—or download the guide using free Wi-Fi).

Sights on the Rock

The various sights on the Rock keep the same hours: Daily 9:30-19:15, until 18:15 late Oct-late March.

▲▲▲The Summit

The cable car takes you to the real highlight of Gibraltar: the summit of the spectacular Rock itself. The limestone massif is nearly a mile long, rising 1,400 feet with very sheer faces. According to legend, this was one of the Pillars of Hercules (paired with Djebel Musa, another mountain across the strait in Morocco), marking the edge of the known world in ancient times.

Local guides say that these pillars are the only places on the planet where you can see two seas and two continents at the same time.

In AD 711, the Muslim chieftain Tarik ibn Ziyad crossed over from Africa and landed on the Rock, beginning the Moorish conquest of Spain and naming the Rock after himself—Djebel-Tarik ("Rock of Tarik"), which became "Gibraltar."

At the cable-car terminal at the top of the Rock you'll find a view terrace and a café. From here you can explore old ramparts and drool at the 360-degree view of Morocco (including the Rif Mountains and Djebel Musa), the Strait of Gibraltar, the bay stretching west toward Algeciras, and the twinkling Costa del Sol arcing eastward. The views are especially crisp on brisk off-season days. Below you (to the east) stretches a vast, vegetation-covered slope—part of a giant catchment system built by the British in the early 20th century to collect rainwater for use by the military garrison and residents. Broad sheets once covered this slope, catching the rain and sending it through channels to reservoirs carved inside the rock. (Gibraltar's water is now provided through a desalination system.)

• *Up at the summit, you'll likely see some of the famed...*

▲▲Apes of Gibraltar

The Rock is home to about 200 "apes" (actually, tailless Barbary macaques—a type of monkey). Taxi tours stop at the Apes' Den, but if you're on your own, you'll probably see them at the top and at various points on the walk back down (basically, the monkeys cluster anywhere that tourists do—hoping to get food). The males are bigger, females have beards, and newborns are black. They live about 15 to 20 years. Legend has it that

SOUTH COAST

as long as the monkeys remain here, so will the Brits. (According to a plausible local legend, when word came a few decades back that the ape population was waning, Winston Churchill made a point to import reinforcements.) Keep your distance from the monkeys. Guides say that for safety reasons, "they can touch you, but you can't touch them." And while guides may feed them, you shouldn't—it disrupts their diet and encourages aggressive behavior, not to mention it's illegal and there's a £500 fine. Beware of the monkeys' kleptomaniac tendencies; they'll ignore the peanut in your hand and claw after the full bag in your pocket. Because the monkeys associate plastic bags with food, keep your bag close to your body:

Tourists who wander by absentmindedly, loosely clutching a bag, are apt to have it stolen by a purse-snatching simian.

• *If you're hiking down, you'll find that your options are clearly marked at most forks. I'll narrate the longest route down, which passes all the sights en route.*

From the top cable-car station, exit and head downhill on the well-paved path (toward Africa). You'll go by the viewpoint for taxi tours (with monkeys hanging around, waiting for tour groups to come feed them), pass under a ruined observation tower, and eventually reach a wide part of the road. Most visitors will want to continue to St. Michael's Cave (skip down to that section), but you also have an opportunity to hike (or ride a shuttle bus) steeply up to...

O'Hara's Battery

At 1,400 feet, this is the actual highest point on the Rock. A massive 9.2-inch gun sits on the summit, where a Moorish lookout post once stood. The battery was built after World War I, and the last test shot was fired in 1974. Locals are glad it's been mothballed—during test firings, they had to open their windows, which might otherwise have shattered from the pressurized air blasted from this gun. You can go inside to see not only the gun but the powerful engines underneath that were used to move and aim it. The iron rings you see every 30 yards or so along the military lanes around the Rock once anchored pulleys used to haul up guns like the huge one at O'Hara's Battery.

• *From the crossroads below O'Hara's Battery, the right (downhill) fork leads down to a restaurant and shop, then the entrance to...*

▲St. Michael's Cave

Studded with stalagmites and stalactites, eerily lit, and echoing with classical music, this cave is dramatic, corny, and slippery when wet. Considered a one-star sight since Neolithic times, the cave was alluded to in ancient Greek legends—when it was believed to be the Gates of Hades (or the entrance of a tunnel to Africa). All taxi tours stop here (entry included in cost of taxi tour). This sight requires a long walk for cable-car riders. Walking through takes about 15 minutes; you'll pop out at the gift shop.

• *From here, most will head down to the Apes' Den (see next paragraph), but serious hikers have the opportunity to curl around to* **Jews' Gate** *at the tip of the Rock, then circle around the back of the Rock on the strenuous* **Mediterranean Steps** *(leading back up to O'Hara's Battery). To do this, turn sharply left after St. Michael's Cave and head for Jews' Gate, the closest thing in Gibraltar to "wilderness." If this challenging 1.5-to-2-hour hike sounds enjoyable, get details at the TI before setting out.*

The more standard route is to continue downhill. At the three-way fork, you can take either the middle fork (more level) or the left fork (hillier, but you'll see monkeys at the Apes' Den) to the Great Siege Tunnels.

*The **Apes' Den**, at the middle station for the cable car, is a scenic terrace where monkeys tend to gather, and where taxi tours stop for photo ops.*

Continue on either fork (they converge), following signs for Great Siege Tunnels, *for about 30 more minutes. Eventually you'll reach a terrace with flags of the United Kingdom and Gibraltar (until Brexit, the EU flag flew as well) and a fantastic view of Gibraltar's airport, the "frontier" with Spain, and the Spanish city of La Línea de la Concepción. From here, the Military Heritage Centre is beneath your feet (described below), and it's a short but steep hike up to the...*

▲Great Siege Tunnels

Also called the Upper Galleries, these chilly tunnels were blasted out of the rock by the Brits during the Great Siege by Spanish and French forces (1779-1783). The clever British, safe inside the Rock, wanted to chip and dig to a highly strategic outcrop called "The Notch," ideal for mounting a big gun. After blasting out some ven-

tilation holes for the miners, they had an even better idea: Use gunpowder to carve out a whole network of tunnels with shafts that would be ideal for aiming artillery. Eventually they excavated St. George's Hall, a huge cavern that housed seven guns. These were the first tunnels inside the Rock; more than a century and a half later, during World War II, 30 more miles of tunnels were blasted out. Hokey but fun dioramas help recapture a time when Brits were known more for conquests than for crumpets.

• *Hiding out in the bunker below the flags (go down the stairs and open the heavy metal door—it's unlocked) is the...*

Military Heritage Centre

This small, one-room collection features old military photographs from Gibraltar. The second room features a poignant memorial to the people who "have made the supreme sacrifice in defense of Gibraltar."

• *From here, the road switchbacks down into town. At each bend in the road you'll find one of the next three sights.*

City Under Siege

This hokey exhibit is worth a quick walk-through if you've been fascinated by all this Gibraltar military history. Displayed in some of the first British structures built on Gibraltar soil, it re-creates the days of the Great Siege, which lasted more than three and a half years (1779-1783)—one of 14 sieges that attempted but failed to drive the Brits off the Rock. With evocative descriptions, some original "graffiti" scratched into the wall by besieged Gibraltarians, and some dioramas, the exhibit explains what it was like to live on the Rock, cut off from the outside world, during those challenging times.

World War II Tunnels

In November 1942, American Army General Dwight D. Eisenhower took charge of Operation Torch, the Allies' plan to occupy French North Africa. From a network of passageways deep within the Rock of Gibraltar, Eisenhower and British admiral Andrew Browne Cunningham conducted the first major collaboration between British and American forces in World War II.

During the war, Britain added 30 miles of tunnels beneath this strategic rock. It was enough space to accommodate an entire city—including a water distillation plant, barracks, generators, repair shops, hospitals, and a telephone exchange—for soldiers and civilians engaged in wartime operations against the Nazis.

Tours of the tunnels leave approximately hourly and are accompanied by an audioguide (included in the nature reserve ticket). You can simply show up and join the next available tour, or check at the TI or Gibraltarinfo kiosk about reserving a time.

Moorish Castle

Actually more a tower than a castle, this recently restored building is basically an empty shell. (In the interest of political correctness, the tourist board recently tried to change the name to "Medieval Castle"...but it *is* Moorish, so the name didn't stick.) It was constructed on top of the original castle built in AD 711 by the Moor Tarik ibn Ziyad, who gave his name to Gibraltar.

• *The tower marks the end of the Upper Rock Nature Reserve. Heading downhill, you begin to enter the upper part of modern Gibraltar. While you could keep on twisting down the road, keep an eye out for staircase shortcuts into town (most direct are the well-marked Castle Steps).*

Nightlife in Gibraltar

Compared to the late-night bustle of Spain, where you'll see young parents out strolling with their toddlers at midnight, Gibraltar is extremely quiet after-hours. Main Street is completely dead (with the exception of a few lively pubs, mostly a block or two off the main drag). Head instead to the **Ocean Village** complex, a five-minute walk from Casemates Square, where the boardwalk is lined with bars, restaurants, and a casino. Another waterfront locale—a bit more sedate—is the **Queensway Quay Marina.** (Both areas are described later, under "Eating in and near Gibraltar.") Kids love the

SOUTH COAST

King's Bastion Leisure Centre (described earlier, under "Helpful Hints").

Some pubs, lounges, and discos—especially on Casemates Square—offer live music (look around for signs, or ask at the TI). **O'Callaghan Eliott Hotel** hosts free live jazz on Thursday and Saturday evenings.

Sleeping in and near Gibraltar

Gibraltar is not a good value for accommodations. There are only a handful of hotels and (disappointingly) no British-style B&Bs. As a general rule, the beds are either bad or overpriced. The rooms I list here range from about £70 to more than £135 a night.

As an alternative, consider staying at one of my recommended accommodations in La Línea de la Concepción, across the border from Gibraltar in Spain, where hotels are a much better value.

IN GIBRALTAR TOWN

$$$$ O'Callaghan Eliott Hotel, with four stars, boasts a rooftop pool with a view, a fine restaurant, bar, terrace, inviting sit-a-bit public spaces, and 123 modern, stylish business-class rooms—all with balconies (air-con, elevator, pay parking, centrally located at 2 Governor's Parade, up Library Street from main drag, +350 200 70500, www.ocallaghanhotels.com, eliott@ocallaghancollection.com).

$$$ The Holiday Inn Express, near the north end of the Rock, has 120 reliably comfortable rooms (air-con, elevator, limited free parking, 21 Devil's Tower Road, +350 200 67890, www.ihg.com, reservations@hiexgibraltar.com).

$$ Bristol Hotel offers 60 basic, slightly worn English rooms in the heart of Gibraltar—noise can be a problem (air-con, elevator, swimming pool; limited free parking; 10 Cathedral Square, +350 200 76800, www.bristolhotel.gi, reservations@bristolhotel.gi).

ACROSS THE BORDER, IN LA LÍNEA

Staying in Spain—in the border town of La Línea de la Concepción—offers an affordable, albeit less glamorous, alternative to sleeping in Gibraltar. The streets north of the bus station are lined with inexpensive *hostales* and restaurants. These options are just a few blocks from the La Línea bus station and an easy 15-minute walk to the border—get directions when you book. All but Oh!tels Campo are basic, family-run *hostales,* offering simple, no-frills rooms at a good price for a mix of tourists and refinery and port laborers.

$$$ Oh!tels Campo de Gibraltar is a huge blocky building, with 227 cookie-cutter rooms spread over seven floors. It's a big,

friendly business-class hotel that is just blocks from the border, around the corner from the bus station. It's also easy to access by car as it's on the main road coming into town. Stay here if you rented a car to avoid lining up to cross the border. Ask for a room on the top floors with expansive views of the Rock (air-con, elevator, pool, large patio, underground pay parking, at the intersection of Avenida Príncipe de Asturias and Avenida del Ejército, +34 956 178 213, www.ohtelscampodegibraltar.es, recepcion.campodegibraltar@ohtels.es).

$ **Hostal Margarita** is a bit farther from the border, but its fresh, modern rooms are a step above the other *hostales* in the area (air-con, elevator, limited pay parking, Avenida de España 38, +34 856 225 211, www.hostalmargarita.com, info@hostalmargarita.com).

$ **Hostal La Campana** has 17 rooms at budget prices. Run by Ivan and his dad Andreas, this place is simple, clean, and friendly but lacks indoor public areas except for its breakfast room (air-con, elevator, limited free street parking, pay parking in nearby underground garage, just off Plaza de la Constitución at Calle Carboneros 3, +34 956 173 059, www.hostalcampana.es, info@hostalcampana.es).

Eating in and near Gibraltar

IN GIBRALTAR TOWN

Take a break from *jamón* and sample some English pub grub: fish-and-chips, meat pies, jacket potatoes (baked potatoes with fillings), or a good old greasy English breakfast. English-style beers include chilled lagers and room-temperature ales, bitters, and stouts. In general, the farther you venture away from Main Street, the cheaper and more local the places become; I've listed a few of my favorites. Or venture to one of Gibraltar's more upscale developments at either end of the old town: Ocean Village or Queensway Quay.

Downtown, near Main Street

$ **The Clipper** pub offers filling meals—including some salads and all-day breakfast—and Murphy's stout on tap (Mon-Fri 9:00-23:00, Sat 9:00-16:00, Sun 10:00-23:00, on Irish Town Lane, +350 200 79791).

$$ **The Star Bar,** which claims to be Gibraltar's oldest bar, is on a quiet side street with an unpubby, modern interior (Mon-Sat

SOUTH COAST

8:00-22:00, Sun 10:00-22:00, 12 Parliament Lane, off Main Street and across from Corner House Restaurant, +350 200 75924).

$ The Living Room is a fast, cheap-and-cheery café run by the Methodist church with a missionary's smile. It's upstairs in the Methodist church on Main Street (Mon-Fri 10:00-16:00, closed Sat-Sun and Aug, volunteer-run, no alcohol, 100 yards past the governor's residence at 297 Main Street, +350 200 77491).

$$$ Gauchos is a classy, atmospheric steakhouse actually inside the wall, just outside Casemates Square (daily 12:00-16:00 & 18:30-23:00, Waterport Casemates, +350 200 59700).

Casemates Square Food Circus: The big square at the entrance of Gibraltar contains a variety of restaurants, ranging from fast food (fish-and-chips joint, Burger King, and Pizza Hut) to inviting pubs spilling out onto the square. The **$$ All's Well** pub serves everything from a full English breakfast to salads or fish-and-chips, and offers pleasant tables with umbrellas under leafy trees (food served daily 10:00-19:00, open later for drinks, +350 200 72987). Fruit stands and cheap takeout food stalls bustle just outside the entry to the square at the **Market Place** (Mon-Sat 9:00-14:00, closed Sun).

Groceries: The Spanish supermarket chain **Eroski** has two locations in Gibraltar: between the border and the airstrip at 12 Winston Churchill Avenue; and in the ICC building, just outside Casemates Square on Line Wall Road (daily 8:00-21:00, ICC location closed Sat). The **Bon Bon Cash & Carry** minimarket is on the main drag, off Cathedral Square (daily 9:30-19:00, Main Street 239). Nearby, **Marks & Spencer** has a small food market on the ground floor, with fresh-baked pastries and lots of UK snacks (Mon-Fri 9:00-19:00, Sat 9:30-17:00, closed Sun).

Ocean Village

This development is the best place to get a look at the bold new face of Gibraltar. Formerly a dumpy port, it's been turned into a swanky marina fronted by glassy high-rise condo buildings. The boardwalk arcing around the marina is packed with shops, restaurants, and bars—Indian, Mexican, sports bar, pizza parlor, Irish pub, fast food, wine bar, and more. Anchoring everything is

Gibraltar's casino. While the whole thing can feel a bit corporate, it offers an enjoyable 21st-century contrast to the "English village" vibe of Main Street (which can be extremely sleepy after-hours).

SOUTH COAST

Queensway Quay Marina

To dine in yacht-club ambience, stroll the marina and choose from a string of restaurants serving the boat-owning crowd. When the sun sets, the quay-side tables at each of these places are prime dining real estate. **$$$ The Waterfront Restaurant** serves upscale bistro fare in its lounge-lizard interior and at great marina-side tables outside (daily 12:00-22:00, +350 200 45666). Other options include Indian, Italian, trendy lounges, and (oh, yeah) Spanish.

IN LA LÍNEA

The pedestrian street Calle Real, several blocks north of the La Línea bus station, is lined with inexpensive cafeterias, restaurants, and tapas bars. La Línea doesn't offer anything out of the ordinary, but you could try the local indoor/outdoor ambience of **La Parada** for *pescadito frito*—typical Andalusian batter-fried fish (Calle Duque de Tetuán 2, Plaza de la Iglesia, +34 856 121 669).

Gibraltar Connections

BY BUS

The nearest bus station to Gibraltar is in La Línea de la Concepción in Spain, five minutes from the border—ask at the Gibraltar TI for schedules. The nearest train station is at Algeciras, which is the region's main transportation hub (for Algeciras connections, see the end of this chapter).

    From La Línea de la Concepción by Bus to: Algeciras (2/hour, fewer on weekends, 45 minutes), **Tarifa** (6/day, 1 hour), **Málaga** (5/day, 3 hours), **Ronda** (no direct bus, transfer in Algeciras; Algeciras to Ronda: 1/day, 3 hours), **Granada** (3/day, 6-7 hours, change in Malaga), **Sevilla** (5/day, 4.5 hours), **Córdoba** (1/day, 5 hours), **Madrid** (1-2/day, 8 hours).

BY PLANE

From Gibraltar, you can fly to various points in Britain and Morocco: British Airways flies to London Heathrow (www.britishairways.com); EasyJet connects to several UK airports (www.easyjet.com); and Royal Air Maroc has service to Casablanca and Tangier (www.royalairmaroc.com). The airport is easy to reach; you can't enter town without crossing its runway (code: GIB, www.gibraltarairport.gi).

ROUTE TIPS FOR DRIVERS

Gibraltar to Nerja (125 miles/200 km): Barring traffic problems, the trip along the Costa del Sol is smooth and easy by car—much of it on a new toll highway. Just follow the coastal highway east. After Málaga, follow signs to *Almería* and *Motril*.

Tarifa

Mainland Europe's southernmost town is whitewashed and Arab-feeling, with a lovely beach, an old castle, restaurants swimming in fresh seafood, in-expensive places to sleep, enough windsurfers to sink a ship, and best of all, hassle-free boats to Morocco. Though Tarifa is pleasant, the main reason to come here is to use it as a springboard to Tangier, Morocco—a remarkable city worth ▲▲.

As I stood on Tarifa's town promenade under the castle, looking across the Strait of Gibraltar at the almost-touchable Morocco, my only regret was that I didn't have this book to steer me clear of gritty Algeciras on earlier trips. Tarifa, with 35-minute boat transfers to Tangier departing about every hour, is the best jumping-off point for a Moroccan side trip, as its ferry route goes directly to Tangier Ville Port in the city center. (The other routes, from Algeciras or Gibraltar, take you to the Tangier MED Port, 25 miles east of Tangier city.) For details on taking the ferry to Tangier from Tarifa—or joining an easy belly-dancing-and-shopping excursion-type tour—see the Morocco & Tangier chapter.

Don't expect blockbuster sights or a Riviera-style beach resort. Tarifa is a seaside town where you just feel good to be on vacation. Its atmospheric old town and long, broad stretch of wild Atlantic beachfront more than compensate for the more functional parts of this port city. The town is a hip and breezy mecca among windsurfers, drawn here by the strong winds created by the bottleneck at the Strait of Gibraltar.

Tarifa is mobbed with young adventure seekers in July and August (but can be quiet off-season). This crowd from all over Europe (and beyond) makes Tarifa one of Spain's trendiest-feeling towns. It has far more artsy, modern hotels than most Spanish towns its size, a smattering of fine boutique shopping, and restaurant offerings that are atypically eclectic for normally same-Jane Spain—you'll see vegetarian and organic, Italian and Indian, gourmet burgers and teahouses, and on each corner, it seems, there's a stylish bar-lounge with techno music, mood lighting, and youthful Europeans just hanging out.

Orientation to Tarifa

The old town, surrounded by a wall, slopes gently up from the water's edge (and the port to Tangier). The modern section stretches farther inland from Tarifa's fortified gate.

Tourist Information: The TI faces the port at the top of Paseo de la Alameda (Mon-Fri 10:00-13:30 & 16:00-18:00, Sat-Sun 10:00-13:30; hours may be longer in summer and shorter on slow or bad-weather days, +34 956 680 993, www.turismodetarifa.com, turismo@aytotarifa.com).

Experiencia Tarifa: This organization, run by can-do Quino of the recommended Hostal Alborada, produces a good free magazine with a town map featuring hotels, restaurants, a wide array of activities, and bus schedules.

ARRIVAL IN TARIFA

By Bus: The bus station is on Calle Batalla del Salado, about a five-minute walk from the old town. (The TI also has bus schedules.) Buy tickets directly from the driver if the station is closed (Mon-Thu 7:30-12:30 & 14:15-18:00, Fri 8:30-12:30 & 14:15-16:45, Sun 14:00-20:00, closed Sat, bus station +34 956 684 038, Comes bus company +34 902 199 208, www.tgcomes.es). To reach the old town, walk away from the wind turbines perched on the mountain ridge.

By Car: If you're staying in the center of town, follow signs for *Alameda* or *Puerto*, and continue along Avenida de Andalucía to Tarifa's one traffic light. Take the next left after the light, down Avenida de la Constitución, to find the TI, ferry ticket offices, and the port. You can pay to park on the street here (€1/hour, max 2 hours; get parking ticket from machine) or look for free street parking throughout the town, including just beyond the port customs building (on the harbor, at the base of the castle). During the busiest summer months (July-Aug), these street spaces fill up, in which case you'll need to use a pay lot or park farther out, in the new town (for more on parking, see "Helpful Hints," next).

HELPFUL HINTS

Laundry: Lavandería Tarifa has self-service machines just off Calle Batalla del Salado in the new town (daily 9:30-22:00, Calle Antonio Maura 2, mobile +34 628 429 777).

Tickets and Tours to Morocco: Two ferry companies—FRS and InterShipping—make the crossing between Tarifa and Tangier. You can buy tickets for either boat at the port. FRS also has a couple of offices in town (see page 303 for information on buying ferry tickets). If taking a tour to Tangier, you can book through a ferry company, your hotel, or one of several travel agencies in Tarifa (for details, see page 305).

Long-Term Parking: Tangier day-trippers looking to leave their cars for the day or overnight can try one of these four long-term lots: on Calle San Sebastián, just off Avenida de Andalucía (€14.50/24 hours, long-stay discounts, secured garage); east of the old-town wall (guarded lot just behind the church, €12.45/24 hours); between the bullring and Avenida de Andalucía on Calle Numancia (€13.50/24 hours, guarded lot); or the port facility (€18/24 hours—show your ferry ticket for a €4 discount).

You can also park for free. Many drivers leave their cars for a few days on the street, especially in free spaces lining the road alongside the port customs building (under the castle). Free street parking is becoming rare in the new town, but look either just north of the old-town walls or near the beach; the little Glorieta de León square, just west of the castle and right near a police station, has a number of free spaces. For any street parking, observe the curb color: Blue lines indicate paid parking, and yellow lines are no-parking areas. If it's white or unmarked, it's free.

Excursions: Girasol Adventure offers mountain-bike rentals (€25/day with helmet), guided bike tours, national park hikes, rock-climbing classes, tennis lessons, and, when you're all done...a massage (€30-60). They also offer tours of Tarifa and Bolonia. Activities generally last a half-day and cost around €25-50. Ask Sabine or Chris for details (Mon-Fri 10:00-14:00 & 18:30-20:30, Sat-Sun 11:00-14:00, Calle Colón 12, mobile +34 615 456 506, www.girasol-adventure.com).

Sights in Tarifa

Church of St. Matthew (Iglesia de San Mateo)

Tarifa's most important church, facing its main drag, is richly decorated for being in such a small town. Most nights, it seems life squirts from the church out into the fun-loving Calle Sancho IV el Bravo.

Cost and Hours: Free, Mon-Sat 8:30-13:00 & 18:00-21:00, Sun 10:00-13:00 & 19:00-21:00; English-language leaflets may be inside on the right.

Visiting the Church: Find the fragment of an **ancient tombstone**—a tiny square (eye-level, about the size of this book) in the wall on the right—next to a chapel with a small iron gate (the third one off the right nave). Probably the most important historical item in town, this stone fragment proves there was a functioning church here during Visigothic times, before the Moorish

To ⑯ via Beach

To Bus Station, Windsurfing, Valdevaqueros Beach & Sevilla

PASEO MARÍTIMO

CALLE DE BOSFORO

CALLE ALMADRABA

CALLE CALLAO

CALLE SAN JOSÉ

CALLE NAVAS TOLOSA

CALLE ARAPILES

C. BERING

BULLRING

CALLE

C. SAN SEBASTIAN

CALLE NUMANCIA

CALLE TRAFALGAR

CALLE BAILEN

CALLE CASTILLEJOS

CALLE ALMADRABA

CALLE SAN ISIDRO

AVENIDA DE

CALLE PADRE FORT

AV. DE LAS FUERZAS ARMADAS

CALLE ALCADE

GLORIETA DE LEON

Playa Chica

To Isla de las Palomas

Beach

① ② ③④ ⑤ ⑥ ⑦ ⑧ ⑨ ⑩ ⑪ ⑫ ⑬ ⑭ ⑮ ⑯ ⑰ ⑱ ⑲ ⑳ ㉑ ㉒ ㉓ ㉔ ㉕ ㉖ ㉗ ㉘ ㉙ ㉚ ㉛ ㉜ ㉝ ㉞ ㉟ ㊱

Accommodations
1. Hotel La Mirada
2. Hostal Alborada
3. La Sacristía
4. Hotel Misiana
5. Dar Cilla Guesthouse & Apartments
6. Casa Blanco
7. Hostal La Calzada
8. Hostal Alameda
9. Hostal Africa
10. Pensión Villanueva

Eateries & Nightlife
11. El Puerto & El Ancla
12. Rist. La Trattoria
13. Restaurante Morilla
14. La Oca da Sergio
15. Mandrágora
16. To Rest. Souk & Surla
17. Bar El Francés
18. Café Bar Los Melli & Bar El Pasillo
19. El Otro Melli
20. Café Central & FIRMM
21. Casino Tarifeño
22. Mesón El Picoteo
23. Confitería La Tarifeña
24. Café Azul
25. Churrería La Palmera
26. Chilimoso
27. Almedina Bar (Flamenco)

Other
28. Supermarket (2)
29. Mercado (Farmers Market)
30. Launderette
31. Girasol Adventure
32. Whale Watch Tarifa & Baelo Tour
33. Turmares Tarifa
34. FRS Ferry Office (2)
35. Tarifa Travel
36. Travelsur

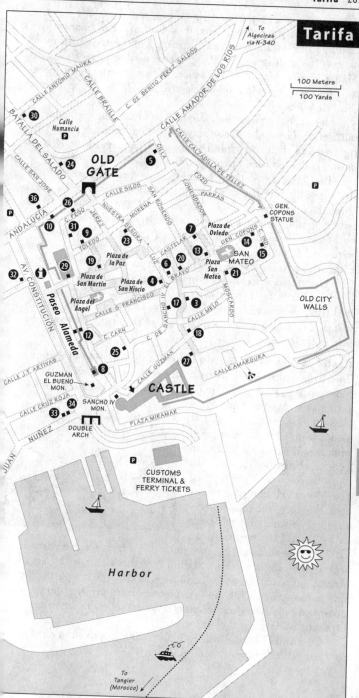

Tarifa

To Algeciras via N-340

100 Meters
100 Yards

OLD GATE

GEN. COPONS STATUE

OLD CITY WALLS

SAN MATEO

Plaza de Oviedo

Plaza San Mateo

Plaza de la Paz

Plaza de San Martín

Plaza de San Hiscio

Plaza del Ángel

Paseo Alameda

GUZMAN EL BUENO MON.

SANCHO IV MON.

DOUBLE ARCH

CASTLE

PLAZA MIRAMAR

CUSTOMS TERMINAL & FERRY TICKETS

Harbor

To Tangier (Morocco)

SOUTH COAST

conquest. The tombstone reads, in a kind of Latin Spanish (try reading it), "Flaviano lived as a Christian for 50 years, a little more or less. In death he received forgiveness as a servant of God on March 30, 674. May he rest in peace." If that gets you in the mood to light a candle, switch on an electric "candle" by dropping in a coin. (It works.)

Head back out into the main nave, and face the high altar. A relief of **St. James the Moor Slayer** (missing his sword) is on the right wall of the main central altar. Since the days of the Reconquista, James has been Spain's patron saint.

The left side of the nave harbors several **statues**—showing typically over-the-top Baroque emotion—that are paraded through town during Holy Week. The **Captive Christ** (with hands bound) evokes a time when Christians were held captive by Moors. The door on the left side of the nave is the **"door of pardons."** For a long time Tarifa was a dangerous place—on the edge of the Reconquista. To encourage people to live here, the Church offered a second helping of forgiveness to anyone who lived in Tarifa for a year. One year and one day after moving to Tarifa, they would have the privilege of passing through this special "door of pardons" and a Mass of thanksgiving would be held in their honor.

Castle of Guzmán el Bueno (Castillo de Guzmán el Bueno)

This 10th-century castle is set on the edge of Europe's southernmost town—a strategically important location since Roman times, acting as a stronghold for Muslims and Christians for almost a thousand years. It was named after a 13th-century Christian general who gained fame in a sad show of courage while fighting the Moors. Holding Guzmán's son hostage, the Moors demanded he surrender the castle or they'd kill the boy. Guzmán

refused, even throwing his own knife down from the ramparts. It was used on his son's throat. Ultimately, the Moors withdrew to Africa, and Guzmán was a hero. *Bien.* Today, the ramparts offer fine harbor views while an interpretive center explains how the castle was constructed and displays a modest collection of artifacts, including some original clothing.

Cost and Hours: €4; daily 10:00-16:00, closed Mon off-season; last entry 45 minutes before closing.

Nearby Views: If you skip the castle, you'll get equally good views from the plaza just left of the Town Hall. Following *ayuntamiento* signs, go up the stairs to the ceramic frog fountain in front of the Casa Consistorial, and continue left.

Bullfighting

Tarifa has a third-rate bullring where novices botch fights on occasional Saturdays through the summer. Professional bullfights take place during special events in August and September. The ring is a short walk from town. You'll see posters everywhere.

▲Whale Watching

Several companies in Tarifa offer daily whale- and dolphin-watching excursions. Over the past four decades, people in this area went from eating whales to protecting them and sharing them with 20,000 visitors a year. The Spanish side of the Strait of Gibraltar is protected as part of El Estrecho Natural Park.

For any of the tours, it's wise (but not always necessary) to reserve one to three days in advance. You'll get a multilingual tour and a two-hour boat trip. Sightings occur on nearly every trip: Dolphins and pilot whales frolic here any time of year (they like the food), sperm whales visit from March through July, and orcas pass through in July and August. In bad weather, trips may be canceled or boats may leave instead from Algeciras (in which case, drivers follow in a convoy, people without cars usually get rides from staff, and you'll stand a lesser chance of seeing whales).

The best company is the Swiss nonprofit **FIRMM** (Foundation for Information and Research on Marine Mammals), which gives a 30-minute educational talk before departure. To reserve, call ahead or stop by one of their two offices (€30-45/person, 1-5 trips/day April-Oct, sometimes also Nov, one office around the corner from Café Central at Pedro Cortés 4, second office inside the ferry port, offices open 9:00-21:00, +34 956 627 008, mobile +34 678 418 350, www.firmm.org, mail@firmm.org). If you don't see any whales or dolphins on your tour, you can join another trip for free.

Both **Whale Watch Tarifa** and **Turmares Tarifa** offer a two-hour whale-watching trip March through October (€30) and a three-hour orca trip in July and August (€45). You'll find Whale Watch Tarifa on Avenida de la Constitución 6 (+34 956 627 013, mobile +34 639 476 544, www.whalewatchtarifa.net, whalewatchtarifa@whalewatchtarifa.net, run by Lourdes), and Turmares Tarifa on Calle del Alcalde Juan Núñez 3 (+34 956 680 741, www.turmares.com, turmares@turmares.com).

Isla de las Palomas

Extending out between Tarifa's port and beaches, this island connected by a spit is the actual "southernmost point in mainland Europe." Walk along the causeway, with Atlantic Ocean beaches stretching to your right and a bustling Mediterranean port to your left. Head to the tip, which was fortified in the 19th century to balance the military might of Britain's nearby Rock of Gibraltar. The actual tip, still owned by the Ministry of Defense, is closed to the public, but a sign at the gate still gives you that giddy "edge of the world" feeling.

▲▲Beach Scene

Tarifa's vast, sandy, and untamed beach stretches west from Isla de las Palomas for about five miles. You can walk much of its length on the Paseo Marítimo, a wide, paved walkway that fronts the sand and surf. Beach cafés and benches along the way make good resting or picnicking stops. Pick up the paseo where the causeway leads out to Isla de las Palomas, near Playa Chica. You'll join dog walkers, runners, and neighbors comparing notes about last night's rainstorm (they get some doozies here). Keep in mind that this is the Atlantic—the waves can be wild and the wind strong (if you're looking for calm, secluded coves, spend your beach time in Nerja instead). On windy summer days, the sea is littered with sprinting windsurfers, while kitesurfers' kites flutter in the sky. Paddleboarding is also popular.

Those with a car can explore farther (following the N-340 road toward Cádiz). It's a fascinating scene: A long string of funky beach resorts is packed with vans and fun-mobiles from northern Europe under mountain ridges lined with modern energy-generating windmills. The various resorts each have a sandy access road, parking, a cabana-type hamlet with rental gear, beachwear shops, a bar, and a hip, healthy restaurant. I like Valdevaqueros beach (five miles from Tarifa), with a wonderful thatched restaurant serving hearty salads, paella, and burgers. Camping Torre de la Peña also has some fun beach eateries.

In July and August, inexpensive buses do a circuit of nearby campgrounds, all on the waterfront (€2, departures about every 1-2 hours, confirm times with TI). Trying to get a parking spot in August can take the joy out of this experience.

SOUTH COAST

Nightlife in Tarifa

You'll find plenty of enjoyable nightspots—the entire town seems designed to cater to a young, international crowd of windsurfers and other adventure travelers. Just stroll the streets of the old town and dip into whichever trendy lounge catches your eye. For something more sedate, the evening paseo fills the parklike boulevard called Paseo de la Alameda (just outside the old-town wall); the Almedina bar hosts flamenco shows every Thursday at 22:30 (at the south end of town, just below Plaza de Santa María, +34 956 680 474); and the theater next to the TI sometimes has musical performances (ask at the TI or look for posters).

Sleeping in Tarifa

Room rates vary with the season: lowest in winter and highest during Easter and from mid-June through September. Many hotels are closed in winter months and reopen the first week of March.

OUTSIDE THE CITY WALL

These hotels are about five blocks from the old town, close to the main drag, Batalla del Salado, in the plain, modern part of town. While in a drab area, they are well-run oases that are close to the beach and the bus station, with free and easy street parking.

$$ Hotel La Mirada, which feels sleek and stark, has 25 mod and renovated rooms—most with sea views at no extra cost. While the place lacks personality, it's well priced and comfortable, with a large roof terrace with views and inviting lounge chairs (elevator, Calle San Sebastián 41, +34 956 684 427, www.hotel-lamirada.com, reservas@hotel-lamirada.com, Antonio and Salvador).

$$ Hostal Alborada is a squeaky-clean, family-run 37-room place with two attractive courtyards and modern conveniences. Father Rafael—along with sons Quino (who speaks English and is generous with travel tips), Fali, and Carlos—are happy to help make your Morocco tour or ferry reservation, or arrange any other activities you're interested in. If they're not too busy, they'll even give you a free lift to the port (RS%, air-con, pay laundry, Calle San José 40, +34 956 681 140, www.hotelalborada.com, info@hotelalborada.com).

INSIDE OR NEXT TO THE CITY WALL

The first three listings are funky, stylish boutique hotels in the heart of town—*muy* trendy and a bit full of themselves.

$$$ La Sacristía, formerly a Moorish stable, now houses travelers who want stylish surroundings. It offers 10 fine and uniquely decorated rooms, mingling eclectic elements of chic Spanish and

SOUTH COAST

Asian style. They offer spa treatments, custom tours of the area, and occasional special events—join the party since you won't sleep (sometimes includes breakfast, air-con, massage room, sauna, small roof terrace, very central at San Donato 8, +34 956 681 759, www.lasacristia.net, tarifa@lasacristia.net).

$$$ Hotel Misiana has 15 comfortable, recently remodeled, spacious rooms above a bar-lounge. Their designer gave the place a mod pastel boutique-ish ambience. To avoid noise from the lounge below, which is open until 3:00 in the morning, request a room on a higher floor (minimum stays of 2-4 nights in high season, double-paned windows, elevator, 100 yards directly in front of the church at Calle Sancho IV el Bravo 16, +34 956 627 083, www.misianahotel.com, info@misianahotel.com).

$$$ Dar Cilla Guesthouse & Apartments is a Moroccan-influenced *riad* (or guesthouse), built into the town wall and re-modeled into eight chic apartments surrounding a communal courtyard. Each apartment has a kitchen and is decorated in modern Moroccan style, with earth-tone walls, terracotta-tiled floors, and Moroccan rugs (family rooms; 2-, 4-, and 7-night minimums; air-con, large roof terrace with remarkable bird's-eye view over the old town to the sea, just east of the old-town gate at Calle Cilla 7, mobile +34 653 467 025, www.darcilla.com, info@darcilla.com).

$$ Casa Blanco, where minimalist meets Moroccan, is a newer, reasonably priced designer hotel. Each of its seven rooms (all with double beds) is decorated (and priced) differently. The place is decked out with practical amenities (minifridges in premium rooms) as well as romantic touches—loft beds, walk-in showers, and subtle lighting (small roof terrace, reception open 9:00-14:00 only, off main square at Calle Nuestra Señora de la Luz 2, +34 956 681 515, mobile +34 622 330 349, www.hotelcasablanco.com, info@hotelcasablanco.com).

$$ Hostal La Calzada has eight airy, well-appointed rooms right in the lively old-town thick of things, though the management is rarely around (closed Dec-March, air-con, 20 yards from church at Calle Justino Pertinez 7, +34 956 681 492, www.hostallacalzada.com, reservashostallacalzada@gmail.com).

$$ Hostal Alameda, overlooking a square where the local children play, glistens with pristine marble floors and dark red decor. The main building has 11 bright rooms and the annex has 16 more modern rooms; both face the same delightful square (air-con, Paseo de la Alameda 4, +34 956 681 181, www.hostalalameda.com, info@hostalalameda.com, Antonio).

$ Hostal Africa, with 13 bright rooms and an inviting roof terrace, is buried on a very quiet street in the center of town. Its dreamy blue-and-white color scheme and stripped-down feel give it a Moorish ambience (RS%, laundry service, storage for boards and bikes, Calle María Antonia Toledo 12, +34 956 680 220, mobile +34 606 914 294, www.hostalafrica.com, info@hostalafrica.com, charming Eva and Miguel keep the reception desk open 9:00-24:00).

¢ **Pensión Villanueva** offers 17 remodeled rooms at budget prices. It's simple, clean, and friendly. It lacks indoor public areas but has an inviting terrace overlooking the old town on a busy street. Reconfirm your reservation by phone the day before you arrive (just west of the old-town gate at Avenida de Andalucía 11, access from outside the wall, +34 956 684 149, hostalvillanueva@hotmail.com).

Eating in Tarifa

I've grouped my recommendations below into two categories: Sit down to a real restaurant meal, or enjoy a couple of the many characteristic tapas bars in the old town.

RESTAURANTS
Near the Port

$$$ **El Puerto,** in an untouristy area near the causeway out to Isla de las Palomas, has a great reputation for its pricey but very fresh seafood. Locals swear that it's a notch or two above the seafood places in town (Thu-Tue 12:00-16:30 & 20:00-23:30, closed Wed, Avenida Fuerzas Armadas 13, +34 956 681 914).

$$$ Next door, **El Ancla** offers a more casual seafood alternative and is especially known for the local specialty *croquetas de choco*—delectable hot-and-fluffy croquettes made with squid ink (Tue-Sat 13:00-16:30 & 21:00-23:30, Sun lunch only, closed Mon; Avenida Fuerzas Armadas 15, +34 956 680 913).

$$$ **Ristorante La Trattoria,** on the Alameda, is a good Italian option, with cloth-napkin class, friendly staff, and ingredients from Italy. Sit inside, near the wood-fired oven, or out along the main strolling street (June-Sept daily 13:00-16:00 & 19:30-23:00; off-season Thu-Tue dinner only, closed Wed; Paseo de la Alameda, +34 956 682 225).

Near the Church

$$ **Restaurante Morilla,** facing the church, is on the town's prime piece of people-watching real estate. This is a real restaurant (tapas sold only at the stand-up bar and sometimes at a few tables), with good indoor and outdoor seating. It serves tasty local-style fish, grilled or baked—your server will tell you about today's fish; it's sold by weight, so confirm the price carefully (daily 8:30-24:00, Calle Sancho IV el Bravo 2, +34 956 681 757).

$$ **La Oca da Sergio,** cozy and fun, is one of the numerous

pizza-and-pasta joints supported by the large expat Italian community. Sergio prides himself on importing authentic Italian ingredients (indoor and outdoor seating; daily 13:00-16:00 & 20:00-23:00; around the left side of the church and straight back on the right, at the end of the street at Calle General Copons 6; +34 956 681 249, mobile +34 615 686 571).

$$$ Mandrágora serves a stylish fusion of Moroccan, Mediterranean, and Asian flavors: lamb shanks with plums and almonds, classic tagines and couscous, generous salads, and the best-anywhere *berenjenas* (eggplant drizzled with honey). It's a sophisticated white-tablecloth place, but casual attire is fine (dinner from 18:30 Mon-Sat, closed Sun, tucked just behind the church at Calle Independencia 3, +34 956 681 291).

In the New Town

These two restaurants are in a residential area just above the beach, about a 15-minute walk along the Paseo Marítimo (or an easy car or taxi ride) from the old town. They're worth a detour for their great food and the chance to see another part of town). As you walk the promenade, keep going until you pass the park and public swimming pool, then turn right into the passageway after the parking lot. You'll find Surla just ahead on the left (in a corner of the large beige building). Souk is straight ahead, across the street and up two flights of stairs. To drive there, head up Calle San Sebastián, which turns into Calle Pintor Pérez Villalta. You'll see the Surla building on the left.

$$ Restaurante Souk serves a tasty mix of Moroccan, Indian, and Thai cuisine in a dark, exotic, romantic, purely Moroccan ambience. The ground floor (where you enter) is a bar and atmospheric teahouse, while the dining room is downstairs (daily 20:00-24:00, closed Tue off-season; good wine list, Mar Tirreno 46, +34 956 627 065, friendly Claudia).

$$ Surla, a hipster surfer bar, serves up breakfast, lunch, and dinner, including wonderfully executed, shareable sushi platters, along with good coffee. Situated just a few steps above the beachfront walkway, it's at the center of a sprawling zone of après-surf hangouts. They also offer delivery (daily 9:00-24:00, Tue-Wed until 20:00, dinner served Thu-Mon, Calle Pintor Pérez Villalta 64—look for the surfboard nailed to the building, +34 956 685 175).

TAPAS

$$ Bar El Francés is a thriving place where "Frenchies" (as the bar's name implies) Marcial and Alexandra serve tasty little plates of tapas. This spot is popular for its fine *raciones*—especially octopus *(pulpo a la brasa)*, fish in brandy sauce *(pescado en* *salsa al cognac),* and garlic-grilled tuna *(atún a la plancha)*—and cheap tapas. It's standing-and-stools only inside, but the umbrella-shaded terrace outside has plenty of tables and is an understandably popular spot to enjoy a casual meal (no tapas on terrace; order off regular menu). Show this book and Marcial will be happy to bring you a free glass of sherry (open Fri-Tue long hours June-Aug; closed Thu and Dec-Feb; Calle Sancho IV el Bravo 21A—from Café Central, follow cars 100 yards to first corner on left; mobile +34 685 857 005).

$$ Café Bar Los Melli is a local favorite for feasts on barrel tables set outside. This family-friendly place, run by Ramón and Juani, is a hit with locals and offers a good chorizo sandwich and *patatas bravas*—potatoes with a hot tomato sauce served on a wooden board (Thu-Tue 20:00-24:00, Fri-Sun also 13:00-16:00, closed Wed; across from Bar El Francés—duck down the little lane next to the Radio Alvarez sign and it will be on your left at Calle Guzmán el Bueno 16, mobile +34 605 866 444). **$$ Bar El Pasillo,** next to Los Melli, also serves tapas (closed midday and Mon). **$$ El Otro Melli,** run by Ramón's brother José, is a few blocks away on Plaza de San Martín.

$$ Café Central is *the* happening place nearly any time of day—it's the perch for all the cool tourists. With a decidedly international vibe, it's less authentically Spanish than the others I've listed. The bustling ambience and appealing setting in front of the church are better than the food, but they do have breakfast with eggs, good salads, and impressive healthy fruit drinks when fruit is in season (daily 9:00-23:00, off Plaza San Mateo, near the church at Calle Sancho IV el Bravo 9, +34 956 682 877).

$$ Casino Tarifeño is just to the sea side of the church. It's an old-boys' social club "for members only" but offers a musty Andalusian welcome to visiting tourists, including women. Wander through. It has a low-key bar with tapas, a TV room, a card room, and a lounge. There's no menu, but prices are standard. Just point and say the size you want: tapa, *media-ración,* or *ración.* A far cry from some of the trendy options around town, this is a local institution (daily 12:00-24:00).

$$ Mesón El Picoteo is a small, characteristic bar popular with locals and tourists alike for its good tapas and *montaditos.* Eat in the casual, woody interior or at one of the barrel tables out front (Wed-Sun 12:00-16:30 & 20:00-24:00, Mon lunch only, closed Tue; a few blocks west of the old town on Calle Mariano Vinuesa, +34 956 681 128).

OTHER EATING OPTIONS

Breakfast or Dessert: **$ Confitería La Tarifeña** serves super pastries and flan-like *tocino de cielo* (daily 9:00-21:00, at the top of Calle Nuestra Señora de la Luz, near the main old-town gate).

$ Breezy **Café Azul** is blissful place to get energized for the day with their generously portioned fruit bowls, Spanish toasts, and fresh juice (daily 9:00-15:00, Calle Batalla del Salado 8).

$ Churrería La Palmera serves breakfast before most hotels and cafés have even turned on the lights—early enough for you to get your coffee fix, and/or bulk up on *churros* and chocolate, before hopping the first ferry to Tangier (daily 7:00-13:00, Calle Sanchez IV el Bravo 34).

Vegetarian: Literally a small hole in the old town wall, **$ Chilimoso** serves fresh and healthy vegetarian options, homemade desserts, and a variety of teas. It's a rare find in meat-loving Spain. Eat at one of the few indoor tables, or get it to go and find a bench on the nearby Paseo de la Alameda (daily 19:00-23:00, opens Sat-Sun at 12:30 in summer, closed Feb; just west of the old-town gate on Calle del Peso 6, +34 956 685 092).

Windsurfer Bars: If you have a car, head to the string of beaches west of town. Many have bars and fun-loving thatched restaurants that keep the wet-suit gang fed and watered (see "Beach Scene," earlier).

Picnics: Stop by the *mercado municipal* (farmers market, Mon-Sat 8:00-14:00, closed Sun, in old town, inside gate nearest TI), or, near the hotels in the new town, the **SuperSol** supermarket, closed Sun, at Callao and San José), or the **Día** supermarket (daily, Calle San Sebastián 30).

Tarifa Connections

TARIFA

From Tarifa by Bus to: La Línea/Gibraltar (6/day, 1 hour), **Algeciras** (hourly, fewer on weekends, 45 minutes, Comes), **Jerez** (1/day, 2.5 hours, more frequent with transfer in Cádiz, Comes), **Sevilla** (4/day, 2.5-3 hours), and **Málaga** (2/day, 2.5-4 hours, Portillo). Bus info: Comes (www.tgcomes.es), Portillo (http://portillo.avanzabus.com).

Ferries from Tarifa to Tangier, Morocco: Two boat companies make the 35-minute journey to Tangier Ville Port about every hour (see the Morocco & Tangier chapter for details).

ALGECIRAS

Algeciras (ahl-*h*eh-THEE-rahs) is only worth leaving. It's useful to the traveler mainly as a transportation hub, with trains and buses to destinations in southern and central Spain (it also has a ferry to Tangier, but it takes you to the Tangier MED port about 25 miles from Tangier city—going from Tarifa is much better). If you're headed for Gibraltar or Tarifa by public transport, you'll almost certainly change in Algeciras at some point.

Everything of interest is on Juan de la Cierva, which heads inland from the port. The **TI** is about a block in (mobile +34 670 948 731), followed by the side-by-side **train station** (opposite Hotel Octavio) and **bus station** three blocks later.

Trains: If arriving at the train station, head out the front door: The bus station is ahead and on the right; the TI is another three blocks (becomes Juan de la Cierva when the road jogs), also on the right; and the port is just beyond.

From Algeciras by Train to: Madrid (4/day, half transfer in Antequera, 5.5-6 hours, arrives at Atocha), **Ronda** (5-6/day, 1.5-2 hours), **Granada** (3/day, 4-5 hours), **Sevilla** (3/day, 5-6 hours, transfer at Antequera or Bobadilla, bus is better), **Córdoba** (2/day direct on Altaria, 3 hours; more with transfer in Antequera or Bobadilla, 4 hours), **Málaga** (3-4/day, 4 hours, transfer in Bobadilla; bus is faster). With the exception of the route to Madrid, these are particularly scenic trips; the best (though slow) is the mountainous journey to Málaga via Bobadilla.

Buses: Algeciras is served by five bus companies, all located in the same terminal (called San Bernardo Estación de Autobuses) next to Hotel Octavio and directly across from the train station. The companies generally serve different destinations, but there is some overlap. Lockers are near the platforms—purchase a token at the machines.

From Algeciras by Bus: Comes (www.tgcomes.es) runs buses to **La Línea/Gibraltar** (2/hour, fewer on weekends, 45 minutes), **Tarifa** (hourly, fewer on weekends, 45 minutes), **Ronda** (1/day, 3.5 hours), **Sevilla** (4/day, 3-4 hours), **Jerez** (2/day 2.5 hours). Avanza (www.avanzabus.com) goes to **Nerja** (1/day, 3.5 hours), and Interbus (www.interbus.es) travels to **Madrid** (6/day, 8 hours).

Portillo (http://portillo.avanzabus.com) offers buses to **Málaga** (hourly, 2-3 hours), **Málaga Airport** (2/day, 2 hours), and **Granada** (4/day, 4-5.5 hours).

Autocares Valenzuela (www.grupovalenzuela.com) runs the most frequent direct buses to **Sevilla** (7/day, fewer on weekends, 2.5-3 hours) and **Jerez** (6/day, fewer on weekends, 1.5 hours).

Ferries from Algeciras to Tangier, Morocco: Although it's possible to sail from Algeciras to Tangier, the ferry takes you to the Tangier MED Port, which is 25 miles east of Tangier city and a hassle. You're better off taking a ferry from Tarifa, which sails directly to the port in Tangier. If you must sail from Algeciras, buy your ticket at the port; companies sailing this route include FRS (www.frs.es) and Balearia (www.balearia.com). Official offices of the boat companies are inside the main port building, directly behind the helpful little English-speaking info kiosk (8-22 ferries/day, port open daily 6:45-21:45).

ROUTE TIPS FOR DRIVERS

Tarifa to Gibraltar (28 miles/45 km): This short drive takes you past a silvery-white forest of windmills, from peaceful Tarifa past Algeciras to La Línea (the Spanish town bordering Gibraltar). Passing Algeciras, continue in the direction of Estepona. At San Roque, take the La Línea-Gibraltar exit.

MOROCCO

Morocco Practicalities

Money: The local currency is the Moroccan dirham (10 dh or MAD = about $1), but euros work here, as do dollars and pounds. For a day trip, bring lots of €1 and €0.50 coins for tips, small purchases, and camel rides. If you plan to do anything independently, change some money into Moroccan dirhams or find an ATM upon arrival.

Language: The native language is Arabic (for useful phrases, see the "Moroccan Mix" sidebar, later), but French is also spoken.

Emergencies and Travel Advisories: Dial 190 for police, medical, or other emergencies. For US State Department travel advisories, see www.travel.state.gov.

Time Zone: Morocco is on Greenwich Mean Time (like Great Britain), so it is an hour behind Spain. It observes Daylight Saving Time with Europe, except during the month of Ramadan, when it is two hours behind Spain (meaning that daylight fasting hours end earlier).

Closed Days and Ramadan: Friday is the Muslim day of rest, when most of the country—except Tangier—closes down. On the final day of the holy month of Ramadan, Muslims celebrate Eid (an all-day feast and gift-giving holiday), and travelers may find some less touristy stores and restaurants closed.

Marijuana Alert: In Morocco, marijuana *(kif)* is as illegal as it is popular. As a general rule, just walk right by those hand-carved pipes in the marketplace. Some dealers sell marijuana cheap—and make their profit after you get arrested. Cars and buses are stopped and checked by police routinely throughout Morocco, especially in the north and in the Chefchaouen region, which is Morocco's *kif* capital.

Health: Take commonsense precautions: Eat in clean—not cheap—places. Peel fruit, eat only cooked vegetables, and drink reliably bottled water (Sidi Ali and Sidi Harazem are two good brands). Carry a small container of hand sanitizer. When you do get diarrhea—and you should plan on it—adjust your diet (small and bland meals) or fast for a day, and make sure you replenish lost fluids.

Embassies: In Rabat—US embassy +212 537 637 200 (Km 5.7, Avenue Mohamed VI, https://ma.usembassy.gov); Canadian embassy +212 537 544 949 (66 Mehdi Ben Barka Avenue, www.morocco.gc.ca).

Phoning: I've listed phone numbers as you would dial them from a US mobile phone. Morocco's country code is 212. To dial from a Moroccan landline, drop 212 and add a zero before the number. To call from a Spanish landline, dial 00 (Europe international access code), 212 (Morocco country code), and then the number.

Tipping: Most Moroccan waiters expect about a 10 percent tip. For a taxi driver, round up the fare a bit.

Tourist Information: www.visitmorocco.com

MOROCCO & TANGIER

al-Maghreb • Tanja

Go to Africa. A young country with an old history, Morocco is a photographer's delight and a budget traveler's dream. It's exotic, and easier and more appealing than ever. Along with a rich culture, Morocco offers plenty of contrast—from beach resorts to bustling desert markets, from jagged mountains to sleepy, mud-brick oasis towns. And a visit to Morocco—so close to Europe, yet embracing the Arabic language and Muslim faith—lets a Westerner marinated in anti-Muslim propaganda see what Islam aspires to be...and can be.

From the town of Tarifa in southern Spain, it's just 35 minutes by boat to the Moroccan port city of Tangier, the focus of this chapter. Tangier defies expectations. Ruled by Spain in the 19th century and France in the 20th, it's a rare place where signs are in three languages and English doesn't make the cut. In this Muslim city, you'll find in close proximity a synagogue, Catholic and Anglican churches, and the town's largest mosque. Wind your way from the port to the Grand Socco, pause in the medina's colorful market, and peek through keyhole gates as you follow twisty lanes up to the Kasbah. In Tangier, the roosters, even more than the minaret's call to prayer, make sure the city wakes up early.

For me, this is the most exciting day trip in Europe: You'll get a legitimate taste of North Africa and an authentic slice of an Islamic culture. As you step off the boat, you realize that, culturally, the crossing has taken you farther than your trip from the US to Spain. Morocco needs no museums; its sights are living in the streets.

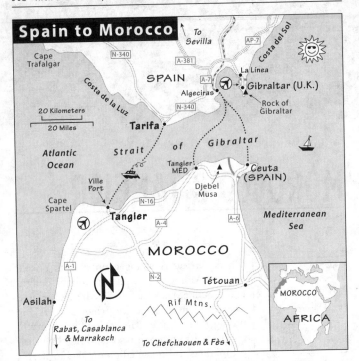

Spain to Morocco

To Sevilla

Cape Trafalgar

N-340

SPAIN

A-381

A-7

La Línea

AP-7

Costa del Sol

Gibraltar (U.K.)

Algeciras

N-340

Rock of Gibraltar

Costa de la Luz

20 Kilometers

20 Miles

Tarifa

Atlantic Ocean

Strait   of   Gibraltar

Ville Port

Tangier MED

Ceuta (SPAIN)

Djebel Musa

Cape Spartel

Tangier

N-16

A-4

A-6

Mediterranean Sea

A-1

MOROCCO

N-2

Tétouan

MOROCCO

AFRICA

Asilah

To Rabat, Casablanca & Marrakech

Rif Mtns.

To Chefchaouen & Fès

Morocco in a Day?

Though Morocco ("Marruecos" in Spanish; "al-Maghreb" in Arabic) certainly deserves more than a day, many visitors touring Spain see it in a side trip. Guided excursions to Tangier from Tarifa make day-tripping foolproof, if clichéd. But it's just as easy to take a boat on your own and meet a local guide at the port. And, though such a short sprint through Tangier is only a tease, a day or overnight in Tangier gives you a good introduction to the country and its people. All you need is a passport (no visa or shots required) and about €80 for either a tour package or the round-trip ferry crossing.

WITH A TOUR OR ON YOUR OWN?

Your big decisions are whether to visit Tangier solo or with a guided tour, and how long to stay (day trip or overnight). Ask yourself: Do you want the safety and comfort of having Morocco handed to you on a user-friendly platter? Or do you want the independence to see what you want, with fewer cultural clichés and less forced shopping?

Taking a **package tour** is easier but less rewarding. On a package tour, visitors are met at the ferry dock by a guide, toured around town by bus and on foot, shepherded through lunch and a shopping excursion, then hustled back down to the boat where—five hours after they landed—they return to the First World thankful they don't have diarrhea.

The alternative is to see Tangier **on your own.** Independent adventurers get to see all the sights and avoid all the kitsch. You can catch a morning boat and return to Spain that evening; extend with an overnight in Tangier; or even head deeper into Morocco (see "Morocco Beyond Tangier" at the end of this chapter for ideas).

My preferred approach is a **hybrid:** Get to Tangier "on your own," but arrange in advance to meet a local guide to ease your culture shock and accompany you to your choice of sights (I list a few reliable guides under "Tours in Tangier," later in this chapter). While you'll pay a bit more than joining a package tour, ultimately the cost difference (roughly €20-40 more per person) is pretty negligible, considering the dramatically increased cultural intimacy.

ON YOUR OWN FROM TARIFA

While the trip to Tangier can be made from various Spanish ports, only the Tarifa ferry takes you to the Tangier Ville Port, in the city center. (Spaniards call it the *Puerto Viejo,* "Old Port"). Note that ferries also travel to Morocco from Algeciras and Gibraltar, but they arrive at the Tangier MED Port, 25 miles from downtown (connected to the Tangier Ville Port by a cheap one-hour shuttle bus). But the most logical route for the typical traveler is the one I'll describe here—sailing from Tarifa to Tangier Ville Port.

Ferry Schedule and Tickets: Two companies make the 35-minute crossing from Tarifa to Tangier, with a ferry departing

about every hour from 8:00 to 22:00. **FRS** ferries leave Tarifa on odd hours (9:00, 11:00, and so on; +34 956 681 830, www. frs.es). **InterShipping** ferries depart Tarifa on most even hours (8:00, 10:00, and so on—but confirm schedule; +34 956 684 729, www.intershipping.es). Return boats from Tangier to Tarifa run from about 7:00 to 21:00 on an opposite schedule: FRS usually departs Tangier on even hours and InterShipping on odd hours. Tarifa's modern little terminal has a cafeteria and WCs.

Prices are roughly €40 one-way or €80 for a round-trip "open-return" ticket valid for any departure (on the same ferry line). If you want the flexibility of returning at any time with either company, stick to one-way tickets.

Tickets are easy to get: Buy them online, at the Tarifa ferry terminal (both companies have offices there), through your hotel in Tarifa, or from a Tarifa travel agency. FRS also has offices in

Time Change

Morocco is one hour behind Spain, except during the month of Ramadan, when it's two hours behind. In general, ferry and other schedules correspond to the local time in each port (if your boat leaves Tangier "at 17:00," that means 5:00 p.m. Moroccan time—not Spanish time). Be sure to change your watch when you get off the boat in Tangier.

Tarifa itself: One is just outside the old-town wall, at the corner of Avenida de Andalucía and Avenida de la Constitución (closed Sun, +34 956 681 830); another is near the port on Calle Alcalde Juan Núñez 2 (open daily; see the "Tarifa" map on page 287 of the South Coast chapter for both locations).

When to Go: You can almost always just buy a ticket and walk on, though in the busiest summer months (July-Aug), the popular 8:00 and 9:00 departures can fill up. Boats are most crowded in July, August, and during the month of Ramadan. A few crossings a year are canceled due to storms or wind, mostly in winter.

Ferry Crossing to Tangier: The ferry from Tarifa is a fast Nordic hydrofoil that theoretically takes 35 minutes to cross. In practice, it often leaves late, and you'll want to arrive early to give yourself time to clear customs, making the whole trip take at least an hour. You'll go through Spanish customs at the port and Moroccan customs on the ferry. Whether taking a tour or traveling on your own, you *must* get a stamp in your passport (only available on board): After you leave Tarifa, find the Moroccan immigration officer on the boat (usually in a corner booth that's been turned into an impromptu office) and get a stamp in your passport and an entry paper (which they keep). The ferry is equipped with WCs, a shop, and a snack bar.

Hiring a Guide: To book a local guide to show you around Tangier, see my recommendations under "Tours in Tangier," later.

Returning to Tarifa: It's smart to return to the port about 30 minutes before your ferry departs. For the return trip, you must complete a passport-control form and get an exit stamp at the Tangier terminal before you board. Back in Tarifa, you'll show your passport once more to reenter Spain and the European Union.

WITH A PACKAGE TOUR FROM TARIFA

A typical day-trip tour includes a round-trip crossing and a guide who meets your big group at a prearranged point at the Tangier port, then hustles you through the hustlers and onto your tour bus. All tours offer essentially the same five-hour Tangier experience: a city bus tour, a drive through the ritzy palace neighborhood, a walk through the medina (old town), and an overly thorough look at a sales-starved carpet shop (where prices include a commission for your guide and tour company; some carpet shops are actually owned by the ferry company). Longer tours may include a trip to the desolate Atlantic Coast for some rugged African scenery

and a short camel ride. Any tour wraps up with lunch in a palatial Moroccan setting with live music and belly dancing, topped off by a final walk back to your boat through a gauntlet of desperate merchants.

Sound cheesy? It is. But no amount of packaging can gloss over the depth and richness of this culture.

Tour Prices: Tour tickets are priced roughly the same no matter where you buy them: about €70-95 (sometimes less than the cost of a round-trip ferry ticket—the tours make their margin in shopping kickbacks). Don't worry about which company you select. (They're all equally bad.)

Tour Schedules: Tours leave Tarifa on a variable schedule throughout the day: For example, one tour may depart at 9:00 and return at 15:00, the next could run 11:00-19:00, and the next 13:00-19:00. If you're an independent type on a one-day tour, you could stay with your group until you return to the ferry dock, and then just slip back into town, thinking, "Freedom!" You're welcome to use your return ferry ticket on a later boat operated by the same ferry company.

Overnight Options: If you want a longer visit, you can book a package through the ferry company that includes a one-night stay in a Tangier hotel. There are also two-day options with frills (all meals and excursions outside the city) or no-frills (no guiding or meals—€85 for a basic overnight, €10-17 extra in peak season; two-day options-€95-115).

Booking a Tour: You rarely need to book a package tour more than a day in advance, even during peak season. Book directly with the **ferry company** (see contact information earlier, under "Ferry Schedule and Tickets," or visit their offices at the port in Tarifa)

Moroccan Mix

While Morocco is clearly a place apart from Mediterranean Europe, it doesn't really seem like Africa either. It's a mix, reflecting its strategic position between the two continents. Situated on the Strait of Gibraltar, Morocco has been flooded by waves of invasions over the centuries: The Berbers, the native population, have had to contend with the Phoenicians, Carthaginians, Romans, Vandals, and more.

The Arabs brought Islam to Morocco in the seventh century AD and stuck around, battling the Berbers in various civil wars. A series of Berber and Arab dynasties rose and fell; the Berbers won out and still run the country today. From the 15th century on, European countries carved up much of Africa. By the early 20th century, most of Morocco was under French control, and strategic Tangier was jointly ruled by multiple European powers as a freewheeling international zone. The country finally gained independence in 1956.

As throughout the Arab world, Morocco has had its share of political unrest in recent years. Widespread but mostly peaceful protests in 2011, influenced by the Arab Spring, called for greater democracy and economic reforms. A new constitution, adopted later that year, gave more power to the legislative branch and the prime minister (although some say King Mohammed VI retained the actual authority). Since that time, crackdowns on protesters (demanding vital services for all) and news-media critics (calling for respect for constitutional rights) have occasionally threatened the country's stability.

Morocco is also struggling to reconcile tensions between Islamist and secular factions within its government and in the region. Bombings attributed to Islamic fundamentalists in 2003 and in 2011 prompted an array of initiatives to counter extremism.

Americans pondering a visit may wonder how they'll be received in this Muslim nation. Al Jazeera blares from televisions in all the bars, but I've sensed no animosity toward American individuals (even on a visit literally days after US forces killed Osama bin Laden). It's culturally enriching for Westerners to experience Morocco—a Muslim monarchy succeeding on its own terms without embracing modern Western "norms."

A feast for the senses, Morocco provides a good dose of culture shock—both good and bad. It's cheap, relatively safe, and private guides are affordable. You'll also encounter sometimes oppressive friendliness, pushy hustlers and aggressive beggars, brutal heat, and the unfamiliarity of the Arabic language. Annoyingly persistent but generally harmless men make a sport of harassing female travelers. Many visitors develop some intestinal problems by the end of their visit. And in terms of efficiency, Morocco makes Spain look like Sweden. When you cruise south across the Strait of Gibraltar, leave your busy itineraries and split-second timing behind. Morocco must be taken on its own terms. Here things go smoothly only *"Inshallah"*—if God so wills.

A Few Words of Arabic

With its unique history of having been controlled by many different foreign and domestic rulers, Tangier is a babel of languages. Most locals speak Arabic first and French second (all Moroccans learn it in school); sensing that you're a foreigner, they'll most likely address you in French. Spanish ranks third, and English a distant fourth. Communication can be tricky for English-speaking travelers. A little French goes a long way, but learn a few words in Arabic. Have your first local friend help you with the pronunciation:

English	Arabic
Hello ("Peace be with you")	*Salaam alaikum* (sah-LAHM ah-LAY-koom)
Hello (response: "Peace also be with you")	*Wa alaikum salaam* (wah ah-LAY-koom sah-LAHM)
Please	*Min fadlik* (meen FAHD-leek)
Thank you	*Shokran* (SHOH-kron)
Excuse me	*Ismahli* (ees-SMAH-lee)
Yes/No	*Yeh* (EE-yeh)/*Lah* (lah)
Give me five (kids enjoy this)	*Ham sah* (hahm sah)
OK	*Wah hah* (wah hah)
Very good	*Miz yen biz ef* (meez EE-yehn beez ehf)
Goodbye	*Maa salama* (mah sah-LEM-ah)

Moroccans have a touchy-feely culture. Expect lots of hugs if you make an effort to communicate. When greeting someone, a handshake is customary, followed by placing your right hand over your heart. It helps to know that *souk* means a particular market (such as for leather, yarn, or metalwork), while a *kasbah* is loosely defined as a fortress (or a town within old fortress walls). In markets, I sing, "la la la la" to my opponents (*lah shokran* means "No, thank you").

or through your **hotel.** There's not much reason to book with a **travel agency,** but offices all over southern Spain and in Tarifa sell ferry tickets and seats on tours. In Tarifa, check with Luís and Antonio at Baelo Tour (RS%—ask, open daily in summer 5:00-21:00, baggage storage available, across from TI at Avenida de la Constitución 5, +34 956 681 242); other Tarifa-based agencies are Tarifa Travel and Travelsur (both on Avenida de Andalucía, above the old-town walls).

Tangier

Artists, writers, and musicians have always loved Tangier. Delacroix and Matisse were drawn by its evocative light. The Beat generation, led by William S. Burroughs and Jack Kerouac, sought the city's multicultural, otherworldly feel. Paul Bowles found his sheltering sky here. From the 1920s through the 1950s, Tangier was an "international city," too strategic to give to any one nation, and jointly governed by as many as nine different powers, including France, Spain, Britain, Italy, Belgium, the Netherlands...and Morocco. The city was a tax-free zone (since there was no single authority to collect taxes), which created a booming free-for-all atmosphere, attracting playboy millionaires, bon vivants, globetrotting scoundrels, con artists, and expat romantics. Tangier enjoyed a cosmopolitan Golden Age that, in many ways, shaped the city visitors see today.

Because so many different colonial powers have had a finger in this city, it goes by many names: In English, it's Tangier; in French, Tanger (tahn-zhay); in Arabic, it's Tanja (TAHN-zhah); in Spanish, Tánger (TAHN-hair). Unless you speak Arabic, French is the handiest second language, followed by Spanish and (finally) English.

Because of its international-zone status, Morocco's previous king effectively disowned the city, denying it national funds for improvements. Over time, neglected Tangier became the armpit of Morocco, and the once-grand coastal city earned a reputation as the "Tijuana of Africa." But that has changed. When King Mohammed VI was crowned in 1999, the first city he visited was Tangier. He's enthusiastic about the city and continues to implement his vision to restore Tangier to its former glory.

While the city (with a population of

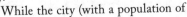

more than one million and growing quickly) still has a ways to go, restorations are taking place on a grand scale: the beach has been painstakingly cleaned, the Kasbah is getting spruced up, pedestrian promenades are popping up, gardens bloom with lush new greenery, and a futuristic soccer stadium hosts professional matches. The city-center port (Tangier Ville) is in the midst of a years-long renovation project that will transform it into a huge, slick marina complex capable of handling mega cruise ships, yachts, and ferries from Tarifa, while more directly connecting the port and old town.

I'm uplifted by the new Tangier—it's affluent and modern without having abandoned its roots. Many visitors are impressed by the warmth of the Moroccan people. Notice how they touch their right hand to their heart after shaking hands or saying thank you—a kind gesture meant to emphasize sincerity.

PLANNING YOUR TIME

If you're not on a package tour, arrange for a guide to meet you at the ferry dock, hire a guide upon arrival, or head on your own to the big square called the Grand Socco to get oriented (you could walk, but it's easier to catch a taxi from the port; see "Arrival in Tangier," later). Get your bearings with my Grand Socco spin tour, then delve into the old town (the lower medina, with the Petit Socco, market, and American Legation Museum; and the upper medina's Kasbah, with its museum and residential lanes). With more time, take a taxi to sightsee along the beach and through the urban new town on Avenue Mohammed VI before heading back to the port. You'll rarely see other tourists outside the regular tour-group circuit.

Orientation to Tangier

Like almost every city in Morocco, Tangier is split in two: old and new. From the ferry dock you'll see the old town (medina)—encircled by its medieval wall. The old town has the markets, the Kasbah (with its palace and the mosque of the Kasbah—marked by the higher of the two minarets you see), cheap hotels, characteristic guesthouses, homes both decrepit and recently

renovated, and 2,000 wannabe guides. The twisty, hilly streets of the old town are caged within a wall accessible by keyhole gates.

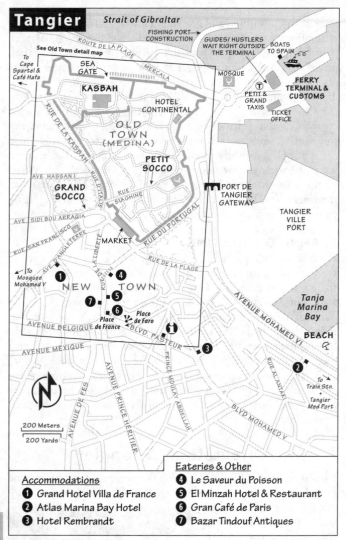

Tangier *Strait of Gibraltar*

Eateries & Other
- ❹ Le Saveur du Poisson
- ❺ El Minzah Hotel & Restaurant
- ❻ Gran Café de Paris
- ❼ Bazar Tindouf Antiques

Accommodations
- ❶ Grand Hotel Villa de France
- ❷ Atlas Marina Bay Hotel
- ❸ Hotel Rembrandt

The larger minaret (on the left) belongs to the modern Mohammed V mosque—the biggest in town.

The new town, with the TI and modern international-style hotels, sprawls past the port zone to your left. The big square, Grand Socco, is the hinge between the old and new parts of town.

Note that while tourists (and this guidebook) refer to the twisty old town as "the medina," locals consider both the old and new parts of the city center to be medinas.

The city could use more street signs, but it's laid out simply, and maps are posted at the major gates. In the maze-like medina, you'll sometimes find street names on ceramic plaques on the corners of buildings, as well as signs directing you to sights in the Kasbah. You're bound to get turned around, but take heart: Nothing listed under "Sights in Tangier" is more than a 20-minute walk from the port, which is always downhill. Petit Taxis (see under "Getting Around Tangier") are a remarkably cheap godsend for the hot and tired tourist. Use them liberally.

TOURIST INFORMATION

The TI, about a 15-minute gradual uphill walk from the Grand Socco, is not particularly helpful (English is in short supply, but a little French goes a long way). But at least you can pick up the free *Tanger Pocket* guide—in French only—with a town map (Mon-Fri 9:00-16:30, closed Sat-Sun, in new town at Boulevard Pasteur 29, +212 539 948 050).

Travel information, English or otherwise, is rare here, but a good English guidebook available locally is *Tangier and Its Surroundings* by Juan Ramón Roca.

ARRIVAL IN TANGIER
By Ferry

If you're taking a tour, just follow the leader. If you're on your own, head for the Grand Socco to get oriented. Note that ongoing construction at the port may cause some changes from the way things are described here.

Given the hilly nature of the city, a small, cheap, blue **Petit Taxi** is the best way to get into town (described later, under "Getting Around Tangier"). Confirm what you'll pay before you hop in. An honest cabbie will charge you 20-30 dh (about $3) for a ride from the ferry into town; less scrupulous drivers will try to charge closer to 100 dh.

If you're determined to **walk,** it's about 10 gently but potentially confusing uphill minutes through the colorful lanes of the medina. Head out through the port entrance gate (by the mosque), cross the busy street, and head left toward the open lot. Then turn *left* to follow the old city walls, keeping the landmark Hotel Continental on your right. After passing the Hotel Continental, look for a street ramp at the end of the lot. Go up this ramp onto Rue de Portugal, and follow it as it curves around the old city wall. At the corner of the wall, take the first right onto Rue de la Plage. This will lead you past the market and into the Grand Socco.

Another option is the new **staircase** on the northern edge of the city wall, which leads steeply but directly up from just across the port to the top of the Kasbah (handy for travelers sleeping in one of my recommended guesthouses). Exit the port as described earlier, then—from the open lot—turn *right* to follow the city walls and find the never-ending stone staircase on your left, just beyond the row of cannons. At the top, head through a gate in the old town walls and emerge in the Place de la Kasbah.

By Plane

The Tangier Ibn Battuta Airport (code: TNG) is small but well organized, with ATMs and cafés. Air Arabia, Iberia, Royal Air Maroc, Ryanair, and others fly from here to destinations in Spain and throughout Europe.

Taxis between the airport and downtown Tangier run about 150 dh and take 30 minutes. If spending the night, ask your hotel to book a taxi and confirm the fare in advance (generally the same price as hiring a taxi yourself).

GETTING AROUND TANGIER

Avoid the big, beige Mercedes "Grand Taxis," which don't use their meters (they're meant for longer trips outside the city center and are OK for the airport, but have been known to take tourists for a ride in town...in more ways than one). Look instead for the cheap **Petit Taxis**—blue with a yellow stripe (they fit 2-3 people). These generally use their meters in town, but from the port, they charge whatever they can get, so it's essential to agree on a price up front.

Be aware that Tangier taxis sometimes "double up"—if you're headed somewhere, the driver may pick up someone else who's going in the same direction. However, you don't get to split the fare: Each of you pays full price (even if the other passenger's route takes you a bit out of your way).

When you get in a taxi, be prepared for a white-knuckle experience. Drivers, who treat lanes only as suggestions, prefer to straddle the white lines rather than stay inside them. Pedestrians add to the mayhem by fearlessly darting out every which way along the street. It's best to just close your eyes.

HELPFUL HINTS

Hustler Alert: Unfortunately, most of the English-speaking Moroccans the typical tourist meets are vendors, hustling to make a buck. Haggle when appropriate; prices skyrocket for tourists (see the "Bargaining Basics" sidebar later in this chapter). You'll attract hustlers like flies at every famous tourist site or whenever you pull out a guidebook or map. In the worst-case scenario, they'll lie to you, get you lost, blackmail you, and pester the heck out of you. Wear your money belt, and assume that con artists are cleverer than you. Never leave your bag-

gage where you can't get back to it without someone else's "help." Consider hiring a guide, since it's helpful to have a translator, and once you're "taken," the rest seem to leave you alone (be aware that anything you buy in a guide's company gets him a hefty commission).

Money: If you're on a tour or only day-tripping, you can stick with euros—most businesses happily take euros or even dollars. But if you're on your own, it's fun to get a pocketful of dirhams. You'll find ATMs in the parking lot of the port (along with exchange services), around the Grand Socco (look just to the left of the archway entrance into the medina), and near the TI along Boulevard Pasteur. ATMs work as you expect them to and are often less hassle than exchanging money. Banks and ATMs have uniform rates.

If you can't find an ATM, exchange desks are quick, easy, and fair. Just understand the buy-and-sell rates—they should be within 10 percent of each other with no other fee. (If you change €50 into dirhams and immediately change the dirhams back, you should have about €45.) Look for the official *Bureaux de Change* offices, where you'll get better rates than at the banks. There are some on Boulevard Pasteur and a handful between the Grand and Petit Soccos. The official change offices all offer the same rates, so there's no need to shop around.

Convert your dirhams back to euros before catching the ferry—it's cheap and easy to do here but very difficult once you're back in Spain.

Keeping Your Bearings: Tangier's maps and street signs are frustrating. I ask in French for the landmark: *"Où est...?"* (Where is...?), pronounced "oo ay," as in *"oo ay medina?"* or *"oo ay Kasbah?"* It can be fun to meet people this way. However, most people who offer to help you (especially those who approach you) are angling for a tip—young and old, locals see dollar signs when a traveler approaches. To avoid getting unwanted company, ask for directions only from people who can't leave what they're doing (such as the only clerk in a shop) or from women who aren't near men. Be aware that most locals tend to navigate by landmarks and don't know the names of the smaller streets (which don't usually have signs). Ask three times and go with the consensus. If there's no consensus, it's time to hop into a Petit Taxi.

Eating with Your Hands: In Islam, the right hand is seen as pure and the left hand as impure. Moroccans who eat with their hands—as many civilized people do in this part of the world—always eat with their right hand; the left hand is for washing.

Mosques: Tangier's mosques (and virtually all of Morocco's) are closed to non-Muslim visitors.

Antiques and Souvenirs: Near the Place de France, **Bazar Tindouf** is a fun place to browse and practice your bargaining skills, with three labyrinthine levels of wall-to-wall, floor-to-ceiling antiques, carpets, pottery, tiles, old photographs, and Moroccan bric-a-brac. Even if you aren't into shopping, it's interesting to browse everyday articles long abandoned by their original owners (daily 10:30-20:30, 64 Rue de la Liberté, +212 539 931 525).

Tours in Tangier

PACKAGE TOURS

For information on guided day-trip tours including the ferry to Tangier from Tarifa in Spain, see "With a Package Tour from Tarifa," earlier.

LOCAL GUIDES

If you're on your own in Tangier, you'll be to street guides what a horse's tail is to flies...all day long. Seriously—it can be exhausting to constantly deflect come-ons from anyone who sees you open a guidebook. If only to have your own translator and a shield from less scrupulous touts who hit up tourists constantly throughout the old town, I recommend hiring a guide.

Getting the Tour You Want: When hiring a guide, be very clear about your interests. Guides, hoping to get a huge commission from your purchases, can cleverly turn your Tangier day into the Moroccan equivalent of the Shopping Channel. Truth be told, some of these guides would work for free, considering all the money they make on commissions when you buy stuff. State outright that you want to experience the place, its people, and the culture—not its shopping. Request an outline of what your

tour will include, and confirm whether the principal guide will be working with you or if you'll be passed off to another team member. Once your tour is under way, if your guide deviates from your expectations, speak up.

What to Expect: While each local guide has specific itineraries, the two basic options are more or less the same: a half-day walking tour around the medina and Kasbah (generally 3-5 hours); or a full-day "grand tour" that includes the walk around town as well as a minibus ride to outlying viewpoints such as the Caves of Hercules and Cape Spartel (7-8 hours, lunch is generally at your expense in a restaurant the guide suggests). Prices are fairly standard from guide to guide.

If you want, your guide can reserve ferry tickets for you for the same cost as booking directly: He'll give you a reference number and you'll pick up your tickets at the ferry office in Tarifa (you'll reimburse him when you meet in Tangier).

Recommended Guides: The guides that I've worked with and recommend here speak great English, are easy to get along with, will meet you at the ferry dock in Tangier, and charge fixed rates. Any of them will make your Tangier experience more enjoyable for a negligible cost. If you're very pleased with your guide, he'll appreciate a tip. If you're displeased with your guide, please let me know at RickSteves.com.

Aziz ("Africa") Benami is energetic and fun to spend the day with. He or a reliable member of his guiding team will happily tailor a tour to your interests (half-day walking tour from €15/person, full-day minibus and walking tour from €35/person, traditional Moroccan lunch-€15/person, market visit and cooking class-€65/person or €55 if added to walking tour, also offers day and multi-day trips to destinations across Morocco, can arrange ferry tickets from Tarifa with RS%, mobile +212 618 504 030, from the US or Canada dial toll-free +1 888 745 7305, www.abtravels.com, info@abtravels.com).

Aziz Begdouri is an old friend who runs private tours of Tangier and the area, and seems to be on a first-name basis with everyone in town. He also manages the recommended hotel La Maison Blanche. Contact him in advance to decide how he can create a tour for you (€45/person, mobile +212 661 639 332, aziztour@hotmail.com).

Ahmed Taoumi, who has been guiding for more than 35 years, has a friendly and professorial style (half-day walking tour including short panoramic car ride up into town-€18/person, full-day grand tour with minibus-€35/person, also offers minibus side trips to nearby destinations and discounted ferry tickets, mobile +212 661 665 429, www.visitangier.com, taoumitour@hotmail.com).

MOROCCO & TANGIER

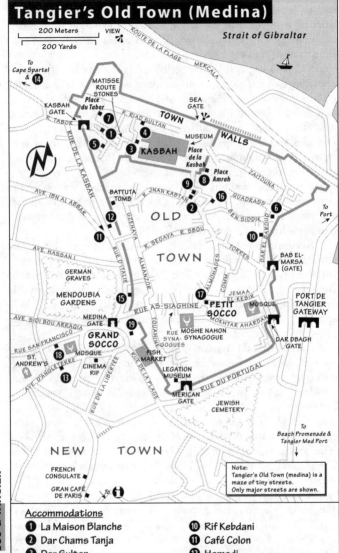

Tangier's Old Town (Medina)

200 Meters
200 Yards

VIEW

ROUTE DE LA PLAGE

Strait of Gibraltar

MERCALA

To Cape Spartel & 14

MATISSE ROUTE STONES

Place du Tabor

KASBAH GATE

R. TABOR

R. RIAD SULTAN

TOWN

SEA GATE

WALLS

MUSEUM

Place de la Kasbah

KASBAH

RUE DE LA KASBAH

AVE. IBN AL ABBAR

Place Amrah

ZAITOUNA

AVE. HASSAN I

BATTUTA TOMB

R. JNAN KABTAN

OLD

QUADRASS

BEN SIDDIK

To Port

GZENAYA

ALMANZOR

R. SEGAYA   R. SBOU

TOWN

TORRES

DAR EL FAROUD

RUE D'ITALIE

GERMAN GRAVES

MENDOUBIA GARDENS

ALMOHADES

COMM.

BAB EL-MARSA (GATE)

AVE. SIDI BOU ARRAQIA

MEDINA GATE

RUE AS-SIAGHINE

JEMAA EL-KEBIR

PETIT SOCCO

PORT DE TANGIER GATEWAY

RUE SAN FRANCISCO

GRAND SOCCO

TOUAHINE

RUE MOSHE NAHON SYNAGOGUE

MOSHE NAHON SYNA-GOGUES

MOSQUE

MOKHTAR AHARDAN

DAR DBAGH GATE

ST. ANDREW'S

AVE. D'ANGLETERRE

MOSQUE

CINEMA RIF

RUE DE LA LIBERTÉE

FISH MARKET

RUE DE LA PLAGE

LEGATION MUSEUM

MERICAN GATE

RUE DU PORTUGAL

JEWISH CEMETERY

NEW   TOWN

To Beach Promenade & Tangier Med Port

FRENCH CONSULATE

GRAN CAFÉ DE PARIS

To

Note:
Tangier's Old Town (medina) is a maze of tiny streets. Only major streets are shown.

Accommodations
1. La Maison Blanche
2. Dar Chams Tanja
3. Dar Sultan
4. La Tangerina
5. Dar Nour
6. Hotel Continental

Eateries & Other
7. El Morocco Club
8. Le Salon Bleu
9. La Terraza de la Medina
10. Rif Kebdani
11. Café Colon
12. Hamadi
13. Restaurant Dama
14. To Café Hafa
15. Bab Al Medina Pastries
16. Café Baba
17. Café Central
18. Pottery Market
19. Produce Market

MOROCCO & TANGIER

Abdellatif ("Latif") Chebaa is personable and is dedicated to making visitors comfortable. In addition to Tangier tours, his offerings include cooking classes, a visit to a traditional Berber house, and a trip to a Berber food market outside Tangier (half-day walking tour-€15/person, grand tour-€35/person, other experiences—€25-55/person, mobile +212 661 072 014, visittangier@gmail.com).

Other Options: I've had good luck with the **private guides who meet the boat.** If you're a decent judge of character, try interviewing guides when you get off the ferry to find one you click with, then check for an official license and negotiate a good price. These hardworking, English-speaking guides offer their services for the day for €15.

Sights in Tangier

GRAND SOCCO AND NEARBY
▲▲Grand Socco

This big, bustling square is a transportation hub, market, popular meeting point, and the fulcrum between the new town and the old town (medina). A few years ago, it was a pedestrian nightmare and a perpetual traffic jam. But now, like much of Tangier, it's on the rise. Many of the sights mentioned in this spin tour are described in more detail later in this chapter.

❥ **Self-Guided Spin Tour:** The Grand Socco is a good place to get oriented to the heart of Tangier. Stand on the square between the fountain and the mosque (the long building with arches and the tall tower). We'll do a slow clockwise spin.

Start by facing the **mosque,** with its long arcade of keyhole arches and colorfully tiled minaret. Morocco is a decidedly Mus-

lim nation, though its take on Islam is moderate, likely owing to the country's crossroads history. Five times a day, you'll hear the call to prayer echo across the rooftops of Tangier, from minarets like this one. Unlike many Muslim countries, Morocco doesn't allow non-Muslims to enter its mosques (with the ex-

Women in Morocco

Some visitors to Tangier expect to see women completely covered head-to-toe by their kaftans. In fact, not all Moroccan women adhere strictly to this religious dress code, especially in cities. Some cover only their hair (allowing their face to be seen), while others eliminate the head scarf altogether. Some women wear only Western-style clothing. This change in dress visibly reflects slowly changing Moroccan attitudes about women's rights.

Morocco is one of the more progressive Muslim countries. As in any border country, contact with other cultures fosters the growth of new ideas. Bombarded with Spanish television and visitors like you, change is inevitable. Another proponent of change is King Mohammed VI, who was only 35 years old when he rose to the throne in 1999. For the first time in the country's history, the king personally selected a female adviser to demonstrate his commitment to change. However, sexual mores are still traditional: Sex outside of marriage is illegal in Morocco, as is homosexual behavior.

But recent times have brought some transformations for women in Morocco. Schools are now coed, although many more boys than girls are enrolled, especially in rural areas. The legal age for women to marry is now 18 instead of 15 (although arranged marriages are still commonplace). Other changes make it more difficult for men to have a second wife. Verbal divorce and abandonment are no longer legal—disgruntled husbands, including the king (who married a commoner for...get this...*love*), must now take their complaints to court. And for the first time, women can divorce their husbands. If children are involved, whoever takes care of the kids gets the house.

Morocco took another step forward with its 2011 constitutional reforms, which guarantee women "civic and social" equality. But it will take time for any progressive changes in the law to be thoroughly translated into practice.

ception of its biggest and most famous one, in Casablanca). This custom may have originated decades ago, when occupying French foreign legion troops spent the night in a mosque, entertaining themselves with wine and women. Following this embarrassing desecration, it was the French government—not the Moroccans—who instituted the ban that persists today.

Locals say that in this very cosmopolitan city, anytime you

see a mosque, you'll find a church nearby. Sure enough, peeking up behind the mosque, you can barely make out the white, crenellated top of the **Anglican church tower** (or at least the English flag above it—a red cross on a white field). A fascinating hybrid of Muslim and Christian architecture, this house of worship is worth a visit (see listing following this section).

Also behind the mosque, you can see parts of a sprawling **market** (featuring pottery and other everyday goods; the far more colorful produce, meat, and fish market is across the square from where you're standing). Traditionally the Grand Socco was Tangier's hub for visiting merchants. The town gates were locked each evening, and vendors who arrived too late spent the night in this area. (Nearby were many caravanserai—old-fashioned inns.) But several years ago, this square was dramatically renovated by King Mohammed VI and given a new name: "April 9th 1947 Square," commemorating the date when an earlier king appealed to his French overlords to grant his country its independence. (France eventually complied, peacefully, in 1956.) Mohammed VI tamed the traffic, added the fountain you're standing next to, and turned this into a delightfully people-friendly space.

Spin a few more degrees to the right, where you'll see the crenellated gateway marked *Tribunal de Commerce*—the entrance to the **Mendoubia Gardens,** a pleasant park with a gigantic tree and a quirky history that reflects the epic story of Tangier (see listing following this section). At the top of the garden gateway, notice the Moroccan flag: a green five-pointed star on a red field. The five points of the star represent the five pillars of Islam, green is the color of peace, and red represents the struggles of hard-fought Moroccan history.

Spinning farther right, you'll see the **keyhole arch** marking the entrance to the medina. (If you need cash, an ATM and exchange booths are just to the left of this gateway.) To reach the heart of the medina—the Petit Socco (the café-lined little brother of the square you're on now)—you'd go through this arch and take the first right.

In front of the arch, you'll likely see **day laborers** looking for work. Each one rests next to a symbol of the kind of work he specializes in: a bucket of paintbrushes for a painter, a coil of wiring for an electrician, and a loop of hose for a plumber.

Speaking of people looking for work, how many locals have offered to show you around? ("Hey! What

you looking for? I help you!") Get used to it. While irritating, it's understandable. To these very poor people, you're impossibly rich—your pocket change is at least a good day's wage. If someone pesters you, you can simply ignore them, or say *"Lah shokran"* (No, thank you). But be warned: The moment you engage with anyone, you've just prolonged the sales pitch.

Back to our spin tour: To the right of the main arch, and just before the row of green rooftops, is the low-profile archway entrance to another **market** *(souk)*. A barrage on all the senses, this is a fascinating place to explore. The row of green rooftops to the right of the market entrance leads toward Rue de la Plage, with even more market action.

Continue spinning another quarter-turn to the tall, white building at the top of the square labeled **Cinema Rif.** This historic movie house still plays films (in Arabic, French, and occasionally English). The street to the left of the cinema takes you to Rue de la Liberté, which eventually leads through the modern town to the TI (about a 15-minute walk). Just to the right of the cinema, notice the yellow terrace, which offers the best view over the Grand Socco (just go up the staircase). It's also part of a café, where you can order a Moroccan tea (green tea, fresh mint, and lots of sugar), enjoy the view over the square, and plot your next move.

▲St. Andrew's Church

St. Andrew's Anglican Church, tucked behind a showpiece mosque, embodies Tangier's mingling of Muslim and Christian tradition.

The land on which the church sits was a gift from the sultan to the British community in 1881, during Queen Victoria's era. Shortly thereafter, this church was built. Although fully Christian, the church is designed in the style of a Muslim mosque. The Lord's Prayer rings the arch in Arabic, as verses of the Quran would in a mosque. Knock on the door—Ali or his son Yassin will greet you and give you a "thank you very much" tour. The garden surrounding the church is a tranquil, parklike cemetery. On Sundays and Thursdays, an impromptu Berber farmers market occupies the sidewalk out front (about 9:00-13:00).

Cost and Hours: 20 dh tip appreciated; open daily 9:30-12:30 & 14:30-sunset, closed during Sun services.

Mendoubia Gardens

This pleasant park, accessed through the castle-like archway off the Grand Socco, is a favorite place for locals to hang out. Walk through the gateway to see the trunk of a gigantic banyan tree, which, according to local legend, dates from the 12th century. Notice how the extra supportive roots have grown from the branches down to the ground.

The large building to the left—today the business courthouse *(Tribunal de Commerce)*—was built in the early 20th century to

house the representative of the Moroccan king. In those days, back when Tangier was officially an international zone administered by various European powers, Morocco needed an ambassador of sorts to keep an eye out for the country's interests.

The smaller house on the right (behind the giant tree) is currently a courthouse used exclusively for marriages and divorces, but it was once the headquarters of the German delegation in Tangier. When France established Morocco's protectorate status in 1912, Germany was kept out of the arrangement in exchange for territory along the Congo River. But in 1941, when Germany was on the rise in Europe and allied with Spain's Franco, it joined the mix of ruling powers in Tangier. Although Germans were only here for a short time (until mid-1942), they have a small cemetery in what's now the big park in front of you. Go up the stairs and around the blocky Arabic monument. At the bases of the trees beyond it, you'll find headstones of German graves...an odd footnote in the very complex history of this intriguing city.

Boulevard Pasteur

In the oldest part of the new town, this street is the axis of cosmopolitan Tangier. The street is lined with legendary cafés, the most storied of which is the Gran Café de Paris, which has been doing business here since 1920 (daily early until late, at Place de France, just across from the French consulate). Moroccans call this the "tennis" street because while sitting at an al fresco café, your head will be constantly swiveling back and forth to watch the passing parade.

A block farther along is the beautiful Place de Faro terrace, with its cannons and views back to Spain. It's nicknamed "Terrace of the Lazy Ones": instead of making the trek down to the harbor, family members came here in the old days to see if they could spot ships returning with loved ones who'd been to Mecca.

MEDINA (OLD TOWN)

Tangier's medina is its convoluted old town—a twisty mess of narrow stepped lanes, dead-end alleys, and lots of local life spilling out into the streets. It's divided roughly into two parts: the lower medina, with the Petit Socco, synagogue, market, American Legation Museum, and bustling street life; and, at the top, the more tranquil Kasbah.

Lower Medina

A maze of winding lanes and tiny alleys weave through the old-town market area. In an effort to help orient hopelessly turned-around tourists, Tangier has installed map signboards with suggested walking tours at the major medina gates. Write down the name of the gate you came in, so you can enjoy being lost—temporarily.

Petit Socco

This little square, also called Souk Dahel ("Inner Market"), is the center of the lower medina. Lined with tea shops and cafés, it has a romantic quality that has long made it a people magnet. In the 1920s, it was the meeting point for Tangier's wealthy and influential elite; by the 1950s and '60s, it drew Jack Kerouac and his counterculture buddies. Nursing a coffee or a mint tea here, it's easy to pretend you're a Beat Generation rebel, dropping out from Western society and delving deeply into an exotic, faraway culture.

The Petit Socco is ideal for some casual people-watching over a drink. You can go to one of the more traditional cafés, but **Café Central**—with the large awnings and look of a European café—is accessible, and therefore the most commercialized and touristy (coffees, fruit drinks, and meals; long hours daily).

Moshe Nahon Synagogue

Steps away from the Petit Socco, down a narrow, dead-end alley, is the Moshe Nahon Synagogue (closed Sat, Rue Synagogues 3). When Sephardic Jews were expelled from Spain in 1492, many fled to Morocco. This area was the Jewish quarter in Tangier, and this is one of the oldest synagogues in the city (it's open to the public—ring the bell outside). Built in the late 19th century by a Jewish scholar, the ornately decorated synagogue draws inspiration from Spanish, Islamic, and Jewish design, reminding visitors how the three cultures are historically connected. Plaques on the wooden benches bear the names of members who paid an annual fee for seats—a mark of wealth and privilege. The wooden panel behind the lectern opens to reveal the Torah, written on leather over 600 years old and protected by a traditional cloth covering. To the left is the circumcision altar, and upstairs is the women's gallery (accessed by a staircase in the courtyard), lined with Hebrew scripture proclaiming, "God for everyone" and decorated with marriage embroideries from the early 1900s.

▲▲Market (Souk)

The medina's market, just off the Grand Socco, is a highlight. Wander past piles of fruit, veggies, and olives, countless varieties of bread, and fresh goat cheese wrapped in palm leaves. Phew! You'll find everything but pork.

Entering the market through the door from the Grand Socco, turn right to find butchers, a cornucopia of produce (almost all of it from Morocco), more butchers, piles of olives slathered with an aromatic and lustrous topcoat of oil, and yet more butchers. The chickens are plucked and hung to show they have been killed according to Islamic guidelines (halal): Animals are slaughtered with a sharp knife in the name of Allah, head toward Mecca, and drained of their blood. The far aisle (parallel and to the left of where you're walking) has more innards and is a little harder to stomach.

Scattered around the market are Berber tribeswomen, often wearing straw hats decorated with ribbons or colorful striped skirts; they ride donkeys to the city from the nearby Rif Mountains, mostly on Tuesdays and Thursdays. (Before taking photos of these women, or any people you see here, it's polite to ask permission.)

Eventually you'll emerge into the large, white fish market; with the day's catch from both the Mediterranean and the Atlantic, this place is a textbook of marine life.

The door at the far end of the fish market pops you out on the Rue de la Plage; a right turn takes you back to the Grand Socco, but a left turn leads across the street to the (figurative and literal) low end of the market—a world of very rustic market stalls under a corrugated plastic roof. While just a block from the main market, this is a world apart, and not to everyone's taste. Here you'll find cheap produce, junk shops, ragtag electronics, old ladies sorting bundles of herbs from crinkled plastic bags, and far less sanitary-looking butchers than the ones inside the main market hall (if that's pos-

Bargaining Basics

No matter what kind of merchandise you buy in Tangier, the shopping style is pure Moroccan. Bargain hard! The first price you're offered is simply a starting point, and it's expected that you'll try to talk the price way down. Bargaining can become an enjoyable game if you follow a few basic rules:

Determine what the item is worth to you. Before you even ask a price, decide what the item's value is to you. Consider the hassles involved in packing it or shipping it home.

Determine the merchant's lowest price. Many merchants will settle for a nickel profit rather than lose the sale entirely. Work the cost down to rock bottom, and when it seems to have fallen to a record low, walk away. That last price the seller hollers out as you turn the corner is often the best price you'll get.

Look indifferent. As soon as the merchant perceives the "I gotta have that!" in you, you'll never get the best price.

Employ a third person. Use your friend who is worried about the ever-dwindling budget or who is bored and wants to return to the hotel. This can help to bring the price down faster.

Show the merchant your money. Physically hold out your money and offer him "all you have" to pay for whatever you are bickering over. He'll be tempted to just grab your money and say, "Oh, OK."

If the price is too much, leave. Never worry about having taken too much of the merchant's time. They are experts at making the tourist feel guilty for not buying. It's all part of the game.

sible). Peer down the alley filled with a twitching poultry market, which encourages vegetarianism.

The upper part of the market (toward the medina and Petit Socco) has a handful of food stands but more nonperishable items, such as clothing, cleaning supplies, toiletries, and prepared foods. Scattered around this part of the market are spice-and-herb stalls (usually marked *hérboriste*), offering a fragrant antidote to the meat stalls. In addition to cooking spices, these sell homegrown Berber cures for ailments. Pots hold a dark-green gelatinous goo—a kind of natural soap.

If you're looking for souvenirs, you won't have to find them... they'll find you, in the form of aggressive salesmen who approach you on the street and push their conga drums, T-shirts, and other trinkets in your face. Most of the market itself is more focused on locals, but the medina streets just above the market are loaded with souvenir shops. Aside from the predictable trinkets, the big-ticket items here are tilework (such as vases) and carpets. You'll notice many shops have tiles and other, smaller souvenirs on the ground floor, and carpet salesrooms upstairs.

▲▲▲Exploring the Medina

Appealing as the market is, one of the most magical Tangier experiences is to simply lose yourself in the lanes of the medina. A first-time visitor cannot stay oriented—so don't even try. I just wander, knowing that going uphill will eventually get me to the Kasbah and going downhill will lead me to the port. Expect to get a little lost...going around in circles is part of the fun. Pop in to see artisans working in their shops: mosaic tilemakers, thread spinners, tailors. Shops are on the ground level, and the family usually lives upstairs. Doors indicate how many families live in the homes behind them: one row of decoration for one, another parallel row for two.

Many people can't afford private ovens, phones, or running water, so there are economical communal options: phone desks

(called *teleboutiques*), baths, and bakeries. If you smell the aroma of baking bread, look for a hole-in-the-wall bakery, where locals drop off their ready-to-cook dough (as well as meat, fish, or nuts to roast). You'll also stumble upon communal taps, with water provided by the government, where people come to wash. Cubby-hole rooms are filled with kids playing video games on old TVs—they can't afford their own at home, so they come here instead.

Go on a photo safari for ornate "keyhole" doors, many of which lead to neighborhood mosques (see photo). Green doors are the color of Islam and symbolize peace. The ring-shaped door knockers double as a place to hitch a donkey.

As you explore, notice that some parts of the medina seem starkly different, with fancy wrought-iron balconies. Approximately 20 percent of the town was built and controlled by Spaniards and Portuguese living here (with the

MOROCCO & TANGIER

rest being Arabic and Berber). The two populations were separated by a wall, the remains of which you can still trace running through the medina. It may seem at first glance that these European zones are fancier and "nicer" compared to the poorer-seeming Arabic/Berber zones. But the Arabs and Berbers take more care with the insides of their homes—if you went behind these humble walls, you'd be surprised how pleasant the interiors are. While European cultures externalize resources, Arab and Berber cultures internalize them.

The medina is filled with surprises for which serendipity is your best or only guide. As you wander, keep an eye out for the legendary **Café Baba** (up a few stairs on Rue Doukkala—not far from Place Amrah, daily 10:30-23:30). Old, grimy, and smoky, it's been around since the late 1940s and was a hippie hangout in the 1960s and '70s—the Rolling Stones smoked hash here (on the wall there's still a battered picture of Keith Richards holding a pipe). Enjoy a mint tea here and take in the great view over the old quarter, including a lush mansion just across the way formerly owned by American heiress Barbara Hutton.

One of the few sights revered by Moroccans that can be entered by non-Muslim visitors is the **tomb of Ibn Battuta.** Hiding at the top of a narrow residential lane (Rue Ibn Battuta—look for tile signs pointing the way), this simple mausoleum venerates the man considered the Moroccan Marco Polo. What started as a six-month pilgrimage to Mecca in 1325 stretched out to some 30 years for Ibn Battuta, as he explored throughout the Islamic world and into India and China. (If you visit the tomb, remove your shoes before entering, and leave a small tip for the attendant.) No one really knows if it's actually Ibn Battuta interred here, but that doesn't deter locals from paying homage to him.

▲Tangier American Legation Museum

Located at the bottom end of the medina (just above the port), this unexpected museum is worth a visit. Morocco was one of the first countries to recognize the newly formed United States as an independent country (in 1777). The original building, given to the United States by the sultan of Morocco, became the fledgling government's first foreign acquisition. It was declared a US National Historic Landmark in 1983.

Cost and Hours: 20 dh, Mon-Fri 10:00-17:00, Sat until 15:00; during Ramadan daily 10:00-15:00, otherwise closed Sun

Islam 101

Islam has more than a billion adherents worldwide, and traveling in an Islamic country is an opportunity to better understand the religion. This admittedly basic and simplistic outline (written by a non-Muslim) is meant to help travelers from the Christian West understand a very rich but often misunderstood culture. Just as it helps to know about spires, feudalism, and the saints to comprehend European sightseeing, a few basics on Islam help make your sightseeing in Morocco more meaningful.

Muslims, like Christians and Jews, are monotheistic. They call God "Allah." The most important person in the Islamic faith is the prophet Muhammad, who lived in the sixth and seventh centuries. The holy book of Islam is the Quran, believed by Muslims to be the word of Allah as revealed to Muhammad. The "five pillars" of Islam are the core obligations of the faith that followers must satisfy:

1. Say and believe this basic statement of faith: "There is no god but God, and Muhammad is his prophet."
2. Pray five times a day.
3. Give to the poor (annually, about 2.5 percent of one's income).
4. Fast during daylight hours through the month of Ramadan. Fasting develops self-control and awareness, and is a step toward achieving selflessness.
5. Make a pilgrimage *(hajj)* to Mecca. Muslims who can afford it and are physically able are required to travel to Mecca at least once in their lifetimes.

year-round; Rue d'Amérique 8, +212 539 935 317, www.legation.org.

Visiting the Museum: This 19th-century mansion was the US embassy (or consulate) in Morocco from 1821 to 1961, and it's still American property—our only National Historic Landmark overseas. Today this nonprofit museum and research center is a strangely peaceful oasis within Tangier's intense old town. It offers a warm welcome and lots of interesting artifacts—all well described in English. The ground floor is filled with an art gallery. In the stairwell, you'll see photos of kings with presidents, and a letter with the news of Lincoln's assassination. Upstairs are more paintings, as well as model soldiers playing out two battle scenes from Moroccan history. These belonged to American industrialist Malcolm Forbes, who had a home in Tangier (his son donated these dioramas to the museum). Rounding out the upper floor are wonderful old maps of Tangier and Morocco. A visit here is a fun reminder of how long the US and Morocco have had good relations.

• *When you've soaked in enough old-town atmosphere, make your way to the Kasbah (see map). Within the medina, head uphill, or exit the medina gate and go right on Rue Kasbah, which follows the old wall uphill to Bab Kasbah (a.k.a. Porte de la Kasbah or Kasbah Gate), a gateway into the Kasbah.*

Kasbah

Loosely translated as "fortress," a *kasbah* is an enclosed, protected residential area near a castle that you'll find in hundreds of Moroccan towns. Originally this was a place where a king or other leader could protect his tribe. Tangier's Kasbah, comprising the upper quarter of the old town, has twisty lanes and some nice guesthouses. It is a bit more sedate and less claustrophobic than parts of the medina near the market below.

Way finding here has always been a challenge for visitors. Look for tile signs with street names and arrows pointing to main sights posted on many corners, and spray-painted blue numbers marking each intersection. Eventually, these numbers will be painted over... once, and if, a permanent system is decided on.

▲Kasbah Museum of Mediterranean Cultures

On Place de la Kasbah, you'll find a former sultan's palace, Dar el-Makhzen, that's now a history museum with a few historical artifacts. While there's not a word of English, some of the exhibits are still easy to appreciate, and the building itself is beautiful.

Cost and Hours: 20 dh, Wed-Mon 10:00-18:00, closed for prayer Fri 12:00-13:30 and all day Tue, ask for English brochure, +212 539 932 097.

Visiting the Museum: Enter straight past the ticket booth. Most of the exhibits surround the central, open-air courtyard; rooms proceed roughly chronologically as you move counterclockwise, from early hunters and farmers to prehistoric civilizations, Roman times, the region's conversion to Islam, and the influence of European powers. Duck through the far-right corner of the courtyard to find a two-story space with a second-century mosaic floor depicting the journey of Venus. A 12th-

MOROCCO & TANGIER

century wall-size map shows the Moorish view of the world: with Africa on top (Spain is at the far right). Mirrors help visitors see the intricate details on the ceiling. Nearby is an explanation of terra-cotta production (a local industry), and upstairs is an exhibit on funerary rituals. Near the entrance to the courtyard, look for signs to *jardin* and climb the stairs to reach a chirpy (if slightly over-grown) garden courtyard. Striking tilework is featured throughout the 17th-century building.

PLACE DE LA KASBAH

The square in front of the Kasbah Museum attracts more than its share of tourists, and that means it's a vivid gauntlet of amusements:

snake charmers, squawky dance troupes, and colorful water ven-dors. These colorful Kodak-mo-ment hustlers make their living off the many tour groups passing by daily. (As you're cajoled, re-member that the daily minimum wage here for men as skilled as these beggars is $10. That's what the gardeners you'll pass in your walk earn each day. In other words, a €1 tip is an hour's wage for these people.) If you draft behind a tour group, you won't be the focus of the hustlers. But if you take a photo, you must pay.

Before descending from the Kasbah, don't miss the ocean viewpoint—as you stand in the square and face the palace, look to the right to find the rebuilt city wall and Bab Bahr, the "Sea Gate." This leads out to a large natural terrace with fine views over the port, the Mediterranean, and Spain. From here, you can descend a lengthy staircase all the way back to the port.

The lower gate of the Kasbah (as you stand in Place de la Kasbah facing the palace, it's on your left) leads to a charming little alcove between the gates, where you can see a particularly fine tile fountain: The top part is carved cedarwood, below that is carved plas-ter, and the bottom half is hand-laid tiles.

MOROCCO & TANGIER

Matisse Route

The artist Henri Matisse traveled to Tangier in 1912-13. The culture, patterns, and colors that he encountered here had a lifelong effect on the themes in his subsequent art. The diamond-shaped stone patterns embedded in the narrow lane leading up along the left side of the palace mark a route that the famous artist regularly walked through the Kasbah, from the lower gate to the upper; those who know his works will spot several familiar scenes along this stretch. Just off the Grand Socco, on Rue de la Liberté, is the instantly recognizable Grand Hotel Villa de France, where Matisse lived and painted while in Tangier (for more on this hotel, see the listing under "Sleeping in Tangier," later).

TANGIER BEACH AND MARINA

The newly inaugurated Tanja Marina Bay, part of the port's rejuvenation project, offers cafés, shops, over 1,400 berths, modern underground parking, and a home for the Royal Yacht Club of Tangier. Stretching gracefully eastward from the marina, the chic La Corniche promenade rests above a stretch of fishy eateries and entertaining nightclubs as it follows the curve of the wide, white-sand crescent beach (Plage de Corniche). The locals call it by the Spanish word

playa. It's packed with locals doing what people around the world do at the beach—with a few variations. Traditionally clad moms let their kids run wild. You'll see people—young and old—covered in hot sand to combat rheumatism. Early, late, and off-season, the beach becomes a popular venue for soccer teams. But while Tangier is making great efforts to upgrade the entire area, and the beach is cleaner than it once was, if you have a beach break in mind, do it on Spain's Costa del Sol.

Nightlife in Tangier

Nighttime is great in Tangier. If you're staying overnight, don't relax in a fancy hotel restaurant. Get out and about in the old town after dark. In the cool of the evening, the atmospheric squares and lanes become even more alluring. It's an entirely different experience and a highlight of any visit. The Malataba area in the new town (along Avenue Mohammed VI) is an easy cab ride away and filled with modern nightclubs. (But remember, this isn't night-owl Spain—things die down by around 22:00.)

El Minzah Hotel hosts traditional music most nights for those having dinner there. The **El Morocco Club** has a sophisticated piano bar. For details on both, see "Eating in Tangier," later.

Cinema Rif, the landmark theater at the top of the Grand Socco, shows movies in French—which the younger generation is required to learn—Arabic, and occasionally English. The cinema is worth popping into, if only to see the Art Deco interior. As movies cost only 25 dh, consider dropping by to see a bit of whatever's on (closed Mon, +212 539 934 683).

Sleeping in Tangier

I've recommended two vastly different types of accommodations in Tangier: cozy Moroccan-style (but mostly French-run) guesthouses in the maze of lanes of the Kasbah neighborhood, and modern international-style hotels, most in the urban new town, a 10- to 20-minute walk from the central sights. June through mid-September is high season, when rooms may be a bit more expensive and reservations are wise.

Although the local currency is the dirham, nearly every hotel gives prices in euros, too. I've ranked the hotels below as **$** Budget: 500-900 dh; **$$** Moderate: 900-1300 dh; **$$$** Pricier: 1300-1700 dh; and **$$$$** Splurge: Over 1700 dh. All include breakfast.

GUESTHOUSES AND A HOTEL IN THE KASBAH

In Arabic, *riad* means "guesthouse." You'll find these in the atmospheric old town (medina). While the lower part of the medina is dominated by market stalls and tourist traps—and can feel a bit seedy after dark—the upper Kasbah area is more tranquil and residential. My recommendations are buried in a labyrinth of lanes that can be difficult to navigate; the map of "Tangier's Old Town (Medina)," earlier, gives you a vague sense of where to go, but it's essential to ask for very clear directions when you reserve. If you're hiring a guide in Tangier, ask him to help you find your *riad*. (If you're on your own, you can try asking directions when you arrive—but be forewarned that locals may see that as an invitation to tag along and hound you for tips.) The communal nature of *riad*s means that occasional noise from other guests can be an issue; bring your earplugs.

When you arrive at your *riad,* don't look for a doorbell—the tradition is to use a door knocker. The guesthouses listed here are in traditional old houses, with rooms surrounding a courtyard atrium, and all have rooftop terraces where you can relax and enjoy sweeping views over Tangier. Besides breakfast, many also serve good Moroccan dinners, which cost extra and should be arranged beforehand, typically that morning. Some also offer hammams

(Turkish-style baths) with massages and spa treatments. Some lack stand-alone showers; instead, in Moroccan style, you'll find a handheld shower in a corner of the bathroom.

$$$ La Maison Blanche ("The White House"), run by Aziz Begdouri, one of my recommended guides, has nine rooms in a restored traditional Moroccan house. Modern and attractively decorated, each room is dedicated to a personality who's spent time in Tangier—including a travel writer I know well. With its friendly vibe, great view terrace, and lavish setting, this is a worthwhile splurge (all with bathtubs, air-con, just inside the upper Kasbah gate at Rue Ahmed Ben Ajiba 2, +212 539 375 188, mobile +212 661 639 332, www.lamaisonblanchetanger.com, info@lamaisonblanchetanger.com).

$$$ Dar Chams Tanja, just below the lower Kasbah gate, has seven elegant, new-feeling rooms (named after women from Morocco) that surround an inner courtyard with lots of keyhole windows. It's impeccably decorated, has a proper French-expat ambience, and boasts incredible views from its rooftop terrace (air-con, hammam, massage service, Rue Jnan Kabtan 2, +212 539 332 323 or mobile +212 654 935 175, www.darchamstanja.com, darchamstanja@gmail.com).

$$$ Dar Sultan rents seven romantically decorated rooms on a pleasant street in the heart of the Kasbah with a small rooftop terrace (some rooms with balconies, Rue Touila 49, +212 539 336 061, mobile +212 671 181 580, www.darsultan.com, dar-sultan@menara.ma).

$$ La Tangerina, run by Jürgen (who's German) and his Moroccan wife, Farida, has 10 comfortable rooms that look down into a shared atrium. At the top is a gorgeous rooftop seaview balcony (cash only, wood-fired hammam, turn left as you enter the upper Kasbah gate and hug the town wall around to Riad Sultan 19, +212 539 947 731, www.latangerina.com, info@latangerina.com).

$$ Dar Nour, run with funky French style by Philippe, Jean-Olivier, and Catherine, has an "Escher-esque" floor plan that sprawls through five interconnected houses (it's "labyrinthine like the medina," says Philippe). The 10 homey rooms feel very traditional, with lots of books and lounging areas spread throughout, and a fantastic view terrace and cocktail bar on the roof (Wi-Fi in lobby only, Rue Gourna 20, mobile +212 662 112 724, www.darnour.com, contactdarnour@yahoo.fr).

$$ Hotel Continental—sprawling at the bottom of the old town, facing the port—is the grand Humphrey Bogart option. It has lavish, atmospheric, and recently renovated public spaces, a chandeliered breakfast room, and 53 spacious bedrooms with rough hardwood floors and new bathrooms. Jimmy, who's always around and runs the shop adjacent to the lobby, says he offers everything but Viagra. When I said, "I'm from Seattle," he said, "206." Test him—he knows your area code (family rooms, Dar Baroud 36; follow my directions for walking into town from the port, but take a right through the yellow gateway—Bab Dar Dbagh—marked *1339*, then turn right again and follow the signs, +212 539 931 024, hcontinental@menara.ma). This hotel's terrace aches with nostalgia. Back during the city's glory days, a ferry connected Tangier and New York. American novelists would sit out on the terrace of Hotel Continental, never quite sure when their friends' boat would arrive from across the sea.

MODERN HOTELS IN THE MODERN CITY

These hotels are centrally located, near the TI, and within walking distance of the Grand Socco, medina, and market.

$$$$ Grand Hotel Villa de France, perched high above the Grand Socco, has been around since the 19th century, when Eugène Delacroix stayed here and started a craze for Orientalism in European art. Henri Matisse was a guest in 1912-13, painting what he saw through his window. After sitting empty for years, the hotel was restored and reopened. Lavish public spaces, including a restaurant and view terrace, have more charm than most of the 58 modern, updated rooms, but a Matisse-inspired leaf design echoes throughout and adds a bit of character to an otherwise businesslike hotel. Suites have a more Moroccan vibe but are not quite worth the splurge (intersection of Rue Angleterre and Rue Hollande, for location see the "Tangier" map near the beginning of this chapter, +212 539 333 111, www.leroyal.com, reservation@ghvdf.com).

$$$ Atlas Marina Bay Hotel, recently restored to its 1970s glamour, is a worthy splurge. Offering 127 plush, modern rooms, sprawling public spaces, a garden, pool, and grand views, it feels like an oversized boutique hotel. Overlooking the harbor, the great lounge—named for Winston Churchill—compels you to relax (some view rooms, air-con, elevator, 3 restaurants, spa and sauna, Avenue Mohammed VI 152, +212 539 349 300, www.hotelsatlas.com, htoula@hotelsatlas.com).

$ Hotel Rembrandt feels just like the 1950s, with a restaurant, a bar, and a swimming pool surrounded by a great grassy garden. Its 70 rooms are outdated and simple but clean and comfortable, and some come with views (air-con, elevator, a 5-minute walk above the beach in a busy urban zone at Boulevard Mohammed V 1, +212 539 333 314, www.rembrandthoteltanger.com, reservation@hotelrembrandt.ma).

MOROCCO & TANGIER

Eating in Tangier

Moroccan food is a joy to sample. First priority is a glass of refreshing "Moroccan tea"—green tea that's boiled and steeped once, then combined with fresh mint leaves to boil and steep some more, before being loaded up with sugar. Tourist-oriented restaurants have a predictable menu. For starters, you'll find a Moroccan tomato-based vegetable soup *(harira)* or Moroccan salad (a combination of fresh and stewed vegetables). Main dishes include couscous (usually with chicken, potatoes, carrots, and other vegetables and spices); *tagine* (stewed meat served in a fancy dish with a cone-shaped top); and *briouates* (small savory pies). Everything comes with Morocco's distinctive round, flat bread. For dessert, it's pastries—typically, almond cookies.

I've mostly listed places in or near the medina. If you'd prefer the local equivalent of a yacht-club restaurant, survey the places along the beach.

IN THE MEDINA

$$$ El Morocco Club has three distinct zones. Outside, it's an inexpensive **terrace** café, serving a light menu of sandwiches, quiches, and salads in the shade of a rubber tree. At night a bouncer lets you into the pricier **fine restaurant** with a Med-Moroccan menu of grilled fish, roasted lamb, and creamy risottos. Guests at the restaurant have entrée to the wonderfully grown-up **piano bar:** a sophisticated lounge with vintage Tangier photos and zebra-print couches (café daily 9:00-17:00, restaurant and piano bar daily 19:30 until late, Place du Tabor, just inside the Kasbah gate, +212 539 948 139).

$$ Le Salon Bleu has decent Moroccan food and some of the most spectacular seating in town: perched on a whitewashed terrace overlooking the square in front of the Kasbah Museum, with 360-degree views over the rooftops. Hike up the very tight spiral staircase to the top level, with the best views and lounge-a-while sofa seating. Run by the French owners of the recommended Dar Nour guesthouse, it offers a simple menu of Moroccan fare—the appetizer plate is a good sampler for lunch or to share for an afternoon snack. While there is some indoor seating, I'd skip this place if the weather's not ideal for lingering on the terrace (daily 10:00-23:00, Place de la Kasbah, mobile +212 662 112 724). You'll see it from the square in front of the Kasbah; to reach it, go through the gate to the left (as you face it), then look right for the stairs up.

$$ La Terraza de la Medina has two floors of spacious dining areas and an outdoor terrace with views. If you're looking for a low-stress restaurant in the heart of the Kasbah, you'll find it here, just behind the recommended hotel Dar Chams Tanja. They serve traditional Moroccan fare such as *pastella*—a savory-sweet chicken pastry, *harira,* couscous, and *tagines* (generally daily 12:00-23:00, Rue Dakakine 6, +212 539 332 386).

$$ Rif Kebdani is a cozy, not-too-touristy place with colorful Moroccan tiles and Berber decor that's matched by a simple yet appetizing menu. With solid *tagine* options plus a variety of seafood dishes at reasonable prices, it's an especially good choice for lunch (daily 12:00-17:00 & 19:00-23:00, Rue Dar Baroud, +212 539 371 760).

$ Café Colon is a window into the real, present-day Tangier, where locals come to play cards and pass the day drinking coffee and tea. There's no food, almost no tourists, and drinks come with a customary glass of water (astute waiters bring bottled mineral water for travelers). Stopping here fills your cultural sustenance tank. As you idly watch passersby from a sidewalk table, you'll feel a part of keeping traditions—and Tangier—alive (long hours daily, Rue d'Italie 54).

Touristy Places in the Medina: Tangier seems to specialize in touristy restaurants designed to feed and entertain dozens or even hundreds of tour-group members with overpriced Moroccan classics and belly dancing. The only locals you'll see are the waiters. But for day-trippers who just want a safe, comfortable break in the heart of town, these restaurants' predictability and Moroccan clichés are just perfect. **$$ Hamadi,** as luxurious a restaurant as a tourist can find in Morocco, has good food at reasonable prices (long hours daily, check bill carefully, Rue Kasbah 2, +212 539 934 514).

IN THE NEW TOWN

These places, while technically in the New Town, are clustered just beyond the Grand Socco.

$$$ Le Saveur du Poisson is an excellent bet for the more adventurous, featuring one room cluttered with paintings adjoining a busy kitchen. There are no choices here. Just sit down and let owner Hassan take care of the rest. You get a rough hand-carved spoon and fork. Surrounded by lots of locals and unforgettable food, you'll be treated to a multicourse menu. Savor the delicious fish dishes—Tangier is one of the few spots in Morocco where seafood is a major part of the diet. The fruit punch—a mix of seasonal fruits brewed overnight in a vat—simmers in the back room. Ask for an explanation, or even a look. The desserts are full of nuts and honey. The big sink is for locals who prefer to eat with their fingers (Sat-Thu 13:00-17:00 & 19:00-22:30, closed Fri and during Ramadan; walk down Rue de la Liberté roughly a block toward the Grand Socco from El Minzah Hotel, look for the stairs leading down to the market stalls, and go down until you see fish on the grill; Escalier Waller 2, +212 539 336 326).

$$$ El Minzah Hotel offers a fancy yet still authentic experience. Classy but low stress, it's where unadventurous tourists and local elites dine. Dress up and choose between two dining zones: The white-tablecloth continental (French) dining area, called El Erz, is stuffy; while in the Moroccan lounge, El Korsan, you'll be serenaded by live traditional music (music nightly 20:00-23:00, belly-dance show at 20:30 and 21:30, no cover). There's also a cozy wine bar here—a rarity in a Muslim country—decorated with photos of visiting celebrities. At lunch, light meals and salads are served poolside (all dining areas open daily 13:00-16:00 & 20:00-22:30, Rue de la Liberté 85, +212 539 333 444).

$ Restaurant Darna, operated by the Maison Communitaire des Femmes, a community center for women, is open to everyone and offers a tasty, hearty, 60-dh two-course lunch. Profits support the work of the center (Mon-Sat 12:00-16:00, closed Sun, last order at 15:30, also open 9:00-11:00 & 15:30-17:00 for cakes and tea, cash only, pleasant terrace out back, near slipper market just outside Grand Socco, Place du 9 Avril, +212 539 947 065).

ON THE WATER WEST OF THE MEDINA

$ Café Hafa, a basic outdoor café cascading down a series of cliff-hugging terraces, is a longtime Tangier landmark. Find your way here with a taxi or your guide, but don't rush—you'll want to settle in to sip your tea and enjoy the fantastic sea views. Tangier's most famous expat, the writer Paul Bowles, used to hang out here (simple pizzas and brochettes, daily 9:00 until late, in the Marshan neighborhood west of the medina on Avenue Hadi Mohammed Tazi).

PASTRIES

Moroccan pastries and cookies are often offered with mint tea in cafés or hotels and are served for dessert after meals. But those with a serious sweet tooth should step into a *pâtisserie* to choose from the variety of local sweets made with almonds, pistachios, cashews, pine nuts, peanuts, dates, honey, and sugar. Ask for *"une boîte petite"* (a little box), and point to what you want to fill it—you'll pay by weight. One easy and delicious spot is **$ Bab Al Medina,** just off the Grand Socco (daily 6:00-22:00, Rue d'Italie 28, mobile +212 667 151 779). It has two sections: a café with pizzas and shawarma, and a bakery that offers Moroccan and French pastries, bread, and Moroccan *crêpes* (called *baghrir*, these have nooks and crannies similar to a crumpet). Eat at the café's tables or on your hotel terrace for a sweet sunset.

MOROCCO & TANGIER

Morocco Beyond Tangier

Morocco gets much better as you go deeper into the interior. The country is incredibly rich in cultural thrills, though you'll pay a price in hassles and headaches—it's a package deal. But if adven-

ture is your business, Morocco is a great option. Moroccan trains are quite good—and a high-speed line connects Tangier with Casablanca. Second class is cheap and comfortable. Buses connect all smaller towns very well. By car, Morocco is easy.

To plan a trip that extends beyond Tangier, you'll need a supplemental guidebook. Lonely Planet and Rough Guide both publish good ones, available at home and in Spain. To get you started in your planning, I've listed a few of my favorite Moroccan destinations here.

MOROCCAN TOWNS

Chefchaouen

Just two hours by bus or car from Tétouan, this is the first pleasant town beyond the north coast. Monday and Thursday are colorful market days. Wander deep into the atmospheric old town from the main square and admire the colorful buildings that inspired the nickname "blue pearl of Morocco."

Rabat

Morocco's capital and most European city, Rabat is the most comfortable and least stressful place to start your North African trip. You'll find a colorful market (in the old neighboring town of Salé), bits of Islamic architecture (Mausoleum of Mohammed V), the king's palace, mellow hustlers, and fine hotels.

Fès

More than just a funny hat that tipsy Shriners wear, Fès is Morocco's religious and artistic center, bustling with craftspeople, pilgrims, shoppers, and shops. Like most large Moroccan cities, it has a distinct new town from the French colonial period, as well as an exotic (and stressful) old walled Arabic town (the medina), where you'll find the market.

For 12 centuries, traders have gathered in Fès, founded on a river at the crossroads of two trade routes. Soon there was an irrigation system; a university; resident craftsmen from Spain; and a diverse population of Muslims, Christians, and Jews. When France claimed Morocco in 1912, they made their capital in Rabat, and Fès fizzled. But the Fès marketplace is still Morocco's best.

Marrakech

Morocco's gateway to the south, Marrakech is where the desert, mountain, and coastal regions merge. This market city is a constant folk festival, bustling with Berber tribespeople and a colorful center. The new city has the train station, and the main boulevard (Mohammed V) is lined with banks, airline offices, a post office, a tourist office, and comfortable hotels. The old city features the maze-like market and the huge Djemaa el-Fna, a square seething with people—a 43-ring Moroccan circus.

Over the Atlas Mountains

Extend your Moroccan trip several days by heading south over the Atlas Mountains. Take a bus from Marrakech to Ouarzazate (short stop), and then to Tinerhir (great oasis town, comfy hotel, overnight stop). The next day, go to Er Rachidia and take the overnight bus to Fès.

By car, drive from Fès south, staying in the small mountain town of Ifrane, and then continue deep into the desert country past Er Rachidia, and on to Rissani (market days: Sun, Tue, and Thu). Explore nearby mud-brick towns still living in the Middle Ages. Hire a guide to drive you past where the road stops, and head cross-country to an oasis village (Merzouga), where you can climb a sand dune and watch the sun rise over the vastness of Africa. Only a sea of sand separates you from Timbuktu.

PRACTICALITIES

This section covers just the basics on traveling in Spain (for much more information, see *Rick Steves Spain*). You'll find free advice on specific topics at RickSteves.com/tips.

MONEY

Spain uses the euro currency: 1 euro (€) = about $1.20. To convert prices in euros to dollars, add about 20 percent: €20 = about $24, €50 = about $60. (Check www.oanda.com for the latest exchange rates.)

The standard way for travelers to get euros is to withdraw money from an ATM (known as a *cajero automático*) using a debit or credit card, ideally with a Visa or MasterCard logo.

Before departing, call your bank or credit-card company: Confirm that your card(s) will work overseas, ask about international transaction fees, and alert them that you'll be making withdrawals in Europe. Also ask for the PIN number for your credit card—you may need it for Europe's "chip-and-PIN" payment machines. Allow time for your bank to mail your PIN to you.

European cards use chip-and-PIN technology; most chip cards issued in the US instead require a signature. European card readers may generate a receipt for you to sign—or prompt you to enter your PIN (so it's good to know it). US credit cards may not work at some self-service payment machines (transit-ticket kiosks, parking kiosks, etc.). If your card won't work, look for a cashier who can process the transaction manually—or pay in cash.

"Tap to pay" cards and smartphone payment apps work in Europe just as they do in the US, and sidestep chip-and-PIN compatibility issues.

To keep your cash, cards, and valuables safe, wear a money belt.

Dynamic Currency Conversion: If merchants offer to convert your purchase price into dollars (called dynamic currency conversion, or DCC), refuse this "service." You'll pay extra for the expensive convenience of seeing your charge in dollars. If an ATM offers to "lock in" your conversion rate, choose "proceed without conversion." Other prompts might state, "You can be charged in dollars: Press YES for dollars, NO for euros." Always choose the local currency.

STAYING CONNECTED

The simplest solution is to bring your own device—mobile phone, tablet, or laptop—and use it just as you would at home (following the money-saving tips below). For more on phoning, see RickSteves.com/phoning. For a one-hour talk covering tech issues for travelers, see RickSteves.com/mobile-travel-skills.

To Call from a US Phone: Phone numbers in this book are presented exactly as you would dial them from a US mobile phone. For international access, press and hold the 0 key until you get a + sign, then dial the country code (34 for Spain) and phone number. To dial from a US landline, replace + with 011 (US/Canada international access code).

From a European Landline: Replace + with 0 (Europe international access code), then dial the country code (34 for Spain) and phone number.

Within Spain: To place a domestic call (from a Spanish landline or mobile), drop the +34 from the phone number printed in this book.

Tips: If you bring your mobile phone, consider getting an international plan; most providers offer a simple bundle that includes calling, messaging, and data.

Use Wi-Fi whenever possible. Most hotels and many cafés offer free Wi-Fi, and you may also find it at tourist information offices (TIs), major museums, and public-transit hubs. With Wi-Fi you can use your phone or tablet to make free or low-cost calls via a calling app such as Skype, WhatsApp, FaceTime, or Google Hangouts. When you need to get online but can't find Wi-Fi, turn on your cellular network (or turn off airplane mode) just long enough for the task at hand.

Most **hotels** charge a fee for placing calls—ask for rates before you dial. You can use a prepaid international phone card (*tarjeta telefónica con código*, usually available at newsstands, tobacco shops, and train stations) to call out from your hotel.

Sleep Code

Hotels in this book are categorized according to the average price of a standard double room without breakfast in high season.

$$$$	**Splurge:** Most rooms over €170
$$$	**Pricier:** €130-170
$$	**Moderate:** €90-130
$	**Budget:** €50-90
¢	**Backpacker:** Under €50
RS%	**Rick Steves discount**

Unless otherwise noted, credit cards are accepted, hotel staff speak basic English, and free Wi-Fi is available. Comparison-shop by checking prices at several hotels (on each hotel's own website, on a booking site, or by email). For the best deal, *book directly with the hotel.* Ask for a discount if paying in cash; if the listing includes **RS%**, request a Rick Steves discount.

SLEEPING

I've categorized my recommended accommodations based on price, indicated with a dollar-sign rating (see sidebar). I recommend reserving rooms in advance, particularly during peak season. Once your dates are set, check the specific price for your preferred stay at several hotels. You can do this either by comparing prices on Hotels.com or Booking.com, or by checking the hotels' own websites. To get the best deal, contact my family-run hotels directly by phone or email. When you go direct, the owner avoids the commission paid to booking sites, giving them wiggle room to offer you a discount, a nicer room, or free breakfast. If you prefer to book online, it's to your advantage to use the hotel's website.

For complicated requests, send an email with the following information: number and type of rooms; number of nights; arrival date; departure date; any special needs; and applicable discounts (such as a Rick Steves discount, cash discount, or promotional rate). Use the European style for writing dates: day/month/year.

In general, hotel prices can soften if you do any of the following: offer to pay cash, stay at least three nights, or travel off-season. Hoteliers are encouraged to quote prices with the IVA tax (value-added tax) included—but it's smart to ask when you book your room.

Room rates are especially volatile at hotels that use "dynamic pricing" to set rates. Prices can skyrocket during festivals and conventions, while business hotels can have deep discounts on weekends when demand plummets. Of the many hotels I recommend, it's difficult to say which will be the best value on a given day—until you do your homework.

Restaurant Price Code

Eateries in this book are categorized according to the average cost of a typical main course. Drinks, desserts, and splurge items can raise the price considerably.

$$$$	**Splurge:** Most main courses over €25
$$$	**Pricier:** €18-25
$$	**Moderate:** €12-18
$	**Budget:** Under €12

In Spain, takeout food is **$**; a basic tapas bar or no-frills sit-down eatery is **$$**; a casual but more upscale tapas bar or restaurant is **$$$**; and a swanky splurge is **$$$$**.

EATING

I've categorized my recommended eateries based on the average price of a typical main course, indicated with a dollar-sign rating (see sidebar). By our standards, Spaniards eat late, having lunch—their biggest meal of the day—around 13:00-16:00, and dinner starting about 21:00. At restaurants, you can dine with tourists at 20:00, or with Spaniards if you wait until later.

For a fun early dinner at a bar, build a light meal out of tapas—small appetizer-sized portions of seafood, salads, meat-filled pastries, deep-fried tasties, and so on. Many of these are displayed behind glass, and you can point to what you want. Tapas typically cost around €4. While the smaller "tapa" size (which comes on a saucer-size plate) is handiest for maximum tasting opportunities, many bars sell only larger sizes: the *ración* (full portion, on a dinner plate) and *media-ración* (half-size portion). *Jamón* (hah-MOHN), an air-dried ham similar to prosciutto, is a Spanish staple. Other key terms include *bocadillo* (baguette sandwich), *frito* (fried), *a la plancha* (grilled), *queso* (cheese), *tortilla* (omelet), and *surtido* (assortment).

Many bars have three price tiers, which should be clearly posted: It's cheapest to eat or drink while standing at the bar (*barra*), slightly more to sit at a table inside (*mesa* or *salón*), and most expensive to sit outside *(terraza)*. Wherever you are, be assertive or you'll never be served. *Por favor* (please) grabs the attention of the server or bartender.

If you're having tapas, don't worry about paying as you go (the bartender keeps track). When you're ready to leave, ask for the bill: "*¿La cuenta?*"

Tipping: To tip for a few tapas, round up to the nearest euro. At restaurants with table service, if a service charge is included in the bill, add about 5 percent; if it's not, leave 10 percent. If you're sampling tapas at a counter, there's no need to tip (though you can round up the bill).

TRANSPORTATION

By Train and Bus: For train schedules, visit Germany's excellent all-Europe website (www.bahn.com) or Spain's Renfe (www.renfe. com). Since trains can sell out, and high-speed AVE ticket prices increase as your departure date draws closer, it's smart to buy your tickets at least a day in advance—even for short rides. You can buy them at a travel agency (easiest), at the train station (can be crowd-ed, be sure you're in the right line; you'll pay a five percent service fee at the ticket window), or online (at www.renfe.com). Be aware that the Renfe website often rejects US credit cards—use PayPal; or from the US try Raileurope.com and Petrabax.com (expect a small fee from either), or use the European vendor Trainline.eu. Futuristic, high-speed trains (such as AVE) can be priced differ-ently according to their time of departure. To see if a rail pass could save you money, check RickSteves.com/rail.

Buses pick up where the trains don't go, reaching even small villages. But because routes are operated by various competing com-panies, it can be tricky to pin down schedules (check with local bus stations, tourist info offices, or the aggregator website Movelia.es).

By Plane: Consider covering long distances on a budget flight, which can be cheaper than a train or bus ride. Check the cost of a flight on one of Europe's airlines, whether a major carrier or a no-frills outfit like EasyJet or Ryanair. Kayak is the top site for flights to and within Europe, easy-to-use Google Flights has price alerts, and Skyscanner includes many inexpensive flights within Europe.

By Car: It's cheaper to arrange most car rentals from the US. If you're planning a multicountry itinerary by car, be aware of often astronomical international drop-off fees. For tips on your insur-ance options, see RickSteves.com/cdw. For navigation, the map-ping app on your phone works fine for Europe's roads. To save on data, most apps allow you to download maps for offline use. Some apps—including Google Maps—also have offline route directions, but you'll need mobile data access for current traffic.

It's also required that you carry an International Driving Per-mit (IDP), available at your local AAA office ($20 plus two pass-port-type photos, www.aaa.com).

Superhighways come with tolls, but save lots of time. Each toll road *(autopista de peaje)* has its own pricing structure, so tolls vary. Payment can be made in cash or by credit or debit card (credit-card-only lanes are labeled *"vias automáticas"*; cash lanes are *"vias manu-ales"*). Spaniards love to tailgate; otherwise, local road etiquette is similar to that in the US. Ask your car-rental company for details, or check the US State Department website (www.travel.state.gov, search for your country in the "Country Information" box, then select "Travel and Transportation").

A car is a worthless headache in cities—park it safely (get tips from your hotelier). As break-ins are common, be sure your valuables are out of sight and locked in the trunk, or even better, with you or in your hotel room.

HELPFUL HINTS

Travel Advisories: For updated health and safety conditions, including any restrictions for your destination, consult the US State Department's international travel website (www.travel.state.gov).

Emergency and Medical Help: For any emergency service—ambulance, police, or fire—call **112** from a mobile phone or landline. Operators, who in most countries speak English, will deal with your request or route you to the right emergency service. If you get sick, do as the locals do and go to a pharmacist for advice. Or ask at your hotel for help—they'll know of the nearest medical and emergency services.

For **passport problems,** contact the **US Embassy** (Madrid—by appointment only, dial +34 915 872 200, https://es.usembassy.gov) or the **Canadian Embassy** (Madrid—by appointment only, dial +34 913 828 400 www.espana.gc.ca).

ETIAS Registration: Beginning in late 2021, US and Canadian citizens may be required to register online with the European Travel Information and Authorization System (ETIAS) before entering certain European countries (quick and easy process, $8 fee, valid 3 years, www.etiasvisa.com).

Theft or Loss: Spain has particularly hardworking pickpockets—wear a money belt. Assume beggars are pickpockets and any scuffle is simply a distraction by a team of thieves. If you stop for any commotion or show, put your hands in your pockets before someone else does.

To replace a passport, you'll need to go in person to an embassy (see above). Cancel and replace your credit and debit cards by calling these 24-hour US numbers with a mobile phone: Visa (dial +1-303-967-1096), MasterCard (dial +1-636-722-7111), and American Express (dial +1-336-393-1111). From a landline, you can call these US numbers collect by going through a local operator. File a police report either on the spot or within a day or two; you'll need it to submit an insurance claim for lost or stolen rail passes or travel gear, and it can help with replacing your passport or credit and debit cards. For more information, see RickSteves.com/help.

Time: Spain uses the 24-hour clock. It's the same through 12:00 noon, then keep going: 13:00, 14:00, and so on. Spain, like most of continental Europe, is six/nine hours ahead of the East/West Coasts of the US.

Siesta and Paseo: Many Spaniards (especially in rural areas) still follow the traditional siesta schedule: From around 14:00 to 17:00, many businesses close as people go home for a big lunch with their family. Then they head back to work (and shops reopen) from about 17:00 to 21:00. (Many bigger stores stay open all day long, especially in cities.) Then, after a late dinner, whole families pour out of their apartments to enjoy the cool of the evening, stroll through the streets, and greet their neighbors—a custom called the paseo.

Sights: Major attractions can be swamped with visitors; carefully read and follow this book's crowd-beating tips (visit popular sights very early or very late, or—where possible—reserve ahead). Opening and closing hours of sights can change unexpectedly; confirm the latest times on their websites or at the local tourist information office. At many churches, a modest dress code is encouraged and sometimes required (no bare shoulders or shorts).

Holidays and Festivals: Spain celebrates many holidays, which can close sights and attract crowds (book hotel rooms ahead). For more on holidays and festivals, check Spain's website: www.spain.info. For a simple list showing major—though not all—events, see RickSteves.com/festivals.

Numbers and Stumblers: What Americans call the second floor of a building is the first floor in Europe. Europeans write dates as day/month/year, so Christmas 2021 is 25/12/21. Commas are decimal points and vice versa—a dollar and a half is 1,50, and there are 5.280 feet in a mile. Spain uses the metric system: A kilogram is 2.2 pounds; a liter is about a quart; and a kilometer is six-tenths of a mile.

RESOURCES FROM RICK STEVES

This Snapshot guide, excerpted from my latest edition of *Rick Steves Spain*, is one of many titles in my series of guidebooks on European travel. I also produce a public television series, *Rick Steves' Europe*, and a public radio show, *Travel with Rick Steves*. My free online video library, Rick Steves Classroom Europe, offers a searchable database of short video clips on European history, culture, and geography (Classroom.RickSteves.com). My website, RickSteves.com, offers free travel information, a forum for travelers' comments, guidebook updates, my travel blog, an online travel store, and information on European rail passes and our tours of Europe. If you're bringing a mobile device, you can download my free Rick Steves Audio Europe app that features dozens of free, self-guided audio tours of the top sights in Europe (including the Madrid City Walk and Sevilla City Walk), plus radio shows and travel interviews about Spain. For more information, see RickSteves.com/audioeurope. You can also follow me on Facebook, Twitter, and Instagram.

ADDITIONAL RESOURCES
Tourist Information: www.spain.info
Passports and Red Tape: www.travel.state.gov
Packing List: www.ricksteves.com/packing
Travel Insurance: www.ricksteves.com/insurance
Cheap Flights: www.kayak.com or www.google.com/flights
Airplane Carry-on Restrictions: www.tsa.gov/travelers
Updates for This Book: www.ricksteves.com/update

HOW WAS YOUR TRIP?
To share your tips, concerns, and discoveries after using this book, please fill out the survey at RickSteves.com/feedback. Thanks in advance—it helps a lot.

Spanish Survival Phrases

English	Spanish	Pronunciation
Good day.	Buenos días.	**bweh**-nohs **dee**-ahs
Do you speak English?	¿Habla usted inglés?	**ah**-blah oo-**stehd** een-**glays**
Yes. / No.	Sí. / No.	see / noh
I (don't) understand.	(No) comprendo.	(noh) kohm-**prehn**-doh
Please.	Por favor.	por fah-**bor**
Thank you.	Gracias.	**grah**-thee-ahs
I'm sorry.	Lo siento.	loh see-**ehn**-toh
Excuse me.	Perdone.	pehr-**doh**-nay
(No) problem.	(No) problema.	(noh) proh-**bleh**-mah
Good.	Bueno.	**bweh**-noh
Goodbye.	Adiós.	ah-dee-**ohs**
OK.	Vale.	**bah**-lay
one / two	uno / dos	**oo**-noh / dohs
three / four	tres / cuatro	trehs / **kwah**-troh
five / six	cinco / seis	**theen**-koh / says
seven / eight	siete / ocho	see-**eh**-tay / **oh**-choh
nine / ten	nueve / diez	**nweh**-bay / dee-**ehth**
How much is it?	¿Cuánto cuesta?	**kwahn**-toh **kweh**-stah
Write it?	¿Me lo escribe?	may loh eh-**skree**-bay
Is it free?	¿Es gratis?	ehs **grah**-tees
Is it included?	¿Está incluido?	eh-**stah** een-kloo-**ee**-doh
Where can I buy / find...?	¿Dónde puedo comprar / encontrar...?	**dohn**-day **pweh**-doh kohm-**prar** / ehn-kohn-**trar**
I'd like / We'd like...	Me gustaría / Nos gustaría...	may goo-stah-**ree**-ah / nohs goo-stah-**ree**-ah
...a room.	...una habitación.	**oo**-nah ah-bee-tah-thee-**ohn**
...a ticket to ___.	...un billete para ___.	oon bee-**yeh**-tay **pah**-rah ___
Is it possible?	¿Es posible?	ehs poh-**see**-blay
Where is...?	¿Dónde está...?	**dohn**-day eh-**stah**
...the train station	...la estación de trenes	lah eh-stah-thee-**ohn** day **treh**-nehs
...the bus station	...la estación de autobuses	lah eh-stah-thee-**ohn** day ow-toh-**boo**-sehs
...the tourist information office	...la oficina de turismo	lah oh-fee-**thee**-nah day too-**rees**-moh
Where are the toilets?	¿Dónde están los servicios?	**dohn**-day eh-**stahn** lohs sehr-**bee**-thee-ohs
men	hombres, caballeros	**ohm**-brehs, kah-bah-**yeh**-rohs
women	mujeres, damas	moo-**heh**-rehs, **dah**-mahs
left / right	izquierda / derecha	eeth-kee-**ehr**-dah / deh-**reh**-chah
straight	derecho	deh-**reh**-choh
When do you open / close?	¿A qué hora abren / cierran?	ah kay **oh**-rah **ah**-brehn / thee-**ehr**-ahn
At what time?	¿A qué hora?	ah kay **oh**-rah
Just a moment.	Un momento.	oon moh-**mehn**-toh
now / soon / later	ahora / pronto / más tarde	ah-**oh**-rah / **prohn**-toh / mahs **tar**-day
today / tomorrow	hoy / mañana	oy / mahn-**yah**-nah

In a Spanish Restaurant

English	Spanish	Pronunciation
I'd like / We'd like...	Me gustaría / Nos gustaría...	may goo-stah-**ree**-ah / nohs goo-stah-**ree**-ah
...to reserve...	...reservar...	reh-sehr-**bar**
...a table for one / two.	...una mesa para uno / dos.	**oo**-nah **meh**-sah **pah**-rah **oo**-noh / dohs
Non-smoking.	No fumador.	noh foo-mah-**dohr**
Is this table free?	¿Está esta mesa libre?	eh-**stah** eh-stah **meh**-sah **lee**-bray
The menu (in English), please.	La carta (en inglés), por favor.	lah **kar**-tah (ehn een-**glays**) por fah-**bor**
service (not) included	servicio (no) incluido	sehr-**bee**-thee-oh (noh) een-kloo-**ee**-doh
cover charge	precio de entrada	**preh**-thee-oh day ehn-**trah**-dah
to go	para llevar	**pah**-rah yeh-**bar**
with / without	con / sin	kohn / seen
and / or	y / o	ee / oh
menu (of the day)	menú (del día)	meh-**noo** (dehl **dee**-ah)
specialty of the house	especialidad de la casa	eh-speh-thee-ah-lee-**dahd** day lah **kah**-sah
tourist menu	menú turístico	meh-**noo** too-**ree**-stee-koh
combination plate	plato combinado	**plah**-toh kohm-bee-**nah**-doh
appetizers	tapas	**tah**-pahs
bread	pan	pahn
cheese	queso	**keh**-soh
sandwich	bocadillo	boh-kah-**dee**-yoh
soup	sopa	**soh**-pah
salad	ensalada	ehn-sah-**lah**-dah
meat	carne	**kar**-nay
poultry	aves	**ah**-behs
fish	pescado	peh-**skah**-doh
seafood	marisco	mah-**ree**-skoh
fruit	fruta	**froo**-tah
vegetables	verduras	behr-**doo**-rahs
dessert	postre	**poh**-stray
tap water	agua del grifo	**ah**-gwah dehl **gree**-foh
mineral water	agua mineral	**ah**-gwah mee-neh-**rahl**
milk	leche	**leh**-chay
(orange) juice	zumo (de naranja)	**thoo**-moh (day nah-**rahn**-hah)
coffee	café	kah-**fay**
tea	té	tay
wine	vino	**bee**-noh
red / white	tinto / blanco	**teen**-toh / **blahn**-koh
glass / bottle	vaso / botella	**bah**-soh / boh-**teh**-yah
beer	cerveza	thehr-**beh**-thah
Cheers!	¡Salud!	sah-**lood**
More. / Another.	Más. / Otro.	mahs / **oh**-troh
The same.	El mismo.	ehl **mees**-moh
The bill, please.	La cuenta, por favor.	lah **kwehn**-tah por fah-**bor**
tip	propina	proh-**pee**-nah
Delicious!	¡Delicioso!	deh-lee-thee-**oh**-soh

For hundreds more pages of survival phrases for your trip to Spain, check out *Rick Steves Spanish Phrase Book*.

INDEX

INDEX

Explore Europe

At ricksteves.com you can browse through thousands of articles, videos, photos and radio interviews, plus find a wealth of money-saving travel tips for planning your dream trip. And with our mobile-friendly website, you can easily access all this great travel information anywhere you go.

TV Shows

Preview the places you'll visit by watching entire half-hour episodes of *Rick Steves' Europe* (choose from all 100 shows) on-demand, for free.

ricksteves.com

your travel dreams into affordable reality

Radio Interviews

Enjoy ready access to Rick's vast library of radio interviews covering travel tips and cultural insights that relate specifically to your Europe travel plans.

Travel Forums

Learn, ask, share! Our online community of savvy travelers is a great resource for first-time travelers to Europe, as well as seasoned pros.

Travel News

Subscribe to our free Travel News e-newsletter, and get monthly updates from Rick on what's happening in Europe.

Classroom Europe

Check out our free resource for educators with 400+ short video clips from the *Rick Steves' Europe* TV show.

Audio Europe™

Rick Steves AUDIO EUROPE

Rick's Free Travel App

Get your FREE **Rick Steves Audio Europe**™ app to enjoy…

- Dozens of self-guided tours of Europe's top museums, sights and historic walks
- Hundreds of tracks filled with cultural insights and sightseeing tips from Rick's radio interviews
- All organized into handy geographic playlists
- For Apple and Android

With Rick whispering in your ear, Europe gets even better.

Find out more at ricksteves.com

Gear up for your next adventure at ricksteves.com

Light Luggage

Pack light and right with Rick Steves' affordable, custom-designed rolling carry-on bags, backpacks, day packs and shoulder bags.

Accessories

From packing cubes to moneybelts and beyond, Rick has personally selected the travel goodies that will help your trip go smoother.

Shop at ricksteves.com

Experience maximum Europe

Save time and energy

This guidebook is your independent-travel toolkit. But for all it delivers, it's still up to you to devote the time and energy it takes to manage the preparation and logistics that are essential for a happy trip. If that's a hassle, there's a solution.

Rick Steves Tours

A Rick Steves tour takes you to Europe's most interesting places with great

with minimum stress

guides and small groups. We follow Rick's favorite itineraries, ride in comfy buses, stay in family-run hotels, and bring you intimately close to the Europe you've traveled so far to see. Most importantly, we take away the logistical headaches so you can focus on the fun.

Join the fun

This year we'll take thousands of free-spirited travelers—nearly half of them repeat customers—along with us on 50 different itineraries, from Athens to Istanbul. Is a Rick Steves tour the right fit for your travel dreams?

Find out at ricksteves.com, where you can also check seat availability and sign up. Europe is best experienced with happy travel partners. We hope you can join us.

See our itineraries at ricksteves.com

A Guide for Every Trip

BEST OF GUIDES

Full-color guides in an easy-to-scan format. Focused on top sights and experiences in the most popular European destinations

Best of England
Best of Europe
Best of France
Best of Germany
Best of Ireland
Best of Italy
Best of Scotland
Best of Spain

COMPREHENSIVE GUIDES

City, country, and regional guides printed on Bible-thin paper. Packe with detailed coverage for a multi-week trip exploring iconic sights and venturing off the beaten path

Amsterdam & the Netherlands
Barcelona
Belgium: Bruges, Brussels, Antwerp & Ghent
Berlin
Budapest
Croatia & Slovenia
Eastern Europe
England
Florence & Tuscany
France
Germany
Great Britain
Greece: Athens & the Peloponnes
Iceland
Ireland
Istanbul
Italy
London
Paris
Portugal
Prague & the Czech Republic
Provence & the French Riviera
Rome
Scandinavia
Scotland
Sicily
Spain
Switzerland
Venice
Vienna, Salzburg & Tirol

HE BEST OF ROME

e, Italy's capital, is studded with
an remnants and floodlit-fountain
res. From the Vatican to the Colos-
t, with crazy traffic in between, Rome
nderful, huge, and exhausting. The
is, the heat, and the weighty history

of the Eternal City where Caesars walked
can make tourists wilt. Recharge by taking siestas, gelato breaks, and after-dark
walks, strolling from one atmospheric
square to another in the refreshing evening air.

Rick Steves books are available from your favorite bookse
Many guides are available as ebooks.

POCKET GUIDES
Compact color guides for shorter trips

Amsterdam	Paris
Athens	Prague
Barcelona	Rome
Florence	Venice
Italy's Cinque Terre	Vienna
London	
Munich & Salzburg	

SNAPSHOT GUIDES
Focused single-destination coverage

Basque Country: Spain & France
Copenhagen & the Best of Denmark
Dublin
Dubrovnik
Edinburgh
Hill Towns of Central Italy
Krakow, Warsaw & Gdansk
Lisbon
Loire Valley
Madrid & Toledo
Milan & the Italian Lakes District
Naples & the Amalfi Coast
Nice & the French Riviera
Normandy
Northern Ireland
Norway
Reykjavík
Rothenburg & the Rhine
Scottish Highlands
Sevilla, Granada & Southern Spain
St. Petersburg, Helsinki & Tallinn
Stockholm

CRUISE PORTS GUIDES
Reference for cruise ports of call

Mediterranean Cruise Ports
Scandinavian & Northern European
  Cruise Ports

Complete your library with...

TRAVEL SKILLS & CULTURE
*Study up on travel skills and gain
insight on history and culture*

Europe 101
Europe Through the Back Door
Europe's Top 100 Masterpieces
European Christmas
European Easter
European Festivals
For the Love of Europe
Travel as a Political Act

PHRASE BOOKS & DICTIONARIES

French
French, Italian & German
German
Italian
Portuguese
Spanish

PLANNING MAPS

Britain, Ireland & London
Europe
France & Paris
Germany, Austria & Switzerland
Iceland
Ireland
Italy
Spain & Portugal